PUBLICATIONS OF THE WISCONSIN CENTER FOR PUSHKIN STUDIES

David Bethea, Alexander Dolinin, Thomas Shaw
Series Editors

Realizing Metaphors: Alexander Pushkin and the Life of the Poet
David M. Bethea

Alexander Pushkin's Little Tragedies: *The Poetics of Brevity*
edited by Svetlana Evdokimova

Pushkin's Tatiana
Olga Hasty

The Imperial Sublime: A Russian Poetics of Empire
Harsha Ram

Pushkin and the Genres of Madness: The Masterpieces of 1833
Gary Rosenshield

The Imperial Sublime

PUBLICATIONS OF THE WISCONSIN CENTER
FOR PUSHKIN STUDIES

Series Editors

David Bethea
Alexander Dolinin
Thomas Shaw

The Imperial Sublime

A Russian Poetics of Empire

Harsha Ram

The University of Wisconsin Press

The University of Wisconsin Press
1930 Monroe Street
Madison, Wisconsin 53711

www.wisc.edu/wisconsinpress/

3 Henrietta Street
London WC2E 8LU, England

5 4 3 2 1

Printed in the United States of America

Library of Congress Cataloging-in-Publication Data
Ram, Harsha.
The imperial sublime : a Russian poetics of empire / Ram, Harsha.
p. cm.—(Publications of the Wisconsin Center for Pushkin Studies)
Includes bibliographical references and index.
ISBN 0-299-18190-1 (alk. paper)
1. Russian literature—18th century—History and criticism. 2. Russian Literature, 19th century—History and criticism. 3. Sublime, The, in literature. I. Title. II. Series.
PG2987.S78 R36 2003
891.709'384—dc21 2002152196

For Nissim,
the youngest emperor

Contents

Acknowledgments

Writing about the sublime is frequently less sublime than living it, yet this book is also the outcome of a prolonged love affair with the Russian language and its poetry, an experience that has certainly afforded me many moments of rapture. Let me then begin by thanking all the teachers who have transmitted to me the passion they felt for the Russian language. Of my early teachers I would single out Michael Ulman in Sydney, Australia, whose classes granted me not only my first systematic insights into Russian literature but dramatized what I soon understood to be the best qualities of the Russian *intelligent:* an unswerving commitment to culture in the face of brute force and a caring relationship to the word, spoken and written.

Although my interest in Russian poetry dates back to my teenage years, the topic of this book emerged during my time as a graduate student in the Department of Comparative Literature at Yale University. Let me thank my dissertation adviser Michael Holquist for supporting my work with unflagging enthusiasm and real insight, Tomas Venclova for sharing his great love for the poetic traditions of eastern Europe, Monika Greenleaf for providing a splendid example of how to engage the Russian poetic canon both seriously and innovatively, and Sara Suleri, without whom my turn to orient and empire would have scarcely been possible. I also wish to thank Katerina Clark and Christopher Miller for the care and attention with which they read my dissertation.

If the book's bare bones were already in place at Yale, then it acquired flesh and blood at the University of California at Berkeley. A semester's fellowship at the Townsend Humanities Center and a Humanities Research Grant, both granted at Berkeley, gave me the much needed time to fill in the many conceptual and narrative gaps of the book. I have the great fortune to be working in one of the most congenial as well as intellectually serious Slavic programs in the United States. Every one of my colleagues has played a significant role in guiding this book to completion: even as I thank them all, let me single out Olga Matich for her warm and sustained interest in my work, Viktor Zhivov for sharing with me his vast knowledge of the eighteenth century, Robert Hughes for his poetic culture and his close scrutiny of the manuscript, and Irina Paperno for her confidence in my abilities and the high standards to which she held me. Thanks must also be given to Berkeley's Slavic graduate students for providing much-needed help with library research and translation as well as for their willingness to exchange ideas. In this context I would like to mention Gabriel White, Anne Dwyer, Polina Barskova, Boris Wolfson, Chris Caes, Ingrid Kleespies, Michael Kunichika, and Stiliana Milkova. On completion, this book swiftly found a home at the University of Wisconsin Press. I owe this to David Bethea, whose kindness and enthusiasm as reader and editor I shall always recall with gratitude. Finally let me not forget the numerous anonymous reviewers, both within and outside Berkeley, who gave me my first real taste of peer review and the giddying sense of community it can afford.

This book is, at least in its post-dissertation phase, the same age as my son Nissim. Not just for the sake of this shared chronology, I dedicate it to him.

The Imperial Sublime

Introduction

Poetry and Empire

In 1721, with a twenty-year war against Sweden concluded in victory, Tsar Peter I of Russia proclaimed himself emperor. To the state chancellor Count Golovkin the new title ratified Peter's feat of ushering his "loyal subjects from the darkness of ignorance onto the theatre of universal glory, from nonbeing . . . into the society of political peoples."[1] Some eighteen years later, in 1739, a subsequent Russian military triumph, this time over Turkey, became the occasion for a related cultural revolution. Hearing of Russia's recent capture of the Ottoman fortress of Khotin, the young poet Mikhail Lomonosov, then studying in Germany, penned an ode hailing the victory, which he sent to Russia together with a letter proposing a new set of rules governing Russian versification. Just as Peter's transformation of Muscovy into the Russian Empire was intended to signal Russia's belated embrace of western modernity, so, too, Lomonosov's ode would eventually be hailed—in Vissarion Belinskii's classic formulation—as "the first Russian poem written in a correct measure" and thus the beginning of modern Russian poetry.[2]

New beginnings, like the ruptures that make them possible, seldom happen quite as neatly as textbook histories would have us believe.[3] Yet it is largely true that empire and modern versification were established almost simultaneously in eighteenth-century Russia. This has been widely, if partially, acknowledged: we need only recall the scholarly commonplace that views modern Russian literature as an outcome of the Petrine reforms, even if its full consolidation would span the long century from Lomonosov's debut to the death of Pushkin. A telling example of this view is Belinskii's observation of 1842 that "to write the history of Russian literature means to show how, as a result of the social reform wrought by Peter the Great, it began as a slavish imitation of foreign models, acquiring a purely rhetorical character; how then, it gradually strove to free itself from formality and rhetoric and to acquire vital elements and independence; and how finally it developed to the level of complete artistry and came to express the life of its own society, becoming Russian."[4] Once romanticism had established the primacy of organic national forms, the grafted nature of eighteenth-century Russian culture seemed embarrassingly evident. Generally identified with classicist poetics and the ode, the literary system of the eighteenth century is widely believed to have declined with the demise of both, ushering in an era of greater writers whom Belinskii could champion as authentically Russian. As the nation emerged, it seems, so the empire receded in importance.

Such an approach, which acknowledges the inaugural period of Russian literature only to demote its significance, has had the effect of obscuring certain continuities displayed by Russian literary culture from the establishment of the imperial state to its collapse in 1917. If empire and modern poetry were established in Russia at practically the same time, then how did these near synchronous events reverberate in the two centuries to come? To what extent was the evolution of modern Russian poetry a response to and an effect of the imperial state?

This book attempts to trace a vital part of the answer to this question, by examining the rise of empire as a literary theme in close tandem with the first systematization of modern literary Russian, specifically poetry. Initially rooted in the vicissitudes of court life, the imperial academy, and state policy, Russian poetry began with and as a subject of empire. While its subsequent history would take it far beyond its early role as the clarion of victories won and treaties signed, the traces of the Russian poet's original subjection to autocracy and its expanding realm would linger, subtly marking the poet's responses to a range of interconnected issues. As imperial discourse came to be manifested within a Russian literary system marked by increasing formal complexity as well as a growing ambivalence to the official state culture in which it was first conceived, the *thematics* of empire became complexly imbricated in questions of *poetics* and *rhetoric*.

The imperial theme, in other words, was quickly linked to a range of other questions, from formal problems of language, genre, style, and lyric subjectivity to the connection, within an autocratic state, between authority and authorship. This range of issues, both formal and ideological, is the subject of this book: together they point to a specifically Russian tradition of relating poetics, rhetoric, and politics. This tradition, which I propose to call the *imperial sublime*, was a melding of the Baroque traditions of late Muscovy with the newer literary codes and cultural fashions imported from France and Germany under the monarchs Peter, Anna, and Elizabeth. First convincingly formulated in the 1730s, the imperial sublime enjoyed a long life marked by significant revisions as well as by a remarkable consistency in its core concerns and formal patterns.

A Poetics of Empire

The first line of Lomonosov's "Oda na vziatie Khotina" (Ode on the taking of Khotin) renders with formulaic clarity the poetics of empire that would mark the Russian lyric for much of the eighteenth century: "A sudden rapture has seized the mind / And leads it up a lofty mountain." Here the fact of poetic inspiration is felt as the violent imposition of an external force. Vertical uplift as its basic axis, the mind is carried upward by a lyric afflatus over which it has no control. The disempowering vertigo of height offers a kind of visual recompense in the panoramic view granted to the poet's eye: this secondary horizontal space will repeatedly become localized as the historical occasion—a victory or a campaign—that is the poem's outward theme. The uplifted poet, slave to his vision, becomes Russia's heraldic eagle surveying the horizontal spread of the retreating Ottoman forces:

> Beyond the hills where a fiery abyss
> Belches smoke, flame and death
> Steal away with your men, Istanbul, beyond the Tigris . . .
> But to restrain the eagles' flight
> There is no hindrance left on earth.

Russian poetry will repeatedly encounter imperial history at the intersection of these two axes. The vertical terror of lyric afflatus is resolved in a compensatory and transformative identification with the horizontal stretch of Russian might. An experience of poetic inspiration is thus presented as analogous to the political power it then describes: impersonal, absolute, a vision that soars to embrace the expanding realm. This spatial articulation of two axes, along with the psychic and historical energies it brings together, provides the basic scaffolding of the imperial sublime.

In the pages to come I chart the formative stages of the imperial sublime, from its post-Petrine beginnings to the demise in 1841 of Russia's greatest romantic poet, Mikhail Lermontov. The first phase (1734–63), discussed in chapters 1 and 2, was dominated by the competing figures of Vasilii Trediakovskii and Mikhail Lomonosov. Discovering Longinus's classical treatise on the sublime during his student years in Germany, Lomonosov was the first Russian to elaborate a specifically local—and imperial—variant of the sublime as a literary construct. This he did by transposing the French classicist reading of the sublime popularized by Boileau onto the older Russian tradition of panegyric oratory, both ecclesiastical and secular. This hybrid amalgam of rhetoric and poetics would provide the immediate theoretical rationale for Lomonosov's poetic revolution, which brought syllabo-accentual—especially iambic—verse and the Pindaric ode to rapid prominence. The lofty ode and the "upbeat" iamb were championed by Lomonosov as the most appropriate means of creating sublimity in verse. Lomonosov's narrower lexical, generic, and metrical orientation soon eclipsed the slightly antecedent and more expansive vision of his rival, Trediakovskii, to provide the essential poetic components of the imperial sublime. Together Lomonosov's artistic choices generated the characteristic style of the ceremonial ode, whose literary preeminence over several decades forged a profound intimacy, ideological and even institutional, between poetry and imperial autocracy. Most of Lomonosov's poems celebrate the state and the sovereign: even where they subtly demur from official policy, they never question the function of autocracy as the agent of progress. Lomonosov's genius was to find a poetic formula for these convictions through an analogy between lyric rapture and imperial glory that became the emblematic mark of the Russian sublime.

The second phase of the imperial sublime (1776–1816), discussed in chapter 2, coincides with the productive years of Gavrila Derzhavin, Russia's greatest poet of the eighteenth century. Derzhavin has been justifiably read as a convinced lyric proponent of enlightened absolutism whose verse was nonetheless able to forge the beginnings of an autonomous literary persona. Less widely acknowledged is that the sublime was central to his poetry as the locus of an encounter between the individual and history. Derzhavin redefined the sublime as pertaining to a realm that was at once greater and lesser than the imperial state. On the one hand, the sublime expanded to become the force of time itself; on the other hand, this ontological dimension became measured and individuated as the destiny of the aristocratic statesman. These transformations did not by any means abolish the ode's defining theme of empire. Rather, they allowed for a layered understanding of authority, in which sovereign power was juxtaposed alongside the impact of time and the career ambitions of the individual. However contemplated, the sublime became the higher instance under whose auspices a sense of selfhood could be conceived.

Derzhavin's innovations can be historicized in the context of two salient aspects of the reign of Catherine the Great: the arrival in Russia of Enlightenment thought and the rapid extension of Russia's southern borders. Early in her reign the empress Catherine strove to reconcile territorial expansion with the fruits of progress. The challenge posed to imperial governance by a multiethnic and multireligious populace was to be resolved through the codification of universal legal principles, equally binding on all. The empress's initial enthusiasm for Enlightenment ideals created the makings of a Catherinian myth whose chief symbol was a hypostasis of the Law. It was Derzhavin's designated task to corroborate this myth. Cognizant of the glaring discrepancy between ethical ideals and administrative practice under Catherine, the poet evolved an ambiguous dialogue with the empress, in which both interlocutors were represented allegorically. Invoking the personae of one of Catherine's own fairy tales, Derzhavin wrote a cycle of odes playfully addressing the empress as "princess of the Kirgiz-Kaisak horde" and identifying himself as a Tatar *murza* or nobleman.

The literary joke was well received by Catherine, but the cultural fantasy it bespoke remained unsettling, highlighting as it did the awkward fusion, on Eurasian soil, of Enlightenment ideology and the ode's obligatory idiom of praise. Just as the empress emerged in the poet's vision as both modernizing sovereign and eastern despot, so Derzhavin himself appeared both as a poet of the European Enlightenment and an *inorodets* or non-Russian, importing the sycophancy and voluptuous indolence said to typify oriental courts. These dual figures intimated, in a humorously deflated manner, the strains of reconciling European law and an Asiatic empire, the utopian goal through which Catherine had once viewed the fate of her subjects. More significant, these allegorical personae individuated what had still been an abstract problem in Lomonosov, translating the political dimension of imperial subjecthood into the psychic and linguistic dimension of lyric subjectivity. Both dimensions, Derzhavin suggested, are born of a willing submission to a higher authority. In other words, the subject accedes to the sovereign will just as the poet accedes to his vision. This model, which had already functioned in Lomonosov as an impersonal outside force, was now simultaneously absorbed as the workings of an ethically self-reflexive mind. Internalizing the sublime was one of Derzhavin's greatest poetic achievements: in his writings, Lomonosov's still primitive model was stretched to accommodate the enhanced possibilities for gentry selfhood—as poet, statesman, general, or bureaucrat—under Catherine the Great.

The third phase of the imperial sublime, examined in chapter 3, culminated in the Decembrist uprising of 1825. Although failing to dislodge the institution of tsarism, the Decembrist movement was remarkably successful in linking the Decembrists' political goals to a literary practice. Rhetorically speaking, the insurrectionary vision of the Decembrists can be read as a revival—and reversal—of the eighteenth-century sublime. In anachronistically linking a revolutionary politics to a significantly archaic poetics, the Decembrist poets were the first to sever the sublime from its monarchist affiliations, even as they retained the empire as one of the defining contexts of their civic engagement and poetic production. The Decembrists' platform highlighted a pervasive if implicit inconsistency found in many Russian writers (the main exception being the mature Tolstoi): their critique of Russian autocracy was mitigated by their enthusiastic support for tsarist imperial policy—in this case the conquest of Transcaucasia and the Greek struggle against Ottoman rule.

A faithful mirror to the geopolitical stakes of the twenties, orientalism was also a crucial aspect of Decembrist *literary* ideology. Simply put, the Decembrists shifted the poetics of the sublime away from the panegyric toward the prophetic mode, whose topoi and stylistic choices were culled from the biblical Psalms of King David, now juxtaposed alongside the Islamic tradition. Russian translations of the Psalms had long served as a veiled form of social dissent and were widely regarded as formally akin to the ode, even as they unsettled its ideological premises. From loyal panegyrist of the monarch, the Russian poet became the insurgent prophet inspired by God to denounce and finally usurp the monarch's place. The Decembrists projected their recoding of the poet's role onto the wars being waged in Russia's southern borderlands. This peculiar amalgam of literature and geopolitics was vividly manifested in the life and work of two writers: Aleksandr Griboedov, also a tsarist emissary to Transcaucasia and Iran, who influenced the Decembrist poets without endorsing their revolutionary agenda, and his close literary ally Wilhelm Küchelbecker. Programmatically reviving the Lomonosovian ode, Küchelbecker radicalized the tensions already present in the eighteenth-century psalmodic tradition between political authority and poetic prowess. His poetry was one of revolt but one that remained complexly attached to the hierarchical model it denounced. It was by identifying with the territorial conquests of the tsarist state that the Decembrist poet was able to acquire the rhetorical authority to decry the purely domestic consequences of autocracy. Empire thus became the sublime matrix of the Decembrist vision, and the poet's own claim to prophetic insight derived from this paradoxical relation, both dissenting and celebratory, to power.

Responding to the Decembrists but rejecting their exclusively civic focus were the greater poets Aleksandr Pushkin and Mikhail Lermontov, who mark a further phase of the imperial sublime (1820–41), examined in the final chapter 4. Pushkin's first of two journeys to the Caucasus, and the literary works to which it gave rise, effectively consolidated the cultural reputation of the Russian "south." A place of conquest to be sure, it was also paradoxically a site of natural freedom. A romantic myth quickly developed around the Caucasus, replete with spectacular mountain scenery and ethnographic color, combining the artist's need to flee the suffocating constraints of civilization and a paradoxical awareness that this path to freedom had first to be cleared by the tsar's armies. The Caucasian works of Pushkin and Lermontov reflect the romantic discovery of the sublime in the natural world. Yet the dialectic they enact between the self and nature points also to the limits of the natural sublime. However awe-inspiring the mountain scenery and however fierce the battle, both fail to match the moody depths of the romantic hero. While rich in descriptive detail of local topography and custom, these works in fact demonstrate a further subjective introjection of the imperial sublime, well beyond the ethical moment found in Derzhavin.

This inward turn corresponds to a tangible shift in poetics: the writings of Pushkin and Lermontov reflect the definitive displacement of the ceremonial ode as the defining poetic genre of empire. Several instances of this change can be indicated. Pushkin's poem "Prorok" (The prophet) (1826) and Lermontov's "Poèt" (The poet) (1838) and "Son" (The dream) (1841) are three vivid examples of a complex dialogue with the eighteenth century as well as with the civic tradition of the Decembrists. These poems revive the figure of the poet-prophet outside the generic context of the psalmodic or sacred ode, thereby depriving his prophetic vision of its traditional content. Lyric afflatus no longer finds an adequate mirror in the social or cosmic order and thus falls back onto a compensatory affirmation of the poet's greatness. In this state of disengagement, empire can no longer be an adequate rationale for the sublime but nonetheless remains its defining context. The disjuncture between the subjective and the objective realms, manifest in the poet's alienation from the state or his isolation from the people, is projected allegorically onto a southern landscape. That the prophetic mode in Russian romantic poetry remains connected to an imperial geography is not widely recognized. To situate empire as the space within and through which the romantic prophet speaks is one task of this book.

Of even greater significance than the poems of prophecy are the famous southern narrative poems of Pushkin and Lermontov, which remained the standard literary representations of Russia's imperial quest until the great age of Russian prose. Quintessentially romantic, these texts situate a disaffected Byronic hero in an exotic mountain landscape. Their elaboration of the sublime is rooted in the specificities of a new genre, the romantic *poèma,* with its greater capacity for emplotment and psychological density. As the affective context of the hero threatens to eclipse his surroundings, so, too, the sublime collapses inward to become the protagonist's own restless longing. This shift from object to subject can be described as a realignment of geography and psychology. The relationship of the Russian center to its imperial borders provides the concrete topography of such poems as Pushkin's *Kavkazskii plennik* (Prisoner of the Caucasus) (1822) but also becomes the basis of the hero's inner life, which is effectively a narcissistic internalization of the same geography. This new "psychic map" charts the trajectory of many of the "heroes of our time" who populate Russian writing of the period. Formally it might be seen as an *elegiac* revision of the imperial sublime.

The elegy has long been acknowledged as a constructive element of the romantic *poèma.* A vehicle of mourning and melancholia, the elegy transforms the sublime into an object of loss and longing rather than of celebratory vision. If the ode is the genre of power triumphant, then the elegy highlights the privative effect of power on those it dispossesses. A sense of elegiac privation haunts the Caucasian theme as a whole, and its effects are curiously double-edged. A prime example is the Russian hero of the *Prisoner of the Caucasus:* fleeing the constraints of his own state, he falls captive to freedom-loving mountain dwellers in their war against the Russian army and comes to admire them even as he plots his escape. In the prisoner's fate, we see the many-sided effects of Russia's coercive state apparatus, which stifles the creative artist from the metropolis just as it subjugates the peoples of the southern periphery. Unlike his odic predecessor, then, the new romantic hero is unable to identify readily with the imperial project. At its unstated limit, his search for freedom leads him to a paradoxical identification with the conquered peoples of the south.

In its attitudes to empire, Russian romanticism wavered characteristically between "odic" triumphalism and "elegiac" mourning: Pushkin's *Kavkazskii plennik,* with its elegiac plotline and belligerently odic epilogue, is a perfect example of this. These tensions become still more acute in the writings of the final poet I examine in this book, Mikhail Lermontov. As a soldier Lermontov fought actively in Russia's military campaigns against the mountain dwellers; as a poet he created some of the most powerfully ambiguous human characterizations of Russian imperialism to be found in the literary tradition. Lermontov succeeded in fleshing out the sublime in the minds and bodies of history's victims, whom he counted on both sides of the imperial divide. Lermontov's *poèmy* are peopled by numerous examples of the Noble Savage. The savage held numerous attractions for the Russian gentry intellectual: as a primitive he was closer to nature, while his ferocious opposition to Russian rule elicited sympathy as a prism through which to contemplate the however limited creative resistance of the Russian poet to his own political system. The romantic artist thus became an ambiguous third element in the otherwise binary conflict between the colonizer and the colonized. The artist had only the limited choice of either identifying "metonymically" with the imperial state or seeing in the fate of the mountain dwellers an alienated metaphor for his own struggles and eventual disempowerment. The Russian romantics, and most Russian writers after them, finally chose *both* options: hence the difficulty of ascribing a single political meaning to their works.

This, then, is the general trajectory of the imperial sublime during the inaugural first hundred years of modern Russian literature. While earlier critics have studied certain aspects of it, such as Lomonosov's theory of the "lofty style" or the archaic elements in Decembrist poetics, the chapters to come are the first attempt at synthesizing what might be called a historical poetics of empire as evinced by the Russian poetic tradition.

Theories of the Sublime

The discourse of the sublime, of course, predates modern Russia as well as modern Europe. Its defining text is a tract of late antiquity, Longinus's

On The Sublime, whose modern currency is owing to the immense influence of Boileau's French translation of 1674. Longinus explains the sublime as a form of elevation, a loftiness or excellence of diction that forces the reader beyond aesthetic appreciation to a sense of wonderment, an apprehension of grandeur. The sublime in Greek is *hypsos*, height itself, whose proportions can be gauged only in the emotional turbulence it provokes. The fascination Longinus held for the eighteenth century and beyond lies perhaps in his anticipating a shift in contemporary aesthetics. His treatise functions essentially to psychologize rhetoric, translating questions of style and diction into a problem of the subject whose psychic responses are no longer gauged in purely normative terms.

The sublime, then, suggests a cluster of affective reactions through which the subject registers the pathos of transport or uplift, an experience that is both empowering and radically privative: "with its stunning power," the sublime has "a capability and force which, unable to be fought, take a position high over every member of the audience."[5] The sublime, in fact, involves a mobile structure of possession that involves at least one and often two displacements of force. The speaker is first absorbed involuntarily into his or her own utterance; the listener, where there is one, is in turn overwhelmed by what he or she hears, elevated by its force to the point of identifying with its speaker.[6]

How did this account of the sublime evolve historically and become culturally differentiated in the modern period? What are the points of convergence and rupture between the Russian tradition traced in the preceding pages and equivalent debates in the west? Samuel H. Monk has seen in the appearance of the sublime in western Europe a major catalyst for the displacement of classical rhetoric by the new discipline of aesthetics.[7] In Europe, then, the sublime evolved away from a taxonomic and prescriptive approach to language toward a conceptual contrast with beauty as an aesthetic norm. Where beauty provides an object of contemplative pleasure, the sublime is the experience of pain inflicted and mediated, a kind of aesthetically cushioned blow. This was the thesis of Edmund Burke's *Philosophical Enquiry into the Origin of our Ideas of the Sublime and the Beautiful* (1757). Burke listed the possible sources of the sublime—the positive excesses of infinity, vastness, or magnificence and the negative privations of darkness or difficulty—to conclude: "In short, wherever we find strength, and in what light soever we look upon power, we shall all along observe the sublime the concomitant of terror."[8] Burke's astonishing legacy is the reduction of the sublime to *fear* as the affective response to strength. Where power is wielded, it does not register in being inflicted but in being received. The sublime is this instance of authority, as it is lived in the terror it provokes.

The locus classicus of early debates on the sublime was Kant's *Critique of Judgment* (1790). Here Kant located the sublime in the mind itself, as opposed to the natural object that had precipitated the experience. Dwarfed by an object incomparably large or violent in its manifested power, the mind initially feels inadequate, experiencing "a momentary inhibition of the vital forces." We soon realize however that "this inadequacy itself is the arousal in us of the feeling that we have within us a supersensible power." The very ineffability of the object was thus embraced by Kant as evidence of the mind's superiority in finally being able to conceive of the *idea* of the infinite, even if—indeed precisely because—the mind cannot conceive its sensuous form. In Kant's conclusion, "the sublime is what even to be able to think proves that the mind has a power surpassing any standard of sense."[9]

Kant's narrative of the sublime, which moved from a blockage in the mind's relation to the sensory world to its cognitive resolution, was further divided into two variants. The *mathematical* sublime involved the mind striving to grasp a vast *magnitude,* for which it finally substituted its own mental infinity. The *dynamical* sublime was elicited by the experience of *power* in nature, "volcanoes in all their destructive power, hurricanes with all the devastation they leave behind, the boundless ocean heaved up, the high waterfall of a mighty river, and so on."[10] Here, too, Kant insisted that these manifestations of nature's might were not in themselves sublime, since the awe or fear they inspired were necessarily superseded in us by our capacity to judge ourselves as morally superior to nature.

Some forty years later, and at a certain remove from Kant's concerns, Hegel transformed the sublime into a marker of cultural difference. In his *Aesthetics* (delivered as a series of lectures during the 1820s) the sublime was canonized as a distinguishing feature of *oriental* art. Within Hegel's art-historical trajectory, the sublime was seen as the aesthetic correlative to a wider failure characteristic of Asiatic civilization. Hegel assimilates the mystical experiences of several eastern religions—Hinduism, Islam, and Judaism—under the rubric of the sublime. These traditions (Hegel will place a special emphasis on the Jewish faith) are akin in contemplating the Absolute according to the flawed theology of a remote and omnipotent god. Such a god, like the sovereign who is his earthly will, is limitless, and hence in excess of any verbal embodiment.

God's grandeur eclipses humanity: the oneness of the universe can be acknowledged only through an erasure of the individual—a fact experienced, in verbal art, as the ineffable. The resulting cleavage, in any human expression of the divine, between form and content generates the sublime as a mystical moment. Here the "Divine can come to consciousness only through the vanishing of the particular individuals in which the Divine is expressed as present." Whereas Christian mysticism realizes the "unification of . . . God with human subjectivity," the "strictly Eastern" forms such as Hindu pantheism as well as the Hebrew Bible depict a world in which "the creature, held over against God, is what is perishing and powerless, so that in the creator's goodness his *justice* has to be manifested at the same time." The sublime is an experience of divine law as purely privative: "man views himself in his *unworthiness* before God" and submits to a greater force, in the spiritual and finally in the secular realms.[11]

The Hegelian sublime differs from Kant's on at least two counts. First, Kant's version apparently lacks geographical or cultural specificity, deriving from nature rather than from a history of the spirit; second, it hypostatizes the mind, hailing its cognitive efficacy and ethical freedom at precisely the moment when Hegel insists on it being overshadowed by its object. How are we to understand these divergences? Between Kant and Hegel, we should remember, lies the tumult of European romantic culture, fueled in no small part by the scholarly enthusiasm of what Raymond Schwab has called the "oriental renaissance."[12] The western philologist's exaltation of the east as the spiritual birthplace of Europe is the polemical context of Hegel's critique. What romantic philology hailed as origin, Hegel would dismiss as a flawed beginning, an early and transient episode in the history of art.

Yet this broad intellectual history can be verified by the most concrete precedent for Hegel's own orientalization of the sublime in the *Aesthetics,* namely Kant himself. In the same section of the *Critique of Judgment,* Kant muses: "Perhaps the most sublime passage of the Jewish Law is the commandment: Thou shalt not make unto thee any graven image, or any likeness of any thing that is in heaven or on earth, etc. This commandment can explain the enthusiasm that the Jewish people in its civilized era felt for its religion when it compared itself with other peoples, or can explain the pride that Islam inspires. The same holds also for our presentation of the moral law, and for the predisposition within us for morality."[13] For Hegel as even for Kant, then, the eastern monotheisms exemplify the sublime by bringing together the aesthetic and the ethical under the aegis of law. Where the spirit is articulated as a divine command, its coercive force is sublimated in art as transcending representation. Heard but not seen, the disembodied imperative of God's word extracts obedience to the precise extent that its formlessness inspires an aesthetic sense of awe.

In locating the sublime chiefly in the orient, Hegel isolated the example of Jewish law from Kant's general claim about morality. Hegel's innovation was to generate instead a series of cultural equivalences of which the sublime was the aesthetic moment. Where religion is divine commandment, we experience politics as tyranny and art as sublime: these analogies constituted the static pattern of Asiatic cultures. Hegel's *Aesthetics* clarified the conceptual basis for the conflation of the artistic sublime with the despotisms and theocracies of the east, which now became its political and spiritual equivalents.[14] Schematizing this complex path it might be said that, during the romantic period and beyond, the European sublime moved largely within the margins of Kant's and Hegel's formulations, between a deepening subjective inwardness and a series of aesthetic, spiritual, or affective responses either to nature or to a civilizational norm whose allure lay precisely in its remoteness from western modernity.[15]

Even in the twentieth century the principal theoreticians of the sublime have been either Anglo-American or European.[16] The insights of the Anglo-American tradition are chiefly based on readings of the English romantic poets, alongside Burke and Kant.[17] Thomas Weiskel's *Romantic Sublime* remains the classic treatise of this tradition. Focusing primarily on the dialectic of consciousness and the world in the poetry of Wordsworth, Weiskel rereads the romantic concept of the poetic imagination through the lens of semiotics and psychoanalysis. Returning to Kant's account of the sublime as the temporary blockage and final triumph of cognition, Weiskel rephrases the dilemma outside the terms of Kantian idealism. The mathematical sublime Weiskel describes as an "excess on the plane of the *signifiers,*" whose monotonous infinity threatens to dissolve "all oppositions and distinctions."[18] Its crisis is resolved by halting or slowing down the syntagmatic flow of signifiers and rediscovering in the very loss of meaning a latent source of signification. This new signification is necessarily metaphorical, for it is derived by substituting one level of discourse (such as the mind) for another (sensuous reality), the former being in no ineluctable way derived from the latter. The dynamical sublime, by contrast, can be seen as an excess of *signified.* Here meaning appears as overdetermined, and the mind seeks to cope by displacing the surplus of meaning "into a dimension of contiguity which may be spatial or temporal. We may be tempted to talk of displacement as projection, for a dynamic element is involved, a motion of presence outward and through substance."[19]

Suzanne Guerlac's *Impersonal Sublime* typifies a more recent tendency to find in Longinus a rhetorical confirmation of the postmodern rethinking of subjectivity. Distancing herself from the phenomenological basis of Weiskel's reading, Guerlac maintains that "the Longinian sublime occurs as a force of enunciation determined neither by subjective intention nor by mimetic effect." Initially "it is as if the speakers merged with the message, while the listeners were overwhelmed or subjugated by the force of the sublime enunciation. . . . In a second moment, the interlocutors come themselves to feel as if they had produced the divine utterance themselves. This is the moment of 'proud flight,' the moment of elevation or transport associated with *hypsos*." The sublime thus involves several shifts, an initial loss of intentionality and a subsequent moment of identification, the latter referring to "an act of enunciation, not to a subject or to the content of an idea."[20]

Despite their divergent models, Weiskel and Guerlac share a common interest in finding an analytical vocabulary adequate to the sublime as a dynamic manifestation of *power.* For both, the sublime conveys an ongoing imbalance of greater and lesser forces, allowing for temporary convergences of discursive position or subjective identification. A more recent trend in critical work on the sublime has involved historicizing the sublime within specific political traditions. In a recent book on the place of the sublime in the construction of an official aesthetic discourse in Communist China, Ban Wang asserts that the "category of the aesthetic . . . helps to illuminate the relations between individual and society—between submission and domination, between governing imperatives and unconscious desire. The notion of the sublime is a nodal point in this interplay between the aesthetic and the political." What, however, remains open to question is the precise political import of the sublime. Wang continues: "the aesthetic offers emancipatory alternatives to an oppressive political structure" but can also be utilized by the state to "anchor its power and laws all the more securely in the sensibilities of its subjects." In this sense, the sublime remains "double-edged," having a tendency "to liberate or to oppress."[21]

A passing observation by Paul Fry might help to clarify this ambiguity. "The force of the sublime as Longinus records it," notes Fry, "covertly transfers power from the oppressor to the oppressed." Yet at the same time it is a "rule of 'transport' in the sublime . . . that to have power one must be enslaved, possessed by another."[22] This observation yields two insights. First, to the extent that the sublime is a dynamic force, it deals with the transferences of power rather than its static possession. Second, the liberating possibilities of the sublime do not lead to any absolute sense of subjective agency but rather enjoin the subject in a transformative circuit of power that remains greater than any of its participants, be they the ruler or the ruled. The sublime, then, seems radical to the extent that it is transformative, yet conservative in the sense that it ultimately reasserts hierarchy and order. Such a conclusion resonates well in the context of Russian history, where the Petrine and Leninist projects of violent modernization were both fundamentally in the service of the state.[23]

Toward a Russian Sublime

Russia's proverbial vastness, its apocalyptic experience of history, and the genre-defying formlessness of so many of its literary masterpieces would seem to predispose the national tradition toward a discourse of the sublime. Yet despite its powerful, even constitutive place in Russian culture, the sublime has remained a diffuse phenomenon, unevenly conceptualized. One symptom of this under-theorization is the absence of a single Russian word corresponding to the English *sublime*. As a modern (seventeenth-century) French and English rendering of the Greek *hypsos*, the term *sublime* was never adopted or calqued successfully during the eighteenth or early nineteenth centuries, when so many comparable words entered the Russian language.[24] Revealing in this regard is a moment in Ivan Martynov's preface to the first complete Russian translation of Longinus's treatise, entitled *O Vysokom ili velichestvennom* (On the high or the magnificent) published in 1803:

> In the original it is written: *peri hypsos*, i.e. *on height*, or *on highness* (*o Vysote ili o Vysokosti*). I translated it with an adjective, following the word customary in French, *du sublime*. Moreover, our treatises on aesthetics often say: *on the elegant*, *on the beautiful*; so why not then say *on the high* (*o vysokom*). Many people advised me to translate it as *on the high-flown* (*o vysprennom*), *on the elevated* (*o vozvyshennom*), *on the superlative* (*o prevoskhodnom*), or even as *on elevatedness, highflownness, grandiloquence* (*o vozvyshennosti, vysprennosti, vysokoparnosti*). Each of them had their reasons for advising me thus, and I too had my reasons for not heeding their advice. The most skilled of our writers have confirmed my choice.[25]

This passage reflects a struggle to register and overcome a certain terminological instability but not the absence of a tradition: Martynov's choice of *vysokoe* is the substantive adjectival form of the term used by Russia's earliest modern writers. In his "Rassuzhdenie o ode voobshche" (Discourse on the ode in general) (1734), Vasilii Trediakovskii had spoken of *vysokost' rechei* (loftiness of discourse), and Lomonosov was to consolidate this terminological choice with his rendering of the *stylum summum* as the *vysokii shtil'* in 1758. Yet in his *Kratkoe rukovodstvo k krasnorechiiu* (Short manual on eloquence) (1748) Lomonosov designated the sublime as affect by the term *voskhishchenie* (ecstasy or delight); the same experience is also more often described in Lomonosov's own poems as *vostorg* (rapture). Insofar as the Lomonosovian sublime was marked by what the eighteenth century called "lyric transport," his style was also dubbed the *pariashchii stil'* (the soaring style) or even *pindarizirovanie* (pindarizing, after the odic poet Pindar). In 1759 Aleksandr Sumarokov published a fragment of Longinus's treatise (translated from Boileau's French): intended as a polemic against Lomonosov, the piece rendered sublimity as *vazhnost' slova* ("solemnity of language") rather than as *vysokost'*.[26] Several generations later Pushkin would criticize Küchelbecker's revival of the odic sublime by accusing the latter of having "confused *vdokhnovenie* ('inspiration') with *vostorg* ('rapture')": "Inspiration can exist without rapture, while rapture without inspiration cannot."[27] The dispute between Lomonosov and Sumarokov, and subsequently between Küchelbecker and Pushkin, characterizes a Russian tradition in which the sublime can be discussed without being consistently named, and where identical or related aesthetic questions are debated without the invocation of the sublime as a unifying rubric.

Several decades later Nikolai Chernyshevskii's celebrated dissertation *Ѐsteticheskie otnosheniia iskusstva k deistvitel'nosti* (The aesthetic relations of art to life) (1855) would critique the basic assumptions of German idealist aesthetics, by then largely assimilated by the Russian intelligentsia, to the point of denying the ontological possibility of the sublime. Since no concept of the infinite existed to which the sublime corresponded, the sublime could only be "that which is much greater than anything to which we compare it." Thus "Mont Blanc or [the Caucasian mountain] Kazbek are sublime [*vozvyshennyi*], grandiose objects; but none of us would think to defy what our own eyes tell us by seeing in them something boundless or immeasurably great." For this reason, "instead of the term 'sublime' [*vozvyshennoe*] (*das Erhabene*), it would be simpler . . . to say the 'great' [*velikoe*] (*das Grosse*)."[28]

Whatever its philosophical merits, Chernyshevskii's materialist critique indicates that by the mid-nineteenth century a certain equivalence of conceptual vocabulary had been established between Russian and western thought. Although twentieth-century Russian philologists have continued to use a pluralizing vocabulary, speaking of *liricheskii pod"em* ("lyrical uplift"), *vostorg* ("rapture"), and *vysokoe* ("the lofty"), the standard term for the sublime has remained *vozvyshennoe* ("the elevated"). A scholarly Soviet edition of Longinus's treatise, the first in Russia since Martynov's second improved translation of 1826, was thus entitled *O vozvyshennom*.[29]

The Russian fin de siècle and its modernist aftermath present a further paradox. At no other time in Russian history was the poet's lofty mission so loudly proclaimed; yet the transcendent vision accorded to the artist did not generate any further aesthetic specification of the sublime as a category—indeed quite the contrary. The writings of the philosopher-poet Vladimir Solov'ëv, which greatly influenced Russian modernism, are a case in point. Solov'ëv believed that art served as a mediating link "between the beauty of nature and the beauty of future life."[30] Among the phenomena of nature Solov'ëv singled out the boundlessness of the starlit sky as "represent[ing] the highest degree of beauty." At this point he added:

> There is a well-known distinction posited by German aesthetics (especially since Kant) between the beautiful [*prekrasnym*] and the sublime [*vozvyshennym*] (Erhabenes); moreover the starry sky is relegated to the latter aesthetic category. It seems to us that a certain nuance of the beautiful has been elevated without an adequate basis to the level of an independent category that is opposed to the beautiful in general. Still, one should not attribute too much importance to this terminological question, and in any case in Russian we have every right to speak of the *beauty* of the starry sky.[31]

Elsewhere Solov'ëv would insist that other examples of nature's infinity such as the stormy sea are "beautiful" rather than "sublime," since "the presence of the chaotic and irrational principle in the depths of being endows the various phenomena of nature that freedom and strength without which life itself and beauty could not exist. . . . Beauty does not require the force of darkness to be annihilated in the triumph of universal harmony."[32] While echoing Chernyshevskii's dismissal of the sublime as an independent category, Solov'ëv was of course reversing Chernyshevskii's intent. The sublime was not abolished but instead reascribed to beauty as one of its intrinsic attributes. This shift, it should be noted, did not serve to consolidate an autonomous aesthetic sphere. For Solov'ëv, the sublime became a necessary feature of art precisely to the extent that aesthetic experience was destined to become one with religion. Dissolved into beauty as part of art's aspiration to transcendence, the sublime could not, for Solov'ëv, be theorized successfully as a distinct phenomenon. This is surely one reason why the sublime appears to be everywhere and nowhere in the writings of the Russian symbolists.[33]

Despite—and to some extent because of—the terminological diversity or imprecision that we have seen prevailing over two centuries, we can legitimately speak of a specifically Russian tradition of the sublime which was distinct from that of western Europe. In Russian culture the sublime was repeatedly linked to extra-artistic concerns; theoretically there was a concomitant desire to extend rather than delimit or specify its import. In Europe Boileau had insisted on distinguishing the sublime from verbal grandiloquence: the sublime, in other words, could be simple. Lomonosov was to break with Boileau over precisely this point. Harking back to the Latin scholastic tradition that had reached Russia via Kiev's Mohyla Academy, Lomonosov grafted the newer tradition of the sublime, with its generic orientation toward the ode, onto the rhetorical category of the *stylum summum* or "lofty style." This conflation would render the Russian sublime more of a linguistic category than a subjective experience. Monk put it clearly: "To write on the sublime style is to write on rhetoric; to write on sublimity is to write an aesthetic."[34] In this sense we might say that the Russian sublime was, at least in its formative stages, a rhetoric, whereas its European counterpart would evolve increasingly under the rubric of aesthetics. In Susi Frank's decisive formulation, "lack of synchrony" between Russian and European debates, as well as the "terminological fuzziness" of the Russian tradition, "not least in the context of the debates between the archaists and the innovators on language and style which in Russia reached well into the nineteenth century," were such that "the Russian sublime was never entirely transformed into an aesthetic category, but always retained the stylistic and pathetic-rhetorical aspect it had possessed since Longinus."[35]

Even in 1803 the evident conceptual discord between Lomonosov and Boileau remained a bone of contention (and a potential source of national differentiation): in the extensive annotations provided to his translation of Longinus, Martynov echoed La Harpe's observation that

"Longinus intended to speak not of the *sublime* (*vysokom*), but of what the Rhetoricians call high or sublime diction (*vysokii slog*), in opposition to simple diction and average or moderate diction. . . . Longinus *properly* conflates the so-called *sublime* with *high diction*. For someone with talent can learn how to write well from rules; but we cannot learn to be sublime."[36] Martynov was here merely reiterating what had effectively become the Russian tradition as it had been formulated in the eighteenth century. For Lomonosov, the sublime was essentially a rhetorical practice, typified by an archaic Church Slavic vocabulary, linked to the contemporary poetic genre of the ode, and linked by historical ties to the church sermon as well as to secular oratory. In other words, the sublime was first a fact of language and only then a subjective experience: it did not assume a preexisting and nuanced world of psychological affect but sought rather to incite and direct a specific emotional response. Tapping the lexicon of religious exaltation and courtly praise, the sublime drew the speaker and the listener into a shared identification with an object of wonder. This identification, in its original as well as its later inverted forms, was based on an analogy between the power of poetic (or oratorical) language and the might of the autocratic state.

The yoking of the sublime to royal power was also a common feature of court culture elsewhere in Europe, and these precedents are discussed in passing in chapter 1. Yet whereas Boileau had believed that the departure from reason occasioned by the sublime was temporary and containable, the rapture of Lomonosov's odes often appears unchecked, corresponding to a far more unstable sense of poetic syntax and cosmic order. Boileau's vision had implied an aesthetic sensibility that was autonomous yet strictly controlled, and reconcilable, what is more, with a rational political order. As Terry Eagleton has put it, "the sublime is a suitably defused, aestheticized version of the values of the *ancien régime*. . . . It is beauty's point of inner fracture, a negation of settled order without which any order would grow inert and wither."[37] In the Russian odic sublime, however, power manifests itself more absolutely, compromising the possibility of a nuanced aesthetic response. If the utopian descriptive topoi commonly found in Lomonosov's poems correspond to the pervasive myth of the harmonious state, then the lyric disorder that is no less typical of Lomonosov might be read as mirroring the basically random nature of autocratic power.

Overall, then, it appears as if the Russian sublime was more overtly politicized and less concerned than its western equivalents with a dialectic of mind and nature or with the emergence of an integrated aesthetic sphere. Certainly Kant's resolution of the sublime into a celebration of the mind's ability to conceive the infinite seems not to have been widely applied in Russian verse. The "egotistical sublime" (to use Keats's description of Wordsworth) is, with some exceptions, far more typical of English romantic poetry than Russian. Harold Bloom has pointed to the "post-Enlightenment crisis-poem" in English-language poetry as "our modern Sublime" and distinguished an "Emersonian or American sublime" predicated on a "refusal of history, particularly literary history." From this arose an "American individuality" that amounts to the "simple, chilling formula . . . *I and the Abyss.*"[38] By contrast, the Russian sublime appears closer to Hegel's characterization of oriental art, in which a transcendental signified, religious or political, overshadows the consciousness that seeks to establish relations with it. In the Russian ode, the lyric subject (and subsequently the reader) appears already inscribed into a circuit of correspondences between language, history, and politics. The Russian sublime might thus be seen as a rhetorical mediation between literary form and political ideology that enables the poet and reader to connect questions of poetic genre, lyric voice, and lexical choice to the wider historical drama of Russian autocracy. However much extended, nuanced, and even subverted in later generations, this was to remain the basic model of the Russian imperial sublime.

Orient and Empire

The sublimity of the Russian state lay in its imperial rather than its purely national character. We have already seen that the constitutive theme of the eighteenth-century Russian ode was empire. Whether it celebrated war or idealized peace, the odic vision of the unfolding of Russian history was inescapably linked to territory. In Lomonosov, Derzhavin, as well as their epigones, this cartographic impulse became deployed in evoking the horizontal stretch of Russia's dominions. In Kant's terms as interpreted by Thomas Weiskel, we might say that the odic topos of horizontality was an effect of the *dynamical* sublime, in which the lyric subject deflects and then projects the impact of power onto a spatial "dimension of contiguity." Replete with toponyms and ethnonyms, this horizontal axis served to quantify and mark Russia's physical extent and yet suggest a boundlessness that became a source of pride as well as anxiety in Russian cultural consciousness.

One feature of the odic map was a relatively consistent distinction between east and west. Lomonosov's geopolitical views distinguished sharply between Russia's involvement in Europe and her expanding military engagements on her southern and eastern frontiers. Although Lomonosov had certain reservations about Russian intervention in Europe, he viewed Siberia, the Far East, as well as Russia's southern regions as vast potential sources of wealth waiting to be tapped. Responding to the geopolitical gambit of Catherine the Great, poetic interest subsequently began to focus more narrowly on Russia's shifting southern border with Ottoman Turkey. For several literary generations beginning with Derzhavin, the Caucasus came to represent a necessary and privileged object of imperial attention.

This intensified focus on Russia's south both assumed and reinforced a deeper east/west dichotomy that is one of the constitutive traits of western orientalism in the ramified sense that this term has acquired since Edward Said. In Said's view, the long history of interrelations between Europe and Asia, culminating in the recent experience of Europe's colonial conquest and domination of the east, was founded on an assumed "line separating Occident from Orient" that is "less a fact of nature than it is a fact of human production," an "imaginative geography."[39] This imaginative geography was central to Russia's quest for national identity and imperial hegemony, and in unique ways. Unlike the paradigmatic cases of Britain or France, Russia conquered contiguous rather than overseas territories: its empire was thus a geographical extension of the nation. In Russia, then, the separation of Europe and Asia as metropolis and periphery was not self-evident: east (above all the Caucasus and the Eurasian steppe) and west (European Russia) met, as empire and nation, *within* one landmass, whose internal differentiation into "Asiatic" and "European" halves was a matter of cultural ideology rather than scientific fact.[40] The quest for empire was undertaken on the edges of the nation itself, whose geographical limits consequently appeared as a moving threshold, an infinitely receding horizon. In literary texts of the romantic period, this shifting horizontal axis was often complemented by the spectacular verticality of the Caucasian mountain range, and a conventional literary expression of imperial space became possible as the convergence of these two axes, horizontal and vertical.

More familiar perhaps than this spatial model are the cultural contradictions it generated. Although Russia's quest for empire was very much intended to establish her status as a European power, Russia was itself frequently viewed as Asiatic by western Europe: Russians thus strove to deflect the "orientalization" to which they had themselves been subjected onto their conquered neighbors. As Fedor Dostoevskii himself phrased the dilemma a century later, in the wake of the Russian General Skobelev's massacre of the Turkmen forces in 1881: "In Europe we were hangers-on and slaves, whereas to Asia we shall go as masters. In Europe we were Tartars, whereas in Asia we too are Europeans. Our mission, our civilizing mission in Asia will bribe our spirit and drive us there."[41] Russia's modernizing impulse, then, was fueled to no small degree by a powerful compensatory urge, an anxiety to belong: yet to be western, Russia paradoxically had to move east. We might thus speak of a triadic model, involving Europe, Russia, and Asia, in place of the familiar binary opposition of east and west. The triadic model imposed on Russia a peculiar form of shifting identity. Straddling two continents but not readily reduced to either, Russia was fated by its geography to engage in a perennial struggle with what might be called the dilemma of contiguity.

In the past decade a small but significant body of scholarship, primarily in the English language, has sought to examine the role of Russian literary orientalism in elaborating the imaginative geographies of nineteenth-century Russia's quest for empire. The primary work on the subject, Susan Layton's pathbreaking *Russian Literature and Empire,* has defined the contours and limits of the debate up until now with its subtitle, "Conquest of the Caucasus from Pushkin to Tolstoi."[42] In Layton's own words:

> Essentially a cultural monologue, Russian writing about the Caucasus engaged in ideologically significant discursive practices which transmitted and reproduced themselves from one epoch to another in various genres—in fiction and non-fiction, in the canonical and the "low." These practices included rhetorical postures, symbolic diction and tropes, specific concepts and a whole mental tendency to compare "us" to "them."
>
> Russian literature does indeed run the gamut between underwriting and resisting the Caucasian conquest: writers were sovereign in their textual domains but wielded their representational authority to different ends. Total complicity in imperialism was the mode of ephemeral orientalia, especially prominent in the 1830s. At the polar opposite, [Tolstoi's] *Hadji Murat* denounced the subjugation of the Muslim tribes as vile aggression. The particularly intriguing middle ground was occupied by young Pushkin, Bestuzhev-Marlinsky and Lermontov. . . . These three romantic outcasts endorsed imperialism in certain ways, while taking issue with it in others.[43]

Susan Layton's book, then, readily corresponds to what was known to Russian philology and history as the "Caucasian theme," even as it renews it methodologically from within.[44] Eschewing the realist bias pervasive in Soviet criticism, Layton argues for the shaping role of the romantic literary imagination as "artful fact" that "invented rather than recorded Caucasian landscape."[45] A "poetics of Caucasian space," says Layton, grew out of Pushkin's *Prisoner of the Caucasus,* allowing "citified travelers" to commune with a rejuvenating "alpine wilderness." Although hints of "Asiatic tribal menace" certainly impinged on this natural idyll, Layton views the alpine sublime as a fundamentally depoliticized experience, a "communion with nature" that—at least initially—"averted the eye from military conquest."[46]

Layton's work suggests ways of linking questions of poetics in a genuinely complex way to those of politics: the range of possible responses to empire of which Russian writers proved capable are gauged first in the light of their valency within the textual sphere of symbolic representations, and only then as evidence of an ideological position. *The Imperial Sublime* derives in no small way from Layton's premise, even as it differs from her book in its range and its particular articulation of the sublime. Limiting herself geographically to Russia's southern frontier and diachronically to the sequence Pushkin-Tolstoi, Layton tells a specific story of the Caucasus as a literary topos and as a fact of imperial history. *The Imperial Sublime,* by contrast, seeks to historicize a specific rhetorical and poetic tradition rather than a geographical region. From this perspective, Russia's southern periphery becomes a privileged moment in a story older than the conquest of the Caucasus itself.

Although Layton has rightly insisted on "alpine sublimity" as the privileged idiom of Russia's Caucasian adventure, she necessarily limits its genealogy to the "long-standing traditions of European writing about the Alps."[47] Such a conclusion risks reducing the sublime to a negotiation between a narrow range of topoi and concerns, foreclosing what is effectively the subject of this book. Not only did the Russian eighteenth century create an imperial context as well as an imperial poetics that preceded the romantic engagement in the Caucasus, it founded a rhetoric of the sublime whose implications far exceeded the European *goût de la montagne.* As the argument of the preceding pages suggests, the sublime takes us far beyond the question of literary *representations* of empire, and indeed beyond a purely mimetic understanding of the encounter between literature and history. If Layton believes that Russia's writers remained "sovereign in their textual domains but wield[ed] their representational authority to different ends," then this book offers an alternative sense of writerly subjectivity and its relationship to poetic form and political power.

As will be clear from the preceding pages, this book deals more or less with the century that began with Lomonosov's public debut as a poet and ended with Lermontov's death in 1841. This chronology has its merits. In literary terms it is widely recognized as the long period during which poetry defined the basic parameters of Russian literary culture, and its final decades also coincide historically with the heyday of Russia's Caucasian wars. To follow the imperial sublime through and beyond Lermontov's *Hero of Our Time* is to note the rapid decline of the lyric sublime and the corresponding rise of the Russian prose tradition, with its very different rhetorical and thematic trajectories. The most striking example of this divergence are Tolstoi's writings on the Caucasus, which can be read as a sustained attempt at prosaicizing and desublimating the tradition outlined in this book.[48] The conclusion to this book sketches out some of the salient moments in the Russian imperial sublime from 1841 up to the revolutions of 1917. Given my specific interest in verse genres and poetic language, however, the conclusion limits itself to an overview of the Russian poetic tradition from Fedor Tiutchev up to the early twentieth century, at which time poetry regained its ascendancy over prose.

Finally, I do not wish to claim that the Russian sublime has always been exclusively imperial or oriental: indeed, I wish in advance to acknowledge the existence of other Russian sublimes, whose correlation might be the object of future work. One thinks of the poet Baratynskii's *Èda* (1825), no less imperial but set in Finland; of Nikolai Gogol's *Arabeski* (1834), whose patchwork of architectural, historical, and geographical sublimes reads as Gogol's most theoretically sophisticated attempt at confronting the classic aesthetic dilemma of integrating part and whole; of the transformative and utopian impulses that typified the Russian avant-garde; and finally of the mass diffusion and ultimate banalization of the sublime that became the standard gesture of official Soviet culture, a story whose details and attendant ironies fall well outside this book's chronology and textual range.[49]

It will be clear by now that the pages to come provide neither an exhaustive history of the imperial theme in Russian literature nor a cultural history of the institutional interactions between literature and the imperial state. Instead they sketch out aspects of a prolonged encounter, largely *within* Russian poetry, between poetics and polity. My concern has been primarily with the means by which, for the first century after Peter the Great, imperial power in Russia became rhetoricized or aestheticized by certain poets within specific genres. The sublime was a potent mechanism by which to bring together—in a fusion or a collision—the apparently distinct problems of poetic vision, sovereign patronage, divine force, and imperial expansion. This complex imbrication of forces was first registered as a fact of language or as an affective state, then projected and played out on the arena of the imperial state and its territories. The sublime was one means of articulating and channeling the energy unleashed at the meeting point of literature and history, and its insistent presence in classical Russian poetry is the story I propose to tell.

This book was completed to daily reports of the extraordinary carnage and destruction being wrought in Chechnia. I would wish both the Russian and the Chechen peoples a future other than sublime.

1

Sublime Beginnings

Not by the silver of merchants but by the iron of Mars
Feofan Prokopovich, from his second Petersburg sermon, 1716

Imperial Beginnings

Some forty years after Peter the Great assumed the title of emperor, Voltaire, whose enthusiasm for Peter's legacy was an important confirmation by a key figure of the Enlightenment of Russia's entry into the concert of European nations, would comment suggestively but inaccurately on this shift in terminology: "As for the title of czar, it comes from the tsars or tchars of the Kingdom of Kazan. When the Russian sovereign John or Ivan Vasilievich [the Terrible] had reconquered this realm in the sixteenth century . . . he assumed its royal title, which his successors kept. . . . The name *czar* was therefore the title of oriental rulers, more plausibly derived from the Shahs of Persia than from the Roman Caesars . . . [while] the name *emperor* . . . is given nowadays to the sovereigns of Russia with more justification than to any other potentate, if one considers the extent and power of their dominion."[1]

Voltaire was implying that the tsardom of Muscovy, for all its traditions of monarchical rule buttressed by territorial expansion, was still an Asiatic power. Although the title of tsar was in fact of Byzantine rather than Islamic origin, Voltaire's folk etymology was not inaccurate in one respect. It intuited that Peter's conferral of imperial status to Russia marked not only her newly augmented "extent and power" but also a fundamental cultural reorientation. In his recent book, *Scenarios of*

Power, Richard Wortman has identified this reorientation as a "shift from a Byzantine to a Roman imperial model."[2] Eliminating the Byzantine vision of a religious symbiosis of church and state, Peter envisioned his empire as a secular western polity measured chiefly by the standards of military might and cultural progress. Muscovite ideology was thereby displaced by a new kind of absolutism, in which modernization itself became a projection of the emperor's will, in foreign policy as in internal reform. At the beginning of the eighteenth century, Russia entered modern Europe as a reforming state ruled by a sovereign of unlimited power whose territories would expand through successive conquests.

Not surprisingly for a reign known for its prolonged wars, the pursuit of empire contributed greatly to the direction of state policy. Peter fought protracted wars against Sweden and Ottoman Turkey: the Baltic, and to a lesser extent the Black Sea, provided the context for Russia's definitive entry into the realm of European diplomacy and politics. To a considerable degree, the imperial context was also to determine the shape of domestic policy: in the classic formulation of the historian Klyuchevsky, "the war was the principal cause of Peter's reforming activity: initially a military reform, it became ultimately a financial reform."[3]

Petrine absolutism, then, was fundamentally imperial rather than national or confessional in tendency, and the deployment of unlimited sovereign power in all aspects of civic life closely followed Peter's vision of martial order and preparedness. This had several consequences in the realm of symbolic representations of the monarch and his rule. Richard Wortman has insisted on the newness of Petrine symbolism, which "recast the image of tsar and elite in terms of a Western myth of conquest and power."[4] Diluting Muscovy's messianic role as defender of Christian Orthodoxy, the new order would seek cultural affirmation in the celebration of its military achievements and worldly greatness, combining reform at home with victory abroad. This transition from "theocratic tsar to sovereign emperor," as Michael Cherniavsky has termed it, was fundamental, although never entirely completed. No longer a saintly guardian of the faith, the emperor became a divinity in his own right, the source and repository of all power, "self-contained and self-generated."[5]

The arrival of secular modernity in Russia involved more than the subordination of church to state. In according the emperor powers wrested from the church, modernity rearticulated the relationship between profane power and spiritual authority. The influential Moscow-

Tartu school of cultural semiotics has highlighted how persistently both Muscovy and imperial Russia legitimated political rule through recourse to the sacred. This tradition survived even Peter's radical secularization of Russian elite culture, so that the emperor was able to enhance his power further by arrogating to himself the creative force of God. The sacred was thus altered rather than abolished, and secularism, like all western ideas, constituted a transformation of, rather than a complete rupture with, the Russian past.[6]

In delineating the displacements and mutations of the sacred, the cultural semioticians have effectively traced the vicissitudes of power from Muscovy to imperial Russia as a symbolic form. It was in the sixteenth century, V. M. Zhivov and B. A. Uspenskii tell us, that the religious connotations attached to the term *tsar* first began to be used to sacralize the institutions of political power. The king's power was perceived to enjoy God's sanction, and its divine provenance, rather than just rule, provided the ultimate rationale for monarchy. Evolving out of religious claims, a specifically imperial ideology emerged only later, during the reign of Tsar Aleksei Mikhailovich (1645–76). Under his reign the ideologeme of *translatio imperii,* whereby the authority of Byzantium was seen to have devolved onto Russia, acquired a specifically political form. Muscovy's claim to be the seat of a universal Orthodox empire, and the Byzantine forms this claim took, formed the local ideological context of Peter's reforms.[7]

In secularizing the imperial model he inherited, Peter would undermine its spiritual base, replacing it with the rationalist ideal of the regulated state. All aspects of policy were concentrated in the hands of the state apparatus, nominally impersonal but in fact vertically derived from the monarch's will. The sovereign became the chief agent of historical transformation, claiming a benign vision of societal progress for a coercive system of state power centered on one individual. Inevitably the figure of the monarch was itself subject to myth making, becoming a symbol to reconcile means and ends, the personalized and arbitrary nature of autocratic power and the goal of creating a "well-ordered state."[8] Paradoxically, then, Petrine secularism contributed to an intensification of the sacred function of the monarch. Where the emperor was seen to possess the theurgic capacity to make and unmake people, institutions, and ideals, the empire became the necessary repository of an order as much cosmic as political. The cult of the emperor and of the divinely bureaucratic imperial state became the dominant symbolic form of the eighteenth century.

Such an exalted symbolism did not immediately correspond to an equivalent linguistic practice. Petrine ideology was distinguished by its propagandist zeal and clarificatory impulse, lending a concrete, earthly expression to a grandiose vision. During Peter's reign, imperial discourse was less a literary problem than a pragmatic one. A rationale for empire evolved from the perceived need to inform and educate weary subjects of the necessity and progress of Russia's prolonged military campaigns. Peter would explain the humiliating defeat at Narva in 1700 at the hands of the Swedes as a result of Russia's "artlessness in all things, military as well as political"; hence subsequent victories in the twenty-year Northern war became a major index of the nation's progress.[9] The vicissitudes of war were articulated as part of the constant drive for military and political modernization that marked Russia's quest for an equal place in Europe. This theme was highlighted in a programmatic publication issued in 1717 to justify the Swedish war, P. P. Shafirov's *Discourse concerning the Just Causes of the War between Sweden and Russia*. Shafirov argued that the disputed provinces of Karelia and Ingria had "of old been part of the Russian Empire"—a term Shafirov applies retrospectively to Muscovy—but lost through Russia's internal weakness. The war to regain these lands was thus part of a wider cultural struggle pitting Russia as much against its own past history as against Sweden: if formerly "Russians were little counted among the nations of Europe . . . nowadays no affair is pursued, even on the furthest edges of Europe, on account of which no attempt is made to elicit his Royal Majesty's friendship or alliance."[10] Only military strength could vouchsafe Russia's place as a European nation.

The task of representing and propagating a discourse of empire under Peter devolved primarily onto two realms, the visual arts, architecture, and spectacle, on the one hand, and panegyric prose, on the other. Engravings of Peter in western dress or armor surrounded by heraldic insignia, and of battle scenes commemorating Peter's triumphs, were among the most popular of his reign. Many of these representations were allegorical, surrounding the emperor with embodiments of Christian virtues, or pagan gods. Triumphal arches were erected to mark Peter's victories, in which contemporary events were encoded through visual references to Roman mythology, ancient history, and medieval heraldry, in keeping with the Baroque sensibility of the courtly and religious culture that Peter had inherited from the late seventeenth century. Learned Baroque culture had already juxtaposed classical pagan and Christian representation but in the interests of didactic knowledge or decorative detail. Peter was to sharpen this gesture into an implied polemic with Muscovite religious tradition, suggesting the epistemological parity of Christian and classical symbolism. Generally inaccessible to the urban population who observed them during victory processions, these abstract "emblemata" were often accompanied by explanatory publications or translated into narrative tableaux that offered a tangible satiric or political message. A picture of Phaeton, son of the sun-god Phoebus Apollo, was said to represent "the force of Sweden which, rising as it were in the noontime of its glory, set fire to the world with its luster, then fell, struck down and put to shame by the arrows of the Russian eagle." A painting of Vesta was identified as Russia "cleansing her native lands of the invasions and predations of her neighbors"; from her circular seat representing the Russian state there emerged a two-headed eagle releasing bolts of thunder to "expel the lion, standard of the Swedish realm," while the four parts of the world, "Asia on an elephant, Europe on a bull, Africa on a lion, [and] America on a crocodile" proffered "wreaths, emblems of greeting, power and divine grace."[11]

Fireworks were Peter's favorite spectacle. One event, held in 1704 to mark the capture of Noteburg, began with the illumination of an eagle, the state emblem, holding under its wings and in its claws figures depicting the White, Caspian, and Azov seas that marked Russia's expanding borders. The eagle continued to burn for half an hour, during which time a boat appeared bearing the sea-god Neptune, who proffered the eagle a fourth sea, the Baltic. Behind the eagle two illuminated shields appeared: one depicted rakes gathering ears of wheat, the other a birdcage with open doors. Together they indicated to viewers that the lands recently wrested from the Swedes had been historically Russian but lost, like fields lying fallow and neglected.[12] Under Peter, then, the aesthetic realm was subordinated to a didactic purpose, and Baroque symbolism became a tool to create an imperial spectacle that would both instruct and exalt.

Panegyric oratory was the other field through which the new discourse of empire was propagated. A prose genre with close links to the religious sermon, it became a powerful tool for the festive propagation of Petrine ideology, and a significant precursor to the victory ode that is central to this chapter. Panegyric literature celebrated Peter's military victories and political achievements, and sought to garner popular support for change. The key protagonist in this field, as in the theoretical elaboration of Petrine ideology, was the "ecclesiastical politician" and "all-Russian imperialist" Feofan Prokopovich (1681–1736).[13] His discourses, which are marked by a powerful geopolitical sensibility, appraised Russia according to her power and physical extent more than for her religious piety, "for it was not through feebleness that this orthodox kingdom has expanded to the point where all the western states are opposed to its grandeur, like rivers against a measureless ocean." Prokopovich popularized the soon influential topos that images Russia's geographical breadth as an index of her might. Russia's confines, he tells us, could not be measured by "any yardstick except a valorous and manly weapon."[14] The remote seas, rivers, and kingdoms that marked Russia's far-flung borders served less to specify her spatial limits than to celebrate her potentially infinite power. Prokopovich's patriotism combined an enthusiasm for Russia's past triumphs with an acknowledgment of the backwardness that his country had only recently overcome. Lacking any knowledge of military science, Russia was ill prepared to confront a "strong and trained adversary." Her ancient "wars and victories against the Tatars" were thus no precedent for modern warfare; "naked and weaponless" at the beginning of the new era, Russia was destined to "arm and adorn herself" only under Peter's tutelage.[15] Prokopovich thus confirmed a sense of radical rupture with the Muscovite past that was an integral part of the self-consciousness of the Petrine era: the correlation between empire, territorial expansion, and social progress remained an important ideological rationale for the Russian imperial state until 1917.

Stylistically, Prokopovich was committed to the didactic clarity and concision that Peter himself viewed as the pragmatic aim of all discourse. Prokopovich's theoretical work, *De Arte Rhetorica* (1706), written for the Mohyla College in Latin, and which he envisioned as a pedagogical manual for public speaking both religious and profane, prescribes three "kinds" or "styles" of speech: a high or sublime style (*summum, quod etiam dicitur grande, grave, sublime, magnificum*) that corresponds to "lofty things," such as "heavenly, eternal, divine matters, as well as human affairs worthy of admiration, or full of pain, pity, or indignation, such as . . . the destruction of kingdoms, the vicissitudes of fortune" and "events of sad import"; a "lowly style" that deals with "humble things"; and, finally, a "middle style" (*stylum medium*). The middle style expresses "happy things" that are the subject matter of "panegyrics and history": it marks victories, hails triumphs, and praises the achievements of illustrious men.[16] In theory if not always in practice, Prokopovich elaborated a linguistic model for a contemporary discourse of empire: during the Petrine period the Russian empire would be stylized linguistically as an affair of "medium import," not yet lofty or sublime. This would radically change with Peter's death and the emergence in Russia of a modern literary culture.

Polotskii and the Baroque Panegyric

Before turning to the post-Petrine period, it is necessary to take note of a seventeenth-century figure whose life and work herald the concerns of this chapter in important ways. Simeon Polotskii (1628–1680) was arguably Russia's earliest modern writer, an educated clergyman and court poet to Peter's predecessors Aleksei Mikhailovich and Fedor Alekseevich. Polotskii's life and work manifest certain patterns that would become paradigmatic for several generations of Russian writers. He was a native Belorussian, educated at the Mohyla College in Kiev and the Jesuit Academy in Vilnius before settling in Moscow. Most Russian writers of note until Derzhavin would follow this biographical model of the writer, drawn from the peripheries of the Russian state to create the language and literature of the imperial center. Polotskii's professional career as Russia's first court poet also dramatized the elusive goal—definitively compromised only with the Decembrist revolt of 1825—of reconciling the demands arising from court patronage with the search for ethical, aesthetic, and professional values that might vouchsafe a writer's creative dignity.

In the absence of an established tradition of versification and a milieu of poetic connoisseurs, Polotskii's achievement appears all the more remarkable. Polotskii is the most celebrated of the seventeenth-century syllabic poets. The syllabic system counted a fixed number of syllables and a caesura in each line, as well as a stress on the penultimate rhyming syllable, as its only regulating principles, and was to prevail for some fifty years until the revolution of form wrought by Trediakovskii and Lomonosov. Polotskii compiled three collections of verse, *Rifmologion* (Rhymology), *Vertograd mnogotsvetnyi* (A many-flowered garden), neither published in full in his lifetime or subsequently, and a translation of the Psalms, the only work to exercise any immediate influence on his poetic descendents. Despite the limited impact of Polotskii's work, his compilations together anticipate the thematic range of Russian court poetry well into the eighteenth century.

Rifmologion is a compilation of panegyric poetry dating from the 1650s to the 1670s. Dedicated to the tsars and the ruling family, these are poems written for public declamation on occasions of state, royal anniversaries and birthdays, or religious holidays. They represent the most substantial attempt at grafting eastern Slavic Baroque poetics onto the official culture of late Muscovy. Hyperbolic and affirmative in tone, they are essentially extended poetic comparisons intended to exalt the tsar and his family. Addressing the tsar conventionally as the defender of Orthodoxy «Царю восточный, царю стран премногих, / нас избавивый от противник многих. / Прогнавый мрачны з Руси еретики / буди ж в победах преславен во веки!» [O Tsar of the East, Tsar of a great many lands, / Who saved us from many enemies. / Who chased the dark heretics from Rus / Be most glorious in your victories for all times!]), Polotskii's praise nonetheless assumes a cosmological dimension that frequently exceeds Muscovite religious tradition. In Polotskii's most pervasive trope, Russia is compared to the firmament, and its rulers to heavenly bodies:

> Небом Россию нарещи дерзаю
> Ибо планиты в оней обретаю.
> Ты солнце; луна—Мария царица;
> Алексий светла царевич денница.[17]

> I dare to call Russia heaven
> For I find planets in it.
> You [o Tsar] are the sun; the moon is Tsaritsa Mariia;
> and Tsarevich Aleksei is the bright morning star.

Polotskii's celestial vision assumes the complementarity of heaven and earth, and a harmonious analogy between political and divine power. Both are seen to originate from the one source, the sun, in order to illuminate as light and emanate as Christian grace. The poet accedes to this vision by "daring" to compare. It is the scaffolding of his similes that largely holds up Polotskii's poetic edifice, and cosmic harmony corresponds, rhetorically speaking, to the poet's power to sustain and elaborate his comparisons.

The most striking cycle or "booklet" (*knizhitsa*) contained in the *Rifmologion* is "Orel rossiiskii" (The Russian eagle) (1667), which addresses the Russian heraldic eagle on the occasion of Aleksei Mikhailovich's son being proclaimed heir apparent:

> Пресветлый орле российския страны
> Честнокаменным венцем увенчаны,
> Орле преславный, высоко парящий,
> Славою орлы вся превосходящий,

Вскую превыше облак водородных
Париши крилы перий славоплодных;
Что во пространстве воздуха велика
Суть стремления тобою толика;
Яко исполнь есть весь орызонт славы
Всемирных концев от твоея главы.
Глава ти небес самых достизает,
простертость крилу весь мир окривает.
Ногама скиптри Царския держиши,
в море, на земли, властелино стоиши.[18]

Most luminous eagle of the Russian nation
Wearing a crown of precious jewels,
Most glorious eagle, soaring high,
Surpassing all other eagles in glory,
Why do you soar far higher than the rain-bearing clouds
With your wings made of feathers that bring glory;
Such that your strivings are so great
in the vast expanse of the air;
For the entire horizon on all sides has been filled with glory
emanating from your head.
Your head reaches the very heavens,
Your spread wings cover the entire world.
You hold the royal scepters with your feet
and bestride, o master, both sea and land.

Thematically speaking, "Orel rossiiskii" is the work by Polotskii that most closely resembles the eighteenth-century ode that will take its place, with the establishment of the Russian Empire, as the defining genre of imperial discourse in literature.[19] Like most of Polotskii's poems in *Rifmologion,* the cycle models the world as a vast visual panorama binding the cosmic and the political. This panoramic vista is horizontally mostly static, relying instead on a vertically mobile vision that can embrace the downward gaze of God and tsar and the upward gaze of the worshipper and subject. The medium in which these gazes meet is the air, in turn populated by abstract symbols and emblems—personifications of Christian virtues, mythological personae, the heraldic insignia of different nations—whose role is to differentiate and organize an otherwise static space. These allegorical figures serve to shrink the infinite or to enlarge the finite: by projecting themselves onto physical space or territory, they effectively reconfigure that space according to their own dimensions. This is the eagle's role in the above passage: in soaring high it acquires a vertical advantage that it then projects horizontally, by spreading its wings, as Russia's spiritual and military destiny.

Polotskii thus mapped classical Muscovite ideology, specifically the need to wrest Constantinople from the Turks for the sake of Orthodoxy, onto a firmament populated by celestial bodies. In one poem Polotskii invokes the twelve signs of the Zodiac as instantiations of the celestial tsar's virtues and deeds, "wet Aquarius" being the sea route taken by the tsar's army to seize Constantinople from the "rotten hands of the sons of Hagar."[20] This idea is elaborated at greater length in the middle section of "Orel rossiiskii," which plots an astrological chart for the heir to the throne, according to which the tsarevich's imperial mission is governed by the sign of Cancer.

> Во Зодий рака ты тогда вступиши
> Солнце России, егда разшириши
> Дасть Бог свою власть, Морем и землею:
> Что рак зодийный клещею своею
> Содержит земель. . . .[21]

> You will enter the sign of Cancer
> O Sun of Russia, when you enlarge,
> God willing, your power on land and sea:
> Just as the sign of Cancer with its claws
> holds many lands.

The expansion of Russian power is astrologically fated: it will propel the tsarevich into a struggle against the "sons of Hagar" in the Muslim world, to whom he will introduce the "rock of faith." Just as it is "customary for the sun to dissipate gloom," so the tsarevich will accomplish two tasks, the religious conversion and the political subjection of the Muslim world. Consistently in Polotskii the horizontal axis of territorial expansion and ideological struggle can be activated only by virtue of the vertical axis of sun and sky. Imperial power resembles radiance more than aggression; its source is astral and only then political. Cultural difference is thus gauged according to a chiaroscuro principle of luminous virtue and black ignorance. Pagan nations are nothing if not "dark": they may remain in the shadow or be drawn into the light.

Polotskii's baroquely conceived "astral imperialism," which maps the grandiose political mission of the Russian tsar onto an allegorically conceived axis of vertical space, anticipates the poetics of the eighteenth-century Russian ode. His Baroque taste for allegory will remain a typical feature of Russian classicism, and his juxtaposition of Christian ideology and classical antiquity looks forward to the Petrine cult of ancient Rome. His lexical choices, particularly the abundance of bookish terms, will also be an important precedent for Lomonosov's "high style." Yet Polotskii's poetics falls distinctly short of what I will shortly identify as the "imperial sublime." First, his vision is essentially moral and static, and hence cannot really sustain the eighteenth century's expansionist notion of empire as an entity evolving competitively in secular rather than redemptive history.[22] Second, the poet is himself barely present to his language. Even if the Baroque writer perceives the linguistic sign to be arbitrary and hence mutable, knowledge is nevertheless inherently finite: hence the poet's task is only to clarify the allegorical correspondence between signifier and signified.[23] Where the poet has an articulated presence, he is instructive rather than inspired, and is finally subsumed by his didactic task.

Polotskii's programmatic poem, "Zhelanie tvortsa" (The artist's desire), comes closest to delineating a contractual relationship between sovereign and poet: the poet praises but in return asks to see his poetry published. Still, publication is not yet, for Polotskii, the acknowledgment of authorship but rather the fact of disseminated knowledge, which is the cultural counterpart to victory in battle: «. . . . Россия славу расширяет / Не мечем токмо, но и скоротечным / типом . . .»[24] (Russia enhances her glory / Not only through the sword, but also through the printing / press.) Poetry's merit lies in spreading knowledge and is distinguished from other forms of cognition only by the formal patterns of rhyme or meter. The role of inspiration, which grants a complex and vital role to poetry and the poet as a dynamic force, is still absent here.

Polotskii's poetics were not destined to survive intact into the Petrine era. Feofan Prokopovich's "Èpinikion" (Victory song) (1709), the most celebrated panegyric poem of Peter's own time, already differs considerably from Polotskii's mode. Translating celebration into description, it reads narratively as a kind of truncated epic in the manner of Homer: «. . . . Уже брань десятое лето начинаше / (Время брани троянской) . . . .»[25] (The war was already beginning its tenth year / [The duration of the Trojan war]). In his *De arte poetica* (1705), also written for the Kiev Academy, Prokopovich counsels against the use in the heroic epic of "lengthy paraphrases, and excessively lofty or inflated words." An epic poem must not "carry us so high that it cannot be followed by the human mind."[26] Prokopovich accordingly reduces his mythological references to epithets and brief similes; they function not as mediating allegories but to dramatize the cult of the emperor. For all these differences, the panegyrist of Peter's time does resemble Polotskii in that he has yet to articulate his own place in the poetic system. The grandeur of the depicted object effaces the speaker:

> Царю Богом венчанный, ты силен о Бозе,
> Сокрушив, повергл еси гордаго под нозе.
> О день благополучний! Кий язык и кое
> Слово изрещи может блаженство такое![27]

> O Tsar crowned by God, you are strong in God,
> You have shattered the proud [enemy] and trounced him under your feet.
> O fortunate day! What tongue and what
> Word can utter such bliss.

Neither Polotskii nor Prokopovich is able to formulate the vivid encounter between political and poetic authority that marks the work of eighteenth-century poets who emerge after Peter.

To achieve a fuller picture of the thematic range available to the court poet in this period of transition from Muscovy to imperial Russia, brief mention must also be made of Polotskii's other major collection. *Vertograd mnogotsvetnyi* is an encyclopedic compendium of didactic verse, containing prescriptive advice as well as fragments of worldly knowledge presented for their informative value. Scattered among these poems one finds pieces with such titles as "Grazhdanstvo" (Citizenship), "Zakon" (Law), "Nachalnik" (Superior), and "Sud" (The trial). Together these poems constitute one of the earliest attempts on the part of a Russian writer to define the ideal sovereign. The good king is one who "seeks and wishes profit for his subjects," unlike the tyrant who is "not at all concerned with the needs of his citizens."[28] In Polotskii, then, we already discern the fundamental dilemma of the court poet. Must he praise the existing order or rather educate the sovereign and the reading public, thereby creating the preconditions for the establishment of a better society? And does praise of the ideal, as if it already existed, constitute a form of hypocrisy or a subtler kind of instruction? This tension between the didactic and the panegyric mode will become all the more dramatic in the post-Petrine era, with the establishment of the ode as the preeminent literary genre and enlightened absolutism as the dominant ideology.

The Emergence of the Ceremonial Ode

The prosaic pragmatism of Peter the Great and the relative absence of belles lettres during his reign should not obscure the essential fact of the near synchronous birth of the Russian Empire and of modern Russian literature. The early struggle to create a normative, secular, and modern literary language endowed with an elaborated system of genres and versification and a prescriptive poetics governing stylistic, lexical, and thematic choice was waged in the 1730s, during which time the principles of autocracy were being definitively established with the neutralization of aristocratic opposition to Empress Anna (1730–40).

At this time, literary practice became deeply embedded in the culture of court patronage and the imperial academy, an intimacy whose contours were never again to be repeated. The role of ecclesiastic discourse, even in the politicized or civic form it had acquired under Peter, continued to erode, yielding its control over symbolic language to new literary forms. Following the "prosaic" hiatus of Peter's reign, the adoption of secular and European models of state ceremony and courtly pomp elicited the introduction of the ceremonial ode as a concomitant literary genre. This was the beginning of a long era in which poetry, poetics, and rhetoric would define the nature of literary Russian, and in which the artistic orientation of the ode would itself resolve a range of issues, from the linguistic and generic parameters of literature to the symbolics of political and poetic power.

"In no other European literature," observes I. Z. Serman, "did the ode enjoy such a varied development and become such an important poetic genre, as in the Russian."[29] Why might this have been the case? Certainly the near absence of a secular court literature in Russia and the newness of the post-Petrine literary system worked against genre pluralism, allowing the ode to quickly establish its monopoly on civic themes. The ode's only potential rival in this realm was the epic, a genre destined never to flourish on Russian soil. The Russian eighteenth century is littered with incomplete or unsuccessful epics, so that a recent critic has been moved to acknowledge the ode as the "Russian equivalent" to the epic poem.[30]

The history of the ode is long and richly entangled.[31] The subgenre that concerns us here is the Pindaric ode of ancient Greece, written to honor the victors of various athletic competitions. For Pindar (518–438 B.C.), an athlete's success was a sign of the gods' favor, a tangible if momentary confluence of the divine and the human. To celebrate an athlete's physical prowess was thus to make vividly tangible a manifestation of the divine. Like the hero he immortalized, the poet was himself close to the gods. In this sense he was like a prophet but one who foresaw "backward" rather than into the future. His temporal perspective was grounded in a competition whose outcome was already known and which needed only to be ranked against similar events in a familiar past. This Pindar achieved through a dense array of mythic references, which situated a given victory in an exalted set of established precedents and analogies. Pindar's poems are rich in metaphor and echoes of mythic tradition, his jagged syntax leaping rapidly from allusion to allusion. With the fading of the worldview of archaic Greece, Pindar came to be remembered—and criticized—chiefly for his elusive style, considered brilliant but structurally uneven.[32]

The odic tradition was intermittently revived in the early modern period, most conspicuously by the French Pléiade poet Ronsard and his successor and antagonist, Malherbe, as a conscious imitation of the ancients. Malherbe (1555–1628), the French odist most often cited by Russians, was to purge the Pindaric ode of its perceived extravagances and submit it to the discipline of a simpler structure. His themes were official, the victories or achievements of France's rulers. It was with Malherbe that the ode "emerged as the literary organ of the centralized monarchy," essential to an "era in which absolutism was crystallizing and being established."[33] The seventeenth-century French critic and satirist Nicolas Boileau-Despréaux (1636–1711), whose opinions were to influence Russian classicism profoundly, commented approvingly of Malherbe's "sober transports," seeing in his capacity to "submit the muse to the rules of duty" a linguistic model for his own time.[34] For all his rationalism, Boileau also provided a powerful justification for the irregularities of the Pindaric style. He pointed to the Hebrew Psalms of King David, which combined prayer and petition, as possessing a similar poetics of rapturous praise. Boileau's analogy between Pindar and David (to which we shall return) was to resonate powerfully in the Russian context, given the importance of the Psalms to Church worship and to the beginnings of the Russian lyric.[35] The "French" Pindar, juxtaposed alongside the Psalms, was the prehistory inherited by the Russian ode in the post-Petrine era. Yet its immediate origins, bureaucratic and official, point to still another source.

The earliest Russian attempts at odic composition were commissioned by the Saint Petersburg Academy of Sciences, written in German by resident foreign academicians and accompanied by Russian approximations in syllabic verse of the German originals. These poems, marking various ceremonial occasions of court life, count as one of several tentative beginnings of the Russian ode. L. V. Pumpianskii has traced the poetics and genealogy of German poetic influence in Russia back to the *Schule der Vernunft*. Comprising minor poets of a transitional era, this school sought to apply the precepts of French classicism to the German context of their time. Just as Boileau's model of syntactical and lexical transparency and aesthetic moderation had summarized a normative model for the culture of French absolutism, so, too, the emergence in 1701 of the new kingdom of Prussia saw the advent of the German ceremonial ode based on the Malherbian style as a constitutive element of the opulent court life of Friedrich I. Given the German cultural and political ascendancy notoriously prevalent in Russia under Empress Anna, it is not surprising that various epigones of German court poetry were to find a ready welcome in Saint Petersburg during the 1730s.[36] In accordance with the practice of European courts, these poets combined a range of activities, from the composition of odes marking anniversaries and other festive occasions, to the translation of commissioned literary works, to the reporting of events for the official gazette, to the devising of political or other allegories that served as the basis of firework displays arranged for the pleasure of the court. These activities were organized under the auspices of the Academy of Sciences, a bureaucratic arrangement that was to leave its mark on the origins of modern Russian poetry. The Franco-German ode provided a ready poetic and political precedent for two successive reforms of Russian versification, and hence to the definitive creation in Russia of the "imperial sublime." As we pursue the legacy of these reforms, first that of V. K. Trediakovskii and then of M. Lomonosov, the relevant aspects of this Franco-German tradition will be indicated.

Vasilii Trediakovskii (1703–1769) was the son of a poor priest who fled his native Astrakhan to acquire an exceptional European education in Moscow, the Hague, and Paris. On arriving in Saint Petersburg he was appointed translator and secretary to the Academy of Sciences, undertaking by contract to "do to the extent of his ability whatever corresponds to the interests of Her Imperial Majesty and the honor of the Academy [and] to purify the Russian language by writing both verse and non-verse."[37] Trediakovskii's role is here defined primarily in relation to the linguistic task of creating a courtly language purged of the Church Slavic and Ukrainian legacies of earlier generations. This goal, which was already pursued in Trediakovskii's earlier and highly successful translation into Russian of Paul Tallemant's *Voyage à l'isle d'amour* (1730), was to become radically compromised as the ode assumed its unique traits on Russian soil.

In 1734 Trediakovsii published his "Oda torzhestvennaia o sdache goroda Gdanska" (A ceremonial ode on the surrender of the city of Gdansk), which he presented as the first Russian solemn or ceremonial ode to be written according to the new Franco-German model. A celebration of Russia's successful military intervention in the Polish war of succession, the ode was accompanied by a commentary entitled "Rassuzhdenie o ode voobshche" (A discourse on the ode in general). The "Discourse" clarifies that an "ode is the combination of many strophes composed of equal and sometimes unequal verses, which always and unfailingly describes noble, solemn, and grandiose matters, in speeches that are highly poetic and very sublime (*vysokikh*)."[38] It is briefer than the epic but resembles the latter in its "nobility of matter and sublimity of speech." Pindar and Horace, adds Trediakovskii, "were able to compose so marvellously, when, in order to manifest their reason when it was, as it were, outside of itself, purposely interrupted the sequence of their discourse, and, in order better to enter reason, departed from reason itself (*chtob luchshe voiti v razum, vykhodili . . . iz samago razuma*), if it may thus be said, in the manner of Boileau-Despréaux, moving away with great effort from the correct order, which would have taken away the entire salt, the entire juice, or better yet, the very soul of Lyric Poetry." It is this quality, proper to the ode and palpable to the reader, that Trediakovskii calls "poetic enthusiasm" (*entuziasm* [*sic*] *piiticheskii*), typified by "audacious figures" such as hyperbole.[39]

We have here the earliest vivid description in Russian of lyric afflatus, and the tension between rapture and order, as it pertains to poetic utterance. (Polotskii had been able to experience "joy" at the presence of the monarch but not yet lyric rapture, which appears prior to the poem's given theme and has its own force.)[40] The statement, like the "Discourse" as a whole and the ode it came with, was not original. In the 1752 redaction of his "Discourse" Trediakovskii openly acknowledges Boileau's poem, "Ode sur la prise de Namur" (1693) and the accompanying article "Discours sur l'ode," as his precedent and guide, proffering his own work as a conscious imitation of Boileau's "superlative" work. Boileau had intended his ode as a polemical experiment, a defense of the ancients, specifically the Pindaric style, against contemporary detractors. In a misreading shortly to be repeated—and magnified—by Lomonosov, Trediakovskii was to perceive Boileau's interest in

Pindaric style as normative and prescriptive, adopting it as the prototype of the new Russian ode.[41]

Where Boileau's ode and "Discours" read as a lively intervention by an author who is defining the limits of a genre and establishing the nature of aesthetic autonomy within French absolutist culture even as he appears to be praising the king, Trediakovskii's equivalent texts read as a form of abject homage, both to the Europe of Pindar and Boileau and to the Russian empress. Still a syllabic poem (the great revolution in metrics is yet to come), Trediakovskii's ode on Gdansk preserves many of the formal (stanzaic and other) attributes of Boileau's ode, as well as its overall thematic movement. An invocation to the muses in the Pindaric style, innovative in the Russian context, begins the poem:

Кое трезвое мне пианство
Слово дает к славной причине?
Чистое Парнаса убранство,
Музы! не вас ли вижу ныне?
И звон ваших струн сладкогласных,
И силу ликов слышу красных;
Все чинит во мне речь избранну.
Народы! радостно внемлите;
Бурливые ветры! молчите:
Храбру прославлять хощу Анну.[42]

What sober intoxication
Gives me the language for so glorious a cause?
Pure adornments of Parnassus,
O Muses! Is it not you I see now?
I feel both the ringing of your sweet-sounding strings,
and the force of your beauteous faces;
All prompts me to make this select speech.
Nations! Heed with joy;
Obstreperous winds! Be silent:
I wish to celebrate the valiant Anna.

Conventional in its imitation of Boileau, this invocation, and the poem to follow, nonetheless contains an element of novelty: the emergence in Russia of an inspired lyric self. The poet is now himself a force, "soaring to the stars" like a "swift, daring eagle," venturing even to prophesy the outcome of battle: «Хочет сбыться, что я пророчил» ("What I prophesied wishes to come true"; cf. Boileau's equivalent line, "Mes présages s'accomplissent").[43] This claim to prophetic status will become an important manifestation of the poet's will-to-power, one that will grow in hubris over the next century just as it collides with the realities of the Russian state.

Even as the inspired voice of prophetic utterance, the poet remains subject to the sovereign's will, which is also the ode's theme. This tension between the lyric self and the monarchical idea is present in Boileau also but in a subtly weaker form, since the poet yields *first* to inspiration and only then to the sovereign:

> Quelle docte et sainte yvresse
> Aujourd'huy me fait la *loy*?[44]

> What learned and holy intoxication
> Today imposes its *law* upon me?

The aesthetic experience of rapture, Boileau suggests, has its own "law" that makes art a distinct but codified realm, outside (but analogous to) the sovereign will. We find nothing really comparable in Trediakovskii: his poetic frenzy cannot legislate; it is itself subject to Anna's "cause."

Inevitably, then, Empress Anna looms far larger in Trediakovskii's poem than does King Louis XIV in Boileau's. Indeed, wherever Trediakovskii fails to follow Boileau, it is in order to embellish and praise the Russian monarch far beyond Boileau's encomiums to his king. The empress is the "beauteous sun of the European and Asiatic heaven," whose "name is terrifying to the world," whose "glory cannot be encompassed by the universe / that desires to be vanquished." The resistance offered by the city of Gdansk is contrasted to those "entire nations," which—like the poet himself—"submit voluntarily, without any fight."[45] This dynamic of resistance and submission, of subjectivity and subjection, will become fundamental to the Russian victory ode in its mature form.

Trediakovskii was ultimately not destined to be either a court poet or a writer of odes. Within a few years the literary politics of his successor, Lomonosov, would render him marginal to the court and to the activities of the Academy. Yet this brief period of Trediakovskii's ascendancy also saw the publication of his "Novyi i kratkii sposob k slozheniiu rossiiskikh stikhov" (A new and brief method for composing Russian verse) (1735), in which syllabic verse is definitively transformed through the introduction of the accentual principle in verse.[46] Trediakovskii's metrical innovation is unmistakably a breakthrough; equally striking is the range of genres Trediakovskii discusses, from the elegy to the sonnet to the ode. Interestingly Trediakovskii does not insist here on any absolute hierarchy of theme or genre, and the preferences he does express correspond to notions of euphony rather than ideology. One might speculate that it was not merely Trediakovskii's lesser talent but also his moderation, or rather his *unwillingness to link poetics and ideology,* which made him less than useful to the official culture of the time. Indicative here is Trediakovskii's refusal to attribute an intrinsic aesthetic significance to the iambic or trochaic meters whenever the question—a significant literary controversy of the 1740s—was subsequently raised: "Neither is the trochee gentle nor the iamb noble in itself, but both metrical feet are noble and gentle according to the words [used in them]."[47] Similarly, in the 1752 redaction of his "Method," written after—and in response to—Lomonosov's formulations, Trediakovskii was to add that the ode "celebrates the loftiest, most noble material but sometimes gentle material also."[48] Given his commitment to the distinctness and heterogeneity of form and content, we need not be surprised that Trediakovskii was destined to evolve outside the bounds of odic court culture.[49]

Poetics and Ideology in Lomonosov's Revolution

Mikhailo Vasil'evich Lomonosov (1711–1765), the son of a fisherman from the remote White Sea region in Russia's far north, is the overarching figure of eighteenth-century Russian literature, and Russia's most gifted poet until Derzhavin. Like Trediakovskii, Lomonosov was propelled by a thirst for knowledge to study in Moscow, Petersburg, and western Europe; unlike Trediakovskii, Lomonosov was to achieve an authoritative place in the literary and scientific communities where his theoretical reforms, scientific encyclopedism, and poetic achievements won him respect and recognition. By the beginning of the 1740s, Lomonosov had taken Trediakovskii's place as the primary Russian poet, lecturer, and translator at the Academy of Sciences, although his professional relationship with the Academy would remain marked by political intrigue.[50]

The first battle cry in Lomonosov's struggle for cultural ascendancy was the appearance of the "Oda na vziatie Khotina 1739 goda" (Ode on the taking of Khotin in 1739), hailed, as we remember, by Belinskii as "the first Russian poem written in a correct measure."[51] The poem, written while Lomonosov was a student in Germany to mark a Russian victory over the Turks, was sent to Russia along with his seminal "Pis'mo o pravilakh rossiiskogo stikhotvorstva" (Letter on the rules of Russian versification) (1739) and circulated among several academicians as a practical example of Lomonosov's intended revolution in prosody. The letter and poem are interesting both for their startling novelty and for the presence in them of several vital if largely implicit prior voices in whose wake Lomonosov was speaking. The coupling of a theoretical treatise with a poem marking a military victory was a clear if sharply polemical acknowledgment of Trediakovskii (and of Boileau before him). Lomonosov's letter, in fact, conflates the narrower generic focus of Trediakovskii's "Discourse on the Ode in General" (1734) with the broader concerns of his "Method" of 1735, even as his ode is clearly a successful attempt at superseding Trediakovskii's ode on Gdansk. Trediakovskii was not indifferent to the nature or breadth of this challenge: his subsequent decision to revise the texts which had served as Lomonosov's Russian context reads like a sophisticated acknowledgment of defeat. The gap between these two redactions illustrates the impact of the Lomonosovian revolution over a decade.[52]

The burden of Lomonosov's "Letter" was to locate a formal specificity within the language on which a uniquely Russian system of versification may be founded. This specificity, for Lomonosov, was the Russian accentual system, distinct from the older mode of syllabic scansion that had been introduced into Russia through Poland and only recently undermined by Trediakovskii. Lomonosov extended the realm of metrical and rhythmical possibility by admitting both binary and ternary meters, allowing monosyllabic words to be considered stressed or unstressed, and by permitting masculine and dactylic rhymes in various sequences, as well as the feminine rhymes prevalent in syllabic poetry.

While extending Trediakovskii's tentative reforms, Lomonosov's poetic revolution in fact amounted to a metrical, generic, and thematic narrowing of lyric possibility. The crucial lines of Lomonosov's "Letter" read as follows:

> I consider the lines which consist of anapests and iambs to be the best, most beautiful, and easiest to compose, and the most capable of expressing in all instances both speed and slowness of action and the intensity of any passion.
>
> Pure iambic verse, although rather difficult to compose, does, by its discreet upbeat, augment the *nobility, magnificence and sublimity* [*blagorodstvo, velikolepie i vysotu*] of the material. Nowhere is it better employed than in victory odes, as I have done in the present one.[53]

Lomonosov saw the iambic sequence of an unstressed and stressed syllable as being essentially superior. Its rising upbeat, unlike the downward movement of the trochee, corresponded, formally speaking, to a "sublimity" of content. This correlation of form and content was further specified by the elevation of the ceremonial ode as the privileged genre of Russian poetry. The greater part of Lomonosov's poetry consists of odes, primarily in four-foot iambs. As he himself was to confess in his "Conversation with Anacreon" (1761):

> Although of heartfelt tenderness
> I am not devoid in love,
> I am more enraptured
> by the eternal glory of heroes.[54]

Lomonosov's revolution is of interest here as an ideology of form. First, it naturalized the iamb—and finally accentual meters in general—as corresponding to the "innate properties" of Russian, its "natural pronunciation," in contrast to those rules that "have been brought to the Moscow schools from Poland."[55] Although deeply grounded in the history of German metrics and Franco-German aesthetics, Lomonosov's thesis manifests an outward nationalism of *form* that was still absent in Trediakovskii, who was willing to acknowledge the prior example of Europe, modern and ancient. Second, Lomonosov's poetic practice would conflate the specific artistic and thematic parameters of the celebratory ode with the concerns of literature as a whole. His odes established a dominant tradition of political poetry with the imperial state as its central theme. This theme was intimately linked to the rhetoric of the sublime, which Lomonosov was to inaugurate definitively as the idiom of empire. No poet before or after Lomonosov is so singularly linked to the subject of this book: to chart the poet's evolution is effectively to trace the political and stylistic parameters of the imperial sublime in its earliest and defining stage.

How did the sublime emerge as a category for Lomonosov? In the above passage it appears embedded in a discussion of meter and genre, where it functions as the moment of *transition* in the argument from formal categories to the ideological premise of imperial victory. It allows Lomonosov to identify both iamb and empire as equally lofty. This is by no means a coincidence: the sublime cannot be schematically reduced to either a purely formal construct or an ideological category. It functions rather as a moment of *mediation,* serving to negotiate and establish analogies *between* the formal problems of genre, lyric voice, lexical choice, and prosody and the ideology of national specificity that Russia will vindicate, yet also complicate, through conquest.

The Imperial Sublime and Its Component Parts

BOILEAU AND LONGINUS

In his *Art poétique* (1671), the great codex of French classicist sensibility in literature, Boileau presented reason or common sense as the sole arbiter of taste, the "yoke" to which rhyme would willingly submit, as slave to master:

> Quelque sujet qu'on traite, ou plaisant, ou sublime,
> Que toujours le Bon sens s'accorde avec la Rime . . .
> La Rime est une esclave, et ne doit qu'obeïr.
> . . . Au joug de la Raison sans peine elle fléchit,
> Et loin de la gesner, la sert et l'enrichit.[56]

> Whatever subject one treats, be it pleasant or sublime,
> Good sense must always be in accord with Rhyme . . .
> Rhyme is a slave, and must only obey.
> . . . She bows without trouble to the yoke of Reason,
> And far from disturbing it, serves and enriches it.

Art, then, was the mastery of content over form, the power of the intellect to tame language, yet without excessive force. Regimentation was necessary but in the service of equilibrium. This moderation in the use of power was aesthetic sensibility, or taste itself. In poetry this involved a limpid syntax that avoided enjambments, observed strict caesuras, and shunned preciosity for its own sake. In the wider realm of culture, Boileau might be said to have summarized the prevalent norms of polite society: the precepts of reasoned elegance and self-restraint corresponded also to the degrees of personal freedom and aesthetic autonomy available to the cultivated individual, the *honnête homme,* under French absolutism.[57]

The ode was the sole genre that, by Boileau's own admission, did not mirror these precepts entirely. Pindar's odes, Boileau tells us in a passage from "Discours sur l'ode" that was cribbed by Trediakovskii, contain "marvellous places where the Poet, in order to designate a mind entirely outside of itself, at times breaks by deliberate design the sequence of his discourse; and, in order better to enter reason, departs, as it were, from reason itself."[58] The ode, then, was a challenge to Boileau's own system; its form disrupted aesthetic order and the concept of reason on which it was founded. Boileau's *Art poétique* describes the ode as follows:

L'Ode avec plus d'éclat, et non moins d'énergie
Elevant jusqu'au Ciel son vol ambitieux,
Entretient dans ses vers commerce avec les Dieux.
Aux athletes dans Pise, elle ouvre la barriere,
Chant un Vainqueur poudreux au bout de la carrière,
Mene Achille sanglant aux bords du Simoïs,
Ou fait fléchir l'Escaut sous le joug de Louïs . . .
Son style impetueux souvent marche au hazard.
Chez elle un beau desordre est un effet de l'art.[59]

The Ode with more sparkle, and no less energy
Raising its ambitious flight up to Heaven
Entertains commerce in its verses with the Gods.
It opens the gate for the athletes in Pisa,
Celebrates a dusty Victor at the end of the race,
Sends bloody Achilles to the edges of the [River] Simois,
or makes the [River] Scheldt bend to the yoke of Louis . . .
Its impetuous style often moves haphazardly.
In the ode a beautiful disorder is an effect of art.

This passage, the last two lines of which quickly became an *idée reçue* of the times, delineates the essential movement of the odic sublime. We first observe the upward flight of the ode by which it establishes "commerce" with the gods in heaven. It is this initial flight of hubris, and the lofty vantage point it affords, that grant the odic poet his authority, one that equals the power of the athlete and the king. The "impetuous style" of the ode is this sudden access to power, whose disruptive potential is then neutralized through its identification, in praise, with the athlete and the ruler. Lyric afflatus, and its subsequent alignment with the power of the sportsman or monarch, corresponds to the "departure" and "reentry" into reason that Boileau had described in his "Discours sur l'ode." This equation of aesthetic reason (the principle of rationalism in art) with the sovereign will is particularly evident from the repetition of the same phrase "fléchir sous le joug" ("bow to the yoke") in the two passages quoted: rhyme bends to the yoke of reason just as the River Scheldt is bent to the yoke of Louis. Yet if King and Reason here occupy a homologous place of authority, we might also note that their power is here exercised *imperially.* The subjugation of rhyme is the equivalent, in poetic terms, of imperial conquest, the victories of Louis XIV over Flanders in 1666–67, designated here by the River Scheldt.

Renowned "lawmaker of Parnassus" and royal historian to King Louis, Boileau was nonetheless no mere codifier of reigning sensibilities.

Boileau's greatness lies in his willingness to contemplate the very limits of representation, and then integrate those limits into the aesthetic order he saw as given. Expressed as a tension between order and disorder, rational control and lyric afflatus, this limit—the sublime—was accorded a place in Boileau's system that was both exceptional and carefully demarcated. In the 1674 edition of his *Oeuvres diverses,* Boileau published a translation of Longinus's celebrated work *On the Sublime* alongside his own *Art poétique.* This act of critical equilibration, in its careful juxtaposition of order and excess, effectively launched the modern career of the sublime.[60]

In the preface to his translation Boileau defined the sublime by distinguishing it from the rhetorical notion of the "sublime style": "It must be understood that by the Sublime Longinus does not mean what the orators call the sublime style, but whatever is extraordinary and marvellous that is striking in discourse and which causes a work to lift up, entrance or transport one (*cet extraordinaire et ce merveilleux qui frape dans le discours, et qui fait qu'un ouvrage enleve, ravit, transporte*). The sublime style always desires big words; but the Sublime can be found in a single thought, in a single figure, in a single turn of phrase."[61] Boileau's definition of the sublime was essentially aesthetic and not rhetorical. The sublime was an *effect* of style rather than a style in itself; it did not depend on the tripartite *genera dicendi* found in the classical Latin manuals of rhetoric, in which the high style was equated with grandiloquence, but pointed instead to the experience of lyric "transport," felt first by the poet and then by the listener or reader.

Boileau's translation of Longinus was read by Lomonosov in 1738 during his sojourn in Marburg as a student, barely a year before he was to write his "Letter on the Rules of Russian Versification." Lomonosov's own notes from Boileau have survived in manuscript form along with his précis of a manual by the German rhetorician Gottsched.[62] From these notes it is clear that Boileau's Longinus came to function for Lomonosov as part of a powerful normative poetics, derived from European debates but never coinciding with them. We have seen that Boileau had insisted on the need to distinguish the sublime from the materialities of style such as ornament or lofty diction; for him, then, there was no contradiction between the sublime and the simple. Lomonosov was to break with Boileau precisely over this question: his poetic model would ultimately be an amalgam in which the weight of Russian tradition would bear heavily on the paradigms imported from France and Germany.[63]

Boileau and Longinus maintain a large if subtle presence in Lomonosov's "Letter." Lomonosov does not mention Longinus himself but cites—in a passage that is generally critical of French influence—the opening lines of Boileau's "Ode sur la prise de Namur." The brief discussion that ensues, concerning only the metrics of the poem, is in fact a buried quote from Gottsched's *Versuch einer Critischen Dichtkunst* (Attempt at a critical poetics) (1733). In an analogous passage Gottsched had quoted the same Boileau ode immediately before an explicit discussion of the Longinian sublime: "This [pathetic] style is the reckoned place of the so-called sublime [*das sogennante Hohe*], about which Longinus has written an entire book. . . . This pathetic style is to be found firstly in odes, where the poet, on becoming agitated, finds release in fiery expression. One example of this is Günther's ode to Eugen, which displays this character almost throughout."[64] The German poet Günther's ode, "Auf den Zwischen Ihro Kaiserl. Majestät und der Pforte an. 1718 geschlossenen Frieden" (On the peace concluded in 1718 between His Royal Majesty and the Porte) (1718), was yet another model for Lomonosov's poetic revolution: composed, like the "Ode on the Taking of Khotin," in four-foot iambs with an identical stanzaic structure, it commemorates an earlier European victory over Ottoman Turkey.

This international context is necessarily muted in Lomonosov's letter, which is above all a search for Russian specificity, a flourish of authorial independence and national pride. To make this context explicit, it has been necessary to reverse the author's intent. Lomonosov's debt to a series of literary and theoretical antecedents suggest that his intervention of 1738 was part of a broadly European revival of the Longinian sublime that began with Boileau's translation of 1674.

LOMONOSOV AND THE "VYSOKII SHTIL'"

We have seen that Lomonosov broke with Boileau even as he borrowed from him. This rupture involved inserting the sublime back into the "sublime style" of classical rhetoric, which had already been assimilated locally a generation before thanks to the Russian Baroque reconciliation of Orthodoxy and secular classical learning. Lomonosov's extensive writings on rhetoric do not dwell explicitly on the sublime at length, although they do provide a great deal of advice on the need for "solemnity" and "grandiloquence" in sermons and panegyrics, and on the use of "conceits" (*vymysly*) in public discourse. In Lomonosov's *Kratkoe rukovodstvo k krasnorechiiu* (A short manual on eloquence) (1748) the sublime is finally described as the figure of rapture or ecstasy (*voskhishchenie*): "Rapture is when an author represents himself as being in an astonished reverie deriving from some exceedingly great, unexpected, fearful or supernatural thing. This figure is almost always coupled with a conceit, and is most deployed by poets."[65] This definition is followed by a series of quotations, primarily from Lomonosov's own odes, as well as Boileau's Namur ode, and Ovid. Every one of these quotations thematizes lyric afflatus, the "sacred horror" that transforms poetic language into prophetic vision.

Lomonosov's definitive theoretical statement on the sublime came considerably later, with the publication of his "Predislovie o pol'ze knig tserkovnykh v rossiiskom iazyke" (Preface on the utility of ecclesiastic books in the Russian language) (1758). Here Lomonosov adapted the rhetorical distinction between high, medium, and low styles to solve the specific dilemma of how Russian and Church Slavic might coexist. The sublime would now be identified by a specific lexical register, the high or lofty style (*vysokii shtil'*):

> The first [lofty style] is composed of Slavo-Russianisms, that is, utterances used in both [Church Slavic and Russian] languages, and Church Slavicisms, which are comprehensible to Russians and not too archaic. Heroic poems, odes, prosaic speeches on important matters should be composed in this style, by which they rise (*vozvyshaiutsia*) from ordinary simplicity to a lofty grandeur. This style gives Russian an advantage over many modern European languages, in making use of the Slavic language from our books of liturgy.[66]

Lomonosov's linkage of the sublime to the ecclesiastical language of Slavic Orthodoxy was to prove a defining moment in the early history of Russian poetics. The ceremonial and sacred odes that constitute most of his own poetic opus are no more than an elaboration of this principle and survived as a legacy over which even the literary battles of Pushkin's day were fought. The Russian sublime was not to be a purely intuitive aesthetic category but a linguistic and rhetorical one, situated at the summit of a strict hierarchy of styles, and endowed with its own lexical traits (Church Slavicisms) and privileged genres (the ode, the epic, and public oratory). Furthermore, the sublime was no longer an exceptional occurrence, a *cas limite,* as for Boileau, but would define the earliest norms by which the literariness of the Russian language would be judged as a national patrimony. The coexistence over centuries of Church Slavic and Russian were seen to distinguish Russia from other nations such as Poland and Germany, for which Church Latin could not serve as a comparable source of lexical wealth.

Lomonosov's article of 1758 (which merely theorized his existing poetic practice) accomplished the considerable feat of reconciling the essentially foreign metrical and ideological legacy of the Franco-German ode with the local tradition, typified by Prokopovich and Polotskii, of the church sermon, the psalm, and the syllabic panegyric. In a sense this amalgam represented a continuation of Peter's policy of secularization. Containing "strong depictions of solemn and sublime [*vysokikh*] ideas," suited for the celebration of the nation's glory, Church Slavic was being advocated for its civic potential and not for its religious vision.[67] Yet, in another sense, this premise was a reversal of Petrine linguistic policy, which had insisted on the definitive separation of Russian and Church Slavic.

Lomonosov's Slavicization of literary Russian constituted an essential chapter in the process of literary modernization in Russia.[68] It was through the "lofty style" of the ode that the norms of literary Russian were first determined. This process marks the convergence of two questions that interest us, both of which link poetic language to cultural ideology. With the reabsorption of the language of the Church into secular literary discourse, the place and function of the sacred were also inevitably to alter. The poet was increasingly to perceive his task in quasi-religious terms, as that of a seer or visionary endowed with a sacred prophetic power. The claim to prophetic status was not necessarily linked to any religious insight: prophecy became a formal vehicle to explore the question of power, its origins, and its exalting or alienating effects. In the odic tradition, the poet's visionary authority deriving from God or the muses would invariably be juxtaposed alongside the power of the emperor or empress, and the imperial state. As we have already seen from Trediakovskii, the simplest resolution of this dual authority was one of alignment: the poet's prophetic voice, not unlike that of the post-Petrine church itself, simply became a clarion of the victories and achievements of the imperial state. Yet we shall see that the history of the imperial theme in Russian literature in fact involved a loosening—but not a severing—of this bond.

Generally the steady alienation of the poet from the court, culminating in the romantic era, has been read as the story of Russian culture's growing autonomy from the state. As Iurii Lotman has it, "the struggle of eighteenth-century Russian literature for its social function was its struggle for the right to social independence, for the right to be the voice of truth, and not the reflection of the opinions of the court."[69] Yet the independence of the poet in Russia, always tenuous at best, was seldom if ever won as a part of recognizing his *artistic* autonomy. Rather, the poetic word became articulated as a manifestation of *force,* derived vertically from God, the muses, or the emperor, and potentially aligned with or opposed to the dominant authority of the imperial state. The poet's authority, even where it claimed no more than aesthetic freedom, was often established through a formal homology with the authoritative discourses of state and church. As Pushkin was to advise the poet, «Ты царь: живи один»[70] ("You are the tsar: live by yourself").

In the following chapters, we shall be examining the rhetorical patterns and discursive modalities by which Russian poetry engaged or evaded the realities of power. Stylistically and thematically, it was to be the role of the sublime first to connect and then to articulate the relationship between the poet as secular prophet and the Russian Empire.

THE POET AS PROPHET

"The notion of the poet as prophet . . . graced by some higher authority is established very early on in eighteenth-century literature," claims Iurii Lotman.

> Trediakovskii, in his translation of Horace, had already rendered *divinis vatibus* (by which Horace had meant "poets inspired from above") as *bozhestvennye proritsateli* [divine prophets]. Trediakovskii thereby fused the Greco-Roman ideal of the sublime poet with the image of the biblical prophet. . . . The hoary classicist metaphor of "poetry as the language of the gods" has been perceived in the Russian context as a precise testament to the authority, and consequently the degree of responsibility, of the poetic word. Precisely because poetry had taken the place of sacred texts in secular culture, truthfulness (*istinnost'*) was perceived not as an optional trait of artistic language, but as an inalienable quality of poetry: anything untrue was not poetry. In replacing the sacred texts, literature inherited their cultural function. This substitution, which took place in the eighteenth century, generally became a persistent feature of Russian literature.[71]

In uncovering the genealogy of the poet as prophet, Lotman is guided by Russian culture's traditional concern with its own autonomy, understood here in its ethical dimension as truthfulness. Yet one cannot underestimate the importance of the reverse process: the constitutive role of the sovereign, figured in his or her relationship to the sacred, in shaping, negatively or positively, the space of literary discourse, and even of the writer himself. It is precisely this reverse process that interests us here.

The textual tradition to reflect this play of forces most closely was the poetic rendering of the Psalms of King David. Simeon Polotskii's *Versified Psalter* (1680) was the first of numerous attempts at translating the Church Slavic versions of the Hebrew Psalms into Russian. Said to have been decisive in drawing the youthful Lomonosov to poetry, Polotskii's *Psalter* established a tradition of measuring the merits of modern poetic language by its capacity to render the Psalms in meter and rhyme. Trediakovskii, Lomonosov, Kantemir, Sumarokov, and later Maikov, Kheraskov, Derzhavin, Petrov, Nikolev, and Kapnist all translated the Psalms or wrote poems influenced by psalmodic motifs.

In his "Discourse on the Ode in General" Trediakovskii had followed Boileau in asserting the essential identity between the psalm and the ode:

> Any Russian who so desires can observe the sublimity (*vysotu*) of language that is befitting to odes, in the Psalms . . . for the Psalms are nothing other than Odes. . . . Here he will see nobility of subject matter, richness of ornamentation, and magnificence of depiction. . . . In them rivers return to their sources; seas part and flee; hills leap; mountains melt like wax and disappear; heaven and earth listen and inspire with respect and silence; all of nature begins to move, swayed by the face of its Creator: he [the reader] will see and say that this is verily the language of God. The perfect Ode, particularly one celebrating noble subject matter, should be thus composed.[72]

The ode and the psalm were thus conflated under the aegis of the sublime. To be sure, Lomonosov was subsequently to distinguish his celebratory odes formally from what he termed *sacred odes* (*dukhovnye ody*), reserving a specific stanzaic and rhyming structure for each subgenre, and the term *sacred ode* was soon to spread beyond the transpositions of the Psalms to cover most religious verse. Yet linking the ode and the psalm was a closely allied set of rhetorical tropes and thematic concerns. As James von Geldern observes, the psalms "in many ways corresponded to the ceremonial frame: It was direct speech but direct speech that recognized hierarchical distinctions between speaker, audience, and subject. The performative nature of the Old Testament explains the curious similarity between ceremonial and spiritual odes. . . . [They] were not two separate genres but a single genre manifest in two performative frames."[73]

In both the sacred and secular odes the poet bore witness to a vaster order that dwarfed him. This order, either cosmic or political (and very often both simultaneously), was manifested as the omnipotence of its creator, be it God or the emperor. Unlike Polotskii's static cosmology, however, the universe of the ode and the odic psalm was essentially mobile, a force made palpable through its dynamism—the moving of rivers, the melting of mountains, the defeat of foes, the extension of empires. This was less a cosmos than a cosmogony, a world in the making. And whereas Polotskii presented his poetic texts as instruction, as something to be known, the odic poet presented his text as something to be *felt,* inspiring awe or fear: "[in the Psalms] all creatures, all forms of matter, all of nature . . . tremble at the presence of the Lord, quake at His brilliance, harken with horror at the all-sovereign (*vsederzhavnoi*) hand that beckons, marvel in fear at the all-powerful Force."[74]

The psychic premise of both the ode and the psalm is subjection: the poet submits to the greater will of God or emperor, who occupy a potentially analogous place of omnipotence. Yet the author of the Psalms, David, was also a "blessed prophet and king," occupying a more exalted position than a poet—or indeed any subject—under Russian autocracy. Dramatizing the quest and plight of a righteous man, the Psalms address God not only to offer praise but also to express need. The element of entreaty, the request for protection and aid, created a dialogue between the worshipper and God whose intimacy scarcely corresponded to the relationship prevailing between monarch and subject. In this process of supplication, a lyric self was created whose contours exceeded what was possible in the ceremonial ode.

Roughly coeval with the ceremonial ode, the sacred ode quickly manifested its potential in what was effectively the first literary competition in Russian history. In 1744, during the course of what appears to have been a friendly dispute, Trediakovskii, Lomonosov, and the younger poet Aleksandr Sumarokov each resolved to attempt his own poetic rendering of Psalm 143. Their convergence was a sign of a common poetics, nascent but already allowing of individual difference. Significantly the project was not seen as a contribution to religious discourse but as a laboratory for testing the new poetic language. A shared culture of versification had already existed for several years, as did an assumption about the sublime kinship of ode and psalm. What remained under dispute was the question of meter. Lomonosov, along with Sumarokov, believed that the iamb "possesses of itself a sublime (*vysokoe*) nobility, because of the fact that it rises up from below, such that its sublimity and magnificence is noticeably audible to any man." Hence it was appropriate to "heroic verse," whereas the trochee was purely "elegiac." Trediakovskii's position, as we know, was less rigid: sublimity was not a metrical property, and "nobility" and "gentleness" could be manifested through "differences in vocabulary."[75]

Trediakovskii's trochaic version, ponderous and prolix, contrasts interestingly with Lomonosov's. Both Lomonosov and Trediakovskii reproduce the basic three subjective agents of the psalm—David, God, and the "alien sons" (*syny chuzhie*) who are David's foes. Yet Trediakovskii attributes to David a sense of radical doubt about his own worth, which extends even to his kingship: «Как? О! как могу быть Царь?»[76] ("How, oh how could I be King?"). By contrast, Lomonosov's David, while acknowledging that not all humans merit God's protection, exhibits an unerring confidence in his own relationship with God. This divine axis is then opposed to David's adversaries:

Благословен Господь мой Бог
Мою десницу укрепивый,
И персты в брани научивый,
Сотреть врагов взнесенный рог.[77]

Blessed be the Lord my God
Who has strengthened my hand,
And taught my fingers to fight,
To erase the raised horn of my enemies.

It is interesting to note that the latter line, concerning "erasing the enemy," is absent in the original Church Slavic version of the psalm, as are the many other references to "enmity" found in Lomonosov's version. Numerous critics have commented on the "intensification of polarities" present in Lomonosov's renderings of the Psalms, in particular the contrast between the "righteous man and his enemy."[78] Not only Psalm 143, but indeed seven out of the nine Psalms that Lomonosov translated, dramatize a world marked by struggle and conflict, which can only be righted by the hand of a just but vengeful God:

Ты видел, Господи, их мерзость:
Отмсти и злобным не стерпи,
Отмсти бессовестную дерзость
И от меня не отступи.

Восстани, Господи Зиждитель,
Взойди на твой святый престол

И буди нашей при решитель
Спаси от нестерпимых зол.[79]

You have seen, O Lord, their baseness:
Wreak vengeance on the malicious, do not tolerate them,
Wreak vengeance on them for their shameless boldness
And do not abandon me.

Rise, O Lord and Creator,
Ascend your holy throne
And be the one who resolves our conflict
And save me from intolerable evils.

These lapidary four-foot quatrains, like many of Lomonosov's psalms, tell the story of a world in which God appears reduced to the level of intercessor in a personal conflict. Many commentators have pointed out that these lines have an autobiographical underpinning and are colored by Lomonosov's prolonged struggle, based on egoism as well as principles, with the "foreigners" in the Academy of Sciences. Indeed, Lomonosov's translation of Psalm 143 coincided with his being placed under temporary house arrest by the authorities, and the image of God as intercessor and protector resonates against Lomonosov's perennial search for powerful patrons close to the ruling sovereign.[80]

This autobiographical element strikingly indicates the emergence of a lyric self within the odic tradition. The psalmist's quest for justice allowed for the individuation of the supplicant, as well as the expression, however veiled, of unofficial political views. This alternative persona arose from the vertical axis of man/God, which was structurally akin to the verticality of subject/monarch. Lomonosov's startling critique of earthly power in Psalm 145, which goes well beyond the original's advice to "put not your trust in princes," is won at the price of an equivalent surrender to God.[81] In this sense the psalm and the ode mutually implicate each other, since both are expressions of a subject that originates in submission. At the same time, the psalm ultimately endowed the lyric subject with a greater flexibility: whereas the writer of ceremonial odes was only ever the monarch's subject and at best her counsellor, David was both king to men and servant to God.

Ontological mobility was the psalm's greatest legacy to the Russian poet. The poet-prophet, as the divine agent of retributive justice, could aspire to a more exalted status than that accorded to him by the state. This sense of elevation was manifested, in literary terms, as inspiration. Lyric rapture was not merely the prelude to a vision; it indicated the newly discovered grandeur of the poet's mission. This notion of inspiration was new to Russia: it began, for all intents and purposes, with the ode and the onset of imperial modernity. As V. M. Zhivov has written, "the concept of poetic inspiration as a specific quality intrinsic to poetry was first clearly witnessed in Russia with the syllabotonic poets, above all Lomonosov."[82]

Lomonosov's recourse to the Church Slavic tradition was thus thematically a selective one. New Testament notions of charity and redemption are weak or absent in his work, and the sacred became a vehicle for the negotiation of power. In this sense the sacred odes were only apparently a form of religious homage. By appropriating the sacred for literary practice, they were also extending the secularization of culture that was a vital part of Peter's legacy.[83] This move was also quite in keeping with the older panegyric tradition, with its divinization of the royal persona. Yet it was precisely the task of the sacred ode to transcend the exaltation of the monarch, and to claim for the poet the holy power of the king. With the rise of critical Enlightenment values and the growing independence of educated society through the eighteenth century and beyond, the sacred ode would ultimately create the terms and frame for an incipient literary discourse of opposition.

In the pages to come, up to and including the chapters devoted to the Decembrists, Pushkin, and Lermontov, we shall be returning repeatedly to the complex relationship between the imperial and what might be called the *prophetic* sublime, and the way the former worked upon the latter. By this I do not mean to suggest that the imperial sublime historically preceded or engendered the prophetic mode but that their rivalry was by no means mutually exclusive. The sublime allowed for a contamination of secular and sacred forms, both of which were based on similarly vertical structures of exalted hierarchy. Inevitably, however, the greater power wielded by secular authority forced the prophetic sublime into an essentially defensive or rebellious mode. Just as post-Petrine autocracy secularized and arrogated for itself the demiurgic power of God, so, too, the poet-prophet reorganized and politicized the sacred into an oppositional force. In this sense the prophetic sublime was both competitive and derivative: even when it militated against autocracy, it did so in a manner that mimicked imperial power. The point here is not that the imperial sublime was a greater force than its rival—it clearly was—but rather that the sublime itself became complicated and diversified as it embraced a greater variety of competing forces.

THE IMPERIAL STATE

The central nature of the sublime in Lomonosov has, of course, not escaped critical attention. Yet no study has been made of the Lomonosovian sublime as a *composite* model that embraces and connects a range of literary, cultural, and ideological levels, from the nature of the iambic meter to the rhetoricization of imperial power. I. Z. Serman identifies "emotional uplift, [or] rapture" as Lomonosov's "basic definition of the creative process"; before him Gukovskii had recognized "lyric uplift" as the "only theme of [Lomonosov's] poetry, merely acquiring various nuances in one or another ode." Hence "the only persona of his lyric theme is the soul, which finds itself in a powerfully affected state, transported to the heavens, or Parnassus."[84] Here the sublime is reduced to a purely literary experience: its ramifications in the realm of history are only "nuances," the outgrowth of a prior emotional state and literary preference. A recent and insightful dissertation monograph by Elena Pogosian defines rapture as the "description of a specific state of the odic narrator" that is at the same time "emphatically unconditional" in its exalted understanding of poetic cognition and yet functionally panegyric in articulating the "relation between the monarch and the poet who addresses him." Yet Pogosian provides no broader premise that might reconcile these contradictions.[85]

By separating form and theme or selectively addressing this or that aspect of the post-Petrine literary revolution, scholars have yet to consider the ode and the new syllabo-tonic metrical system as the inaugural moment of a tradition that makes the sublime the basis of a new poetics of empire. Perhaps the critic L. V. Pumpianskii came closest to discerning the relationship between Lomonosov's new poetics and the new Russia that had arisen in Peter's wake:

> To understand the origin of the affair of genius that took place in 1739 [i.e., Lomonosov's revolution in prosody], one must try to imagine that first moment when rapture at the West suddenly (explosively) became rapture at oneself as a Western country. . . . Hence it was possible to profess belonging to both Europe and Russia with the same rapture! Let us call this the "post-Petrine" revelation (the "second" revelation) of the Russian people. The awakening of rhythm in linguistic consciousness is connected to this very thing, i.e. the rapturous profession of *selfhood*.[86]

Selfhood, for Pumpianskii, is here primarily the *national* self, an intuition of Russia's greatness that provoked the discovery of "style." This self,

Pumpianskii grants, was born first of an *external* identification (with the west). Subsequently it became *internally* differentiated, since national self-consciousness led immediately to a split between "those who understood (and led) and those who were subordinate. This division was, without a doubt, linked to the first stirrings of song, the birth of the ode written by the governing class."[87] Joachim Klein has recently elaborated on Pumpianskii's analogy between the new state and the new poetics: "The new [syllabo-tonic] verse had to be not only more beautiful than the old one, but also more 'rational.' With its regulated smoothness it was intended to merge with the rational structure of [Peter's] 'regulated' state."[88]

The new prosody, then, emerged as a response to Peter's avowed intent to bring Russia into the sign-system of European culture and history. In these early decades, the iambic ode would dramatize the hopes and aspirations of the Petrine state, whose defining ideology was essentially imperial. In the following chapter we shall see how the Lomonosovian sublime became the rhetorical basis for a poetics of imperial nationhood.

2

The Ode and the Empress

The Odes of Lomonosov

In the preceding chapter we saw that the imperial sublime came together in Lomonosov as the sum of many parts: the sublime of Longinus and Boileau, with its notions of lyric transport and Pindaric rapture, the *vysokii shtil'*, which allowed for the grafting of the European ode onto the domestic tradition of ecclesiastical writing and panegyric verse, the prophetic mode derived from the translations of the Psalms, and the ideology of the imperial state. The latter element, empire itself, becomes dramatically evident as the defining context and primary theme of the ceremonial ode.

The heyday of odic production coincides with the reign of Russia's three empresses, Anna (1730–40), Elizabeth (1741–61), and Catherine the Great (1762–96). Becoming a mass phenomenon only under Catherine, the Russian ode took several decades to evolve its range of topoi and themes, and to test out the possible modes of addressing the sovereign. Although it remains unclear whether the ode was necessarily declaimed during ceremonial occasions or simply presented to the monarch, odes were certainly intended to coincide with an event of significance to the court or its anniversary, or for convocations of the Academy of Sciences.[1] As such they were generally included in officially published accounts of court celebrations and festivities. Although they were occasionally commissioned, odes could also be written at the poet's own initiative; in both cases they served as a means of securing royal favor and the patronage of court magnates. Externally these poems functioned as a form of praise, recounting the sovereign's virtues and the poet's enthusiasm for them, combining both in a paean to the Russian state. Not surprisingly the static elements of formulaic praise often overwhelmed the historically contingent nature of the occasion of the poem. Nonetheless, the Lomonosovian ode displayed a certain capacity to evolve and change. The ode's laudatory framework could accommodate a tacit political agenda that was distinct from the status quo, as long as it could be subsumed into the mission of the modernizing state. For all its formal inertia, the odic vision had its stylistic nuances and thematic innovations: the classical version of the odic sublime, and its variations, are the topic of this section of the chapter.

Although not the first poetic work to win Lomonosov widespread recognition (it was not published, in fact, until 1751, and its status as the "founding text" of modern Russian poetry is owing less to its immediate impact than to the insight of later historians), the "Oda na vziatie Khotina" (Ode on the taking of Khotin) (1739) was Lomonosov's earliest ode, already possessing the classic (Güntherian) odic form of a ten-verse stanza of iambic tetrameters with the rhyming sequence of ABABCCDEED. Intended as a programmatic illustration of his new poetics, it was quickly recognized by those who read it as a radical innovation in style. The very first lines of the poem establish the sublime as Lomonosov's privileged idiom:

Восторг внезапный ум пленил,
Ведет на верьх горы высокой,
Где ветр в лесах шуметь забыл;
В долине тишина глубокой.
Внимая нечто шум молчит,
Которой завсегда журчит
И с шумом вниз с холмов стремится.
Лавровы вьются там венцы,
Там слух спешит во все концы;
Далече дым в полях курится.[2]

A sudden rapture has captivated the mind
And leads it up a lofty mountain,
Where the wind in the forests has forgotten to roar;
In the deep valley there is silence.
The noise, harkening to something, falls silent,
[The noise] that forever gurgles
And courses noisily down from the hills.
There wreaths of laurel wind about,
There hearing [or rumor] rushes in all directions;
Further out smoke curls along the fields.

The ode's first two stanzas characterize the sublime as a purely lyrical afflatus, the relationship of a poet to his art that initially appears prior to any historical occasion or institutional affiliation. Vertical uplift is its quintessential axis: the mind is here "captivated" and thrust upward to the top of Mount Parnassus by the sudden onset of poetic rapture over which it has no control. It was this experience of "lyric disorder," and the dialectic of authority it enacted, that struck readers as both new and uniquely Lomonosovian: in its radicalism it certainly surpasses the models provided by Boileau, Malherbe, and the German poet Günther. In his ode on Namur Boileau can still order his "faithful lyre" to "follow his transports," and Günther peremptorily bids his Muses to "go after" the Austrian commander Eugen.[3] By contrast, the Lomonosovian sublime involves more rapid and unconditional shifts in authority: the poet surrenders more completely, and passively, to his inspiration, just as he will submit more abjectly to his vision of Russia's conquering rulers. The power of language and the might of empire will thus be more intimately connected in Russia than in Europe.

The drama of poetic inspiration is ritually enacted in the second stanza. In a series of imperatives—"drink," "wash your eyes with Castalian dew," "stretch your gaze over steppe and hill"—the Muses subject the poet to a kind of Orphic initiation. The authority that the mind ritually yields to poetry it then reestablishes over space. Where the difficulty of height consumes the first seven lines, the final period provides a compensatory horizontal axis of extension. The mind's elevation grants it a panoramic view: cleansed by the waters of inspiration, it can see and hear into a potentially infinite distance. This horizontal space will become localized as the historical occasion that is the poem's real object, the capture by Russian forces of the Ottoman fortress of Khotin in August 1739 that concluded a three-year war with Turkey.

Horizontality is the site of conflict; its field of attraction is territorial aggression, the surge of battle, the line of advance, victory or retreat. Poetry encounters history at the intersection of two axes, the point at which the disorder of lyric afflatus is resolved in a compensatory and transformative identification with imperial power. The uplifted poet, slave to his vision, becomes Russia's heraldic eagle surveying the horizontal spread of the retreating Ottoman forces:

За холмы, где паляща хлябь
Дым, пепел, пламень, смерть рыгает,
За Тигр, Стамбул, своих заграбь,

Что камни с берегов сдирает;
Но чтоб орлов сдержать полет,
Таких препон на свете нет.
(19–20)

Beyond the hills where a fiery abyss
Belches smoke, flame and death
Steal away with your men, Istanbul, beyond the Tigris
That tears the rocks off its own shoreline;
But to restrain the eagles' flight
There is no hindrance left on earth.

The poet's eagle eye constructs odic space as a vast geography, political and cosmic, to be surveyed. In a panegyric to the empress Elizabeth, Lomonosov had described geography as a science that "subjects the vastness of the entire universe to a single gaze," while history and poetry seize the "laudable feats of great statesmen" from the jaws of oblivion.[4] The ode was thus a form of heroic memory that could miniaturize the protagonists and setting of imperial history into a kind of tableau. Not unlike the firework displays that were its visual equivalent, the ode was fundamentally spectacular, a theater that embraced both the given battle and a larger participating universe. In the Khotin ode Lomonosov compares Turkish forces hurling "metal and flame" at the Russian forces to Mount Etna, while the earth "quakes like the sea," the moon blushes, and the rising sun marvels at the Russian victory.

Lomonosov's taste for simile and allegory certainly recalls the sensibility of the Russian Baroque, but the poet is already many steps removed from the world of Simeon Polotskii. Where Polotskii's universe is essentially static and preordained, Lomonosov's is dynamic and diachronically oriented, evolving as the pageant of history. The battle progresses, the sun rises and sets, and the inevitability of victory is ascribed to Russia's rulers rather than to the grace of God. Although the Turks are once again termed the "race of the outcast slave" Hagar, the struggle being waged is ultimately between empires and not between faiths. Hence the importance of toponyms for Lomonosov: in predicting that "Damascus, Cairo, Aleppo will burn," and that the "Euphrates will be muddied" with the enemy's blood, he is not speculating on the real consequences of the capture of Khotin but is conjuring the larger geopolitical context of the given conflict. Place-names do not localize space but designate territory, namely, the empire to which they belong.

If the horizontal axis in Lomonosov provides *what* is seen, the vertical axis is the visionary itself. Once the battle has culminated in a Russian victory, the poet looks skyward to witness a second spectacle, an allegorical encounter between a series of Russian tsars:

Что так теснит боязнь мой дух?
Хладнеют жилы, сердце ноет!
Что бьет за странной шум в мой слух?
. . . .
Небесная отверзлась дверь,
Над войском облак вдруг развился,
Блеснул горящим вдруг лицем,
Умытым кровию мечем
Гоня врагов, Герой открылся.

(22)

Why does fear so weigh upon my spirit?
My veins go cold, my heart aches!
What kind of strange noise strikes at my ears?
. . . .
The door of heaven opened up,
A cloud suddenly appeared over the troops,
And flashed suddenly like a burning face,
With a sword bathed in blood
Scattering his enemies, the Hero appeared.

The hero at hand is Peter the Great, who then begins to converse with Ivan the Terrible about the course of Russian history:

«Не тщетно я с тобой трудился,
Не тщетен подвиг мой и твой,
Чтоб россов целый свет страшился.
Чрез нас предел наш стал широк
На север, запад и восток.
На юге Анна торжествует,
Покрыв своих победой сей.»
Свилася мгла, Герои в ней
Не зрит их око, слух нечует.

(23)

"Not in vain did you and I strive,
Not in vain was my feat and yours,
So that the whole world should fear the Russians.
Through us our boundaries have grown wide
To the north, west and east.
In the south Anna is triumphant,

Sheltering her subjects with this victory."
The gloom coiled round, the Heroes (dissolved) into it
The eye no longer sees them, and the ear hears them not.

Where Polotskii's sovereigns generally embodied Christian virtues, Peter and Ivan are symbols of an evolving secular history, a series of military victories that they recount in order to insert Russia's most recent triumph into a ready sequence of historical milestones. Long dead, these monarchs appear as phantoms, abstract dramatizations of Russian expansion that the poet is uniquely privileged to witness.

This vision of Russia's rulers involves a kind of secondary afflatus that is no longer purely lyrical, as in the case of the poem's opening lines. Psychologically speaking it is marked by awe, the poet's sublime terror at witnessing the embodied form of sovereign power. In this, the first vivid lyric expression of the Russian imperial sublime, poetic inspiration anticipates and rehearses a power dynamic that will then be manifested as imperial might. In other words, the *poetic* moment of sublime rapture is made homologous with the poet's abject relation to the monarch as an embodiment of *political* power. In both cases, the poet must submit to an external authority. The same act of willing submission, to poetry and to power, marks the beginning and end of the poem:

Велика Анна, Ты доброт
Сияешь светом и щедрот:
Прости, что раб твой к громкой славе,
Звучит что крепость сил Твоих,
Придать дерзнул не красной стих
В подданства знак Твоей державе.
(30)

Great Anna, You
Shine with the light of good qualities and liberality:
Forgive your slave for daring to augment your loud glory
That trumpets the firmness of your strength,
With a crude line of verse
As a sign of subjection to Your rule.

This act of submission, articulated in a typically contorted Lomonosovian syntax, finds a third, quite unexpected analogue in the surrender of the Turkish troops to Russian forces, where the phrase *v poddanstva znak* (as a sign of subjection) reappears:

Кто скоро толь тебя, Калчак,
Учит Российской вдаться власти,
Ключи вручить в подданства знак
И большей избежать напасти?
(27)

Who teaches you, Kalchak [the Turkish commander],
To give yourself up so swiftly to Russian power,
Surrender your keys as a sign of subjection,
And avoid any further misfortune?

The poet accedes to language just as the subject bows to the autocrat, and just as the vanquished yield to a superior force. This chain of parallels leads us to the startling analogy (marked chiefly by the repetition of the phrase *v poddanstva znak*) between the poet and the conquered Turk.[5] Destined to remain undeveloped until the nineteenth century, when the alienating effects of Russian imperialism would rebound more sharply onto the Russian creative intelligentsia, this analogy is quickly neutralized through the poet's identification with the sovereign's achievements in the imperial arena. This identification allows for the more comforting polarity pitting Russians against "the whole world," with the poet and the Russian monarch finally united in victory against a common foe.

The critical tradition has yet to pay adequate attention to the extent to which empire—and not merely Russian national destiny—defines the context of the Lomonosovian sublime and its subsequent evolution. In the most suggestive account he ever offered of the phenomenon, which he termed the *soaring style* (*pariashchii stil'*), Pumpianskii wrote: "Civilizational reason, the principle of progressive statehood that is bringing this reason into being, and the stoic heroes who embody this process of realization (Peter the Great)—that is the ideational basis, and hence the semantic function, of the soaring style."[6] While correctly identifying the strong relationship between poetics and politics that lies at the heart of the Russian sublime, Pumpianksii's definition suffers from the pervasive Hegelian Marxist optimism of the Soviet era, retrospectively applied.

The imprint left by imperial autocracy on the origins of modern Russian poetry was surely more troubling than Pumpianskii's formulation allows. We might ask, for example, whether Lomonosovian rapture, with its highly emotional and visionary qualities, is the most appropriate vehicle for the celebration of reason. Unlike Boileau, for whom rationalist classicism and *raison d'état* were more easily reconciled, Lomonosov's rhetorical excesses suggest a more complex vision of autocracy as the guardian of order and the agent of change. Lomonosov's martial odes in particular, with their oxymora and hyperboles, their metaphoric leaps and syntactical complexity—vastly exceed the formulaic *beau désordre* recommended by Boileau: rising to a cosmic level of upheaval, they deploy the Psalms' metaphorical representations of God's power to convey the impact of imperial might:

И чувствуя приход Петров,
Дубравы и поля трепещут.
Кто с ним толь грозно зрит на юг,
Одеян страшным громом вкруг?
Никак смиритель стран Казанских?
(23)

And feeling the approach of Peter,
The groves of oak and fields quake.
Who with him looks so terrifyingly to the south,
Swathed all about in thunder?
Surely [Ivan], the pacifier of the Kazan lands?

These visions of Russia's monarchs, contrasting heavenly grandeur and earthly abasement, suggest a discourse of power derived not from profane reason but from a secularized model of divine authority, unlimited and thus not circumscribed by reason. Hence the lingering ambivalence that resonates in Lomonosov's odes: praise for the empress and enthusiasm for progress coexist with self-abjection and a profound dread of power. Sublimated as imperial majesty, projected as conquest, or reabsorbed into poetry itself as prophetic inspiration, these ambivalences mark a continuing tension between the state's modernizing mission and the unchecked nature of autocratic power.

War and Peace

This dynamic—of poet, sovereign, and the geography of empire—is the very core of the imperial sublime. It is born out of the psychic experience of subjection that finds its closest analogy in conquest, as expressed in the victory odes of Lomonosov and his poetic successors. Lomonosov's vision of empire, however, is by no means exhausted by war. Indeed, the most visionary moments of his odic corpus point to a *pax russica* that takes us considerably beyond the crude belligerency of his early odes. The theme of a peace won *through* war is already present in the Khotin ode, which concludes with a vision of pastoral beauty established "under Anna's strong protection" that allows wheat and peace to be sown together, and the shepherd to tend to his flock without fear (29–30). With the palace revolution that brought the empress Elizabeth to power, Lomonosov's odes began to articulate a more complex vision of war and peace. The new reign was greeted as a Golden Age, hearkening back to the times of Peter the Great, Elizabeth's father; this hereditary lineage allowed the poet to read "bironovshchina," the German hegemony said to have prevailed under Empress Anna, as an interregnum of foreign tyranny. In odes such as "Oda na pribytie iz Golstinii i na den' rozhdeniia . . . velikogo kniazia Petra Feodorovicha 1742 goda" (Ode on the arrival from Holstein and the birthday of . . . Archduke Petr Feodorovich), this Golden Age remains pastoral, a land of milk and honey (67); in the "Oda na pribytie ee velichestva Imperatritsy Elisavety Petrovny iz Moskvy v Sanktpeterburg 1742 goda po koronatsii" (Ode on the arrival of Her Majesty the Empress Elizabeth Petrovna in Saint Petersburg from Moscow on the occasion of her coronation in 1742) the poet foresees a time when swords and spears will be forged into ploughs and sickles, and "flora will scatter her flowers on the site of battles and discord" (99).

As Lomonosov was able to consolidate his academic and poetic reputation in the forties, his vision of a *pax russica* became less of a utopian topos and more of a policy agenda: «От той Европа ожидает, / Чтоб в ней восставлен был покой.» (Europe expects of her [Elizabeth], / that peace be reestablished in it"), writes Lomonosov in 1746 (144). In the celebrated "Oda na den' vosshestviia na prestol . . . Imperatritsy Elisavety Petrovny 1747 goda" (Ode on the anniversary of the empress Elisaveta Petrovna's ascension to the throne in 1747) the poet was able to elaborate most vividly what has been somewhat generously called his "pacifist" politics. An apostrophe to "beloved tranquillity" ("vozliublennaia tishina"), the ode praises Elizabeth for choosing peace to the glory of battle. Peace is defined in at least two ways: chronologically, in that it follows war (the Petrine era), and developmentally, in that it is connected to the growth of science: «Здесь в мире расширять науки / Изволила Елизавет.» (Elizabeth has deigned / to expand the sciences through the world) (199). The static pastoral myth of Lomonosov's previous verse here gives way to a grandiose vision of industrial and mercantile expansion:

Толикое земель пространство
Когда Всевышний поручил
Тебе в счастливое подданство,
Тогда сокровища открыл,
Какими хвалится Индия;
Но требует к тому Россия
Искусством утвержденных рук.
Сие злату очистит жилу,
Почувствуют и камни силу
Тобой восставленных наук.
(203)

When the Lord entrusted
So great a stretch of land
To you in happy subjection,
He revealed treasures,
Such as those of which India boasts;
But for this sake Russia demands
Hands trained in artful skill.
The latter will cleanse the veins of gold,
And even stones will feel the force
Of the sciences you have revived.

Lomonosov's ode of 1747 describes a Russia in which knowledge emanating from the center taps the hidden mineral wealth of the periphery. Far from the theater of European war, Lomonosov's imagination invokes the exploitable expanses of the North, Siberia, the Far East, and even beyond, where a "Russian Columbus" sails to inform "unknown peoples" of the Empress's munificence. Less a pacifist position than a critique of military intervention in Europe as the primary basis of foreign policy, Lomonosov's vision sought to avoid unnecessary entanglement in European military alliances, advocating in its place a scientific and industrial basis for empire. Such a position, as the historian Sergei Solov'ev and many after him have observed, involved a certain amount of civic courage.[7]

The critic Pumpianskii long ago suggested that the "question of what was ultimately 'better,' military glory or the benefits of peace" was never definitively resolved by the odic poet; indeed, "this very unresolvedness was the essential theme of the classical ode as a whole. The demagnetizing of the metaphysical polarities [of war and peace] and hence the resolution of the conflict was effected by a new reality, specifically the reality of industrial capitalism."[8] This sociological reading, reductive but stimulating in a way typical of early Soviet scholarship, identifies

Lomonosov with the interests of the upper gentry, who saw the autocratic state, and the Academy of Sciences as its counterpart, as entrepreneurial agents in Russia's technological development, in opposition to the middle gentry, which remained tied to a feudal and agrarian vision of the status quo. Both constituencies struggled to influence the autocracy with its vision.[9] What Pumpianskii and Berkov failed to indicate outright, however, was that Lomonosov's "pacifism" was not a negation of empire but a deflection or redirection of its interests.

The dilemma of war and peace, and the relationship of both to empire, would become the central—and unresolved—theme of Lomonosov's odes. In his odes of the late forties and fifties, the poet's language strains to convert the energies of an obligatory martial rhetoric to peaceful use. This strategy and its rather tortured results are particularly evident in the odes written during Russia's involvement in the Seven Years' War against Prussia (1756–62), about which Lomonosov appears to have had strong reservations. These odes, like the ode of 1747 before them, represent Lomonosov's boldest attempt at injecting a note of dissent into a genre that largely precluded independent thought. We see it most vividly in the poet's use of paradoxes, such as «воздвигнуть против брани брань» ("to wage war against war") (635), and «война и мир дают победы» ("both war and peace bring victories") (742). These paradoxes have a semantically leveling effect. War appears to be less about conquest than about the furtherance of peace; at the same time peace appears less about tranquil coexistence than about the armed security that enables Russia to enjoy the fruits of earlier conquests.

As the war against Prussia dragged on and the fiction of a "peaceful war" became more threadbare, Lomonosov developed the beguilingly facile contrast between the internal state of Russia and its foreign policy:

Там слышен вой в оружном треске;
Из туч при смертоносном блеске
Кровавы трупы множат страх.
А ты, Отечество драгое,
Ликуй при внутреннем покое
В Елисаветиных лучах.

(638)

Over there a howl is audible in the crackle of weapons;
[Emerging] from the clouds in the deadly dazzle
Bloody corpses increase fear.

But you, dear fatherland,
Exult in your internal peace
[Bathed] in Elizabeth's rays [of light].

And again in 1759:

О коль блаженны мы тобой!
Искусства, нивы, торг, науки,
Победоносны слыша звуки,
Блажат свой внутренний покой.
(655)

O how blissful are we in you [Elizabeth]!
The arts, the meadows, trade, and the sciences,
On hearing the sounds of victory,
Bless their internal peace.

The same contrast reappears in his first ode to Catherine the Great, written in 1762, in which the newly crowned empress is lauded for being "a storm over there, but here tranquillity" (773).

This awkward juxtaposition of war and peace that coexist at a spatial remove has been perceived by Lomonosov scholars such as Walter Gleason as a polemical opposition of "the ideal of domestic security to the potential disarray consequent to foreign military ventures."[10] This cautiously dissonant note nonetheless falls into a generic context in which imperial glory and expansion remain the primary object of odic contemplation. In an earlier ode composed in 1748, Lomonosov writes:

Но море нашей тишины
Уже пределы превосходит,
Своим избытком мир наводит,
Разлившись в западны страны.
(219)

But the sea of our tranquility
Already surpasses its confines,
And brings about peace through its own abundance,
Overflowing into the nations of the west.

While starkly contrasted to war, peace resembles war in being a question of expanding borders. Like war, peace can erase and renegotiate frontiers, just as the sea erodes and reshapes land. Even as a military strategist might contemplate how to wage and contain war, Lomonosov's vision of *pax russica* was confronted with the dilemma of how, and whether, to "contain" peace.

Lomonosov's most vivid representations of the Russian Empire emerge from the felt need to convey poetically the territorial effects of war and peace. In an ode of 1748, following a moving plea for peace, we find the following lines:

Однако дух еще стремится,
Еще кипит сердечный жар,
И ревность умолчать стыдится:
О муза, усугубь твой дар,
Гласи со мной в концы земные,
Коль ныне радостна Россия!
Она, коснувшись облаков,
Конца не зрит своей державы;
Гремящей насыщенна славы
Покоится среди лугов.

В полях, исполненных плодами,
Где Волга, Днепр, Нева, и Дон,
Своими чистыми струями
Шумя, стадам наводит сон,
Седит и ноги простирает
На степь, где Хину отделяет
Пространная стена от нас;
Веселый взор свой обращает
И вкруг довольства исчисляет,
Возлегши лактем на Кавказ.
(221–22)

But the spirit yearns still further,
The heart's ardor still seethes,
And one's zeal is ashamed to fall silent:
O muse, increase your gift,
Pronounce with me to all ends of the earth,
How happy Russia now is!
Having touched the clouds, she
Cannot see an end to her own realm;
Filled with thundering glory
She rests among the meadows.

In the fields, filled with fruit,
Where the Volga, Dnieper, Neva, and the Don
With the noise of their pure streams
Lull the herds to sleep,
She sits and extends her legs
Over the steppe, where China is separated
By a vast wall from us;
She turns her merry gaze

And counts the prosperity around her,
Resting with her elbow on the Caucasus.

In these lines the familiar vertical axis of the Lomonosovian sublime raises Russia herself—rather than the poet—to the clouds. Russia is embodied here allegorically as a human colossus straddling her own territory and surveying the horizontal expanse that she commands. The strangeness of the personification lies in the typically Lomonosovian collapse of the abstract into the concrete: Russia "sits and extends her legs over the steppe," then "rests her elbow on the Caucasus" with the ponderous affability of a giantess. In his *Rhetoric* of 1748 Lomonosov had recommended the conceit of magnifying objects, pointing to the depiction of giants as a favored device of epic poetry.[11] Here the aggrandized personification of Russia has the contrasting effect of miniaturizing space: the empire appears much as the land of Lilliput would have appeared to Gulliver.

Mapping is, in fact, the most frequent outcome of allegorical personification in Lomonosov: whether it be an embodiment of the nation or of its ruling monarchs, what results is a surveying of territory, in which cartographical abstraction is combined with descriptive detail. Most original in this regard is the apostrophe to the sciences in Lomonosov's ode of 1750 to the empress Elizabeth, in which Mechanics, Chemistry, Astronomy, Geography, and Meteorology are themselves implored to "stretch their arms / and their gaze to the furthest places. Walk across the land and the ocean depths, / the steppe and the deep forest, / the bowels of the Urals and their peaks, / and the very heights of heaven," in order to "gather the space of Russian land onto small grids" (400–402).

The moral and religious criteria that governed Polotskii's spatializations of Russia are here replaced with a more scientific and utilitarian sense of the bounty of empire. Although existing ultimately for the use of the Russian state and its rulers, empire is an abundance to be measured and exploited rationally, and the poet's odic "maps" are in fact highly tendentious guides to imperial policy. We might note first of all the absence of any absolute distinction, in Lomonosov's maps, between an ethnically Russian heartland and the borderlands. Historically Russian lands are figured pastorally but are devoid of ethnic specificity, while the rivers of Siberia and the Far East "swirl in obedience" to Russia, and its peoples, who "scarcely have a roof above them, strive to catch expensive animals as tribute" to the empress (223). Lomonosov's imprecision on this point will, in fact, become a characteristic feature of

Russian imperial culture: the desire for geographic and ethnographic markers within which to contain a nation at peace gives way to the potential infinity of the empire's receding borders. The distinction between ethnic Russia and its borderlands is clearly less important, particularly in this early period, than that between the various borders themselves. Even in his peace-loving odes, Lomonosov makes a clear distinction between Russia's *western* boundary with Europe, where peace is desirable, and its *southern* and *eastern* limits, which continue to provide an outlet for military adventurism:

Когда взираем мы к востоку,
Когда посмотрим мы на юг,
О коль пространность зрим широку,
Где может загреметь твой слух!

Там вкруг облег Дракон ужасный
Места святы, места прекрасны
И к облакам сто глав вознес!
Весь свет чудовища страшится,
Един лишь смело устремиться
Российский может Геркулес.
(562–63)

When we gaze at the east,
When we look to the south,
O what a vast expanse we see,
Where news of you may thunder!

There the terrible Dragon has surrounded
The holy land, the splendid land
And raised its hundred heads to the clouds!
The whole world fears the monster,
The Russian Hercules is the only one
Who can boldly rush on.

From the Khotin ode of 1739 to his penultimate ode of 1761 to Catherine II, in which an Arctic maritime route is suggested as leading to Russia's conquest of China, India, and Japan (757), Lomonosov's odic map consistently maintains an overarching distinction between west and east (which, for Russia, meant also the southern peripheries of the empire). Precisely in order to progress as a western power, Russia must look eastward for its destiny. This argument absorbs but also surpasses the old quarrel of Orthodoxy with Ottoman Turkey: indeed, one might say that it marks the beginnings of a modern orientalist ideology in Russia as Edward Said has understood the term, whereby the civilizational distinction between Asia and Europe is resolved as a matter of political superiority and military aggression. As Mark Bassin observes, "the deliberate 'Europeanization' of Russia's own image set in motion by the Petrine reforms not only engendered but to a significant extent actually depended upon an inverse and no less deliberate 'Asianizing' of its vast colonial domains in the east."[12] Indeed, this orientalism strikingly corresponds to the distinction, too often hailed as an instance of Lomonosov's humanity, between war and peace. Lomonosov's "pacificism," in fact, amounted to little more than a plea for Russia's military disengagement from Europe: peace would enable the reorientation of Russian attention toward its vast Eurasian territories, through industrial exploitation but also through further conquest. Lomonosov's views thus ultimately corresponded to the formal constraints of his chosen genre, the ode: both precluded a genuine contrast between war and peace. We might say, rather, that both war and peace served to configure Russia territorially as an empire, articulating its European political engagements alongside the military and economic stakes of its eastern hinterland.

Nonetheless, a real shift can be noted in Lomonosov's odic production, from the crude belligerency of the thirties and early forties to the more nuanced imperialism that characterizes his mature work. As the theme of "peace" became more insistent, the poet's praise of the empress acquired a tendentious quality: what was being ascribed in laudatory terms to the ruling monarch was, in fact, the poet's own vision which, although not inimical to the empress, was hardly a royal attribute or achievement. Inevitably the dilution of the martial theme in Lomonosov's odes affected the functioning of the sublime as a psychic and political model. Emotionally Lomonosov's poems are generally combinations of rapture (*vostorg*), dread (*boiazn'* or *uzhas*), and blissful happiness (*blazhenstvo* or *schast'e*). These emotions must be read as responses to and displacements of force: their dialectical interrelation thus becomes a ready index of the poet's own subjective relation to authority. The already cited "Oda na pribytie ee velichestva Imperatritsy Elisavety Petrovny iz Moskvy v Sanktpeterburg 1742 goda po koronatsii" (Ode on the arrival of Her Majesty the Empress Elizabeth Petrovna in Saint Petersburg from Moscow on the occasion of her coronation in 1742) provides a vivid example of the psychic shifts possible in the Lomonosovian sublime:

Какая бодрая дремота
Открыла мысли явный сон?
Еще горит во мне охота

Торжественный возвысить тон.
Мне вдруг ужасный гром блистает
И купно ясный день сияет!
То сердце сильна власть страшит,
То кротость оное живит;
То бодрость страх, то страх ту клонит,
Противна страсть противну гонит!

(97)

What vigorous dreaminess
Has opened the vigilant sleep of my thought?
The desire still burns within me
To elevate my solemn tone.
A terrible thunder suddenly gleams before me
And at the same time the day is brightly shining!
Now a strong power terrifies the heart,
Now meekness revivifies it;
Now vigor bends my fear, now fear bends my vigor,
One opposed passion chases its opposite!

Odic rapture, elicited as usual by a spectacular apparition of the empress, here acquires an added complexity. These lines precede a visionary encounter between Peter the Great and his granddaughter, Elizabeth, and the dialectic of fear (*strakh*) and vigour (*bodrost'*) in fact correspond to the divergent hypostases these monarchs embody: whereas Peter represents sheer power (*sil'na vlast'*), Elizabeth represents meekness (*krotost'*), ruling as she does "gentler than a zephyr" (745). Elizabeth is repeatedly called "meek" in Lomonosov's odes, an appellation clearly intended to elicit a tempering of sovereign authority. Corresponding, in a sense, to the "pacificist" theme in foreign policy, the sovereign's meekness permitted an enhanced role for the poet as lyric hero. In the rhetoric of the sublime, no absolute reduction of power is possible: authority is merely delegated to or usurped by another agent. The poet, then, is not freed from power; nor, yet, does he aspire to seize it (like the revolutionary Decembrists): he merely acts as the prophetic medium for its dispersal and reconfiguration. In a striking passage from an ode of 1757, God is heard speaking to all "rulers and judges" through the poet-as-prophet:

Сие глаголет вам Господь
Святым своим в пророках духом;
Впери всяк ум и вникни слухом:
Божественный певец Давид

Священными шумит струнами,
И Бога полными устами
Исайя восхищен гремит.
(636)

This the Lord sayeth unto you
With his Holy Spirit [speaking] through the prophets;
May each man turn his mind and penetrate with his hearing:
The divine singer David
Strums on his holy strings,
And with the full voice of God
The enraptured Isaiah thunders.

Stretching the limits of the ceremonial ode, Lomonosov here turns to the idiom of the psalm and the sacred ode: only the prophetic voice of the Old Testament God wields the authority needed to imbue the sovereign with meekness and to instruct her to "keep your oath faithfully," "open your door to supplicants," and "comfort the suffering." The ventriloquism inherent in prophetic utterance—God speaking through man—reminds us that, for the sublime, power, whether dominant or subversive, is citational. The poet does not speak—he is spoken.

In his penultimate ode, marking the coronation of the new empress Catherine in 1762, Lomonosov does appear to erode the citational aspect of sublime power. Although framed on both sides by a reference to God and to the "monarch's faithful slaves," a similar admonition to the world's "judges and rulers" appears outside quotation marks:

Услышьте, Судии земные
И все державные главы:
Законы нарушать святые
От буйности блюдите вы,
И подданных не презирайте
Но их пороки исправляйте
Ученьем, милостью, трудом.
Вместите с правдою щедроту;
То Бог благословит ваш дом.
(778)

Hear, ye judges of the world
And all the sovereign heads of states:
Keep from violating the sacred laws
Out of boisterous excess,
And do not despise your subjects

But correct their vices
With teaching, kindness, and hard work.
Combine justice with generosity;
Then God will bless your house.

A new voice speaks in these lines, one that holds the ruler accountable to "sacred laws" and seeks to correct her errors just as she, in turn, would correct those of her subjects. This is the voice of the Enlightenment, coinciding with the coronation of Catherine the Great who was actively, if inconsistently, to promote it. Lomonosov's ode of 1762, along with his earlier ode on the ascension of Peter III, displeased the new empress intensely; the poet fell out of favor and was nearly forced into retirement ten months later.[13] His ode thus provided an early litmus test for the limits and contradictions of Catherinian Enlightenment as a discourse of the state.

Lomonosov's New Year's ode of 1763—his second to Catherine and the last ode he was ever to write—regresses predictably to the ventriloquistic model of the sublime. The Solomonic voice of royal wisdom is equated with that of the empress—«Премудрый глас сей Соломонов, / Монархиня, сей глас есть твой» (This wisest of Solomonic voices, / Monarch, this is yours) (795)—and the poem concludes with a prophetic vision proclaimed by the Muses, in which two models of sovereign rule are contrasted. The Russian empress is hailed as "beloved and enlightened" for "opening the doorway to scholarship throughout her realm," while that "inflated giant," the Chinese emperor, is denounced for believing that he alone "holds all earthly power in his hand . . . not knowing that vast force without the art of valor through which Europe flourishes is fated to decay" (796–97). Lomonosov's last ode establishes a polarity that will become vital to the Catherinian era and to its chief poet, Gavrila Derzhavin. Whereas European Russia is associated with the spread of knowledge and law-based governance, Asia emerges not merely as a rival force but as a politically alien system. This system, oriental despotism, will provide the new generation of court poets with an important symbolic construct through which to measure the success or failure of Russia's aspirations to enlightened modernity.

In leaving Lomonosov, we must acknowledge him as the most influential figure in the history of the Russian sublime as a rhetoric and poetics of empire. To a greater extent than any of his predecessors or contemporaries, Lomonosov is distinguished by the topos of *vostorg*, lyric rapture, the onset of inspiration that marked the emergence of the modern Russian poet as well as his initial subservience to the state. While Trediakovskii provided many of the individual elements of the Russian sublime—the European ode, the biblical psalm, and the beginnings of a new system of versification—it was Lomonosov who put these elements into active use and then reconciled them to the "lofty style" of the older Church Slavic and panegyric tradition.

Lomonosov's literary preeminence was by no means absolute, neither during his lifetime nor after his death. In 1759 his chief rival, Aleksandr Sumarokov, published an extract from Longinus's treatise on the sublime with Boileau's preface. Its polemical intention was to remind readers of the discrepancy between Lomonosov's "sublime style" and Boileau's classicist premise that the sublime could be reconciled with a clear and simple diction.[14] In the same year Sumarokov wrote three very funny "nonsense odes" (*vzdornye ody*) vividly parodying Lomonosov's poetics. Eliding the sacrosanct theme of Russian autocracy, these odes attacked only Lomonosov's rhetorical premise—lyric rapture—along with its cosmic and geographical projections. The inspired poet soars into the sky to witness a world in turmoil, which Sumarokov describes in a hotchpotch of Lomonosovian hyperboles and oxymora. When stripped of their political context and ideological rationale, the poet's lyric effusions appear pompous and incoherent.[15]

Although he was successful in blocking the publication of Sumarokov's nonsense odes, Lomonosov was unable to forestall the longer-term transformation of the ode as a genre that took place after his death. Of course, conventional ceremonial odes continued to be written well into the Catherinian era by a number of lesser poets such as V. Petrov, V. I. Maikov, and E. Kostrov, whose works provided a battleground for the ongoing struggle between Lomonosov's baroque legacy and the classicist ideals of Sumarokov. Although Petrov's work is often striking, the legacy of the later odic poets is overall of limited interest.[16] More significant are the efforts of the poet Sumarokov and his pupil, M. M. Kheraskov, to broaden the ode as a genre by composing Anacreontic and didactic odes on intimate or moral themes. These developments, however, fall outside the history of the imperial sublime, whose next decisive moment is the dialogue between Lomonosov and the poet Derzhavin.

Derzhavin and Lomonosov

Gavrila Romanovich Derzhavin (1743–1816) hailed from the petty landowning gentry of Kazan. During his difficult rise to social and literary prominence, the poet would serve as a soldier and then a noncommissioned officer in the Preobrazhenskii Guards before becoming governor of two provinces, personal secretary to Catherine the Great, senator, and minister of justice under Alexander I. Derzhavin's ascent from humble and provincial origins was not atypical for a petty nobleman able to link innate talent to the spoils of patronage.[17] Yet unlike earlier poets from analogous backgrounds, Derzhavin was the first to thematize his own biography as a fact of intrinsic poetic interest. The great historical events of the time, such as the establishment of the Leglisative Commission in 1767 and the closely related publication of Catherine's celebrated "Nakaz," an instruction or guidebook to the rule of law, the Pugachev Uprising of 1773–75, the statute of local administration of 1775, or the two Turkish Wars of 1768–74 and 1787–92, were no longer perceived in isolation from the individuals of prominence who lived them. The intertwining of national history and personal destiny was Derzhavin's great conundrum: metaphysically, it was manifested as the enigma of time or death; ethically, it became the quest for an equilibrium that would permit the individual to endure and survive the impact of force, be it the sovereign will or the blows of fate.

Derzhavin was to spend some forty years serving the imperial state: the writing of poetry remained for him a Horatian respite from the demands of state service, even as it also became the means to ponder, among other things, the meaning of a career marked by vertiginous ups and downs. Favored—however inconsistently—by royal attention and bestowed with useful sinecures, Derzhavin made the mistake of taking his job too seriously. Devoted to the monarchy he had defended against Pugachev but zealous and uncompromising in his understanding of administrative norms, Derzhavin repeatedly managed to confront or antagonize the superiors on whom he depended. Put simply, Derzhavin failed to acknowledge, let alone reproduce, the pervasive disjuncture between ethical ideals and the everyday practice of imperial governance. What resulted was a prolonged cat-and-mouse game with an empress who despaired at Derzhavin's lack of political savoir faire but who discerned in him a poet capable of giving lyric expression to her vision of enlightened absolutism. Less than a free agent but much more than a lackey, Derzhavin would investigate the contours and limits of the Catherinian enlightenment as a state-sponsored discourse.[18]

While Lomonosov's limited dissent had never broken with the defining framework of the state, Derzhavin placed the rhetorical model of the imperial sublime alongside the distinct if related problem of the individual as an ethical subject. It is this added dimension of individuation that interests us, the "inner conflict" of the Catherinian era that, in James Billington's words, first created the modern Russian intelligentsia as a "personal and moral" tension "within the ruling aristocracy."[19] A letter by Derzhavin of 1815 bears rich testament to this historical moment, in which the Russian artist and the politician were yet to be sundered, remaining as interlocutors in a conflicted dialogue conducted within the same individual: "Being a poet by inspiration, I had to speak the truth; as a politician through my service at the court, I was compelled to cover the truth in allegories."[20]

Derzhavin's role in transforming the panegyric ode and shattering the classicist system of poetic genres has long been acknowledged.[21] What Pushkin had once dismissed as Derzhavin's wildly uneven poetic culture can now be viewed as a radical if implicit assault on the stylistic markers of the Lomonosovian sublime.[22] Without ever calling the ode theoretically into question, Derzhavin renewed it from within by violating the distinction between the Pindaric ode, distinguished by what he called "flashes of piety and edifying lessons for the tsars," and the Horatian tradition, with its capacity to derive the "rules of wisdom" from contemplating "life's sweetness" (7:579). This led to a crisis of the "lofty" style that had typified the Russian ode, undermining, in turn, the thematic hierarchy that separated politics from the sensuous givenness of everyday life. While never ceasing to praise the sovereign and the state, Derzhavin stretched the panegyric ode to accommodate sharply satirical asides against potentates and court favorites even as he also sought to provide new philosophical moorings for his own class, the post-Petrine service gentry.

Derzhavin was, in fact, to write relatively traditional Lomonosovian odes throughout his life, preserving the older tradition primarily for the theme of military victory. Celebrating Catherine's success in dividing Poland and rapidly extending Russia's southern borders, these poems are perhaps the least original of Derzhavin's major works.[23] Yet Derzhavin understood early on that the Lomonosovian ode in its traditional form was not to be his calling. From the hindsight of 1805, he wrote (speaking of himself in the third person) that he had initially "wanted to imitate Mr. Lomonosov, but . . . when desiring to soar, was unable continuously to sustain, through an attractive choice of words, the grandiloquence and sumptuousness that are unique to the Russian Pindar alone. For that reason, beginning in 1779, he chose a very specific path . . . imitating Horace most of all" (6:431).

Derzhavin's long quest to surpass Lomonosov began predictably with failed acts of homage. Among his juvenilia we find poetic effusions dedicated to the empress in the older odic vein. Although they count for little as poetry, they signal an early convergence of theme and geography that would leave a lifelong mark on Derzhavin's poetic dialogue with the empress. In 1767 Catherine undertook a journey of inspection through the Volga provinces to coincide with the elections to the Legislative Commission. Drawn from government institutions as well as all recognized social groups, including non-Russian *inorodtsy* (here "foreign subjects"), the Commission was a consultative body intended to elaborate the great legal and political reconceptualization of the Russian Empire that had been set out in Catherine's "Nakaz." Destined never to be formalized into a code of law, the "Nakaz" remained a set of ideal precepts whose real function, as Richard Wortman suggests, was to propagate an image of Catherine as ruler based on a "myth of universal justice": "The empress followed the myth of empire, not of the universal Christian Empire but a Roman Empire, led by an enlightened monarch and an enlightened administrative elite, bringing the benefits of law and improved material life to the new territories, as well as to the Russian provinces."[24]

Sailing down the Volga to Kazan in a flotilla of eleven galleys, the empress and her courtiers amused themselves by translating Jean-François Marmontel's controversial *Bélisaire* (1766), a historical novel set in Byzantium intended as a didactic parable for contemporary monarchs, and by observing the festive displays of regional color organized for them by the local nobility. In a letter to Voltaire written from Kazan, Catherine shared her impressions of Asiatic Russia:

> These laws, of which so much is being said at present, are not quite completed as of yet. . . . Consider only, if you will, that they are destined to serve both Asia and Europe: and what a difference there is between them in terms of climate, people, customs, and even ideas!
>
> Here I am finally in Asia; I have wanted so terribly to see it with my own eyes. There are in this city twenty different peoples who do not resemble one another in the least. We shall nonetheless have to design a garment that would fit them all. General principles can certainly be found, but what of the details? And what details! I was about to say: we will have to create, unify, and preserve a whole world.[25]

There is a certain poignancy to this letter, marking as it does the arrival of the Enlightenment in Russia's southern peripheries, and with it the familiar double-edged sword of the European civilizing mission.

Catherine desires to acknowledge and permit those cultural and religious differences that she can classify, even as she seeks to establish an overarching commonality which would make that very diversity redundant. The attitude is one of cultural superiority, to be sure, but one that also admits to a taxonomist's lucid anxiety about "details," the refractory specificities of custom and religion that cannot be subsumed by the spectacles of picturesque natives organized on her behalf. As Catherine wrote with still greater candor two days later, "this is an Empire in itself and only here can one see what an immense enterprise it is as concerns our laws, and how little these conform at present to the situation of the Empire in general."[26]

This was also Derzhavin's homeland, and his earliest poems are, in fact, minor documents of Catherine's vision for the outlying Asiatic provinces. Commenting on a masquerade for the empress in which Nogays and other nomadic peoples danced and played before her on their instruments, the young poet wrote:

Достойно мы тебя Минервой называем
На мудрые твои законы как взираем.
Достойно мы тебя Астреею зовем:
Под скипетром твоим златые дни ведем.
. . . .
И дикие с степей сбегаются фауны
И пляшут пред тобой, согласно движа струны.
Россия! похвались владычицей твоей:
И варварски сердца уже пленились ей.
(3:183–84)

It is fitting that we call you Minerva
When we gaze upon your wise laws.
It is fitting that we call you Astrea:
We live our Golden Age under your scepter.
. . . .
And wild fauns come running from the steppe
And dance before you, striking strings in accord.
Russia! Well may you boast of your sovereign:
Even the hearts of barbarians have already fallen captive to her.

A Catherinian Golden Age is inaugurated here. Unlike the Elizabethan Golden Age of Lomonosov, it is presided over by the sovereign personified as imperial legislator, for whom the fate of the non-Russian peoples of the empire looms newly on the horizon. The poem establishes an abyssal gap between nature and culture—"wild fauns," on the one hand, and a Russia aligned with Greek gods, on the other—and then reconciles both through a hypostasis of universal law. According to Catherine's "Nakaz," the incorporation of the Turkic nomads, no less than the loyalty of the empress's Russian subjects, could be idealized as a voluntary submission to the law.

Even as he showered the empress with laudatory epithets, the young Derzhavin was already wary of surrendering entirely to the idiom of praise. Truth, he insisted, was his principal Muse; "what Russians feel," and not the dictates of eloquence, would guide his pen (3:184–85). Both Derzhavin's sincerity and the Catherinian myth of the Golden Age were powerfully tested with the Pugachev Uprising, the century's most significant internal challenge to imperial governmentality that brought unprecedented upheaval to Derzhavin's native region. The poet fought Pugachev as a nobleman and an officer committed to the monarchy and eager for the rewards that proven loyalty could bring. His "Chitalagai Odes" of the same period—a cycle of four translated and four original odes published in 1776—are a case in point.[27] Although the few explicit references to the Pugachev Uprising to be found in the "Chitalagai Odes" remain bound by the odic cliches of the time, other aspects of the cycle suggest that Derzhavin had found a more indirect way to register the limits of imperial control as well as the crises of his own career.

The translated odes of the cycle, written by King Frederick II of Prussia, were devoted to praising or denouncing virtues and vices such as flattery, calumny, or constancy. These odes evince a strong ethico-political and metaphysical orientation that would become a consistent feature of Derzhavin's work. Critical of power without ceasing to be monarchist, they provided an alternative model to Lomonosov's gingerly attempts at political didacticism. They urge sovereigns to be wary of the "false mirror" of flattery and denounce the arrogance of power that is the downfall of all rulers (3:207). Derzhavin's original poems of the Chitalagai cycle continue in the same vein. An ode to Catherine "composed during the revolt of 1774" focuses more on her spirit of mercy than on her military victory: the poem, comments Ronald Vroon, praises an "ideal model of behaviour prescribed by the poet" more than it commemorates Catherine's actual triumph over Pugachev.[28] In his "Oda na znatnost'" (Ode on nobility) Derzhavin tellingly contrasts the formal titles of grandees with a nobility that is of the spirit: "I am a prince, if my spirit shines; / A master if I am master of my passions" (3:225–26). A few years later these lines resurfaced in the still more pointed context of a poem addressed to the newly born tsarevich Alexander, "Na rozhdenie v Severe porfironosnogo otroka" (On the birth of a royal son in the north) (1779): «Будь страстей твоих владетель, / Будь на троне человек!» (Be the master of your passions, / Be a human on the throne!) (1:51). These lines formulate the typically Derzhavinian strategy of *internalizing political power and the social world as an ethical facet of personality.* Self-control, not the domination of external reality, is seen as the supreme goal, and with this contrast is born the richly productive dialectic between the public and the private self.

Since Gukovskii, scholars of Derzhavin have rightly emphasized Derzhavin's discovery of personhood, while neglecting to account for the sublime as the continued locus of the encounter, in Derzhavin, between the individual and history.[29] One of Derzhavin's ongoing goals, in poetry as in life, was to negotiate between the public and the private persona. The political sphere embodied by the ceremonial ode had provided little space for the intimacy and leisure necessary for the articulation of private life. To push the ode beyond the rubric of the state without renouncing the defining sphere of public service was one of Derzhavin's primary poetic tasks. This he accomplished by redefining the place of the sublime as pertaining to an ontological realm that was at the same time greater and lesser than the political state.

Derzhavin and the Sublime

In the fourth of Derzhavin's "Chitalagai Odes," a prose translation of Frederick's ode, "Life Is a Dream," we read: "11. Land, titles, honors, power, you are deceptive like smoke. The mere glance of truth dissipates the luster of your transient beauty. There is nothing reliable in this world, and even the greatest kingdoms are the playthings of inconstancy. 12. . . . If we soar to the heavens and from this grandiose height cast our gaze down onto Paris, Peking, and Rome, then from this remote distance all those great things disappear. The entire earth resembles a point; and what of man himself? 13. Filled with vanity, we rush about between the abyss of the past and that of future centuries, which hurtle constantly onward" (3:219–20).

This awareness of the radical impermanence of worldly affairs was to become Derzhavin's philosophical motto. Like all poets of the sublime, the poet here soars to the heavens to contemplate the earth below, but this familiar vertical axis now yields the opposite lesson to Lomonosov's odic maps of empire. The capital cities of nations become annihilated at this infinite remove of contemplation, dissolving the imperial state into a vaster movement of the cosmos. The experience being intimated here is no less quintessentially sublime, but it is configured ontologically rather than geopolitically, as the erasive force of time or fate. Derzhavin would return again and again to these concerns, as in "Na smert' kniazia Meshcherskogo" (On the death of Prince Meshcherskii) (1779):

> Монарх и узник—снедь червей,
> Гробницы злость стихий снедает;
> Зияет время славу стерть:
> Как в море льются быстры воды,
> Так в вечность льются дни и годы;
> Глотает царства алчна смерть.
> (1:54)

> [Both] monarch and convict are food for worms,
> Tombs are devoured by the malice of the elements;
> Time yawns to erase fame:
> As fast-flowing waters pour into the sea,
> So the days and years pour into eternity;
> Kingdoms are swallowed by ravenous death.

Temporal infinity, rather than empire, is for Derzhavin the supreme sublimity, although he remained content to juxtapose both categories rather than abolish one in favor of the other. Time exposes the evanescence of empire and earthly power, and displaces the empress as the supreme arbiter of destiny. The sovereignty of fate resembles imperial rule in inducing fear and awe but also differs in functioning randomly and violating the distinctions of the social world. Whereas the rulers of the panegyric ode had presided over a relatively static universe, the Derzhavinian sublime creates a mobile hierarchy of being that contains elements both greater and lesser than the empire and the empress: «Сегодня бог, а завтра прах» (1:54) ["God today, ash tomorrow"]. The sublime is a relativistic force, but its energy is not simply destructive. It speeds things up, dislodges experiences, and uproots structures with the fury of a flash flood, making social stability, professional security, political glory, and ontological fixity seem like so much debris borne along by a rapid current. The sublimity of fate is the motor energizing much of Derzhavin's universe. Its effects can be felt in the metaphysical poems such as "Bog" (God) (1784), where the poet declares in a famous line that he is, all at once, "tsar, slave, worm, and God" (1:132). In Derzhavin's world, hierarchy, be it metaphysical or political, is less a ladder than a roller coaster, allowing for the psychological extremes of exaltation and abasement, self-aggrandizement and abjection to exist contiguously rather than as opposites.

It is from this perspective that Derzhavin contemplates the distinction between the public and private. If Derzhavin's later collection of Anacreontic verse lends itself to Il'ia Serman's conclusion that, at least in the 1790s, Derzhavin "distanced himself from all politics and from history, and was drawn to the theme of a peaceful domestic life," then his earlier work suggests a more complex articulation of this polarity.[30] Far from contrasting the two as a simple binary opposition and securing the private world as a respite from politics, Derzhavin examines both from the radical infinity of Time as a sublime force.

Death touches the king and the householder equally, and it is this ontological dimension, not politics as such, that creates as its opposite the concrete dimension of lived life. The lyric subject in Derzhavin is born already knowing the brittleness of power and the voluptuous transience of the sensory world. Embodying both is the *vel'mozha,* the grandee or magnate of the Catherinian era whose mercurial career and sybaritic tastes Derzhavin will describe in numerous poems: it is the magnate, not the state or the empress, who generally provides a counterpoint to the poet's own life. While in the poem "Na Novyi god" (On the New Year) (1780–81) the magnate clambers up the sublime ladder of ambition—«Еще вельможа возвышаться, / Еще сильнее хочет быть» (The magnate desires to rise still higher / To be still stronger), the poet opts "not to chase happiness in the world / [But] to find it in himself" (1:76). For Derzhavin, to live inwardly is never an ascetic goal: it involves savoring the gamut of the senses even as one seeks to become reconciled ethically to the workings of fate.

Derzhavin's late essay, "Rassuzhdenie o liricheskoi poèzii ili ob ode" (1811–15) (Discourse on lyric poetry or on the ode [1811–15]), his only substantial excursion into literary criticism, summarized his poetic debt to the odic past, as well as the revisions he brought to the discourse of the sublime. Here Derzhavin follows Trediakovskii in equating the ode and the psalm, and follows Lomonosov in viewing the ode as practically synonymous with the lyric. In the same essay, however, the poet goes on to distinguish explicitly "two kinds of sublimity (*vysokost'*)", one that is "*sensuous* and consists of the lively representation of material substances . . . the incessant representation of a multitude of brilliant pictures and feelings in a sonorous, grandiloquent, flowery diction that induces rapture and astonishment." The other sublime is "*intellectual,* and consists of showing the actions of a lofty spirit, . . . the silent and peaceful movements of a great soul that is higher than others" (7:550). In this passage Derzhavin fails to identify the sublime as Time itself: instead, he dwells on its *effects*. First, it assails the senses as an experience of grandeur, combining beauty with terror in such a way as to induce "rapture." Its second dimension is intellectual or moral, embodied in the spiritual drama of the superior individual. This discussion corresponds strikingly to a passage in Ivan Martynov's heavily annotated translation of Longinus's treatise on the sublime, then recently published. At one point Martynov comments that the sublime can be further separated into a "sublime of feelings" and a "sublime of thoughts" which is provoked by a "large physical or abstract object" such as "the firmament, high craggy cliffs, bottomless abysses, ruins, . . . the clash of troops, earthquakes, . . . hurricanes, noisily flowing rivers, and waterfalls." Both forms of the sublime are the property of "genius," distinguished by "grandeur of spirit."[31]

In Derzhavin's work, both the sensuous and the intellectual sublime are manifested in the life trajectory of the *vel'mozha*, the generals, courtiers, and functionaries of Catherinian Russia, as much as in the empress or her empire. It is their lifestyle, career, and ultimate fate that will compel the poet to ask the empress to teach him "how to live sumptuously and righteously" ("Felitsa," 1:83).

We can say, then, that Derzhavin first "ontologized" the sublime as Time itself and then mapped its transformative effects on the privileged individual and his destiny. These innovations did not in themselves abolish the imperial theme that had been the ceremonial ode's essential core. Rather, it engendered a newly complex vision in which empire could be juxtaposed as an entity alongside the vaster reality of Time as well as the lesser but poetically essential dimension of the historical individual, be it the poet himself or his aristocratic peers.

The Sublime Individuated

Derzhavin's celebrated poem "Vodopad" (The waterfall) (1791–94) is one poem that successfully combines all these elements. Conceived in response to the death of Prince Grigorii Potemkin, statesman, military commander, and a lover of Catherine, the poem begins by describing a waterfall that will provide an allegorical frame for the piece as a whole:

Алмазна сыплется гора
С высот четыремя скалами,
Жемчугу бездна и сребра

Кипит внизу, бьет вверх буграми;
От брызгов синий холм стоит,
Далече рев в лесу шумит.

(1:318)

A diamond mountain is scattering
[Plunging] from the heights along four ledges,
A chasm [or multitude] of pearls and silver
Seethes below and thrusts up mounds;
A dark-blue hill stands [created by] the jets of water,
Farther away a roar reverberates in the forest.

Derzhavin's waterfall generates yet another example of the mountainous sublime with which we are now well familiar. Indeed, this first stanza of "Vodopad," and the poem as a whole, can be read as a complex parody of Lomonosov's ode on Khotin. The latter began, we recall, with the poet's flight to the top of Mount Parnassus, from which he harkens to the visual and auditory details of a receding horizon: «*Далече* рев в лесу шумит» (*Further out* a roar resounds through the forest), says Derzhavin at the end of his first stanza; «*Далече* дым в полях курится» (*Further out* smoke curls along the fields), reads Lomonosov's equivalent line. Both poems begin with a figurative vertical axis that affords an experience of the sublime; both then use this vantage point to view and comment on an ongoing conflict between Russia and Ottoman Turkey.

Unlike Lomonosov's poem, however, "Vodopad" does not celebrate a single military victory nor does it articulate its theme in exclusively patriotic terms. Its allegorical premise is at once greater and smaller, and embraces a range of voices, human experiences, and philosophical conclusions. Long before the appearance of Potemkin or the theme of the second Russo-Turkish war of 1787–92, we encounter a "gray-haired man"—Count Rumiantsev, a respected army commander and civilian administrator of the time, whom Potemkin had sidelined from power during the recent war. Rumiantsev's function in the poem is didactic: his loss of political clout provides him with the moral distance necessary to interpret the poem's unfolding allegory. Seated by the waterfall clad in golden armor, he broodingly glosses the "terrible beauty" (*strashnaia krasa*) of the natural scene:

Не жизнь ли человеков нам
Сей водопад изображает?
Он также благом струй своих
Поит надменных, кротких, злых.

Не так ли с неба время льется,
Кипит стремление страстей,
Честь блещет, слава раздается,
Мелькает счастье наших дней,
Которых красоту и радость
Мрачат печали, скорби, старость?
. . . .
Не упадает ли в сей зев
С престола царь и друг царев?
(1:319–20)

Is not the life of humans
Depicted for us by this waterfall?
With its benign waters it too
Provides drink for the haughty, the meek, and the evil.

Does not time pour in a like way from heaven,
The ambition of passions seethe,
Honor gleam, and glory resonate,
The happiness of our days flash,
Whose beauty and joy
Is obscured by sadness, grief, and old age?
. . . .
Do not the king and the king's friend
Fall from the throne into these jaws?

The rush of water was one of Derzhavin's preferred metaphors: generally representing the all-consuming vortex of time, it was also likened metapoetically to the ode itself, which, like a fast river, "carries everything away in its wake" (7:593). Time's flow leaves nothing and no one untouched: it is the supreme force, shaping and smashing people's lives just as water might carve out or erode formations of rock. To interpret these shapes is to map the effects of time on the scale of life as it is lived by individuals. What results, in this poem as in many of Derzhavin's works, are lyric biographies: whereas Lomonosov gauged historical events in terms of the benefits accruing to the empress *qua* empire, Derzhavin particularizes these events as watersheds in the political life of the noblemen of his day. The heroes of Lomonosov's Khotin ode, we recall, were Ivan, Peter, and Anna, who were little more than the sum of their victories in battle. Derzhavin's heroes, by contrast, are very human; they are the Russian statesmen whose conflicting ambitions marked the course of the Turkish war. Unlike Lomonosov's ode, then, the imperial theme in "Vodopad" does not simply glorify Russian expansion; it establishes the context for the statesman's career that becomes the new matrix for understanding the relationship between the individual and the general.

"Vodopad" is a long poem, whose very diffuseness permits a series of protagonists, allegorical visions, and philosophical assertions that are only tenuously integrated, creating what Anna Lisa Crone calls a "reticulating and meandering effect."[32] Rumiantsev dominates only the first half, articulating a sense of the transience of glory whose pessimism is counterbalanced by a dream in which he revisits his heroic exploits. This structure of alternating negative and positive moments is repeated throughout the poem: the poet or his heroes acknowledge the impact of mortality only to wrest some compensatory consolation from the jaws of death. Thus Rumiantsev, on seeing the winged figure of death announce Potemkin's demise,

> sighs . . . :
> . . . .
> "Blessed is he who, in aspiring to glory, preserved the common good,
> Was merciful in bloody war,
> And preserved the life of his very enemies."
>
> (1:323)

Rumiantsev ultimately bridges the evident gap between his past glory and his present decline by projecting an alternative vision of his own posthumous fame, vouchsafed not only by martial valor but also by greatness of spirit (1:323).

Yet if Rumiantsev represents the ideal ethical reconciliation of personal glory (*slava*) and the general good (*pol'za*), then Potemkin is a less benign and more complex figure. Unlike Rumiantsev, who was deprived of royal favor, Potemkin represents a more compelling fusion of glory and good fortune (*schast'e*). Potemkin, again unlike Rumiantsev, does not speak and hence cannot provide his own life with any sense of philosophical closure. Potemkin is thus doubly enigmatic: his titanic persona, the meteoric extremes of his rise and fall, render him more compelling than Rumiantsev, yet his charisma remains a source of aesthetic wonderment rather than ethical synthesis.[33] Potemkin's alienation from his own destiny is underscored by the split between his spirit and his body, which the poet represents separately, and in turn. His "wondrous spirit" flies southward to the scene of his great victories against the Turks, reviewing the kingdoms he has conquered, while his "corpse" lies prostrate in the ground, fallen "abruptly among the steppes," his "deathbed the earth," his "palace the surrounding desolation" (1:324).

While Rumiantsev's words most closely match Derzhavin's philosophical conclusions, it is Potemkin's dead body that marks the beginnings of a new model for the imperial sublime. Marked by a restless sense of personal ambition, Potemkin's fate anticipates the narcissistic cult of the romantics (Potemkin's corpse is surely an intertext for Lermontov's great poem, "The Dream," with its description of a soldier's bleeding body lying in a valley of Daghestan, unburied and hence unreconciled with his homeland, a text we turn to in the next chapter). With Potemkin we have a man whose life and death appear suddenly coterminous with empire, which is now measurable in terms of personal loss or gain as much as territorial contraction and expansion. Derzhavin notes in his commentary that "none better than Prince Potemkin grasped Catherine's ambitious spirit and the might of her empire, on whose foundation he based his own great plans" (3:521). Here Derzhavin was referring to the "Greek Project," a plan to wrest Constantinople from Ottoman hands and establish there a fraternal Orthodox empire, which became closely identified with Potemkin's rise to power in 1774. As Andrei Zorin observes, such enterprises as the annexation of the Crimea in 1783 were perceived in certain quarters as "Potemkin's political adventure, undertaken despite the opposition of the entire cabinet of ministers, and whose outcome would determine the continuation of Catherine's favour and his influence."[34] Derzhavin's views reflect a similar ambivalence: in the following lines, the prestige of the sovereign and the state seem equally to be a platform for Potemkin's own ambitions:

> Не ты ль, который взвесить смел
> Мощь Росса, дух Екатерины,
> И опершись на них, хотел
> Вознесть твой гром на те стремнины,
> На коих древний Рим стоял,
> И всей вселенной колебал?
>
> (1:324–25)

> Is it not you who dared to weigh
> The might of the Russian and the spirit of Catherine,
> And leaning on them, wanted
> To raise your thunder to that precipice
> On which ancient Rome had stood
> And swayed the entire universe?

While Rumiantsev's discourse remains essentially self-contained, Potemkin's "open but silent mouth" needs to be ventriloquized. The poet thus addresses Potemkin directly and revisits his exploits, which he had himself celebrated in the past:

В созвучность громкого Пиндара
Мою настроить лиру мнил,
Воспел победу Измаила,
Воспел,—но смерть тебя скосила!
(1:325)

In consonance with loud Pindar
I thought to tune my lyre,
I celebrated your victory at Izmail,
I celebrated [it]—but death cut you down!

In recalling "Na vziatie Izmaila" (On the taking of Izmail) (1790), the most famous and the most conventional of his victory odes, Derzhavin here signals its essential limits. In Derzhavin's work, the odic sublime is perpetually threatened by death and the evanescence of power. The strains of sustaining the odic enterprise of praise, and the glory of empire that is its object, are vividly manifest in the nervously rhetorical quality of the poem's final pages. Just as the poem as a whole seems to waver between ode and elegy, so, too, the poet repeatedly renounces his most pessimistic conclusions with a hasty "or no!"—much like a suicide who changes his mind at the edge of a cliff.

Derzhavin's "Vodopad" thus contains several heterogeneous elements: the traditional concerns of the ode (Russian "rapture" and Turkish "terror") coexist alongside a pessimism concerning the efficacy of human endeavor that threatens to negate all worldly affairs, while the piece finally concludes by returning to the poet's ethical agenda. The waterfall is reminded that its sublimity should only exist in proportion to its beneficial effects: «Чтоб был . . . сколь дивен, столь полезен» (May you be . . . as wondrous as you are useful) (1:329).

Given the importance of state service for Derzhavin's own career, it is not surprising that the career of the state functionary, subject to the whims of the sovereign and the tides of fortune, continued to provide a model for the poet's notion of selfhood. The concerns of "Vodopad," which struggles to reconcile imperial policy with an ethics of public behavior, became an ongoing theme of Derzhavin's poetry. "Na vozvrashchenie grafa Zubova iz Persii" (On the return of Count Zubov from Persia) (1797) and its immediate predecessor, "Na pokorenie Derbenta" (On the conquest of Derbent) (1796), are a case in point. Both poems are addressed to the young military commander Valerian Zubov, brother to another of Catherine's favorites, and address the vicissitudes of his career as a means of inserting a search for ethical norms into the ode's traditional celebration of military conquest.

Zubov's career had brought home yet again the extent to which empire could be made and unmade by the personality of the monarch and the shifting tides of royal favor. On ascending the throne, Catherine's son, Paul, decided to renounce his mother's ambitious southern policy: Zubov was ordered home in the midst of a successful campaign against Persia and then forced to live under police surveillance. Derzhavin's innovation was to contemplate this shift in imperial policy as a human and ethical problem rather than as a question of geopolitics. Motivated, like "Vodopad," by a sympathy for the underdog, the ode to Zubov could neither be published at the time nor read at court: this itself suggests the extent to which the ode, even when marking Russia's imperial engagements, was outgrowing its ceremonial function.

Addressing Zubov on his return from Persia, the poem begins at a considerable philosophical remove from the count's recent campaign. The aim of life, we are told in the very first line, is peace of mind (*pokoi*). The poem figures life as a series of landscapes to be traversed in this search for ultimate peace, a journey in which a steep rise or descent is equivalent to temporary success or failure: «Сей с холма в пропасть упадает, / А тот взойти спешит на холм» (This man falls from a hill into an abyss, / And that one races to climb the hill) (2:20). Yet true happiness involves abandoning the dizzying heights of the vertical sublime («За ней на высоту не мчится» [does not pursue it by rushing to a high place]) for the calm certitudes of the "middle path." The poem thus begins by denying *philosophically* what would be its greatest *poetic* innovation: its vivid description, the first in Russian literature, of the Caucasus as a privileged locus of the sublime.

As the poet recalls Zubov's recent campaign in the Caucasus, the poem makes an abrupt shift from ethical detachment to aesthetic rapture:

> О юный вождь!—сверша походы,
> Прошел ты с воинством Кавказ,
> Зрел ужасы, красы природы:
> Как с ребр там страшных гор лиясь
> Ревут в мрак бездн сердиты реки:
> Как с чел их с грохотом снега
> Падут, лежавши целы веки;
> Как серны, вниз склонив рога,
> Зрят в мгле спокойно под собою
> Рожденье молний и громов.
>
> (2:20–21)

O young leader!—in waging your campaigns,
You have marched through the Caucasus with your soldiery,
You have gazed upon the horrors, the beauties of nature:
The angry rivers, as they pour forth there from the ribs of terrifying mountains
As they roar into the gloom of abysses:
The snows as from their brows [of the hills] thunderously
They fall, after having lain there for whole centuries;
The chamois, their horns bent down,
View calmly in the gloom below them
The birth of lightening and thunder.

The Caucasus mountains and their region are presented here in a way that corresponds perfectly to Derzhavin's later definition of the sublime as being either "sensuous," "intellectual," or (occasionally) both (7:550). These lines are nothing if not "the incessant representation of a multitude of brilliant pictures"; as such they contain the germ of the Caucasian problematic that would become a major current of Russian romanticism. Derzhavin here signals the beginning of what is a more specifically sensuous or natural form of the imperial sublime, whose rich visual excess was definitively formulated for Russian poetry in Pushkin's southern verse. The luxuriant profusion of natural detail here is no longer abstractly symbolic (as with Lomonosov) and not yet simply picturesque or enumerative (as often with Pushkin). It is organized in strict accordance with the visual criteria of horror and beauty («ужасы, красы природы» [the horrors, the beauties of nature]), which the sublime will first juxtapose and then conflate. Descriptive detail proliferates up and down a sheer vertical drop that is contrasted with the horizontal perspective of the itinerant eye.

The stanzas devoted to describing the landscape of the Caucasus are structured as a series of vertical glances, arrested and then displaced, providing a series of vignettes that are recounted as part of the poem's account of Zubov's life as a career. This sequence of visions provides the natural counterpart to the intellectual sublime, the latter consisting of "showing the actions of a lofty spirit." A great soul is one who, having climbed the ladder of power and savored both success and failure, gains the self-mastery necessary to view his own destiny with detachment. Soaring ambition thus becomes the intellectual counterpart to the mountainous sublime:

Ты домы зрел царей, вселенну,
Внизу, вверху ты видел все;

Упадшу спицу, вознесенну,
Вертяще мира колесо.
(2:21)

You saw the homes of tsars, the universe,
Above, below, you saw it all;
You saw the fallen spoke and the raised one,
The world's wheel turning.

The poem thus effectively creates two vertical axes, the *sensuous* sublime that celebrates the natural grandeur of the Caucasus mountains and the *intellectual* sublime that symbolizes the hierarchical power of kings and potentates "seated on the throne / high above mortals" (2:20). Both sublimities function to link the imperial metropolis to the colonial periphery, re-creating the typically Lomonosovian effect of imperial cartography. Yet, for Derzhavin, this map is not, at least here, a representation of the Russian state. It is a psychological lesson, serving as a guide to the individual's "victories over the self" (2:22), a gauge of one's capacity to survive the caprices of power and finally surrender the realm of politics for the "wisdom of other kingdoms." The glory of conquest is devalued in favor of self-control, and this introjection of power is what allows the imperial sublime to become psychologized as an ethical imperative.

This ethical vision permits Derzhavin to question the attractions of the vertical sublime without dismantling it. The latter is philosophically subordinated to the poet's search for a reflective equilibrium but, rhetorically speaking, remains the privileged mode of expressing that very search. This is why it is dismissed as transient or episodic in the ode to Zubov even as it rhetorically defines the poem's basic movement. What finally remains, the soul stripped of earthly illusions, can best be defined as a subtler version of what the poet once defined as the intellectual sublime:

Сиянье вкруг тебя заснуло,
Прошло,—остался только ты.
Остался ты!—и та прекрасна
Душа почтенна будет ввек . . .
(2:22)

The luster about you has faded,
It has passed,—you alone remain.
You remain!—and that splendid
Soul will be esteemed forever.

The great soul is like the poem itself, an immortal residue that has survived the experience of the vertical sublime, to measure its rise and fall.

The Oriental Despot

"Vodopad," and poems like it, point to the role of the service nobility in redefining the imperial sublime: whereas the Lomonosovian sublime amounts to little more than a celebration of the state, the Derzhavinian sublime suggests a more complex dialectic between personal ambition and royal favor. This same dialectic is even more dramatically evident in the mature work of Derzhavin that addresses Catherine the Great, the so-called "Felitsa" poems for which, then as now, he is best remembered.

Long before Derzhavin, the poet Trediakovskii had pointed out that the empress Anna's presence in his poem on Gdansk was metaphorical, given that she had been ascribed a role on the battlefield that in fact her general had performed.[35] From then on, the tropological mode of "presencing" the monarch through address, what rhetoricians call "prosopopeia," would become central to the odic representation of power. Yet, although most of the odes written by Trediakovskii and Lomonosov in fact addressed one of Russia's three empresses, their representations were anything but distinct or particular:

Надежда, свет России всей
В Тебе щедрота Божья зрится,
Хоть внешней красотой Твоей
Довольно всяк, кто зрит, дивится.
Душевных лик Твоих доброт
Краснее внешних всех красот,
Где всяки совершенства явны,
Любезны всем, во всем преславны.[36]

Hope and light of all Russia
In You God's generosity can be seen,
Although Your external beauty
Is marveled at enough by any who gaze upon it.
The image of your inner virtues
Is more beautiful than all external charms,
Where all forms of perfection are evident,
Pleasing to all, and glorious in every way.

These lines, largely formulaic but dedicated in fact to the empress Elizabeth, perform the cliché that governs Lomonosov's rendering of

Russia's ruling monarchs.[37] As Louis Marin has said of the role of royal eulogy under French absolutism:

> It would seem that political power, in its desire for the absolute, can find no representation more adequate than the one offered by the epideictic mode in its positive form of panegyric and praise. . . . It is a narrative that does not aim to re-present the past by making it present once again but, rather, by insisting on or redoubling the presence of the prince in his immediate action, thereby giving him his essential legitimacy as the brilliant manifestation of his perfections.[38]

Yet, in praising the sovereign, the poet risks emptying his or her figure of all specificity: a fleshless and idealized vision of perfection, the sovereign body becomes diaphanous and even flat, so that the seeing eye can pass unimpeded from its outer beauty to its inner virtues, rendering them equally visible and hyperbolically equivalent. For the ode, sheer surface is the supreme space of allegorical projection, transforming the abstract and concrete attributes of the ruler, as well as the topography of her realm, into commensurable objects of spectacle. Before Derzhavin, the odic poet had elaborated imperial history as successive embodiments of power, highly abstract if essentially mobile. These allegorical bodies were the tsars themselves, who coexisted in the space of empire and were coextensive with it, displaying their face and limbs as attributes of might or retributive justice.

Derzhavin's innovation lay in representing the monarch as *individuated* without being any less allegorical. The empress's attributes, idealized yet recognizably specific, were derived from works written by Catherine herself. The "Felitsa" odes were a unique example of "coauthorship," textualizing the sovereign body, as well as the lyric persona, in a newly collaborative way. The texts at stake are readily identified: the famous "Nakaz" of 1767, which provided Derzhavin with a means of situating Catherine's reign in a specific—if largely theoretical—ideological terrain, and a fable, "The Tale of the Crown Prince Khlor," whose plot line supplied the cultural fantasy of the "Felitsa" cycle. Let us examine these texts in turn.

Beginning with the earliest odes of his youth, Derzhavin continually invoked Catherine as the author of the "Nakaz." Interpreted initially as a statement of principles outlining Catherine's vision of a law-based state and then as an increasingly mythical attribute of the royal persona, the "Nakaz" had served the essential function of updating the ideological basis of Russian autocracy with respect to the latest shifts in European thought. Although autocracy had long been identified as the basis of Russian statehood, Russia had become newly vulnerable to the critique of absolutism that was emanating from the French Enlightenment. Catherine responded to this critique with a now characteristically Russian gesture, acknowledging the necessity for progressive reform based on western ideas without abrogating the absolute power vested in the Russian ruler. This polemic interests us as a source for the ideological symbols and cultural anxieties to which Derzhavin would give expression in his poetic representations of Catherine and her empire.

Inevitably, one important crux of Catherine's argument concerned the distinction between despotism, or arbitrary government with no limits on power, and an absolute monarchy espousing enlightened values that were believed to reconcile power with the legitimate ends of good governance. This distinction acquired a geographical dimension in Montesquieu's *De l'Esprit des Lois* (1748), in which he defined despotism as whatever the European monarchies were not, or should not be. This definition, apparently restrictive yet in fact open-endedly polemical, established despotism as a purely negative category, functioning only to clarify what European monarchy ideally ought to be. Operating outwardly as a theorization of Asia where it is "so to speak naturally domiciled," despotism designates the reign of a tyrant who governs by the force of fear alone. Whereas the monarch is the sole ruler but governs "by fixed and established laws," the despot "*is* the law, the state, and the prince."

The transition from sheer, undifferentiated power to a law-based monarchy was, for Montesquieu, Russia itself:

> Observe, I beg of you, how industriously the government of Muscovy is seeking to move out of despotism, which weighs upon it more than on the people themselves. The large bodies of armed men have been broken up, the penalties for crimes diminished, tribunals have been established, laws have begun to be acknowledged, and the people instructed. But there are particular reasons which will perhaps lead it [Muscovy] back to the ill fate it sought to flee.[39]

Russia, for Montesquieu's Europe, is this spatial oscillation, "moving out" yet relapsing into despotism, almost Europe but never arriving.

A central feature—and justification—of despotism, in Montesquieu's eyes, was the fact of *empire*. Despotism emerges when a nation expands through conquest, a shift that Montesquieu defines in spatial terms: "A monarchical state must be of a mediocre size," whereas "a large empire supposes a despotic authority in him who governs. The swiftness of decisions must compensate for the distance of the places to which they are conveyed, fear must hinder the negligence of the governor or magistrate far-away; the law must reside in one person alone."[40] Imperial territory, with its extended distances and peculiar concentration of authority, finds its rationale and correlative in the figure of the despot, its guardian and ultimate personification. Empires, moreover, are a characteristic feature of Asia: "In Asia, we have always seen large empires; in Europe they have never been able to subsist. . . . Power must therefore always be despotic in Asia. . . . In Europe, natural division forms several states of a mediocre size, in which a law-based government is not incompatible with the maintenance of the state."[41]

Montesquieu's work circulated widely in Russia, and was acknowledged by Catherine herself as her "breviary." Catherine's "Nakaz" was to retain the terms of Montesquieu's geography while fundamentally reshaping its limits. It effectively repeated the contradiction that Montesquieu had discerned in the Petrine reforms, by collapsing the essential distinction between European monarchy and oriental despotism:

> 6. Russia is a European power [*derzhava*] . . .
>
> 7. The proof for this is as follows. The changes which in Russia were undertaken by Peter the Great were all the more successful because the manners which prevailed at the time were quite unsuitable to the climate and had been imported to our land thanks to the intermingling of peoples and the conquest of foreign lands. In introducing European manners and customs to a European people, Peter I then found facilitating factors such as he himself had not expected. . . .
>
> . . . .
>
> 9. The sovereign is autocratic [*Gosudar' est' samoderzhavnyi*]; for no other power [*vlast'*] save that which is united in his person [*v ego osobe*] can act in a manner commensurable with the extent [*prostranstvom*] of so great a state.
>
> 10. An extended dominion [*Prostrannoe gosudarstvo*] presupposes autocratic power [*samoderzhavnuiu vlast'*] in the person who rules it. A swiftness in resolving affairs dispatched from distant parts must make amends for the delay caused by the distance of these places.[42]

Catherine's debt to Montesquieu has been long acknowledged, but we should not underestimate the important displacements effected by her mimicry: Montesquieu's definition of *oriental* despotism is deployed here to assert Russia's place as a *European* nation. Catherine first relies on Montesquieu's theory of geographical determinism, implying that despotism could not flourish naturally in a colder climate such as Russia's, except as an "imported" tradition.[43] Yet the Tatar-Eurasian heritage implied in the allusions to "intermingling" and "conquest" returns us to the imperial-Asiatic context that Montesquieu had defined as the natural home of despotism, and which Russia would presumably have to shed in order to become truly European. Significantly the term *despotism* is here crucially elided: autocracy (*samoderzhavie*) replaces despotism at each point as the defining feature of Russia, claiming the contours and features of a despotic empire while asserting Russia's place in the European theater of nations. Defending Russia against the charge of despotism became an ongoing challenge for Catherine at this time. Her *Antidote* (1770), published as an anonymous rebuttal to Abbé Jean Chappe d'Auteroche's anti-Russian tract, *Voyage en Sibérie* (1768), proffered an argument similar to her "Nakaz." Admonishing Chappe for the "odious term despot" that he did not "cease to employ," Catherine justified the "seven hundred years" of Russian autocracy as the "sole form of government possible in Russia given the extent of the Empire."[44] This statement contrasts interestingly with an earlier comment, not intended for publication, which Catherine wrote on the margins of the book *Lettres russiennes* (1760). Here the term *despotism* is retained to argue the very same point: "So great an empire as Russia would perish if any form of rule were instituted in it other than the despotic, because it alone can provide with the necessary speed for the needs of distant provinces."[45]

These vacillations in terminology reflect more than Catherine's intellectual strategies. They might equally be read as signs of a prolonged crisis of cultural belonging. Sandwiched between Europe and Asia, Russia could not be defined exclusively in the civilizational terms of either continent, appearing "Asiatic" to the extent that it was an imperial state, and European to the extent that it remained committed to the modernizing process, whether in the form of institutional reform or in reproducing the sign-systems of the European Enlightenment. The paradoxes of this dual status were many, and one of its symbols was the oriental despot. A vivid designation of unlimited power, the oriental despot nonetheless seldom functioned in a purely mimetic fashion, namely as a figure corresponding to a specific geographical region or historical era. It is generally best read allegorically, as a complex cultural fantasy of the times.

Writers of the French Enlightenment were the first to explore the allegorical potential of oriental despotism. Montesquieu's *Lettres persanes* (1721), and subsequently Voltaire's philosophical tales beginning with

"Zadig" (1747), had established the tradition of oriental narratives whose satirical edge and exotic locale allowed for a defamiliarization of European politics and its cultural assumptions. The east in these stories had a double function—as an *external* contrast to the west, which appeared progressive by comparison, and as an *internal* critique of the west, from the perspective of Enlightenment reason that was revealed to be culturally universal. The despot was similarly dual: a tyrant different in every way from western norms of rule but also a cautionary if metaphorical reminder of the abuses prevalent under European absolutism.

Originating in France, the oriental tale enjoyed wide popularity in Russia from the 1760s. While remaining satirical, the Russian tales strove more actively than their French counterparts to reconcile Enlightenment ideology with absolutist power. As V. N. Kubacheva observes, the oriental tales published in Russia in the 1780s and the early 1790s posed the problem of social organization primarily in terms of "the personality of the sovereign."[46] Structural criticism was largely precluded, and the Enlightenment's social ideals of reason and justice were generally defined as moral qualities that the monarch could acquire through education; negative attributes, such as vices or social injustices, were ascribed to courtiers and ministers rather than to the ruler. What resulted was an attractively simple scenario, in which moral edification was not merely an ideological attribute of the story but an actual panacea for social ills.

The empress Catherine herself wrote two such stories, "Skazka o tsareviche Khlore" (Tale of the Crown Prince Khlor) (1781) and "Skazka o tsareviche Fevee" (Tale of the Crown Prince Fevei) (1783).[47] These were edifying fairy tales composed for her grandchildren, Alexander and Constantine, and pointedly concerned with the upbringing of dynastic heirs. Crown Prince Khlor is told to seek a "thornless rose that does not prick," and Prince Fevei must also undergo various tests to prove his moral caliber. While the question of education provides the ethical focus of these stories, their geographical location is of equal interest. Unlike the majority of oriental tales set in the Middle East or India, these stories take place in Russian Eurasia. While the tsar of Russia is away from his palace attending, we are told, to a border dispute, the khan of a nomadic Kirgiz tribe kidnaps the tsar's son, Khlor, a boy of rare intelligence and beauty. Khlor emerges as a kind of royal fetish: his body, in being stolen, establishes theft as the medium of the tale's encounter between the Russian tsar and the Kirgiz khan. Nomadic Kalmyks and

"Tatars" from the Golden Horde similarly threaten the young prince Fevei and his father's kingdom.

Both stories, even as they seek to impart a timeless moral code of behavior, are also about territorial conflict, disputed boundaries and bodies. In both stories the restoration of the prince to his family and kingdom provides the necessarily happy ending. Almost too easily achieved, the final equilibrium of the stories also raises—if not for Catherine then for her interpreters—more disquieting questions about the perennial Eurasian tension between sedentary and nomadic modes of social organization. The Russian autocratic state, the tale of Khlor implies, never exists as a prior given. Rather, its identity is endlessly produced and reaffirmed through a violent encounter with an alien nomadic culture—a war, a skirmish, a theft—an encounter from which the very basis of Russian statehood is derived. Khlor is not fully a prince until he is kidnapped and then restored: it is from the nomads who kidnap him that he learns of the whereabouts and nature of the "thornless rose that does not prick," which symbolizes virtue: he returns to Russia enlightened but quasi-oriental. Although the story is set in a remote prehistory ("before Kii, the founding prince of Kiev"), it is not difficult to discern here the makings of a historical allegory: temporarily subjugated by the eastern nomads yet learning from them, Russia frees itself only after absorbing elements of the very culture it opposes. This absorption has a moral or ideological character in the story, but its territorial implications are not difficult to extrapolate.

Catherine's fairy stories contain many of the rich cultural paradoxes of the oriental tale, including those specific to Russia. The Turkic peoples remain an alien and threatening force in both stories yet have (at least in the "Tale of the Crown Prince Khlor") a capacity to impart moral values which, in the true tradition of the Enlightenment, are assumed to be universal. Hence the peculiar compromise, common to both stories, between territorial aggression and cultural tolerance, which was also to be Catherine's standard response to the subject peoples of her empire.[48] If these stories are minor allegories of Catherinian absolutism, then it is worth noting that the young "enlightened despot" who is the hero of both tales does not belong unequivocally to this or that nation or culture: he is imaged rather as a transactional figure, through whom borders are renegotiated, values exchanged, and cultural identities established. The "orient," it seems, is less a place on the map than a border to be crossed, and a lesson to be imparted.

Addressing the Despot

Derzhavin wrote a series of poems whose theme and central protagonists he culled from Catherine's "Tale of the Crown Prince Khlor." The first of these poems, "Felitsa," succeeded spectacularly in establishing Derzhavin's poetic reputation as well as defining his political relationship to Catherine and her court. It was followed at varying intervals by the related poems "Blagodarnost' Felitse" (Gratitude to Felitsa) (1783), "Videnie murzy" (The Murza's vision) (written in 1783–84, reworked and published in 1791), "Izobrazhenie Felitsy" (A portrayal of Felitsa) (1789), and, much later, "Poslanie indeiskogo bramina k tsarevichu Khloru" (Epistle of an Indian brahmin to the crown prince Khlor) (1802), a poem dedicated, appropriately enough, to Catherine's grandson, Alexander.

Critics have generally hailed the "Felitsa" cycle as Derzhavin's vindication of the individual personality. "Derzhavin's originality," writes Il'ia Serman, lies in "having placed himself" inside his portrait gallery of Catherine's noblemen.[49] Iurii Lotman writes, still more pointedly, that "Derzhavin paradoxically reversed the situation" of the Russian ode by "predicat[ing] the very possibility of odic poetry on the assumption that the tsarina was a private person, a human being and not an embodied principle. Derzhavin abolished the antithesis of the state and the private individual by subordinating the positive sphere of the former to the latter."[50] Yet was this inversion so absolute? That Derzhavin succeeded in personalizing his dialogue with power is beyond doubt, but was his individuation of the human persona an unequivocal triumph over the state? And how does his unsettling of these antinomies relate to the oriental tales that Catherine herself authored?

In writing "Felitsa" Derzhavin fulfilled his need to win the empress's favor and attention even as he reworked the genre of the panegyric ode. This double success, pragmatic and literary, is easily understood from the very title "Felitsa." A transient but crucial figure in the Khlor tale, Felitsa is the Kirgiz khan's daughter, a princess of "merry character and exceedingly pleasant," who provides Khlor with the kindly counsel he needs to find the thornless rose, and offers him her son, Reason, as his guide. In Felitsa the quintessential folkloric motif of the magical intercessor becomes a vehicle for Enlightenment ideology: her aid consists solely of fostering Khlor's innate capacity to discern what constitutes proper conduct and to persevere on the correct path. Derzhavin's brilliance consisted of recognizing Felitsa as the empress's own self-projection, and of magnifying and then turning back on Catherine the mirror she had crafted for herself. Overall the "Felitsa" cycle dramatized in poetic form the awkward reconciliation of "oriental" despotism and Enlightenment principles that had become identified as Catherinian ideology. This was a playful but forced marriage between a progressive European content and a regressive "oriental" form, one whose strains are evident throughout much of the cycle.

"Felitsa" begins by addressing Catherine as the "God-like Princess of the Kirgiz-Kaisak horde," imploring her to instruct the poet just as she had once taught the crown prince Khlor. In the course of the poem, the poet's self-representation acquires two dimensions. He is first an eager student, submitting like Khlor before him to the empress's discipline; second, he identifies himself as the Murza Lazybones, a genially indolent aristocrat who functions in Catherine's story as a minor obstacle to Khlor's quest for virtue. This second dimension sits awkwardly with the first and is a radical emendation of the original story: a reprobate and morally static character in Catherine's text, the Murza now abruptly turns to Felitsa in search of self-improvement:

Подай, Фелица, наставленье,
Как пышно и правдиво жить,
Как укрощать страстей волненье
И счастливым на свете быть.
Меня твой голос возбуждает,
Меня твой сын препровождает;
Но им последовать я слаб:
Мятясь житейской суетою,
Сегодня властвую собою,
А завтра прихотям я раб.
(1:83–84)

Give me instructions, Felitsa,
On how to live sumptuously and righteously,
How to subjugate the agitation of the passions
And be happy on the earth.
Your voice makes me animated,
Your son sends me off,
But I am too weak to follow them:
Rushing about absorbed in life's vain pursuits,
Today I am in control of myself,
But tomorrow I am a slave to my caprices.

The poem as a whole is not much more than a continuing elaboration of this initial contrast between benign instructress and errant pupil. The Murza presents himself as indolent and prone to sybaritic excesses, while exalting Felitsa for being a sovereign who is permissive in relation to others yet disciplined enough to be able herself to "subjugate the passions." The contrast between Felitsa and the Murza is more than a theme: it is also the structuring principle behind a new sense of lyric subjectivity. In a typically Derzhavinian gesture, the above lines turn the political realm inward, converting the imperial state into a psychic sovereignty over the self. The lyric subject is born in this quest for self-mastery but also, as we shall see, in the repeated failure of this quest.

The tone of bashful self-reproach that dominates the poem has been primarily read as a social satire of gentry mores; yet it might also be read in a more psychological vein, as the construction of a gentry selfhood reached through critical self-examination. (That Derzhavin was not a part of Catherine's inner circle when writing "Felitsa," and hence not fully implicated in the Murza's self-deprecating confessions, makes the overlapping of collective and individual selves all the more complex.) In fact, as James Billington has observed, these two aspects, social and psychological, are deeply connected: "The personal moral crisis for the ruling aristocrat of Catherine's era was not, in the first instance, created by economic and political privilege but rather by the new style of life within the aristocracy itself: by the vulgar hedonism and imitative Gallomania of their own increasingly profligate lives."[51]

The Murza's aristocratic consciousness is precisely this: a self-reflexivity that turns inward to critique the indulgent rhythms of gentry life, and then looks for external models in order to overcome its malaise. While the details of the Murza's lifestyle have given rise to much critical discussion of Derzhavin's new individualism, it is worth noting that the poet's search seldom culminates in any real sense of personal autonomy. For Derzhavin there is always a higher authority to which the self is answerable. Felitsa is one image of this authority and, as such, has two hypostases, political and moral. As ruler, she has broadened the range of permitted behavior, knowing the "rights of both people and kings" and allowing at least her aristocratic subjects to "travel to foreign parts" (1:88–89). Ethically she functions as a model of proper conduct, a regulatory ideal to be absorbed and emulated:

> You do not play cards,
> Like me, from one morning to the next.
> (1:84)

These two hypostases are inflected in inverse ways: the political sphere is expansive and permissive whereas the moral sphere emphasizes restraint and self-discipline. These two spheres are not necessarily in contradiction: doctrinally speaking, the power of the absolute monarch was defined as unlimited, with any restriction on his power emanating from him alone, as an act of voluntary self-limitation. The sovereign's moral restraint, then, was the necessary complement to the political freedom of his subjects.

Although Derzhavin's civic odes can vary in terms of which hypostasis is dominant, it is generally true that the ethical aspect prevails in his verse. This moral strain corresponds to what many critics have seen as Derzhavin's "privatization" of politics, a process that merits more careful examination. Far from abandoning the state for the comforts of private life, Derzhavin introjects the state's authority, internalizing the sovereign as an ego-ideal that penetrates even the private sphere of domestic life. The enlightened despot, omnipotent but consciously self-limiting, is projected beyond the sphere of governance, to become an ethical ideal for the everyday life of the gentry. This regulatory model bears little resemblance to Catherine herself: operating externally as an exalted vision of the sovereign, it is also a moral imperative emanating from within the poet.[52]

In "Videnie murzy," for example, Felitsa appears to the Murza in his chamber as a nocturnal vision and unexpectedly upbraids him for his facile panegyrics:

When
Poetry is not a whim,
But the highest of the gods' gifts, then
this gift of the gods should be used
only for honor
And for teaching their ways,
Not for flattery
And the perishable praise of people.
(1:109)

These words bear no relationship to Catherine's actual understanding of poetry, which was limited, or her relationship to poets, which was mainly instrumental. Yet if Derzhavin "literally puts words into [Catherine's] mouth," as Pierre Hart would have it,[53] then it is also true that the question of authorship and agency here becomes increasingly moot. Commenting on the closing lines of "Videnie murzy," addressed by the Murza to Felitsa, «Превознесу тебя, прославлю / Тобой безсмертен буду сам!» (I shall exalt and praise you / Through you I myself shall be immortal!) (1:111), Hart suggests that it is the poet and his immortality that is privileged here, for which Felitsa is merely a vehicle.[54] Yet however bold these lines appear, they nonetheless perpetuate a condition familiar to us from Lomonosov's time: lyric subjectivity remains an extension of political subjecthood (*poddanstvo*). What is new here is the transformation and *internalization* of the monarch's voice: the enlightened despot is no longer just the empress—she is also the inner voice of the poet's own conscience, a superego if you will, urging the Murza to question his actions and test his motivations.

The inverse, however, is also true: taken as a whole, "Videnie murzy" can also be read as a sly message to Catherine on how to read and what to ask of poetry, a message that is then attributed to Felitsa herself. In this sense one might say that Derzhavin and Catherine were involved in a complex game of mutual ventriloquism. The "Felitsa" cycle invokes Catherine's writings as if it were yielding to a higher power but in quoting them ultimately turns their authority back on the empress. Given the discursive levels—fictional (Felitsa and the Murza) and authorial (the empress and the poet)—simultaneously present in Derzhavin's poems, it is not easy at any given time to discern who is speaking, and who is teaching whom.[55] Hence the strangely contradictory gestures of sycophancy and didactic presumption that typify Derzhavin's addresses to the empress. Derzhavin may well have achieved a personalized dialogue with the empress but one in which neither interlocutor possesses a distinctly individuated voice.[56]

The apotheosis of both hypostases of Felitsa, moral and political, was achieved in the poem "Izobrazhenie Felitsy" (1789). Derzhavin's longest poem, and by no means his most original, "Izobrazhenie Felitsy" was written in the hope—vain as it turned out—of securing the empress's personal intercession in the poet's career, which appeared particularly shaky after political intrigues deprived him of the governorship of Tambov Province. "Izobrazhenie Felitsy" rhetorically reposes the longstanding question of the odic representation of the monarch. The poem repeats the clichés of the panegyric tradition concerning the godlike nature of the empress, but also seeks to reconcile them with a typically Derzhavinian emphasis on the integrity of the artist. Claiming to be "enraptured" by Felitsa, the poet Murza feels he can continue to sing his "Tatar songs" in her praise with a "clear conscience" (1:201–2). For this to be so, Felitsa can no longer be "merely" a royal persona but a fundamental aspect of the poet's inner life:

Но что, Рафаэль, что ты пишешь?
Кого ты, где изобразил?
Не на холсте, не в красках дышишь,
И не металл ты оживил: Я в сердце зрю алмазну гору;
На нем божественны черты
Сияют изступленну взору;
На нем в лучах—Фелица, ты!
(1:202)

But what, Raphael, what is it you are painting?
Whom have you depicted, and where?
Not on a canvas, and not in paint do you breathe,
It was not to metal that you brought life: I see a diamond hill in my heart;
In it divine features
Shine before my ecstatic gaze;
In it, surrounded by rays [of light] are you, Felitsa!

However hyperbolic, these lines are not a mere rhetorical flourish: Felitsa is consistently presented as the "mistress of hearts" (1:191): her empire extends over the inner self as much as over physical territory. Her gaze is said to

swiftly penetrate thoughts
even in the most secretive of hearts;
so that from afar she might discern
whoever is innocent of all [crimes].
(1:196)

Felitsa's moral hypostasis allows Derzhavin to jointly articulate a range of apparently unconnected questions, from the fate of the odic poet to the status of the subject peoples of the Russian Empire. Both the artist and the non-Russian subject (and let us remember that the Murza is *both* a poet and a Tatar) submit voluntarily to Felitsa's sovereignty («обладать собой избрал» [1:191]). By surrendering their will to the "Felitsa within" («Став сами вы *себе* послушны» [1:192; my emphasis]) they translate the political dimension of imperial subjecthood into the psychic dimension of subjectivity. Just as the inner workings of conscience can reconcile individual will with moral constraint, so, too, the rule of the enlightened despot reconciles political freedom and imperial sovereignty.

"Izobrazhenie Felitsy" elaborates this idealized scenario in great detail; what results is the most sustained poetic treatment of what enlightened absolutism entails for empire and for poetry:

Престол ее на Скандинавских,
Камчатских и Златых горах,
От стран Таймурских до Кубанских
Поставь на сорок двух столпах;
Как восемь бы зерцал стояли
Ее великие моря;
С полнеба звезды освещали,
Вокруг—багряная заря.

Средь дивного сего чертога
И велелепной высоты
В величестве, в сияньи Бога
Ее изобрази мне ты;
Чтоб, сшед с престола, подавала
Скрыжаль заповедей святых;
Чтобы вселенна принимала
Глас Божий, глас природы в них.

Чтоб дики люди, отдаленны,
Покрыты шерстью, чешуей,
Пернатых перьем испещренны,
Одеты листьем и корой,
Сошедшися к ее престолу
И кроткий вняв законов глас
По желто—смуглым лицам долу
Струили токи слез из глаз;

Струили б слезы и, блаженство
Своих проразумея дней,
Забыли бы свое равенство
И были все подвластны ей:
Финн в море бледный, рыжевласый,
Не разбивал бы кораблей,
И узкоглазый Гунн жал класы
Среди седых, сухих зыбей.

(1:192–93)

Place her throne on the hills of Scandinavia,
Kamchatka and the Golden Hills,
from the countries of Timur to the Kuban
On forty-two columns;
Like eight mirrors
Her great seas would stand;
Stars covering half the sky would illuminate [them],
All round—a purple dawn.

In the midst of this splendid palace
And magnificent elevation

In her grandeur and divine luster
Depict her for me;
So that, descending from her throne, she might offer
The tablet of sacred commandments;
So that the universe might accept
The voice of God and the voice of nature in them.

So that distant and savage people,
Covered in furs and scales,
Speckled with the feathers of birds,
Clothed in leaf and bark,
Converging on her throne
And hearing the voice of gentle laws
Might shed streams of tears
Down their swarthily yellow faces.

They would shed tears, and foreseeing the bliss
Of their [future] days,
Would forget their own equality
And all submit to her:
The pale and red-haired Finn,
Would not destroy ships at sea,
and the slant-eyed Hun would reap the ears of grain
Among the dry, gray rippling [fields].

In typical odic fashion, these lines project the sovereign's body onto the realm she rules, so that her throne appears physically to straddle Russia's forty-two provinces, transforming terrain into territory. At this point, however, the allegory becomes historically more precise. Derzhavin's own notes (3:494) identify the above passage as a reference to the Legislative Commission of 1767, an emblematic moment in the early years of Catherine's reign which Derzhavin had also celebrated in his youth. The commission, we remember, had marked a historic first encounter between the European Enlightenment and the peoples of Russia's outlying provinces, whose significance had been confirmed by Catherine's journey of discovery down the Volga. Signaling a symbolic convergence between the ruler and the ruled, the commission promised a new legal covenant that would supersede the politics of conquest and coercion. Returning to this early and unfulfilled promise to reconcile a multinational empire to the rule of law, Derzhavin depicts Catherine as a second Moses, and her Nakaz as a secular revelation binding the racially marked bodies of the subject peoples to the sovereign who rules over them. In the new dispensation, submission takes the place of subjugation: Catherine's subjects, the Finn and the "Hun" (the Turk?) are shown willingly abandoning their primitive freedoms to become subject to the legal constraints of empire. V. M. Zhivov has called these lists of "savage peoples" the "ethnographic correlative" to the geographical markers of empire that were a long-established odic topos: "in geographical space the monarch appears in the hypostasis of Mars," the god of war, "while in ethnographic space she appears in the hypostasis of Minerva," the goddess of wisdom.[57]

The Legislative Commission, as an early watershed in Catherine's reign and as a topos in Derzhavin's poetry, might well be reexamined as a way of historicizing the figures of Felitsa and the Murza, which critics have often viewed as nothing more than playful literary masks.[58] Catherine had consistently nurtured territorial ambitions as well as a civilizational vision for Russia's southern peripheries, which were noted for their ethnic and religious diversity. Two prolonged wars against Ottoman Turkey, the annexation of the Crimea, a steady advance through the Kuban into the Northern Caucasus, and the ambitious if unrealized "Greek Project" to retake Constantinople were the milestones of a southern policy that was one of the guiding principles of Catherine's rule. This extraordinary chapter in the history of Russian expansionism paradoxically coincided with a rare period of domestic tolerance toward people of other faiths. Abandoning overt coercion for bureaucratic assimilation, Catherine sought to stabilize the volatile borderlands by absorbing the local nobility as well as the Muslim clergy into the Russian state apparatus. The Tatars of Kazan, as the most assimilated non-Russian community of the time, played a significant role as intermediaries in this new dispensation.[59] As a native of Kazan claiming noble Tatar ancestry, an active participant in quelling the Pugachev Revolt, and the owner of several villages in the Orenburg district bordering the Kirgiz horde over which Felitsa's father was said to have ruled, Derzhavin would have been acutely aware of the immense stakes of Catherine's southern policy.[60] His choice of the Murza as a lyric persona might well be seen as a lyric refraction of this historical moment, when the civilizational discourse of the European Enlightenment, adopted and modified for the Russian autocratic tradition, created a new kind of pacified imperial subject. The Murza gives voice to a specifically Russian imperial variant of enlightened absolutism, juxtaposing the predicament of the odic poet alongside the impact of imperial rule on Russia's *inorodtsy.* These are the beginnings of a persistent analogy found in Russian literature: the relationship between the emperor and his empire is seen as parallel to the one obtaining between the emperor and the writer as subject.

While Derzhavin's "Felitsa" cycle contributed enormously to the consolidation of an official Catherinian myth, the orientalist fantasy that was its basis paradoxically foregrounded the underlying contradictions of the odic tradition. Whereas Felitsa was intended to symbolize the triumphant application of Enlightenment principles to an Asiatic empire, the figurative elaboration of the oriental despot inevitably exacerbated the tension between the ode's newly professed ideology and its rhetorical form. The Enlightenment ideals of human dignity, civic merit, and law-based rule were difficult enough to express through the traditional apparatus of panegyric description and address but appeared even more incongruous alongside the playful evocations of murzas, pashas, sultans, and harems. Nevertheless, Derzhavin's "Felitsa" cycle represents the most vivid and sustained attempt at resuscitating what was an increasingly moribund genre. Its stylized orient was a subtle means of updating the ode's historical content, evoking an imaginary geography in which the Russian autocratic state could continue its southward expansion while retaining its claim to European modernity.

More than one generation of poets after Derzhavin would intuit the layered and allegorical nature of the Felitsa/Murza encounter, embracing as it does the broader question of autocracy and empire, and the specifically literary dimension of the poet's subjective relation to political power and literary genius. As a brief index of its reverberations we might cite the celebrated Pushkin poem "Prorok" (The prophet) (1826), which echoes several elements (including one rhyming sequence, albeit with different stress) from "Videnie murzy." Says Felitsa to the Murza in that ode:

«*Вос*трепещи, мурза несчастный!
И страшны истины *внемли*,
Которым стихотворцы страстны
Едва ли верят на *земли*.»

"Tremble, unfortunate Murza!
And hearken to terrible truths,
Which passionate poets
On earth scarcely believe."

And in "Prorok" Pushkin's God exclaims:

«*Вос*стань, пророк, и виждь и *внемли*,
Исполнись волею моей,
И, обходя моря и *земли*,
Глаголом жги сердца людей.»

"Arise, o prophet, both see and harken
Be filled with my will
And, traversing sea and land,
Burn the hearts of men with the word."

The sublime confrontation between ruler and subject remained the context in which the prophetic sublime was to evolve in Russian romantic poetry. To restore the romantic poet-prophet to this imperial context will be one of our tasks in the chapters to come.

Derzhavin's reworking of the imperial sublime was not limited to the "Felitsa" cycle or to those poems that satirize or exalt the gentry culture of the time. His poem, "Vlastiteliam i sudiiam" (To rulers and judges), a blunt condemnation of social injustice first published in 1780, continues the tradition of using the Psalms of David as a vehicle for dissent. More interesting are the two short poems "Pamiatnik" (The monument) (1795) and "Lebed'" (The swan) (1804), both translations of Horace, which strikingly anticipate what the imperial sublime will become in the romantic era. Both poems assert the Horatian topos of poetic immortality with a confidence new to Russian verse, locating the poet's sense of his life's accomplishments and posthumous future in a new vision of imperial space.[61] Each poem erects its own sublime vertical axis—a monument "higher than the pyramids" and a swan that soars far above the earth—but for an entirely new purpose. Where the vertical sublime formerly yielded maps of empire, replete with toponyms and ethnonyms, whose sole purpose was to elaborate the glory of the empress and the state, now the same map charts the poet's vision of his *own* greatness. "Pamiatnik" declares that the poet's glory "will grow undiminished / as long as the race of Slavs is honored by the universe" and that news of him "will spread from the waters of the White Sea to the Black," where every man "among innumerable peoples" will remember his achievements (1:534). "Lebed'" elaborates Derzhavin's "poetic empire" with still greater boldness. The poet-swan leaves behind the "dazzle of kingdoms" and the rewards of courtly life to establish a new relationship to the earth below:

С Курильских островов до Буга,
От Белых до Каспийских вод,
Народы, света с полукруга,
Составившие россов род,

Со временем о мне узнают:
Славяне, гунны, скифы, чудь,

И все, что бранью днесь пылают,
Покажут перстом—и рекут:

«Вот тот летит, что, строя лиру,
Языком сердца говорил,
И, проповедуя мир миру,
Себя всех счастьем веселил.»
(2:315)

From the Kurile Islands to the River Bug,
From the waters of the White Sea to the Caspian,
The peoples from half the circumference of the earth
Who compose the Russian race,

Will learn of me in time:
The Slavs, the Huns, the Scythians, and the Chud,
And all those who today are aflame with [the fire of] war,
Will point their finger and say:

"Behold him flying who, tuning his lyre,
Spoke the language of the heart,
And, propagating peace to the world,
Made himself and everyone merry with happiness.

The odic markers of geography and ethnicity are all present here, but as witness to the poet's glory. However bound to empire, the poet renounces the odic celebration of conquest, pointing to a future reconciliation of all the peoples of Russia that is the utopian political correlative to his own poetic immortality. "Pamiatnik" and "Lebed'" are two audacious and early examples of a fissure between Russian literature and the state that would only grow wider during the course of the nineteenth century. Yet it is also worth recalling that, like all symmetrical reversals, these poems remain indebted to the model they implicitly critique. Neither denies empire as the sole matrix of fame and glory—they merely crown the poet in place of the tsar. This gesture strikingly anticipates the poetry of the Decembrists who will literalize—and politicize—a usurpation of power that remains a literary conceit in Derzhavin's hands.[62]

Empire and poetic language were established almost simultaneously in eighteenth-century Russia. This fact, generally acknowledged yet unstudied in all its ramifications, was the object of the last two chapters. In Lomonosov's theory and odic practice, a parallel dynamic of poetic inspiration and political power came together as the imperial sublime. Implicitly assimilating questions of territory to poetics and selectively adapting newer European models to the older panegyric tradition, Lomonosov succeeded in establishing a poetic language equal to the post-Petrine model of imperial statehood.

The Lomonosovian sublime is at the same time the most consistent of models as well as the most primitive in its absence of nuances. Often little more than a prolonged exclamation of praise and wonderment, its vision does not intimate the real complexities of war, statecraft, or court life under the empresses Anna and Elizabeth. Nonetheless, its very idealization of state policy contains prescriptive elements that sound a note of subtle dissent. As Iurii Lotman notes, independent literary culture was first manifested in Russia as a utopian vision of the state that was clearly opposed to the realities of empire.[63] Despite these veiled disagreements with imperial policy, the ode as a genre necessarily generated a lyric self that was intimately connected to the empress and her empire. Indeed, we might say that a new lyric subjectivity was born out of the dynamic of supplication that bound the poet to the monarch and was then projected onto the horizontal stretch of conquered territory. The narrow range of emotions available to the odic poet, from dread to rapturous enthusiasm, corresponds in the main to this imperial context.

It was Derzhavin's task to transform and personalize the abstract limitations of the Lomonosovian sublime. Although Derzhavin was deeply engaged in the realities of imperial administration, his poetry was never limited to being a crudely celebratory mouthpiece, hailing a victory won or a treaty signed. It achieved a distance on the politics of the day by widening the ode beyond the defining matrix of the state. Sublimity, for Derzhavin, was the impact of force in general, be it the sovereign will or the vaster workings of time: individuality is what absorbs and survives the shattering experience of the sublime in one of its many forms. The ethical dimension typical of Derzhavin's poetry is a result of this transformative internalization, in which the political or ontological dimension of power is contemplated and then introjected to become a regulating mechanism within the human personality.

The life story thus becomes a necessary foil to the abstractions of empire, and many of Derzhavin's odes are, in fact, short lyric biographies. As the vicissitudes of ambition and the struggles of conscience loom larger in the poet's consciousness, the fortunes of empire are gauged less for their importance to Russia than as benchmarks in the career of the Russian statesman. This vocational aspect of empire, typified by such figures as Rumiantsev, Potemkin, or V. Zubov, was to have a profound impact on the next literary generation (namely, Griboedov, the Decembrists, Pushkin, and then Lermontov) all of whom would experience, in poetry or in battle, the imaginative pull of Russia's southern borderlands. It was Derzhavin who first intuited the natural sublimity of the Caucasus as a *subjective* experience that is felt through and beyond its picturesque value. Celebrating the Caucasus (and before it the Kivach waterfall) as the aesthetic fusion of horror and beauty, Derzhavin was also able to draw the more sobering lesson that self-mastery is a greater accomplishment than foreign conquest. It is this inward turn that translates the imperial sublime into an ethical dilemma for the gentry intellectual.

This internalizing mechanism is most evident in Derzhavin's poetic dialogue with the empress. The individuation of both the empress and the poet is accomplished allegorically, through the use of oriental literary masks. In historical terms, the image of Felitsa proclaims the myth of the enlightened despot who can reconcile omnipotence and self-restraint, imperial rule and political freedom. Psychologically speaking, the same myth permits the despot to function internally as an ego-ideal to which the poet willingly submits. To the extent that it repeatedly dramatizes the encounter between the self and a vaster power, Derzhavin's poetry remains deeply engaged in the workings of the sublime. Yet the poet's ultimate response is as much a philosophical reconciliation as an act of political submission: in this way the Derzhavinian sublime greatly surpasses in subtlety the older model of Lomonosov's, even as it lacks the volatility of the romantic sublime to come.

3

Sublime Dissent

New Literary Ideologies

Early in the nineteenth century, under the reign of Alexander I, the imperial sublime became progressively detached from its commitment to tsarist autocracy. Politically this was related to a general radicalization of expectations of what Russia could be and a concomitant crisis of faith in autocracy as an agent of progress. Socially it reflected the growth of a restricted but vibrant literary culture that defined itself, aesthetically if not always politically, outside the purview of the court and the imperial bureaucracy. New models and movements began to proliferate, and the authority of the older classicist precepts correspondingly weakened. The ode, while remaining, at least until the 1820s, the primary genre of civic engagement, was never again to enjoy a position of dominance in Russian poetry. If in the eighteenth century the "lofty tyle" had been dominant, in the early nineteenth century it was compelled to stand in polemical opposition first to Karamzinian sentimentalism and subsequently to what became the dominant current of romanticism championed by Vasilii Zhukovskii and later Pushkin. Eighteenth-century poetics were increasingly seen as an anachronism, to be rejected or revived as the case may be.

The crisis of classicism became acute with the rise to prominence of the most influential of the pre-romantics, Nikolai Karamzin (1766–1826). In a clear rejection of the lofty style, Karamzin, and shortly after him the poet Konstantin Batiushkov (1787–1855), argued for a new set of discursive norms, a "middle style" based on the conversational patterns of French polite society under the ancien régime.[1] Language, they believed, did not exist to persuade or to exalt but to please: mellifluousness, refinement, aesthetic perfection, and genre diversity were declared the new goals of literary discourse. The writer was no longer a public orator but the bearer of sentiment: he proffered experiences that could not immediately be assimilated to the social sphere, in a variety of genres that matched his moods. Yet far from signaling a retreat into private life, the "middle style" advocated by Karamzin and Batiushkov was, in fact, a means of socializing and regulating the recently emerged inner world of feeling. Based on propriety and good taste rather than "lyric disorder," the theory and practice of the Karamzinists ratified a new division and correlation between the public and private sphere.

Marking a sociological shift from the court to the literary salon as the arbiter of prevailing sensibility, the new poetic language was the expression of an emergent aristocratic culture, lively if limited, that saw itself as distinct from the apparatus of the state. Expelling the discourses of the church and the imperial bureaucracy from its confines, it celebrated an inner life of brooding contemplation and a social world based on exalted affective relations.[2] Despite its implicit aesthetic rejection of the state, this was not the poetic idiom of social opposition: its human ideal was the refined gentleman amateur, aesthetically liberal but socially conservative. State service continued to be an important gentry vocation but was counterbalanced, as William Todd has observed, by a growing sense of personal honor. If the trajectory of the romantic poet Zhukovskii (1783–1852), who enjoyed a long and close relationship with the ruling family, made him the last of Russia's court poets, then Karamzin's career was perhaps more emblematic of new attitudes: twice refusing governorships in order to remain the state's appointed historian, Karamzin "demonstrated a more acceptable mode of civil service behavior, one marked both by a spirit of independence and by a sense of national responsibility."[3]

Despite its new dominance, the literary culture of Karamzin and Zhukovskii by no means neutralized all vestiges of the literary past. In addressing the sublime's persistence into the new century, this chapter turns to the "losing side," the *archaists* as the critic Iurii Tynianov once termed them, who remained faithful to a literary culture that to many now seemed reactionary, even as some of them paradoxically combined it with a radical politics.[4] By the 1820s, the sublime, while remaining a sign of empire, had been freed of its unequivocal identification with the Russian monarchy. How the sublime survived, and how it changed its political valency, is the subject of this chapter.

An earlier and still isolated example of this shift was Aleksandr

Radishchev (1749–1802). In "Slovo o Lomonosove" (Discourse on Lomonosov) which ends his celebrated *Puteshestvie iz Peterburga v Moskvu* (Journey from Petersburg to Moscow) (1790), the book for which Catherine exiled him to Siberia, Radishchev distinguished the panegyric content of Lomonosov's odes from the linguistic revolution that his odes represented: "I do not envy you for following the general custom of fawning on the tsars, who were often unworthy not just of elegant praise but even of a few strains on a fiddle. . . . [Yet] if indeed anyone ever succeeds in attaining your unbroken euphony in poetry, still none has succeeded until now."[5]

In his poem, "Vol'nost'" (Liberty) (1781–83), written in the years between the American and French Revolutions, Radishchev gave a practical illustration of his separation of odic form from its content. Structurally a classical Lomonosovian ode, the poem radically reversed Lomonosov's politics, hailing freedom as a natural right, declaring monarchy a contractual relationship with the people that could be terminated if its terms were violated, and predicting the eventual collapse of the existing order. Remarkably and quite atypically for Russia's poets, Radishchev identified imperial expansion as the primary cause of Russia's future demise. Russia would continue seeking to "widen its borders to the west, south, and east" only to find that it lacked any naturally ordained limits. This geopolitical dilemma, and the military adventurism it invited, was fraught with danger, since "the further the source of power, / the weaker the union of its elements," just as a "ray that emanates from the sun / Accompanied by luster and strength / Loses its power in space."[6] The solar metaphor typical of the Russian panegyric is here subject to the scientific gaze of a republican skeptic. Just as imperial overstretch would lead to Russia's collapse, the poem concluded, so freedom would eventually be rekindled in a post-imperial Russia. Stylistically, the ode reflects Radishchev's adherence to the poetic "coarseness" of Lomonosov and Derzhavin. Defending the clumsy line «Во свет рабства тьму претвори» (Transmute the darkness of slavery into light), Radishchev claims that "others opined this verse to be successful, finding in the roughness of the verse a pictorial expression of the difficulty of the act itself."[7] The question of stylistic or lexical difficulty, a perennial marker of the "lofty style," would acquire new ideological motivations in the years to come.

Radishchev's inversion of odic ideology was a powerful precedent for the more organized and complex literary-political debates of the early nineteenth century. By this time, the ready equivalence of stylistic signifier and political signified no longer obtained: those who remained committed to classicist poetics were themselves split ideologically and generationally into two camps, which Iurii Tynianov long ago termed the *older* and *younger* archaists. The older archaists, who formed the Colloquy of Lovers of the Russian Word in 1811 (in which the aging Derzhavin also played a defining role), essentially argued for a modified version of Lomonosov's stylistic hierarchy and the linguistic philosophy on which it was based. The chief ideologue of the Colloquy, Admiral A. S. Shishkov, soon to become secretary of state, insisted on the intimate link between Russian and Church Slavic, which precluded the introduction of new linguistic and stylistic elements into the language.[8] His inaugural speech at the Colloquy divided Russian literature into three currents, the ancient ecclesiastic tradition, noted for its "elegance and sublimity [*vysotoiu*]," the folk tradition, "not as sublime . . . but exceedingly pleasant," and modern Russian literature, which was "no more than one century old." Russian could thus be "sublime and magnificent in the depiction of solemn objects, but sweet and simple in describing ordinary things."[9] Disavowing the exclusive monopoly of the lofty style, Shishkov argued for the inclusion of *both* the lofty and the coarsely popular into the literary language.

Shishkov's position was a sharply polemical one: the lofty and the lowly registers were equally opposed to the middle style of Karamzinism. Both levels were understood as markers of Russianness, a patriotic blend of folksiness, piety, and monarchist sentiment that contrasted with the perceived foreignness of the new words and models imported from France and Germany. In the words of Il'ia Serman, "Shishkov and his allies, including Derzhavin, saw themselves as restoring a lost stylistic unity."[10] At the same time, Shishkov's position was only in part a return to past norms. His interest in popular language and folk tradition hints at the impact of newer currents in European thought: Shishkov, in fact, inflected his conservative stylistic orientation with the insights of a nascent romantic philology, a combination that exercised considerable influence on the following generation.

Although the conservative literary politics of the older archaists and their close ties to the court culture of Alexander I are of limited interest today, the greater impact of the younger generation was largely owing to their ability to sever the link between literary archaism and political reaction. As Tynianov puts it, "the second element fell away and the first element became manifested all the more sharply."[11] Several of the younger archaists were to play a constitutive role in the first organized attempt at overthrowing Russian autocracy, which culminated in an abortive uprising on Senate Square in December 1825. In the pages to come we shall see how the literary currents allied with what came to be known as the Decembrist movement reversed the ideological valency of eighteenth-century poetics, updating it in the light of romantic aesthetics even as they preserved many of its essential rhetorical features. This reversal would breathe a second life into the imperial sublime, relocating the familiar question of political and poetic authority in a new insurrectionary context.

Decembrist Orientalism and the Poetics of Opposition

While failing to dislodge the Russian monarchy, the Decembrist movement of the early 1820s was remarkably successful in one respect: in combining a political platform with a literary one, diverse enough to embrace a discrete range of stylistic and ideological options yet consistent enough to resonate as a united voice. By linking an oppositional politics to a prescriptive poetics, Decembrist ideology was able to fuse literary word and political deed into a singular civic act.[12]

For obvious reasons, Decembrist literary and political culture was one of the most exhaustively studied topics in Soviet philology and historiography. The most significant critical interventions have focused on defining the nature and breadth of Decembrist literary ideology, its poetics and its precise cultural genealogy. While Tynianov focused on the "younger archaists" as a purely literary phenomenon and emphasized their debt to the eighteenth century, G. A. Gukovskii popularized the term *civic* or *revolutionary romanticism* to designate a current that was both wider than the conspiratorial circles of the Decembrist secret societies and fundamentally at odds with Russia's literary past. Gukovskii specifically insisted on the romantic—rather than classicist—nature of Decembrist poetics: "Despite the presence of the 'lofty' style that externally resembles the lofty style of classicism, . . . the style of civic romanticism is in its essence foreign to classicism and is based on the essential ideas of the romantic era."[13] While acknowledging the continuous presence of the sublime in Russian poetry, Gukovskii strove to separate what I have called the odic sublime from the romantic sublime of the Decembrist poets:

> The "lofty" style of the romantics is not related to the generic system of thought proper to classicism, which is based on a mechanistic world view and furthermore on a hierarchical under-

> standing of the state, of class, and of politics in general. The "lofty" style of the romantics arises out of the pathos of the self-liberating personality of man, of the citizen, and is not decided a priori on the basis of a theme, a genre, etc.[14]

Gukovskii's premises were subsequently called into question by Lidiia Ginzburg. The "Russian poetic system of the eighteenth century," observes Ginzburg, was, in fact, "intimately related" to Decembrist poetics "through its sublimity [*vozvyshennost'iu*]—its lofty genres, and the lofty diction with its Church Slavic and biblical lexicon. It was this linguistic element, treated in a specific way, that gave the Decembrists a means to express their heroic, libertarian patriotism."[15]

At stake in these debates, without ever being carefully elaborated as a nodal point, is the aesthetic and political nature of the Decembrist sublime. If the latter was incommensurable with the poetic past, as Gukovskii would have it, then how are we to explain the marked predilection of the Decembrist poet Wilhelm Küchelbecker (Vil'gel'm Kiukhl'beker) for the ode, and for the rhetorical and even thematic aspects of odic rapture? Yet if it was intimately linked to the eighteenth century, as Tynianov and Ginzburg would have it, then how was it able to generate an oppositional discourse, informed by a new awareness of nationhood and national form, and by a tangibly different kind of lyric and political subjectivity? I wish to suggest that much of Decembrist poetic culture was marked by a reversal of the *ideological* presuppositions of the eighteenth-century odic tradition, even as many of the *formal* trappings of the odic sublime were retained. From loyal panegyrist of the monarch, the Russian poet came to be seen as the insurgent rebel who must denounce and finally usurp the monarch's place. While the Decembrist movement was, in fact, diverse enough to embrace both constitutional monarchists and regicide republicans, what interests us here is not their concrete political goals—which were in any case unrealized—but the shared *symbolic* basis of their contestation.

The contemplated overthrow of autocracy required, among other things, an enhanced civic role for the Russian writer, and a reappropriation of the available discourses of political engagement. Alexander Zholkovsky has recently observed of the twentieth-century Russian poet's relationship to Soviet power that "strategies of resistance and survival through an *obverse replication of the regnant power structure* were not exceptional."[16] Gregory Freidin has formulated this problem with great clarity as part of a wider cultural pattern that had its roots in the early nineteenth century: "Given the fact that the Russian intelligentsia tended to rely on sources of rhetorical authority it shared with the autocratic state and the Orthodox Church, the question begs to be asked: By what means did the symbolic order of the intelligentsia gain enough power to be able to challenge the autocratic state and its ally, the Church?"[17] It did so, Freidin suggests, through a "a secular appropriation" of the power of church and state by the left intelligentsia, creating a "potent mixture of revolutionary, autocratic, and ecclesiastical vocabularies."[18] For all the political courage it clearly required, Decembrist literary discourse was, in the rhetorical sense, derivative in that it viewed the civic poet's laurels as nothing less than the tsar's crown, first toppled and then usurped. For this reason, it is difficult to entertain Gukovskii's thesis that Decembrist libertarianism was essentially alien to odic statism. Rather, as V. M. Zhivov has put it in commenting on the development of the Russian cult of the poet, it was precisely "out of the mythology of the state" that the "mythology of the poet was to emerge."[19]

Linking both mythologies was the shared structuring principle of empire. Since the Decembrist uprising has been primarily understood in terms of its opposition to autocracy and its role in the Russian romantic discovery of the *narod,* considerably less attention has been paid to the role of empire in shaping Decembrist politics and poetics. In recuperating the national past, the Decembrist poets and ideologues dwelt frequently on the theme of Russian military expansion; in formulating a politics for the present, they did not push their quarrel with tsarism into a critique of its imperial foundations. While questioning the impact of autocracy at home, the Decembrist radicals remained active supporters of tsarist policy in Transcaucasia and agitated actively for Russian intervention in the Greek war of independence against Ottoman Turkey. An interest in Russia's southern borderlands was, in fact, a crucial aspect of Decembrist culture: reflecting the evident geopolitical tensions of the 1820s, orientalism was also a crucial aspect of the *literary* ideology that the Decembrists were to champion even after their political demise.

The aspects of the Decembrist revision of the political and literary tradition which interest us are readily encapsulated by the ode "Grazhdanskoe muzhestvo" (Civic courage) (1823), written by the celebrated poet-conspirator Kondratii Ryleev (1795–1826), who led the fateful uprising of December 14 and became one of five principal organizers to be executed in its aftermath:

> Певцов возвышенные звуки
> Прославят подвиги вождя,
> И, юношам об них твердя,

В восторге затрепещут внуки.
. . . .
Но подвиг воина гигантский
И стыд сраженных им врагов
В суде ума, в суде веков—
Ничто пред доблестью гражданской.[20]

The sublime sounds of bards
Will celebrate the feats of a [military] leader,
And, when recounting them to the young,
Their grandsons will tremble with rapture.
. . . .
But the gigantic feat of a warrior
And the shame of the enemies he vanquished
In the judgment of the mind, in the judgment of the ages—
Is nothing before civic valor.

In these lines Ryleev apparently dismisses the theme of military victory central to the eighteenth-century sublime. As martial bravery gives way to civic courage, the leaders worthy of odic praise are no longer an Attila or a Napoleon but Cicero, Brutus, or Cato, the great stalwarts of republican Rome. Yet this ideological shift is markedly contained by the conservatism of its imagery. Embodying a typically Decembrist amalgam of civic virtue and paternalistic authoritarianism, the new revolutionary hero towers over his fellow citizens, a "wondrous giant" no less monumental than the emperors and empresses of the eighteenth century. The following lines, redolent of revolutionary neoclassicism, revive the grandiose allegorical forms of the classicist past for the sake of a new political agenda:[21]

Кто сей, украшенный венком,
С мечом, весами и щитом,
Презрев врагов и горделивость,
Стоит гранитною скалой
И давит сильною пятой
Коварную несправедливость?

Не ты ль, о мужество граждан,
неколебимых, благородных. . . .

Who is this, adorned by a wreath,
With a sword, scales and a shield,
Disdaining his enemies and haughtiness,
Standing like a granite cliff

And trouncing with his strong heel
Wily injustice?

Is it not you, o courage of citizens,
Unwavering, noble . . .

A libertarian impulse is here contradictorily articulated through an axis as sublimely vertical as found in any ode by Lomonosov or Derzhavin. Oppositional but far from democratic, the Decembrist affirmation of liberty would shift rapidly from a critical engagement in the existing order to its radical contestation. Ryleev's poetry from 1823 to 1825 marks precisely such a shift: in this poem the Decembrist stills sees himself as a "support for power and for the people," while his poem of the following year, "Na smert' Beirona" (On the death of Byron) (1824) celebrates a poet "who was obedient to his genius alone / and did not recognize any other power."[22] Yet these shifts also conceal a deeper continuity: in both cases the civic hero can claim his freedom only by mimicking the authority of the tyrant he opposes. A giant alone can dislodge another, and the poet, from being a citizen among equals, becomes the people's tribune and prophet.

Ryleev's poem ends by somewhat unexpectedly comparing the revolutionary hero, "steady and impregnable," to the Caucasian peak Mount Elbrus:

Так в грозной красоте стоит
Седой Эльбрус в тумане мглистом
Вкруг буря, град и гром гремит,
И ветр в ущельях воет с свистом,
Внизу несутся облака,
Шумят ручьи, ревет река;
Но тщетны дерзкие порывы:
Эльбрус, кавказских гор краса,
Невозмутим, под небеса
Возносит верх свой горделивый.

Thus with menacing beauty stands
Gray Elbrus in the gloomy mist
Around it there roars a storm, hail and thunder,
And the wind howls whistling in the ravines,
Below clouds race,
Streams course noisily, a river rampages;
But these impudent impulses are in vain:
The Elbrus, beauty of the Caucasus mountains,
Is imperturbable, and raises
Its proud summit toward the heavens.

These lines recall Derzhavin's juxtaposition of the "natural" and "intellectual" sublime in his ode to Count Zubov: in both cases the jagged alpine landscape of the Caucasus is compared to the inner resolve of the civic hero. Yet whereas Derzhavin's comparison was based on the life trajectory of a military commander who had just returned from a campaign in the Caucasus, here the same analogy is unmotivated by any textually available information. We are dealing here with what Russian critics have called a "signal" or "catchword," a phenomenon widespread in the political poetry of the romantic era. Neither purely personal nor abstractly allegorical, these signal words or symbols assumed a political import that resonated emotionally against an implied background of shared ideas.[23] The Caucasus came to be one such topos, bearing a politically charged but essentially polyvalent message.

Evocations of specific Caucasian mountain peaks were not infrequent in Russian romantic verse: one need only recall the dedication to *Kavkazskii plennik* (Prisoner of the Caucasus) (1820–21), in which Pushkin speaks of the "gloomy Beshtu, majestic hermit, / five-headed master of villages and fields," as having been the "new Parnassus" for his poetry of exile, or Mikhail Lermontov's celebrated poem, "A Quarrel" (1841), in which the mountains Kazbek and Elbrus have an animated argument over the significance of Russian imperial encroachment.[24] Just as lyric transport had once generated the odic map of empire, so, too, the naming and evoking of Caucasian mountaintops served, in the poetry of Pushkin, the Decembrists, and Lermontov, to link a poetic dilemma to a political geography. Unlike the ode's enthusiastic survey of the horizontal expanse of territory, however, the new toponyms of Elbrus, Kazbek, or Beshtu betokened a more critical engagement in imperial history on the part of the Russian romantic poet. Enabling a lyrical evocation of alpine scenery and ethnographic detail, these mountains functioned also as a symbol of civic resistance to autocracy, suggesting a parallel between the radical Russian gentry's confrontation with tsarism and the freedom struggle of the Caucasian mountain dwellers. This parallel energized a great deal of the romantic literary engagement in the Caucasus, and we shall return to it repeatedly. It should be stressed from the start, however, that what is at stake here is less a case of political solidarity than of symbolic analogy. Even as they were drawn to the mountain dwellers' libertarian spirit, Decembrist intellectuals, in fact, supported Russia's conquest of the Caucasus with great enthusiasm.

This paradox is vividly captured by the figure of the Transcaucasian commander-in-general A. P. Ermolov, military administrator of Georgia and commander of the Caucasian Military Corps from 1817 to 1827, to whom Ryleev's last stanza might well be referring. Ermolov's capacity to combine extreme ruthlessness in colonial warfare with a sharply critical attitude toward Russia's ruling establishment and a relatively convivial esprit de corps made him a beacon for disaffected young intellectuals of the time. Hailed as the potential commander of a Russian military intervention on behalf of the Greek struggle for independence against Ottoman Turkey, Ermolov became a personalized emblem of the complex cluster of political aspirations—combining conquest *and* revolt—which the Decembrists projected onto Russia's southern borderlands.[25] The geopolitics of the day and the Decembrist response to it have been usefully summarized by Boris Tomashevskii: "While hostile to [Tsar] Alexander's policy toward the west, where the Russian government was suppressing the revolutionary movement under the banner of the Holy Alliance, the Decembrists viewed the tasks facing Russia in the east differently. Russia's movement eastward, in their eyes, was preordained by history."[26]

It is a curious fact that the most systematic method and rationale for Russia's conquest of the Caucasus was expounded not by the tsarist government but by the leader of the Southern Society of the Decembrists, Pavel Ivanovich Pestel' (1793–1826). Pestel''s underground manifesto, *Russkaia pravda* (completed by 1823), intended as a concrete guideline for a post-insurrectionary government, insisted that a multiethnic Russia remain an "indivisible" rather than a federated state, thereby subordinating the right of smaller peoples to nationhood (*Pravo narodnosti*) to Russia's greater need for order and security (*Pravo blagoudobstva*).[27] Whereas Poland as a fraternal Slavic nation was to be permitted self-determination, Pestel' singled out the southern lands bordering Turkey and Iran as falling within the Russian ambit. The Caucasian mountain dwellers, he observed, "practise various faiths, speak various languages, have diverse customs and modes of governance, and resemble one another only in their predisposition toward belligerency and plunder."[28] Taking into consideration the innate inclination of the mountain dwellers toward "perpetual war" and the failure of all past attempts to "turn [them] into peaceful and calm neighbors," Pestel' advocated the "decisive subjugation of all peoples and all lands lying to the north of the border extending between Russia and Persia, and also Turkey," imposing "Russian administration and order" on the peaceable natives and transporting those who remained belligerent "by force into Russia's interior, scattering them into small groups throughout the Russian provinces."[29] Opposition to the tsar thus could and did coexist, for the Decembrists, with the most vigorous support for the state's southern policy.

A symbol of heroic resistance *and* of inevitable conquest, the Caucasus (and the regions to the south) became the object of what might be called an "oppositional imperialism." This ideological position found, in turn, a literary expression, an aspect of the civic strain in Russian romantic poetry that is generally known as the "oriental style" (*vostochnyi stil'*). It has long been noted that the "oriental style" functioned as a coded form of political opposition. As Gukovskii put it, in civic romanticism the oriental style "became the style of freedom." The orient of the Russian romantic tradition, Gukovskii adds, was "not clearly differentiated on a national, geographical, or historical basis. . . . It was the style of the Koran and the Bible taken together, and at the same time the style of Persian poetry and Caucasian legend. The traits of all these historical phenomena interwove to constitute a singular image of the East. . . . It was precisely this image that had the status of a slogan in the struggle of nations against tyranny."[30]

How did Decembrist orientalism come to constitute a sign of revolt, and what was its relationship to the imperial sublime? How did the apparent indeterminacy of the Decembrist orient nonetheless lead to a politics and poetics of civic engagement? I wish to suggest that the oppositional imperialism of the Decembrists was not merely a political stance but corresponded equally to a poetic problem inherited from the odic past. Breaking fundamentally with the panegyric mode, the Decembrist poets nevertheless retained empire as the symbolic structure through which to recode their own relationship to the Russian sovereign. To examine the Decembrist reworking of the imperial sublime, I turn to two of the most celebrated writers among the younger archaists, the poets Aleksandr Griboedov and Wilhelm Küchelbecker.

Aleksandr Griboedov: The South as a Career

Known chiefly as the author of the singular classic *Gore ot uma* (Woe from wit) and as a diplomat martyred for his efforts on behalf of the Russian Empire in Transcaucasia and Iran, Aleksandr Griboedov (1795–1829) dramatized for his contemporaries the new political, professional, and creative possibilities offered by Russia's southern borderlands following the annexation of eastern Georgia in 1801. Arriving in the Georgian capital Tiflis in 1819, Griboedov preceded and, to varying degrees, defined the southern itineraries of later poets, including Küchelbecker, Pushkin, and Lermontov, providing future travelers with a vivid map of what was to become Russian romanticism's "Caucasian theme."

The external milestones of Griboedov's career are well known: his reluctant acceptance, in 1818, of a position as secretary to the Russian diplomatic mission in Iran; his work, in Tabriz and Teheran, on behalf of Russian prisoners of war; his complex relationship to General Ermolov and his colonial military policies; the writing of *Woe from Wit,* begun in Tiflis in the company of the poet and future Decembrist Küchelbecker and completed in Russia itself, where, by 1824, it would remain unpublished but enjoy wide acclaim; Griboedov's arrest and subsequent release, during 1826, for possible involvement in the Decembrist cause; his subsequent diplomatic efforts under the new leadership of General Paskevich during the Russo-Persian War of 1826–1828 culminating in his decisive role in formulating the peace treaty of Turkmanchai; his marriage in 1828 to the daughter of the celebrated Georgian poet and administrator Aleksandre Chavchavadze; and, finally, his death, perhaps the most improbable in the lengthy martyrology of Russia's great writers, during the storming of the Russian mission in Teheran by a mob of frenzied Persians.

This brief outline of Griboedov's achievements hints at a singular paradox of his career: an ability to combine service to the tsarist state at the highest level with a literary output noted for its creative freedom and intellectual independence. To be sure, the strains of this double life are evident—most clearly in Griboedov being implicated, however indirectly, in the Decembrist uprising, and in the amply documented accounts of Griboedov's many frustrations with the bureaucratic apparatus of the tsarist state. In this sense, Griboedov's career can be said to have updated Derzhavin's concern with the ethics of state service. If Derzhavin's account of Count Valerian Zubov's Persian campaign highlighted the often random and personalized nature of imperial policy under Catherine and Paul, then Griboedov's life reflects the greater complexity that marked the relations between the writer-statesman and the state apparatus during Russia's continuing southern expansion under Alexander and Nicholas.

Caught between literature and diplomacy, Griboedov left behind a small body of writing that includes, besides the celebrated play, the outlines of two orientalist dramas, poetry, travel notes, literary criticism, a body of letters, as well as a historic proposal, destined never to be implemented, for a "Russian Transcaucasia Company" that sought to reform the bureaucratic state apparatus of empire along British mercantilist lines. Critics have long pondered the relationship between this creative legacy and Griboedov's political life, between his literature and his diplomacy. In 1840 Belinskii posited a rather vaguely articulated negative causality binding Russia's southern borderlands to Griboedov's critique of the Moscow gentry: the "wild grandeur" of the Caucasus and the "austere poetry" of its inhabitants was said to have "inspired his offended humanity" to depict the "apathetic and insignificant" milieu of the Moscow elite.[31] More recently, M. S. Lazarev has asserted that Griboedov's literary work "had few connections with the East, while his life was connected to it in the most direct and fatal way."[32]

In fact, Griboedov's life and work were intimately connected. Taken together they constitute a paradigm of a then newly emergent Russian orientalism, in the multiple senses the word has recently acquired in English: first, as the institutional discipline of oriental studies, or *vostokovedenie;* second, as a more diffuse set of ideological and cultural assumptions about the east derived from European models and adapted to striking effect by the Russian romantics in their development of the "Caucasian theme" in Russian literature; and, finally, as the practical deployment of these discursive models in the imperial policies that informed Russia's southward expansion.[33] To present Griboedov as a defining figure in Russian orientalist discourse is not to reduce him to a single ideological or thematic position. On the contrary, Griboedov's legacy is interesting precisely for the ambiguous way it straddles poetics and politics. The diplomat's often embarrassed familiarity with the harsh realities of empire stands in a complex relationship to the writer's literary vision, and in this internal dialogue of writer and statesman lies Griboedov's unique contribution to the imperial sublime.

The young Griboedov was a faithful mirror of the literary debates of the time. In an early and programmatic article of 1816, he championed Pavel Katenin's ballad "Ol'ga", written in polemical opposition to Zhukovskii's mellifluous style, defending the line «Турк без брани побежден, / И, желанный плод победы,/ Мир России возвращен» (The Turk is vanquished without battle, / And, the desired fruit of victory, / Peace is returned to Russia) in the following way: "the word *turk* [as against *turok*] is often found . . . both in Lomonosov's exemplary odes and in popular folk-songs."[34] This statement is characteristic of the archaist platform, which not only insisted on the perennial validity of the odic lofty style but sought also to reconcile it to the new romantic interest in folk culture.

Griboedov first linked his literary convictions to the question of empire in a letter of January 1819, written in the Georgian capital Tiflis. Appearing in *Syn otechestva* (Son of the Fatherland), this was a letter intended for publication and dramatizes the mutually implicating nature of Griboedov's political and literary careers. In an early passage we read:

> It has been half a year since I left Petersburg, and in a few days I was transported from the north to the southern lands belonging to the Caucasus (not mentally, but by post: one is more disturbing than the other!); following the thundering Terek I entered the cluster of towering mountains on which, in Lomonosov's words, "Russia leaned her elbow," but now she has moved it much further. Around me were barren rocks, above me soared the king of birds as well as buzzards, descendants of Prometheus's tormentor; before me glowed snow-covered mountaintops which I soon reached and where I found snowdrifts, freezing cold, all the signs of advanced winter, and yet at a distance of several versts, the harshness of winter receded: the sharp descent from Kashaur leads directly to the springtime shores of the Aragva.[35]

In these lines Griboedov continues—albeit in prose—the task already begun by Derzhavin and Zhukovskii, of transforming the "abstractly allegorical nature" of the eighteenth-century sublime. At stake is a new vision of landscape, subjectivity, and finally politics itself. The Lomonosov quote, "Russia leaned her elbow," recalls for us the traditional odic map of empire, with its anthropomorphic image of Russia stooped awkwardly over her territory, yet this image now nestles in a description of the Caucasian mountain landscape whose naturalism assumes the priority of eyewitness experience over cartographic allegory. Travel—"not mentally, but by post"—has displaced the intellectual ecstasy of lyric transport.

As a letter to the editor the above text citationally situates the poetic past in a prosaic world of pressing political exigencies. Probably written at General Ermolov's behest, it seeks to debunk publicly certain rumors published in Saint Petersburg but originating in Istanbul concerning a popular uprising in Georgia, one whose consequences could "resonate in all corners of the empire." A skirmish with the Chechens had indeed occurred, reports Griboedov, but was quickly resolved by the resolute actions of General Ermolov, such that "never had the supreme power of our sovereign in those countries been based so reliably on the submission of its peoples as today."[36] Griboedov concludes by asking:

> But what is the real source of these inventions? Who was the first to circulate them? Some Armenian, dissatisfied with his trade in Georgia, comes to Constantinople and with a gloomy face informs a friend that things are going badly over there. This piece of news is conveyed from one friend to another, who interprets a private complaint as general discontent. It isn't hard for a third party to transform a languid complaint into a revolt! This hypothesis soon acquires the reliability of a newspaper report and reaches the *Hamburg Correspondent* from which nothing can be concealed, and from which we Russians are accustomed to translate every single line. So it was hardly possible to pass by an article emanating from Constantinople.[37]

Griboedov's letter is striking for its peculiar mixture of personalized literary travelogue, poetic reminiscences, astute Realpolitik, and tendentious fantasy. The traditional vertical axis of the sublime is here finally eclipsed by what we might call a *horizontal* axis that seeks to channel information according to the exigencies of imperial policy. Significantly, however, this alternative axis is no less imaginary than the poetic axis it displaces. In a private letter of October 1818 Griboedov describes the Caucasus as a "vile hole where one sees only filth and fog,"[38] and in another letter of the same time he notes: "What they wrote in *Invalid* about a revolt was nonsense, to which I wrote a no less nonsensical rebuttal in *Syn otechestva*."[39] The improbable picture of Tiflis as a cosmopolitan mercantile idyll guaranteed by a benign Russian civilian administration is presented as long existing, rather than the projected and ultimately utopian goal of what was to become Griboedov's final political testament, the "Project for the Establishment of a Russian Transcaucasia Company."[40] Making (dis)information its central theme, Griboedov's letter shows how the circulation of language can serve to shape political geography. To trace the itinerary of a rumor is at the same time to map out the relationship between metropolis and periphery, as well as between imperial rivals such as Russia, England, Turkey and Iran.

Iurii Tynianov has commented insightfully on the importance of rumor, its appearance and growth, as a recurrent structuring principle in Griboedov's literary activity no less than in his diplomacy. Speaking specifically of Chatskii's rumored madness, Tynianov observes that "the plot of *Woe from Wit*, where the most important thing is the emergence and diffusion of a fiction or slander, was elaborated through the everyday practice of Griboedov's diplomatic work."[41] Strangely Tynianov failed to point to the one moment in the first redaction of the play that most dramatically confirms his insight. In a remarkable extended simile, Chatskii compares the speed of a rumor to an avalanche in the Caucasus:

. . .—Я был в краях,
Где с гор верхов ком снега ветер скатит,
Вдруг глыба этот снег, в паденьи всё охватит,
Гул, рокот, гром, вся в ужасе окресность.
И что оно в сравненьи с быстротой,
С которой, чуть возник, уж приобрел известность
Московской фабрики слух вредный и пустой.[42]

I have been in parts,
Where the wind can rip a lump of snow off mountaintops,
Suddenly this snow becomes a block, and in falling seizes everything in its way,
Rumbling, din, thunder, the entire surroundings are gripped by terror.
But what is that compared to the speed
With which, as soon as it arises, a noxious and empty rumor of Moscow fabrication can gain currency.

Omitted in the final redaction, this passage is the only concrete reference in the play to the Caucasus, where much of *Woe from Wit* was composed. Perhaps Griboedov was loathe to ascribe to his main character a geographical itinerary so like his own or perhaps the metaphorical projection of rumor, which circulates horizontally, onto the vertical axis of the alpine sublime struck him finally as poetically unconvincing. Whatever the case, it appears that the classical vertical sublime was, for Griboedov, the privilege of poetry: the letter of 1819 is, in fact, based on precisely the opposite spatial principle: rumor creates a "prosaic" horizontal axis corresponding to the geopolitical dimension of imperial space that effectively eclipses the descriptions of alpine scenery with which the letter begins.[43]

It is possible to read much of Griboedov's remaining work as a dialogue between a vertical poetic sublime and a prosaic "horizontal" axis dominated by the exigencies of politics. Griboedov's direct involvement in the cut and thrust of colonial war and imperial diplomacy distinguishes him sharply from his odic predecessors as well as his romantic contemporaries, compromising but not effacing his independence of judgment. Typical of his ambivalent engagement in colonial policy was his attitude to the monumental figure of General Ermolov. Of his first impressions of Ermolov, Griboedov wrote: "[he] pacifies resistance with arms, hangs people, burns their villages—what is one to do? By law I cannot justify some of his actions, but remember that he is in Asia,—here every child reaches for a knife. But he is really kind; as far as I can tell, he is a man of the gentlest disposition, or I've become quite the panegyrist, although I think that is something with which I cannot be reproached: I haven't written any poems to Izmailov or Khrapovitskii."[44]

Succumbing to Ermolov's personal charm even as he expressed qualms about his military tactics, Griboedov here also distances himself in a fundamental way from the panegyric tradition of the eighteenth-century ode. The reductive orientalism that was now a commonplace of Russian culture—"he is in Asia"—demanded that Russia be distinguished sharply from its Islamic neighbors to the south. If Iranian political culture was a "ladder of blind slavery and blind power," a tyranny where "even . . . historians are panegyrists," then the Russian writer could no longer adhere to comparable discursive forms.[45] To contemplate Russia as a modernizing empire that differed from the despotisms of the east, new genres and paradigms were necessary.

Noting privately in 1825 that "no people has conquered so easily and has been so unable to make good use of its conquests as the Russians," Griboedov had long been dissatisfied with Russian colonial policy.[46] The most elaborate example of Griboedov's innovative political thinking was the "Proèkt uchrezhdeniia Rossiiskoi Zakavkazskoi kompanii" (Project for the establishment of a Russian Transcaucasia Company) (1828). Modeled on the Russian American Company in Alaska and Britain's East India Company, the project sought fundamentally to alter the economic and political basis of the Russian Empire, at least in the Transcaucasian region. Noting that until then the Russian administration in the Caucasus had subordinated commercial advantage to military exigency, the project advocated the establishment of a company that would encourage the development of trade and industry while simultaneously arrogating to itself many of the privileges reserved for the imperial state. In place of the military-bureaucratic apparatus presided over by the generals Ermolov and Paskevich, Griboedov envisioned a company that could unify the region's capital and harness its frustrated productive capacity. Consisting primarily of "Transcaucasian landowners and merchants," the company would facilitate "peaceful, pleasant relations for the sake of profit," a relationship of mutual advantage that could erase the "prejudices that had created a sharp divide between us [Russians] and our subject peoples."[47]

Griboedov's dream of replacing the military subjugation of the Caucasus with a capitalist model of enterprise was essentially foreign to the culture of tsarist autocracy and remained, like many of his literary projects, unrealized. Yet Griboedov's advocacy of a principled and "progressive" imperialism finds echoes in a small number of related literary works. The poem "Khishchniki na Chegeme" (Predators on the Chegem) (1825), his finest piece after *Woe from Wit,* is a war song of defiant resistance to Russian rule. Attributed to the mountain dwellers of the Caucasus themselves, it surpasses even Pushkin's attempts at reproducing the spirit of North Caucasian culture. The startling thematic shift from imperial glory to anticolonial resistance is reflected in the poem's genre: not an ode but a ballad, it fulfills the ballad's generic function in Russian romanticism of expressing indigenous national spirit.[48]

The context of the poem's composition vividly reflects Griboedov's mixed feelings about General Ermolov's military strategy. Voluntarily joining a Russian punitive expedition sent in response to a recent attack by Circassians on a Cossack outpost, Griboedov speaks of the campaign in a private letter that serves as a commentary to the poem itself: "Now I am somewhat engaged in this, the struggle of the freedom-loving peoples of the mountains and forests against enlightenment to the drumbeat [*barabannym prosveshcheniem*] and artillery fire: we will keep stringing them up or pardoning them, and we don't give a damn about history."[49]

The poem amplifies Griboedov's own reservations by attributing them to the mountain dwellers themselves. Although the poem brands the mountain dwellers as "predators" and clearly details their practice of enslaving prisoners of war, these negative details are oddly muffled by the overall "ventriloquizing" effect that the poem achieves. In terms of imagery, the text is predicated on a topographical—and finally anthropological—distinction between Russia, a "land of villages and meadows" and the Northern Caucasus, a place of "precipices and steep falls." However powerful the Russians appear, the mountain dwellers cling tenaciously to their heights:

Живы в нас отцов обряды,
Кровь их буйная жива.
Та же в небе синева,
Те же льдяные громады,
Те же с ревом водопады,
Та же дикость, красота
По ущельям разлита!

Наши—камни, наши кручи!
Русь! зачем воюешь ты
Вековые высоты?
Досягнешь ли?—Вон над тучей—
Двувершинный и могучий
Режется из облаков
Над главой твоих полков.[50]

The rites of our father live on within us,
Their impetuous blood lives on.
The same blue is in the sky,
The same colossi of ice,
The same thundering waterfalls,
The same wildness, beauty
Is spread throughout the ravines!

The rocks are ours, the plunging slopes are ours!
Russia! Why do you wage war against
The age-old heights?—There above the cloud—
The double-peaked and powerful [Mount Elbrus]
Cuts through the clouds
Above the heads of your regiments.

In these lines, the mountain dwellers confront the might of Russia by appropriating for themselves the natural sublimity of the Caucasian landscape, whose descriptive detail had been well established in Russian poetry thanks to Derzhavin's ode to Count Zubov, Zhukovskii's "Poslanie Voeikovu" (Epistle to Voeikov) (1814), and Pushkin's poetry of the 1820s (to which I turn in the next chapter). Even as it rehearses the already standard epithets of the alpine sublime, Griboedov's poem goes further than other contemporary romantic evocations of the Caucasus in identifying the mountain landscape explicitly as a trope of *resistance* to Russian rule. Conflating their martial customs with the natural grandeur of the Caucasus, the mountain dwellers symbolize their struggle for freedom by countering the horizontal axis of empire with the soaring heights of Mount Elbrus. For Griboedov, as for much of the poetic culture of Decembrist romanticism, the alpine sublime was to become a necessarily ambivalent symbol of resistance, a libertarian impulse that the poet could embrace as a disaffected member of the Russian gentry and yet also disavow as a Russian patriot for whom empire could nonetheless be distinguished from the evils of autocracy. The politically polyvalent nature of the alpine sublime is brought out in another stanza of the same poem, which was censored when the poem first appeared in 1826. Here the mountain dwellers describe the fate of the Russians they have captured:

Узникам удел обычный,—
Над рабами высока
Их стяжетелей рука.
Узы—жребий им приличный;
В их земле и свет темничный!
И ужасен ли обмен?
Дома—цепи! в чуже—плен!

Prisoners will suffer the usual fate,—
High above the slaves
Is the arm of those who have acquired them.
Chains are a lot that befits them;
In their land even the light is that of a prison!
And is the exchange so terrible?
Chains at home, captivity abroad!

These lines explicitly politicize the parable which Pushkin's *Kavkazskii plennik* had already elaborated in more muted tones: a Russian who falls captive to the Caucasian mountain dwellers, the poem tells us, is merely exchanging one form of tyranny for another. In the tradition of Decembrist romanticism and its aftermath, the alpine sublime would thus come to embody a complex, even contradictory, political message: the freedom struggle of the mountain dwellers became viewed allegorically as a displaced symbol of the radical gentry's own disaffection with the tsarist order (and with serfdom in particular), even as General Ermolov and his successors were hailed for extending the bounds of Russian civilization.

Griboedov's remaining orientalist works, written over some eight or nine years, survive largely as incomplete fragments or undeveloped plans. The narrative poem *Kal'ianchi* (The Hookah-Bearer) (1820–21), the tragedy *Gruzinskaia noch'* (Georgian night) (1826–27), and the play *Rodamist i Zenobiia* (Rodamist and Zenobiia) (date unknown) cannot be judged on their aesthetic merits. Yet they are striking for their thematic continuity and for their clear connection with Griboedov's diplomatic concerns. They all take place in Transcaucasia—Georgia or Armenia—a region that is shown in every case to be doubly oppressed: a victim both of its own feudal hierarchy and of imperial encroachment by foreign powers—Iran, Russia, and, in times past, ancient Rome. As in "Khishchniki na Chegeme," the plight of the region is dramatized in several accounts of individual slavery, national subjugation being thus figured symbolically in the buying and selling of human beings. Since it was also Griboedov's ongoing task as a diplomat to negotiate the release of Russian and other Christian captives living in Iran, here, too, we find a direct correspondence between the writer's vision and the concerns of the diplomat.

In summarizing Griboedov's literary and political engagement in Transcaucasia and Iran, we might end by quoting a telling observation found in *Rodamist i Zenobiia,* a text that, while set in ancient Armenia, clearly allegorizes Griboedov's professional predicament. Describing the Roman emissary Casperius who has just arrived to pursue diplomatic negotiations with Armenia, King Rodamist observes: "What need is there for such a man as Casperius in an autocratic empire: he is dangerous to his own government, and a burden to himself, for he is the citizen of another age."[51] Alien to the political culture of imperial Rome but still faithful to its state interests, Casperius is said to have developed a personal ethic that is "unshakable." This ethic marked the personal and political pathos of Griboedov's orientalist career. Critical of the despotism that he perceived as pervading oriental culture ("They are slaves, my dear fellow, and serves them right!"),[52] Griboedov was equally dissatisfied with Russia's own colonial policies. A principled stand, for Griboedov, thus involved advocating a kind of progressive imperialism, one that would dismantle the military-bureaucratic apparatus of empire in favor of a mercantile capitalist model and thereby circumvent both the bureaucratic arbitrariness of the tsarist state and the local tyranny of the Transcaucasian feudal elites.

When read together, then, Griboedov's literary and diplomatic careers point to the ambiguities of Russian orientalism deployed: a legacy ambiguous enough both to render service to the Russian Empire and to corroborate, however indirectly, the oppositional politics of the Decembrists, for whom Griboedov's orientalism served as an important aesthetic and political model.

Küchelbecker, Griboedov, and the Poet-Prophet

If Griboedov remained an unhappy moderate in his politics, the poet Wilhelm Karlovich Küchelbecker (1797–1846) was, by contrast, a radical. His participation in the uprising of 1825 would divide his life in two, a rebellious youth immersed in the cultural politics of the day and a long maturity, lonely but productive, spent in prison and Siberian exile. Surviving most of his literary contemporaries, Küchelbecker remained doggedly faithful to the ideals of his youth and, perhaps more than any other poet of his time, formulated the aesthetic vision of Decembrist culture. While fellow Decembrist writer Alexander Bestuzhev remained more catholic in his romanticism and the lesser poet Ryleev was substantially influenced by Pushkin's verse, Küchelbecker was programmatically narrower in his literary sensibility.[53] He polemicized sharply with the alternative "elegiac" current of Russian romanticism and effectively resisted Pushkinian poetic values even as he acknowledged Pushkin's greatness. Küchelbecker interests us, then, for adhering to a literary platform that consciously recuperated many of the salient traits of eighteenth-century poetics even as it sought to fashion a lyric persona that was essentially romantic.[54] The already archaic mode of the odic and psalmic sublime was now to become the vehicle of the poet-prophet, who would refract the nineteenth-century question of the nation, national specificity (*samobytnost'*) and national liberation, through the eighteenth-century theme of empire.

Even during his adolescence as Pushkin's schoolmate at the Lycée of Tsarskoe Selo, Küchelbecker had been an ardent propagandist of Longinus's treatise on the sublime. "This book," Iurii Tynianov has observed, "—the canon and source for the theory of sublime poetry—became the foundation for all of Küchelbecker's later literary views."[55] In 1820–21 Küchelbecker toured Europe, delivering a provocative lecture in Paris that remains a valuable summary of early Decembrist thinking on language and its relationship to national self-determination. "The history of the Russian language," Küchelbecker told his French audience, "will perhaps reveal to you the character of the nation that speaks it. Free, strong, and rich, its earliest formation preceded the establishment of serfdom and despotism, and it subsequently offered a constant antidote to the pernicious effects of oppression and feudalism."[56]

It was only in the winter of 1821, however, that the poet's sensibility evolved to the point of constituting a poetics and a politics for which he would be prepared to risk imprisonment and exile. Shortly after returning to Russia Küchelbecker was assigned to serve under the watchful eye of General Ermolov in the Georgian capital Tiflis, where he met and befriended Aleksandr Griboedov. Under Griboedov's influence, Küchelbecker definitively abandoned his remaining elegiac and Zhukovskian sympathies to adopt a literary position that would be largely at odds with the direction Russian poetry was to take under the aegis of Pushkin. In Küchelbecker's prison diary of 1832 we find a precious autobiographical testimony to this moment:

> I read the first thirty chapters of the Book of Isaiah. Without a doubt none of the biblical prophets can be compared to Isaiah in terms of power, sublimity [*vysprennostiiu*] and fire; the first five chapters constitute an ode the likes of which does not exist in any language or among any nation (they were a favorite of my late friend Griboedov, and we first became acquainted when he read them to me in Tiflis in 1821).[57]

Küchelbecker is here reliving what had effectively been a moment of literary conversion: the idiom of the Church Slavic Bible and the figure of the Old Testament prophet exemplified by the Book of Isaiah were said to constitute an "ode" that would become Küchelbecker's catechism for a poetic intervention in the politics of his day.

The encounter in Tiflis between Griboedov and Küchelbecker provided the definitive impulse for a new Decembrist rendering of the imperial sublime. No less than through references to Greek and Roman antiquity, this rendering was based on the convergence of two orients—the Bible of the ancient Hebrews, on the one hand, and the Islamic tradition, on the other, the latter embracing both the Persian literary tradition and the tense political rivalries of the contemporary Near East. Let us take these two elements in turn.

Russian poets, we know, had long utilized adaptations of the Hebrew psalms as a form of political commentary. In the early 1820s this practice became even more widespread: the Decembrist poet Fedor Glinka's collection, *Opyty sviashchennoi poèzii* (Experiments in sacred poetry) (1826), was only the most systematic attempt at promoting a spiritually charged form of civic opposition, couched in the eighteenth-century tradition of "sacred odes."[58] Only one work by Griboedov survives as evidence of his direct involvement in the cultivation of the Hebrew psalms. The poem "David," which appeared anonymously in 1824 in the literary almanac *Mnemozina* (Mnemosyne) published by Küchelbecker and Vladimir Odoevskii, is a free rendering of Psalm 151.[59] In it David's inspired music reaches God, who in turn sends an angel to anoint him for the sacred task of defeating his great enemy, Goliath, in battle. The text's apparent remoteness from the controversies of Griboedov's day should not deceive us. The poem is, in many ways, a parable of contested authority: David is the underdog, singled out among his more valiant brothers for his pious artistry. His music will finally prevail not only over his enemy but also over the brute strength of his elder brothers.

Küchelbecker's response to Griboedov's poetic example was both enthusiastic and consistent. The poem "Griboedovu" (To Griboedov) (1821) is constructed as a dialogue of kindred spirits fated to live out parallel but distinct destinies: while Küchelbecker, "inhabitant of the sublime world [*vozvyshennogo mira*]," anticipates his martyrdom at the hands of "vile serpents" below, Griboedov, the poet predicts, "will soar high above the songs of the crowd," since he has been initiated into "the golden mysteries of high art [*vysokogo iskusstva*]."[60] Another poem, of 1823, imagines the flight of Küchelbecker's spirit to Griboedov in Tiflis over whose "prophetic head" the "sumptuous muses of sacred Farsistan" are seen hovering even as the poet "imbibes the fragrance of [Sa'adi's] *Gulistan*."[61] More significant still is the opening fragment of an incomplete narrative poem of the same period dedicated to Griboedov. As befits a long poem, its structure is more complex, a tale within a tale framed by an oriental narrator, who claims credit for having revealed to Griboedov "the wisdom of the sweet lessons / of the wise men and prophets of the east." Overall the fragment is striking for its stark juxtaposition of the region's glorious past with the colonial captivity of the present:

> Can I recall you Dara,
> Ruler of all sublunary worlds,
> You, Khusro's martial forces,
> You, battles of the terrible Shahpur?
> Here on the captive banks of the Kura
> The Russian rattles his weapon;
> Recalling the glory of the past,
> I succumb to involuntary sadness.[62]

In these works by Küchelbecker the several dimensions of Griboedov's legacy—his orientalist literary interests (specifically in the Hebrew Bible and the Persian classical tradition) and the arena of his service to the tsarist state (Transcaucasia and Iran)—converge to generate an imaginative geography that straddles at least two cultural traditions and several historical periods. However indeterminate it might appear, the orient of Decembrist romanticism was generic only in a defined and limited way. The linguistic register and historical narrative of the Old Testament provided a lexical, thematic, and subjective basis for a doctrine of national liberation, led by the poet-prophet and inspired by a righteous God. The Islamic east, by contrast, became the stylistic register of imperial politics, the vicissitudes of history mapped as the rise and fall of empire. In other words, the two orients, Hebrew and Islamic, corresponded, to a significant degree, to the concepts of *nation* and *empire.* Converging without fusing, these orients constituted a symbolic landscape on which the Decembrist poets were able to create a distinct type of lyric subjectivity that was at the same time a discourse of literary and political opposition. In the remaining pages of this chapter, I turn first to Wilhelm Küchelbecker's theoretical updating of the imperial sublime in the light of the romantic discovery of nationhood and then to his poetry, in which the contours of the poet-prophet are vividly delineated.

Nation and Empire

In a programmatic essay of 1824 Küchelbecker launched a bold if anachronistic polemic against the ascendancy of the newer romantic genres, such as the elegy and the ballad, as well as the mania for all things foreign. Defining poetry as being marked by "strength [or force: *sila*], freedom and inspiration," Küchelbecker claimed that lyric verse becomes "all the more outstanding the more it rises [*vozvyshaetsia*] above everyday events, above the lowly language of the rabble which does not know inspiration." Among existing lyric genres, the ode alone was found to contain the qualities Küchelbecker championed.

> The ode, in being animated by sublime [*vysokimi*] objects, in transmitting to the ages the feats of heroes and the glory of the Fatherland, in soaring toward the throne of the Unsaid and prophesying before the awe-struck people, glides, thunders, flashes, and enslaves the ear and soul of the reader. Moreover, the odic poet is disinterested: he does not rejoice in the insignificant events of his personal life, or lament over them; he proclaims the truth and judgment of providence, triumphantly declares the greatness of his native land, hurls bolts of lightning at his foes, lauds the righteous and curses the monster.[63]

The ode of which Küchelbecker speaks here scarcely resembles a genre in the classicist sense, corresponding instead to what we might call the rhetoric of the odic sublime, now stripped of its former political loyalties. The Decembrist "ode" must denounce even as the monarchist ode had praised. While Lomonosov and Derzhavin were, to varying degrees, compelled to efface their selfhood through an identification with empire, now the Decembrist poet must transcend his private life by championing the nation: "Let us begin to hope that finally our writers . . . will throw off their demeaning German chains and desire to be Russian."[64]

A striking feature of Küchelbecker's polemic is his tendency to conflate aesthetic and generic categories with national ones. "Any free, national poetry" after Dante, he claims, "began to be called romantic."[65] Russia is said to have freed itself of the "yoke of French letters" only to risk becoming fettered to the "chains of English or German rule." In a transplanted culture as was Russian romanticism, true *narodnost'* could be found only by jettisoning internalized foreign influences, freeing Russian literature from "Germanisms, Gallicisms, and barbarianisms."[66] In a telling statement of the same year, Küchelbecker once more glossed the literary clashes of the time as forms of national rivalry, thus equating aesthetic influence with political domination: "The Germano-Russians and the Russian Frenchmen are ceasing their internecine conflicts, in order to unite against the Slavs, who in turn have their classicists and romanticists! Shishkov and Shikhmatov can be counted among the former, and Katenin, Griboedov, Shakhovskoi, and Küchelbecker among the latter."[67]

Much has been made, particularly by Soviet-era critics, of the romantic—and specifically Decembrist—vindication of the *narod,* or nation. "The intactness of cultural specificity," writes Gukovskii, "was perceived as the consequence of a nation's courage in heroically defending its character, its independence, its freedom. . . . The romantic concept of national culture and its liberating function was ahistorical and asocial (but still ethnographically based)."[68] Especially suggestive has been Lidiia Ginzburg's attempt to link the problem of lyric individuality in romantic poetry with the political concept of national individuation or self-determination. "For all its individualism," Ginzburg clarifies, "the romantic persona was invariably conceived of as enriched by supra-individual values."[69] A heroic, libertarian patriotism was one such model of supra-individuality, allowing the individual to identify private vicissitudes—exile, persecution, even love—with the trials of the nation.

The Soviet critical emphasis on the progressive and libertarian aspects of the Decembrist legacy is understandable, but such an approach remains deaf to the markedly authoritarian elements of Decembrist ideology. The Decembrists' vision of national liberation was predicated on a deeply hierarchical understanding of political leadership, a fact reflected in their understanding of the role of the poet no less than in the actual uprising on Senate Square. Let us recall that for Küchelbecker poetry was defined not only by "freedom" but also by "strength" or "force" (*sila*). This strength was neither personal nor purely liberatory: unleashed and directed vertically by sublime poetic inspiration, it allowed the poet-prophet to soar over and dominate the people he claims to serve. Küchelbecker's article of 1824 makes it clear that power is not channeled through the poet in order to grant the nation any kind of political agency. Rather, it is passed on through a cycle of domination and subjection that remains the primary model of change, in literature as in history.

For Küchelbecker, the supreme status of the poet corresponds to a vision of Russia as "the primary power in the universe," whose cultural ascendancy will have eclipsed its derivative relationship to older civilizations. While as a culturally colonized nation Russia has only *imitated,* as a world power Russia should instead *appropriate,* thereby establishing a new relationship between the foreign and the native. Even while retaining "ancestral faith, local custom, popular chronicles, songs and tales" as the "true sources of Russian literature," Russia should take advantage of her "geographical position" to "appropriate all the intellectual treasures of Europe and Asia. Ferdousi, Hafez, Sa'adi, Jami all await Russian writers."[70] We find here a precocious sign of a cultural politics that in the twentieth century would come to be called Eurasianism: a subordinate cultural relationship to Europe is abandoned through a vindication of the Russian national tradition and the simultaneous absorption of the Islamic east.

Two little-read works by Küchelbecker conceived about ten years apart—*Evropeiskie pis'ma* (European letters) (1820) and *Russkii Dekameron 1831-go goda* (The Russian Decameron of 1831) (written in the early 1830s and published in 1836)—deserve attention for what they tell us about the poet's evolving sense of the cultural implications of Russian imperial nationhood. The *Evropeiskie pis'ma* describes the journey of an American traveler visiting Europe in the twenty-sixth century. This futuristic setting allows the traveler to ruminate on the broader patterns of universal history while reflecting on the related problem of cultural translation and appropriation. Progress is inevitable, we learn in Letter 9, but coexists with the cyclical rise and decline of distinct civilizations. Rome imitated and then vanquished Greece, before being in turn absorbed by Christian Europe. This historical narrative, in itself quite conventional, is then updated from the perspective of the remote future. Europe, we learn, has now itself been displaced, such that the "sun of truth" now shines "over Asia, Africa, and Europe's natural successor America."[71] Mired in provincial barbarism, Europe is now little more than a museum of ruins dotted with colonies of settlers from its former peripheries who are busy mining its cultural legacy.

As an account of world history, the *Evropeiskie pis'ma* clearly implies that political power is always transient, even as the overall progress of humanity is ensured through the absorption of older cultural paradigms by newly dominant civilizations. Yet if the rise and fall of empires and civilizations constitute the primary Decembrist paradigm for understanding history and temporal change, then how is one to situate nationhood and national self-determination within this paradigm? Reaching the ruins of the Escurial, the traveler muses: "Spain in its struggle for freedom and independence, for the sacred rights of nations—a great and edifying example for posterity! A cold wind from the north interrupted my thoughts, and I continued to wander for a long time in a pensive state among the ruins, feeling the insignificance of my own presence and of all things earthly!"[72] However laudable, the Spanish revolution of 1820 has left no tangible material legacy in the twenty-sixth century, so that nationhood appears no more constant than power itself. While commenting extensively on the mores of the French and Italians, Küchelbecker makes it clear that these traits, too, are things of the past, details now available only in textbook histories and ethnographies. The only mechanism of continuity, it seems, is imperial appropriation. Polemically reversing the relationship of the dominant and the dominated that prevailed in his own time, Küchelbecker ranks Russia alongside America, Asia, and Africa as one of the new powers to have superseded and effectively colonized Europe. These new conquerors retain a nominal sense of nationality even as they in reality constitute an essentially cosmopolitan elite. Dobrov, the leader of a Russian colony in Calabria, is a case in point. A refined Epicurean and the finest example of a new civic culture that has reconciled aesthetics, morality, and politics, Dobrov reads "the poetry of all nations and all periods, but not in the original but through splendid translations into his native language."[73]

Anticipating Küchelbecker's article of 1824, we might read the problem of poetic translation as a literary instantiation of the broader problem of Russian imperial nationhood. Far from being focused exclusively on the national, the Decembrist vision of Russian culture actively promoted the absorption of the foreign, even as it insisted that the foreign be translated and thereby subordinated to a national idiom. National self-affirmation was thereby linked to imperial hegemony, and this became an essential tenet of Decembrism, in literature no less than in politics. The striking amalgam of libertarian and authoritarian elements in Decembrist ideology corresponds to a considerable extent to this peculiar marriage of nationalism and imperialism.

Russkii Dekameron 1831-go goda, written during Küchelbecker's years in prison, further nuances the poet's understanding of the poetics of imperial appropriation. A compositionally complex work, *Russkii Dekameron* follows Boccaccio's fourteenth-century masterpiece in staging an encounter between several Russian noblemen and women who have fled to the countryside from a plague that is ravaging Moscow. Here the poet Chinarskii, whose biography and interests bear a striking resemblance to Griboedov's, offers to entertain his friends by reciting them his narrative poem, *Zorovavel'* (Zerubbabel), the retelling by a contemporary Persian bard from Tabriz of the biblical tale from the Book of Ezra of a Jewish leader's confrontation with the Persian king Darius. This intricate structure of interpolated text, framing narrative and commentary together, constitutes what is perhaps the most densely layered attempt by a Russian romantic to work out the philological and political ramifications of literary orientalism. Doubtless mirroring the conversations that must have taken place between Griboedov and Küchelbecker, Chinarskii offers the following explanation of the literary strategy underlying his poem. "The topic of my story is taken from Persian history, the events are Persian, as are the customs, and I have tried to endow even the language with an oriental, Persian flavour."[74] Like a good romantic, Chinarskii views philological accuracy as an index of national specificity and has sought to preserve both within a larger poetic synthesis of east and west. His interlocutor, Osval'd, then reassures him that "reaching the goal [of synthesis] along the path you have chosen is not easy, but it is at least possible. *Soaring is something homogeneous; what people call the sublime is common to all nations* [*Parenie odnoobraznoe; to, chto nazyvaiut vysokim, u vsekh narodov odno*]."[75]

In this immensely suggestive exchange the sublime is presented as culturally universal, and hence capable of rhetorically mediating between the romantic premise of national specificity and the political context of imperial appropriation. Chinarskii's poem, *Zerubbabel,* can be read as an attempt at precisely such a mediation, coupling an acknowledgment of the *cultural* parity of nations with a ready acceptance of the *political* hierarchy that imperialism necessitates. The poem itself involves two historical moments, the Russo-Persian war of 1829 and Old Testament antiquity, the former framing the latter just as empire absorbs empire. The text begins with the occupation of Tabriz by Russian troops in the aftermath of General Paskevich's victorious campaign against Iran. "Above the troops of the Russian tsar / within the vanquished walls of Tabriz" a professional bard recites to his conquered countrymen the cautionary tale of the Jew Zerubbabel, who, alone among the sycophants of King Darius's court, dared to defend the power of truth against all other forces, be they the inebriating freedom of wine or the supremacy of the royal will.[76]

The poem *Zorovavel'* is an ambiguous text. The encounter between Zerubbabel and King Darius presents a highly idealized reconciliation between sovereign and subject, as well as between empire and subject-nation. When Zerubbabel, "inspired from above," proclaims that "king and slave are equal" before the power of truth, Darius rewards him by permitting the Jewish people to return to Jerusalem and rebuild their temple. The poem's conclusion, however, shifts back to the present and reframes the biblical narrative within the overall perspective of world history.

Так некогда веленьем Дары
Восстал из пепла падший храм;
Но храм сей лет позднейших кары
Вновь грозным предали рукам,
И руки те за злодеянья,
За грех Эверевых сынов,
Огнем сожгли священный кров
И разметали основанья.[77]

Thus once by the command of Darius
The fallen temple rose from the ashes;
But the tribulations of later years consigned this temple
Once more to menacing hands,
And those hands, on account of the wicked deeds,
The sin of the sons of Heber,
Set the sacred abode afire
And scattered its foundations.

The Persian bard concludes by recalling that the Jews were permitted by King Darius to rebuild the temple only to have it destroyed, centuries later, by the Roman emperor Titus. History, it seems, teaches us the fragility of national freedom, which falls prey repeatedly to the vicissitudes of empire. The choice, it seems, is not always between freedom and subjugation but between a benign imperialism and a despotic one. This lesson is then applied in the closing lines to the present, as a young Russian soldier stationed in Tabriz, his soul "full of rapture," mentally "soars over the ancient land," contemplating its fate at the hands of the Russian army. "Darius," he concludes, "would recognize his Iran" today, suggesting that Russian occupation resembles Darius's policy toward the Jews.[78]

In his critical writings as in his literary works, Küchelbecker consistently complicated the premise of national liberation that has been generally attributed to Decembrist ideology. Literary orientalism, even as it corroborated the romantic taste for national specificity, also provided a paradigm for understanding past and present history as the rise and fall of empire. This complex imbrication of nation and empire had significant consequences for the status of the poet, to which I now turn.

The Prophet and the Despot

Apart from the works dedicated to Griboedov himself, Küchelbecker's conversion to the poetics of the sublime inspired a significant number of poems on the nature of the poet and poetic inspiration. "Ermolovu" (To Ermolov) (1821), "Olimpiiskie igry" (The Olympic games) (1822), "Prorochestvo" (Prophecy) (1822), "Prokliatie" (A curse) (1822), "Upovanie na Boga" (Hope in God) (1822/23), "Uchast'e poètov" (The fate of poets) (1823), "Zhrebii poèta" (The poet's lot) (1823/24), and "Smert' Bairona" (The death of Byron) (1824) count as the most systematic attempt by a Russian romantic poet to equate poetic utterance with prophecy. The traits of the poet-prophet are most vividly delineated in the opening lines of "Prorochestvo":

Глагол господень был ко мне
За цепью гор на бреге Кира:
«Ты жизнь влачишь в мертвящем сне,
В объятьях леностного мира:
На то ль тебе я пламень дал
И силу воздвигать народы?—
Восстань певец, пророк Свободы!
Вспрянь, возвести, что я вещал!
Никто—но я воззвал Элладу;
Железный разломил ярем:
Ее душа не дастся аду;
Она очистится мечем,
И, искушенная в горниле,
Она воскреснет предо мной:
Ее подымет смертный бой;
Она возблещет в новой силе!»[79]

The word of God reached me
Beyond the chain of mountains on the banks of the Kura:
"You eke out your life in deadening slumber,
In the embrace of an indolent world:
Was it for this that I gave you the flame
And the power to make people rise up?—
Arise, bard, prophet of Freedom!
Leap up, and announce what I have preached!
None—but I have summoned Hellas;
Broken her iron yoke:
Her soul will not surrender to hell;
But will be purified through the sword,
And, tested in the forge,
She will resurrect before me:
She will be lifted up by a mortal struggle;
And glow in her new strength!"

The poet is here summoned by God to become the voice and agent of divine providence. The ancient covenant binding God, the biblical prophets, and the Hebrew nation is applied to a new historical juncture, in which Russia's escalating presence in Transcaucasia is juxtaposed alongside the Greek struggle against Ottoman rule. Sublime rapture (*vostorg*) is the prophet's condition, but where lyric transport had once celebrated imperial victories that enhanced the sovereign's glory, now it serves to "shake and shatter thrones."[80] Formerly creating a fearful intimacy between the odic poet and monarch, the sublime is now what *separates* the poet from the despot, even as it establishes the terms of their conflict: "No, monster,—not to you was given / rapture, the usurper of immortality."[81] The poet is now the tyrant's rival and lives out the life of the monarch in reverse: whereas the latter "possesses the throne only momentarily" and will be condemned by history, the prophet is mocked and persecuted during his lifetime but vindicated by posterity.[82]

Küchelbecker's most complex early lyric elaboration of the poet-prophet and his encounter with the despot is "Smert' Baĭrona." Published in the third volume of the almanac *Mnemozina,* the poem performed the required task of memorializing Byron within the politically charged context of his death in Greece. Juxtaposed alongside the fact of Byron's engagement in the Greek cause is Pushkin's banishment in 1820 to the Caucasus and Bessarabia. The analogy is, of course, entirely justified in literary terms: it was during his own southern exile that Pushkin discovered Byron, whose oriental tales largely provided the genre and idiom for Pushkin's own southern works. "Smert' Baírona" is thus, most immediately, Küchelbecker's act of homage to two of his contemporaries, situating their poetic exile within a shared symbolic geography that is evoked in the opening lines:

Вспылал далекий минарет;
Иман, над прахом возвышенный,
Трикрат провозгласил вселенной:
«Бог только Бог—иного нет . . .»
Услышали; в мгновенье ока
Все пали ниц сыны пророка.[83]

A distant minaret began to gleam;
The imam, elevated above the ashes,
Proclaimed thrice to the universe:
"God alone is God—there is no other . . ."
They heard; and in the blinking of an eye
All the sons of the prophet fell to the ground.

The poem begins somewhat remotely, with a depiction of the Islamic custom of evening prayer to a God who tolerates no other name and demands the absolute surrender of his worshippers. The theological principle of God's radical transcendence culturally situates the entire poem in the Islamic east. As Ryleev's equivalent poem, "Na smert' Beirona" (On Byron's death) (1824) makes clear, divine transcendence is the religious equivalent of a political despotism that was regarded in Europe as the distinguishing feature of Ottoman political culture:

What does the tyrant of the luxurious East
rejoice at on his shaky throne,
What do the young and old of Istanbul
rush to thank the prophet for?[84]

Oriental despotism, however, is not merely a political tyranny to be condemned but the first of a series of radically vertical axes of power that quickly becomes the poem's structuring principle, in poetry as in politics.

The poem quickly moves away from this scene of prayer to discover Pushkin himself standing on the shores of the Black Sea, where he will shortly have a terrifying vision of Byron's demise:

Певец, любимец россиян,
В стране Назонова изгнанья,
Немым восторгом обуян,

С очами, полными мечтанья,
Сидит на крутизне один;
У ног его шумит Евксин —[85]

A bard, beloved of all Russians,
In the land of Ovid's exile,
Is seized by mute rapture,
His eyes filled with reverie,
Sits on the precipice alone;
With the Euxine [Black] Sea crashing noisily at his feet—

Echoing Pushkin's own poems on the Black Sea,[86] Küchelbecker here introduces the romantic theme of poetic exile, even as he superimposes this theme anachronistically onto what closely resembles an odic map of empire:

Тогда (но страх объял меня!
Бледнею, трепещу, рыдаю;
Подавлен скорбию, стеня,
Испуган, лиру покидаю!)—
Я вижу—сладостный певец
Во прах повергнул свой венец.

Он зрит: от дальних стран полдневных,
Где возвышался Фебов храм,
Весь в пламени, средь вихрей гневных,
По мрачным, тяжким облакам
Шагает призрак исполина;
Под ним сверкает вод равнина![87]

Then (but fear has seized me!
I turn pale, I quake, I weep;
I am oppressed by grief, moaning,
I abandon my lyre in fright!)—
I see—the sweet bard
Has cast his wreath in the ashes.

He sees: from the distant lands of the south,
Where the shrine of Phoebus once stood erect,
Enveloped in flame, among angry whirlwinds,
Through gloomy, oppressive clouds
The phantom of a giant is marching;
Below him the flat expanse of water gleams!

Küchelbecker's dread recalls Lomonosov's terror at the onset of his sublime visions. Yet where Lomonosov's visionary experiences were limited to Russia's monarchs, whose phantom presence served to map out the expansion of Russia's borders, it is now Byron himself, along with the protagonists of his poems, who appear before a rapt Pushkin. The realignment of hero and odic landscape is crucial here. Küchelbecker's map is less of one empire than of several imperial peripheries, the diffuse boundary zone between Russia's southern borderlands, the territories occupied by Ottoman Turkey, and, finally, England—at once a place of political tension and literary dissent. This is one of the most characteristic landscapes of Decembrist poetry, one that is in a close if critical dialogue with the monarchist topography of the eighteenth-century ode as well as with the alienated psychological landscape of Pushkin's Byronic poems. One of the most stylistically "odic" of Küchelbecker's poems, "Smert' Bairona," revives the eighteenth-century sublime, even as it inverts its ideological intent. How precisely was the sublime transformed into a vehicle for Decembrist poetics and ideology?

"Smert' Bairona" is structured as a rapid series of sublime visions whose content mirrors their form. The visions depict a sequence of poets—Küchelbecker, Pushkin, and Byron—and end with a glimpse of a remote future when the English nation is no more and its lands are ruled by a foreign despot who reflects grimly on the discrepancy between Britain's literary genius and her political demise. This theme is then formally reproduced in the sublime force that generates the poet's visions. The poem traces the ebb and flow of a visionary force that electrifies all it touches. Restlessly mobile, this sublime power is at once eschatological, political, and poetic. It displaces and conflates, passing readily from God to his worshippers to the rulers of diverse empires—Ottoman, Russian, and British—and, finally, to the poets Küchelbecker, Pushkin, and Byron themselves. The movement of force allows for a leapfrogging of sublime visions whose rapid succession is readily felt in the passage quoted above, where Küchelbecker views Pushkin viewing Byron and his fallen heroes. The force of the sublime, however, does not grant the seeing eye any easy sense of subjective agency—its visionary force disempowers the viewer as the precondition of his sight. Küchelbecker abandons his lyre in fright, and his terror is what permits Pushkin to see, just as Pushkin's own poetic paralysis is the prerequisite for the resurrection of the poet Byron. The poem as a whole enacts a dialectic of sacrifice and enablement in which the dynamism of power derives from the shifting balance of gain and loss. Whereas the eighteenth-century ode, by and large, subordinated the poetic force of the sublime to the unifying figure of the sovereign, the Decembrist sublime appears inherently unstable, based on a relationship of *rivalry*—rather than of simple identification—between aesthetic and political power.

The essentially competitive relationship between poetry and polity is dramatized in the poem's conclusion: the poet Byron, we are told, is destined to "soar forever," whereas England—which is addressed in these lines—is eventually to be either destroyed or ruled over by a foreign king:

Увы! ударит час судьбы!
Веков потоком поглощенный,
Исчезнет твой народ надменный,
Или пришельцовы стопы
лобзать, окован рабством, будет,—
Но Байрона не позабудет

Тебя гнетущий властелин;
Он на тебя перстом укажет;
Друзьям, главой поникнув, скажет:
«Ужель родиться исполин
Мог в сей земле, судьбой забвенной?»
И смолкнет, в думу погруженный.[88]

Alas! The hour of fate will strike!
Consumed by the flow of the centuries,
Your haughty nation will vanish,
Or, shackled to slavery, will kiss
The feet of newcomers,
But Byron will not be forgotten

By the sovereign who oppresses you;
He will point to you with his finger;
And say to his friends with lowered head:
"Could such a giant have been born
In this land abandoned by fate?"
And he will fall silent, deep in thought.

These lines stage a typically Decembrist confrontation between political authority and poetic genius, whose tense proximity is underlined by the rhyme *vlastelin/ispolin* (sovereign and poet-giant). Not content with vouchsafing Byron's immortality, Küchelbecker contrasts the durability of the poetic word with the transience of political power. Yet this contrast leaves intact a troubling side to Byron's posthumous fame, which survives the demise of the English nation only to depend on the wistful recollection of England's future conqueror. However much Byron's fate is linked to the Greek national struggle, nationhood finally seems a rather labile entity while empire remains the most potent form of political structure and historical memory.

How, then, are we to understand the relationship of the Decembrist poet to empire and to the imperial sublime? We have seen that the Decembrist viewed himself as the sovereign's rival and equal rather than as his subject: this change in self-understanding corresponds to the dramatic shift from the panegyric to the prophetic mode. Yet, in denouncing the imperial despot, the Decembrist poet strives to take his place, and his poetry is an exercise in displacing rather than dissolving the despot's power. No less than the panegyric poets of the past, the poet-prophet remains a servant of the imperial sublime, denouncing its political apex without fundamentally renouncing the rhetorical structure that expresses it. Even as it springs from an alternative source of inspiration, prophetic utterance is formally not unlike the allegorical visions of the eighteenth-century ode: where once the poet had been subject to the sovereign command, now he is the vessel of God's will. As Küchelbecker vividly states in the poem "Zhrebii poèta" (The poet's lot) (1823/24):

> O! It is terrifying to be a fragile vessel,
> A prophet for the joyful gods!
> Consumed by a sacred fire,
> That inspires golden verse
> He is given in sacrifice to a terrible power [*groznoi vlasti*]
> In whom the ardor of song incites the passions.[89]

Yet in being organized along more than one vertical axis of power, the Decembrist sublime appears looser and more diffuse than its odic predecessor. No longer unquestioned, the tsar's authority must contend with divine intervention, poetic vision, and popular revolt as well as the military aggression of rival empires, all of which circulate as competing claims to power. As a consequence, Russian and world history appear more vast and unstable than the incremental and aggrandizing vision intimated by the eighteenth-century ode.

While acknowledging the Decembrists' stylistic debt to the eighteenth century, Russian critics have chiefly emphasized the radical newness of Decembrist literary and political ideology. This chapter might be read as a corrective to the received tradition: if Gukovskii and Ginzburg have sought to derive the Decembrists' individual lyric persona from the political quest for *national* self-determination, I have suggested that Decembrist culture continued to ponder the question of national and personal revolt within the inherited paradigm of *imperial* history. In political terms we might say that the Decembrists sought to undermine the tsar without subverting the premise of imperial statehood. The poet's own prophetic voice derived from this paradoxical relation, both dissenting and celebratory, to power. Küchelbecker's interest in the biblical and Islamic east is doubly significant here: politically it provided a concrete geography through which to articulate Russia's geopolitical claims; stylistically it provided a symbolic landscape of resistance and revolt, in which the tsar's authority could be contested without abandoning the imperial vision on which post-Petrine Russia rested. The peculiar vacillations of Russia's nineteenth-century literature of empire, so often hesitating between imperial triumphalism and alienated dissent, derive, to no small degree, from the legacy of Griboedov and the Decembrists.

4

Pushkin, Lermontov, and the Elegiac Sublime

Pushkin and Prophecy

A challenge to any scholar, Pushkin is doubly so for any consideration of the imperial sublime. Along with a number of works born of the poet's two journeys to the south, Pushkin's *Kavkazskii plennik* (Prisoner of the Caucasus), written in 1820–21 and published in 1822, is rightly credited with consolidating the Caucasian theme in Russian literature. No other poet, save Pushkin's anointed successor, Lermontov, is so closely identified with Russia's southern borderlands, and hence with a major aspect of this book. At the same time Pushkin is the first poet of concern to us to have broken definitively with the inherited tradition of the odic sublime. A writer naturally prone to exceed and evolve beyond any aesthetic paradigm, Pushkin viewed the prescriptive taxonomies of eighteenth-century poetics, as well as the looser sensibility of Byronic romanticism, as literary modes to be mastered and eventually shed.

This chapter addresses the fundamental recasting of the imperial sublime effected first by Pushkin and then by Lermontov. The Caucasian theme is one of the most studied aspects of Russian romantic literature in terms of its stylistic and formal properties, and more recently in terms of its cultural politics. Yet the remarkable innovation that Pushkin's southern works represent might still benefit from being placed in a creative tension with the poetic tradition delineated in the previous chapters. In Lidiia Ginzburg's decisive formulation, "Pushkin rejected the romantic [i.e., Decembrist—H.R.] sublime [*vysokosti*] (and the classicist one as well). Failing to understand the historical significance of this rejection, the Russian romantics of the 1820s and 1830s attributed it to Pushkin's adherence to the Karamzinian school."[1] How, then, did Pushkin shatter the odic sublime? For what reasons did he do so? And what, if any, alternatives did he propose? In the following pages I first explore Pushkin's dialogue with the Decembrist poet Küchelbecker and, through him, with the odic past. I turn then to several works by Pushkin and Lermontov, in which the *rhetorical* sublime of the "lofty style" is largely abandoned in favor of an *aesthetic* form of the sublime, based on a dialectic between the subjectivity of the elegiac or Byronic hero and the Caucasian landscape and its people.

Pushkin's attitude to the ode, and to all poetic genres, was never as one-dimensional as Küchelbecker's. Even as he experimented with the intimate genres championed by Karamzin, Batiushkov, and Zhukovskii, the youthful Pushkin also wrote political verse. "Vospominaniia v Tsarskom Sele" (Memories in Tsarskoe Selo) (1814), the earliest poem published under the poet's name, was at least partly in the odic style, whereas Pushkin wrote several poems in the same period that might be termed proto-Decembrist, of which the poem "Vol'nost'" (Liberty) (1817) was conspicuously subtitled "An Ode."[2] "Vospominaniia v Tsarskom Sele" deals chiefly with Russia's victory over Napoleon, while "Vol'nost'" attacks royal absolutism from a politically moderate perspective that seeks to reconcile monarchy with the rule of law. The panegyric-ceremonial aspect of Pushkin's first poem and the rhetorical indignation of "Vol'nost'" together cover the full ideological range of the Russian ode from Lomonosov to Radishchev. Yet both poems are equally interesting for the presence of stylistic and thematic elements that break with odic norms. "Vospominaniia v Tsarskom Sele," read before an audience that included the aging Derzhavin, deepens Lomonosov's contrast between war and peace (*tishina*) into a more melancholy apprehension of historical change. In place of the cumulative list of victories that had formerly served to spatialize territory, the poem opens with a lingering description of Tsarskoe Selo, the country retreat of Catherine the Great, which functions in the poem as a distinct if complementary site of historical memory:

> Here each step gives birth in the soul
> To recollections of past years;
> Looking about oneself, A Russian proclaims with a sigh:
> "Everything has disappeared, the great [Catherine] is no more!"
> And, falling into deep thought, leaning over the grassy shores
> He sits in silence, lending his ears to the wind.
>
> (1:84)

Contemplating the eighteenth century as it has been commemorated in the monuments scattered about the gardens of Tsarskoe Selo, the poet is reminded of the recent Napoleonic wars, whose victorious conclusion he hails as a sign of the historical continuum linking Catherine's reign to the new century. The reader is nevertheless struck by the stylistic detour required to achieve this thematic continuity. Instead of simply writing a patriotic ode celebrating Russia's victory over Napoleon, Pushkin feels compelled to frame that victory in a remembrance of the past. "Vospominaniia v Tsarskom Sele" is less an ode, it seems, than an elegiac commemoration of the ode as a genre: the poet's stylistic distance from the ode precisely mirrors the temporal remove that separates him from the victory monuments he so wistfully contemplates.[3]

Even the militantly political poem "Vol'nost'" injects the same unexpected note of historical melancholia into its denunciation of tyranny. The "pensive poet" abruptly shifts his gaze to the "forgotten palace" of Tsar Paul I whose assassination he relives by contemplating the "desolate monument to the tyrant" who lived there (1:323). While the poem successfully integrates Paul's fate into its political thesis, the historical sensibility it evinces, in marrying political indignation to a more contemplative nostalgia, is no longer consistently odic. Pushkin's other political verse of the time is similarly hybrid: "Derevnia" (The countryside) (1819) begins as a pastoral idyll and ends with an odic denunciation of serfdom (1:359–61), whereas Pushkin's celebrated poem to Chaadaev of 1818 superimposes the imagery of love poetry onto the political theme of liberty (1:346).

All this suggests a fundamental openness to formal experimentation, a Pushkinian trait whose consequences for the imperial sublime will be explored through much of this chapter. It was this aesthetic freedom that determined Pushkin's response to Küchelbecker's poetry, as well as to the Decembrist politicization of the poet's mission. Even as he maintained a tender interest in the vicissitudes of Küchelbecker's life both before and after 1825—they had been fellow students at the Lycée of Tsarskoe Selo—Pushkin became increasingly vexed by his friend's "conversion" in 1821 to the poetics of the sublime. In a letter of 1822 to his brother, Pushkin expresses his impatience with Küchelbecker's stylistically jarring and historically regressive attempt to celebrate the Greek cause in "Slavo-Russian verse taken entirely from [the Book of] Jeremiah" (10:44).[4] Pushkin is here questioning the constitutive elements of Decembrist literary ideology, namely, the odic "high style," the biblical topos of the prophet, and the political theme of nation and empire.

In the months preceding the historic uprising on Senate Square, Pushkin formulated his poetic and critical response to the Decembrist sublime with considerable clarity. The parodic "Oda ego siiat. gr. Dm. Iv. Khvostovu" (Ode to His Excellency Count Dm. Iv. Khvostov) (1825) addressed the popular theme of Byron's recent death in Greece (2:248–50).[5] A pointed satire of the poems by Küchelbecker and Ryleev on the same theme, its eighteenth-century cadences highlighted the anachronism of using the ceremonial ode to defend the cause of Greek liberation. The poem is a hodgepodge of the older panegyric style and the contemporary Decembrist cult of the poet-prophet: these two modes—one a medium of often venal praise and the other a vehicle of cultural revolt—seem all the more incongruous in being so closely juxtaposed, and are both equally deflated through an amusing overkill of the "lofty style."

In a series of notes penned in response to Küchelbecker's controversial articles of 1824, Pushkin articulated in critical terms what his ode to Count Khvostov had performed as poetry. "The critic," complained Pushkin, "confuses inspiration (*vdokhnovenie*) with rapture (*vostorgom*). . . . Rapture does not presuppose the force of the mind, which arranges parts in their relation to the whole. Rapture is short-lived, inconstant, hence not capable of creating truly great perfection (without which there is no lyric poetry)." Pushkin then went on to identify the amorphousness of rapture with the ode, whose essential drawback was its lack of structure: "no *plan* is possible in the ode. . . . What kind of plan is there in Pindar's Olympian odes? What plan is there in Derzhavin's best work, 'The Waterfall'? The ode excludes the possibility of constant work, without which the truly great cannot exist" (11:41–42). The terms of Pushkin's critique were not original: they merely reversed Boileau's permissive attitude to the *beau désordre* that had long been seen to typify the Pindaric ode. Never published in Pushkin's lifetime, these lines nonetheless signal the inevitable demise of the ceremonial ode. If odic rapture was no longer seen as coterminous with poetic inspiration and indeed believed incapable of generating formal perfection, then the ode itself could no longer be cultivated as a self-sufficient genre. (Two notable exceptions in Pushkin's own work, which I discuss in the conclusion to this book, are his odic outbursts "Klevetnikam Rossii" [To the slanderers of Russia] and "Borodinskaia godovshchina" [The anniversary of Borodino], both written in 1831).

What still remained possible, for Pushkin, was an "odic style," one that retained select rhetorical and thematic features of the odic sublime in a form that was radically truncated and often juxtaposed alongside the distinguishing markers of other genres.[6] One thinks in this regard of the introduction to *Mednyi Vsadnik* (The bronze horseman) (1833), with its celebration of Petersburg and the Petrine legacy. More relevant for our purposes is Pushkin's celebrated poem "Prorok" (The prophet) (1826), written in the aftermath of the Decembrist uprising and often read as an elliptical commentary on the Decembrist cause. Arguably Pushkin's most exquisite exercise in the "lofty style," the poem renders homage to the poetics—if not the politics—of the Decembrist sublime, at a time when the poet's sympathy for the defeated conspirators would have most certainly overshadowed the literary reservations he had previously entertained. As most readers will certainly recall, the poem narrates a moment of intense spiritual crisis, dramatized in mythic terms by the appearance of a six-winged seraph who finds the lyric hero languishing in the desert. Sent by God as his emissary, the seraph performs what amounts to a ritual transfiguration of the poet's body, augmenting his sight and hearing and replacing his tongue and heart, so that the lyric hero is finally transformed into a vessel of prophetic cognition.

For all its heightened pathos, "Prorok" remains somewhat reticent about its underlying message. As V. E. Vatsuro has recently noted, "What exactly [the prophet] says, we never do find out. It may seem strange, but a poem about a prophet breaks off precisely at the moment when the hero becomes the Prophet."[7] A topos that had functioned as a vehicle for dissent in the psalmic or religious odes of the eighteenth century and that had been further politicized by the Decembrists becomes, in Pushkin's hands, strangely equivocal. The essential ambivalence of "Prorok" has been a central source of controversy in the considerable scholarly literature devoted to the poem. The numerous attempts—particularly in the commentaries to Soviet editions of Pushkin—to read the poem as a piece of political invective have been based chiefly on biographical context, or on the existence of more ideologically explicit textual variants that were later eliminated, or on the purported existence of a cycle of poems on the Decembrist uprising to which "Prorok" was said to belong.[8] This thesis has been most recently questioned by Boris Gasparov, who reads "Prorok" as part of a deeper shift in Pushkin's self-understanding as a poet from a messianic model grounded on expectations of imminent salvation to a prophetic paradigm in which the lyric hero "observes an infinite series of cataclysms and discerns their inner meaning," without intervening in a salvific capacity.[9]

One of the earliest critics to strike an appropriate balance between an attentive reading of the canonical text and the broader question of Pushkin's stylistic and ideological intent in writing "Prorok" was N. L. Stepanov, who noted that while "the image of the Pushkinian poet-prophet, like the entire biblical-sublime style of the poem, goes back to the poetics of the Decembrists . . . an interpretation of 'Prorok' in a purely political Decembrist vein that ignores its wider philosophical content risks limiting and narrowing Pushkin's intent."[10] In Stepanov's view, Pushkin's poem presents prophetic afflatus as a metaphor for the onset of poetic inspiration. If we recall Pushkin's own distinction between odic *vostorg* and *vdokhnovenie,* we might say that "Prorok" recreates the mythic origins of sublime rapture, allowing it to transport the prophet as well as the people he will soon encounter without clearly identifying its content with any object outside the desert landscape with which the poem opens, or the vaster cosmic spaces revealed to the poet through the seraph's intervention. "Prorok" thus reads like a truncated ode, where the sublime is divinely inaugurated but then denied a concrete semantic correlative in the realm of politics or even religion. David Bethea has recently suggested that Pushkin's reticence here corresponds to a "post-Decembrist time-space" in which the writer "must place his poetry at the service of an energy force that to him is both real and nonspecific—it doesn't belong to the tsars, just as it doesn't belong to the Decembrists, no matter how Pushkin may feel for the latter as friends. This makes Pushkin's 'The Prophet' one of those mysterious poems in his oeuvre . . . that don't take sides and that only he could write."[11]

Bethea's description of Pushkin's post-Decembrist sublime in "Prorok" as "nonspecific" is both subtle and fair, and takes us far from the flattened ideological readings of the Soviet era. Yet we might ask if the poem's politics should be sought only in its mimetic effects or referential omissions. The striking indirectness of "Prorok" might equally be read as the result of a longer literary-historical process that rechanneled the allegorical content and historical import of the cluster of topoi and symbols it deploys. Recontextualized in this older poetic history, "Prorok" might well begin to speak to us in a different way.

Most scholarly research on the literary sources of "Prorok" has focused on its biblical and even Koranic sources, the former pointing to the Book of Isaiah and the latter clarified with reference to Pushkin's earlier "Imitations of the Koran" (1824), the first explicit elaboration of the prophetic topos in Pushkin's work.[12] Interpretive effort has focused mainly on asserting or disputing the religious implications of the said topos or on establishing the extent of Pushkin's fidelity to the original biblical or Koranic passages. We already saw in chapter 3 that the "Judeo-Islamic" orient functioned in Decembrist poetry as a potent allegory, providing a symbolic means of gauging the power of national revolt, imperial aggression, and prophetic vision against the claims of tsars and rival empires. How, if at all, is this oriental topography evident in "Prorok," and might its presence be unraveled in such a way as to read the poem's "nonspecific" energy?

To answer this question, it becomes necessary to situate "Prorok" in a larger genealogy of poems by Derzhavin, Pushkin, Küchelbecker, and Lermontov. These five poems, written over half a century, share a set of motifs that together make up a symbolic topography that is among the richest in Russian poetry. Let us examine the relevant sections of these poems in their historical sequence (the words italicized should be carefully noted: in as much as they appear in at least two if not more of these poems, they are the constitutive aspects of the topos under discussion). The first poem, "Na vziatie Izmaila" (On the taking of Izmail), is one of Derzhavin's more conventional victory odes, composed to mark a Russian victory in the second Turkish war. This event serves as an occasion to explore Russia's military vicissitudes throughout history, beginning with the lengthy Tatar-Mongol occupation. Derzhavin personifies the subjugated Russian land as a giant soldier who has lapsed into a state of prolonged torpor before finally awakening to his historical mission. Here are the relevant lines:

Я вижу страшную годину:
Его три века держит *сон,*
Простертую над ним *долину*
Покрыл везде колючий терн;
. . . .
Разбойники вокруг суровы
Взложили тяжкие *оковы,*
Змия на *сердце* у него.

Он *спит*—и несекомы *гады*
Румяный потемняют зрак,
Войны опустошают грады,
Раздоры пожирают злак;
Чуть зрится блеск его короны,
Страдает вера и законы,
И ты, к отечеству любовь!
Как зверь, его Батый рвет гладный,
Как змей, сосет лжецарь коварный—
Повсюду *пролилася кровь!*

Лежал он во своей печали,
как темная в *пустыне* ночь;
. . . .
Князья, бояра в *неге спали*
И ползали в пыли как червь,—
Но Бог, но дух его великий
Сотряс с него беды толики,—
Расторгнул лев *железну* вервь!

Восстал! . . .

Он сильны орды пхнул ногою,
Края азийски потряслись;
Упали царствы под рукою,
Цари, царицы в *плен* влеклись;
И победителей разитель,
Монархий света разрушитель,
Простерся под его пятой;
В Европе грады брал, тряс троны,
Свергал царей, давал короны
Могущею своей душой.
. . . .[13]

(Derzhavin, "Na vziatie Izmaila,"
1790 or 1791)

I see a terrible time:
He [the Russian] is seized by slumber for three centuries,
The *valley* stretched out above him
Is covered by prickly thorns;
. . . .
Stern bandits have *placed*
Heavy *chains* around him
A *snake* lies on his *heart.*

He *sleeps*—and insect *vermin*
Darken his crimson eyes,
Wars empty the cities,
Discord devours the planted fields;
The gleam of his crown is hardly visible,
Faith and laws suffer,
As well as you, love of the fatherland!
Like a beast, hungry Batyi rips into him,
Like a snake, the perfidious false king sucks him—
Blood flows bespattered everywhere!

He *lay* there in his sadness,
Like a dark night in the *desert;*
. . . .

The princes and boyars *slumbered in their leisure*
And crawled about in the dust like worms,—
But God, but his great spirit
Shook off the many misfortunes from him,—
The lion shattered the *iron* chain!

He *rose!* . . .

He kicked the strong hordes with his leg,
The Asiatic lands shook;
Kingdoms fell under his hand,
Kings, queens were driven into *captivity;*
And the defeater of victors,
The destroyer of the monarchies of the world,
Was crushed by his heel;
In Europe he took cities, shook thrones,
Toppled kings and gave crowns
With his powerful soul.

Let us compare this fragment to the opening lines of Pushkin's *Kavkazskii plennik,* which describe a Russian being held in chains by mountain dwellers in the Caucasus. Russian captivity is once more imaged as a kind of deathly slumber, but national destiny is now reduced to the individual fate of the alienated romantic hero:

И вдруг пред ними на коне
Черкес. Он быстро на аркане
Младого *пленника влачил.*
«Вот русский!»—хищник возопил.
. . . .
Как труп недвижим оставался
. . . .
Над ним летает *смертный сон*
И *холодом* тлетворным дышит.

И долго *пленник* молодой
Лежал в забвении тяжелом.
Уж *полдень* над его главой
Пылал в сиянии веселом
. . . .
Воспомнил юноша свой *плен,*
Как *сна* ужасного тревоги,
И слышит: загремели вдруг
Его *закованные* ноги . . .
(Pushkin, *Kavkazskii plennik,*
1822; 4:93–94)

And suddenly before them on a horse
Appeared a Circassian. He quickly *dragged*

The young *prisoner* by a lasso.
"Here's a Russian!" the predator exclaimed.
. . . .
[The prisoner] *stayed motionless* like a corpse
. . . .
Above him a *deathly sleep* hovered
And breathed a putrefying *cold.*

And for a long time the young *captive*
Lay in a heavy oblivion.
Now *midday* was shining above his head
With a merry glow
. . . .
The young man recalled his *captivity,*
Like the anxieties of a terrible *dream,*
And heard the sudden clanging
Of his *shackled* feet . . .

Küchelbecker's "Prorochestvo" (Prophecy), a poem already familiar to us from chapter 3, is the first poem in this genealogy to present the state of deathly slumber as a condition that precedes the onset of prophetic afflatus. The opening lines, in which God chastises the prophet for his indolence, correspond readily to Küchelbecker's own critique of the Byronic hero (whose melancholy detachment he found unequal to the civic mission of the poet):

Глагол господень был ко мне
За цепью гор на бреге Кира:
«Ты дни *влачишь* в *мертвящем сне,*
В объятьях леностного мира:
. . . .
Восстань, певец, *пророк* Свободы!
Вспрянь, возвести, что я вещал!
Никто—но я воззвал Элладу;
Железный разломил ярем:
Ее душа не дастся аду;
Она очистится мечем,
И, искушенная в горниле,
Она воскреснет предо мной:
Ее подымет смертный бой;
Она возблещет в новой силе!»[14]
(Küchelbecker,
"Prorochestvo," 1822)

The *word* of God reached me
Beyond the chain of mountains on the banks of the Kura:

"You *eke* out your days in *deadening slumber,*
In the embrace of an indolent world:
. . . .
Arise, bard, *prophet* of Freedom!
Leap up, and announce what I have preached!
None—but I have summoned Hellas;
Broken her *iron* yoke:
Her soul will not surrender to hell;
But will be purified through the sword,
And, tested in the forge,
She will resurrect before me:
She will be uplifted by a mortal struggle;
And glow in her new strength!"

Pushkin's "Podrazhaniia Koranu" (Imitations of the Koran) takes up the now established motif of a prolonged deathly sleep, which here occurs as a result of divine intervention. In the cycle's concluding poem, we find the hero exhausted and lost in the middle of a desert:

И путник усталый на Бога роптал:
Он *жаждой томился* и тени алкал.
В *пустыне* блуждая три дня и три ночи,
И зноем и пылью тягчимые очи
С тоской безнадежной водил он вокруг,
И кладезь под пальмою видит он вкруг.

И к пальме пустынной он бег устремил,
И жадно *холодной струей* освежил
Горевшие тяжко язык и зеницы,
И лег, и *заснул* он близ верной ослицы:
И многие годы над ним протекли
По воле владыки небес и земли.
(Pushkin, "Podrazhaniia Koranu,"
1824; 2:212)

And the tired traveler muttered a complaint about God:
He was *tormented by thirst* and longed for shade.
Wandering in the *desert* for three days and three nights,
His eyes made heavy by the heat and the dust,
He cast about with hopeless anguish,
And suddenly caught sight of a well under a palm tree.

And he ran in the direction of the desolate palm,
And greedily refreshed with a *cold stream*
His eyes and pupils that were harshly burning,
And lay down, and fell asleep beside his faithful ass:
And many years passed by over him
By the will of the lord of the heavens and earth.

"Prorok," written some two years later, might be read as a symbolic abstraction of the traveler's plight as described by the "Imitations of the Koran." His thirst and physical exhaustion are here transformed into an inner torment of the spirit:

> Духовной *жаждою томим*
> В пустыне мрачной я *влачился,*
> И шестикрылый серафим
> На перепутье мне явился.
> Перстами легкими как *сон*
> Моих зениц коснулся он.
> . . . .
> И *гад* морских подводный ход
> . . . .
> И жало мудрые *змеи*
> В уста замершие мои
> *Вложил* десницею *кровавой.*
> И он мне *грудь* рассек мечом
> И *сердце* трепетное вынул
> . . . .
> Как *труп в пустыне я лежал,*
> И *Бога* глас ко мне воззвал:
> «В*осстань, пророк,* и виждь, и внемли,
> Исполнись волею моей,
> И обходя моря и земли,
> *Глаголом* жги сердца людей.»
> (Pushkin, "Prorok," 1826; 2:338–39)

> *Tormented* by spiritual *thirst*
> I *dragged* myself through the gloomy *desert,*
> And a six-winged seraph
> Appeared before me at a crossroads.
> With fingers light as a *dream*
> He touched the *pupils* of my eyes.
> . . . .
> And the underwater movements of marine *animals*
> . . . .
> And the sting of a wise *snake*
> Into my benumbed mouth
> He *thrust* with a *bloody* right hand.
> And he smote my *breast* with a sword
> And took out my trembling *heart*
> . . . .
> I lay like a *corpse in the desert,*
> And *God's* voice summoned me:
> "*Rise,* o *prophet,* see and hear,

Be filled with my will,
And traversing sea and land,
Burn the hearts of people with the *word.*"

Finally, let us look at Lermontov's beautiful poem "Son" (A dream), which takes us away from the mythic landscape of prophecy back to the historical space of imperial conflict, even as it preserves the essential motifs of the tradition:

В *полдневный* жар, *в долине* Дагестана,
С свинцом в *груди лежал недвижим я;*
. . . .
. . .—но *спал* я *мертвым сном.*
. . . .
И *снилась* ей *долина* Дагестана;
знакомый *труп лежал в долине* той;
В его *груди* еще дымилась рана,
И *кровь лилась хладеющей струей.*[15]
(Lermontov, "Son," 1841)

In the *noonday* heat, in a *valley* of Dagestan,
With a bullet in my *breast, I lay motionless;*
. . . .
. . .—but I *slept* a *deathly sleep.*
. . . .
And she *dreamed* of a *valley* in Daghestan;
A familiar *corpse lay* in that *valley;*
In his *breast* the wound was still freshly smoking,
And *blood poured* from it in a *stream that grew slowly cold.*

By reading the above poems in sequence we can see that the topos of prophecy in Russian poetry, whose heyday coincided with Decembrist romanticism, derives from the ceremonial ode no less than from Russian renderings of the Bible or even the Koran.[16] Although Derzhavin's ode and Lermontov's "Son" do not explicitly identify the hero as poet-prophet, they share such a wealth of precise symbolic detail with the remaining poems in the tradition that we are led to the unexpected conclusion that *the prophetic topos in Russian verse is tied as much to a poetic reconceptualization of imperial history as to religious or aesthetic experience.*

Derzhavin's ode is the earliest and longest poem in the sequence I have traced, providing the historical narrative and symbolic details that later poems will abbreviate, re-elaborate, or transform. In the passage quoted above, Derzhavin describes the Tatar yoke as a slumber lasting "three centuries" during which the body of the Russian nation lay inert and abandoned to the predations of the Golden Horde. Through a superhuman effort, the poet tells us, Russia then revived itself, exacting its revenge on Turkic Asia by "imposing chains on those very men / Who were so terrifying to the world at large." This simple story of Russian national might reasserted contains its share of complex symbolism: if political subjugation can be compared to sleep, then historical conflicts can be represented as varying forms of embodiment and consciousness. Although Derzhavin's ode does not explicitly equate the Russian national body with the prophet's, it does provide the vivid details of bodily ravishment that will come to typify the prophetic topos. These details are the physical equivalents of an oneiric state in which levels of consciousness, specifically the gradations of awareness of one's own powerlessness or strength, appear fluid and malleable.

Let us enumerate these details, which recur throughout the poems quoted with an extraordinary consistency: (1) the Russian body lies prostrate in a desolate mountain valley or desert remote from his place of birth, somewhere in the orient and, for the majority of poets, explicitly in the Caucasus; (2) the Russian being asleep, his captivity or paralysis appears to him and to the reader in and as a dream suspended between life and death (in "Prorok" sleep is only metaphorically present in the phrase "light as a dream," but the prophet is likened to a corpse at the end of the poem); (3) the Russian's disempowerment is enacted physically: his sleeping body is violated or at least challenged by a superior force, either a Turkic or an Asiatic enemy (in Derzhavin, Pushkin's *Kavkazskii plennik,* and Lermontov) or God himself (in the case of Küchelbecker and Pushkin's "Prorok"); (4) just as prolonged sleep is followed by an awakening, so, too, the hero's captivity or stasis is shown to precipitate some kind of historical or ontological change: in Derzhavin's ode, Küchelbecker's "Prorochestvo," and in the epilogue to Pushkin's *Kavkazskii plennik* this change is understood militarily and is brought about by Russian imperial aggression, whereas in the remaining poems violence is inflicted primarily on the body of the prophet, who thereby becomes the passive receptacle of prophetic utterance. Lermontov's "Son" (to which we shall return later in this chapter) can be read as a confluence of both variants: the dying soldier is both imperial aggressor and martyred victim, and the landscape of the poem negotiates between the brute violence of colonial war and a visionary state that grants the soldier a final dreamlike glimpse of his beloved and his homeland.

In surveying the poets that came in Derzhavin's wake, we can see that they effectively abstracted the living death of the Russian national body away from Derzhavin's odic narrative of the Tatar occupation, its overthrow, and the subsequent consolidation of the Russian state. The romantic tradition came to equate the nation's body with the poet's, lingering over the details of his martyrdom in sleep, and finally *elided the history of Russia's imperial expansion into the problem of prophetic utterance.* For all poets after Derzhavin, the prophet either revived or perished *in place* of Russia's political resurrection. This shift, while radically truncating the narrative of Derzhavin's ode, is not as ahistorical as it might appear. Most of the poems we have looked at can be traced back to a political event or cause of great import to the imperial state, such as the Greek struggle against Ottoman rule, the Decembrist uprising, or the North Caucasian wars. These events are either represented explicitly within the poem (as in Küchelbecker's "Prophecy," Pushkin's *Kavkazskii plennik,* and Lermontov's "Son") or are figured through a purely symbolic encounter with the east (as in Pushkin's prophetic poems) and then recoded as the catalyst for prophetic utterance.

The romantic topos of prophecy thus owed a great deal to the eighteenth-century ode, whose historical sensibility and symbolic landscape it broke down and reworked with remarkable consistency. The Decembrists, we know, updated the odic topography of imperial rivalry by positing national revolt and poetic prophecy as two additional axes of sublime power with which Russian autocracy had to contend. Pushkin himself flirted with this model even as he moved away from it. On hearing of the death of Alexander I, Pushkin wrote half-seriously in a private letter that he should be considered a prophet since his recent poem, "Andre Shen'e" (André Chenier) (1825) contained the lines "And the hour will come . . . and it is not far away: / You will fall, tyrant" (2:263), which could be read as prophesying the emperor's demise. Similarly his quasi-odic poem, "Mordvinovu" (To Mordvinov) (1826 or 1827) hails an administrator who showed great courage in opposing the execution of the five Decembrist leaders: his independence of judgment is seen as fulfilling a "prophecy" made by the eighteenth-century poet Petrov, who had dedicated an ode to Mordvinov in 1796 (3:16). By and large, though, Pushkin's prophetic poems followed a somewhat different path, creating an oriental landscape that was at once more abstract and more individuated. This process of abstraction is most evident in "The Prophet," where the *political* hierarchy of sovereign and subject is replaced by the *cosmic* verticality of prophetic vision. Yet even here a "gloomy desert" remains to mark the presence of the odic and Decembrist orient, inviting us to read Pushkin's topos of prophecy, no less than Küchelbecker's, as a reworking of the imperial sublime.

The historical import of "Prorok" might thus be more complex than the question, relentlessly explored by Soviet critics, of Pushkin's sympathy for the Decembrist cause. I am not suggesting that "Prorok" is actually about imperialism, or indeed "about" anything else. Rather, I am interested in what "Prorok" *doesn't* say about history, an *indirectness* that can be read as a *redirecting* of the sublime forces evident in the odic and Decembrist works with which the poem is in dialogue. What Derzhavin and the Decembrists had represented as historical cycles of aggression attending the rise and fall of empire become, in Pushkin's hands, the ritualized acts of violence by which the prophet is broken and reworked into a vehicle for divine cognition. Imperial history is thus temporarily recoded as a spiritual-aesthetic transfiguration of the poet's self. (My reading might be confirmed by a further juxtaposition, this time with Pushkin's extraordinary later poem, "Anchar" [The upas tree] [1828], in which the same Asiatic desert landscape reverts to its function as an allegory of imperial history. Here the vertical axis of sublime power shifts from God and prophet back to the oriental despot and his slave, whose task is abjectly to facilitate, even at the cost of his own life, his ruler's conquest of "alien lands" [3:82–83]).[17]

"Prorok," then, deflects the ode's traditional enthusiasm for the imperial state, without taking any explicit ideological stance. With this shift comes a radical realignment in the status of the poet-prophet. Whereas the odic poet had been subservient to the emperor or empress but could still elevate himself by identifying with the project of empire building, the lyric afflatus of the romantic prophet was unable to find an adequate reflection in the social order and typically fell back onto a compensatory affirmation of the poet's own greatness. Unlike the Decembrists, who were still able to see themselves as protagonists of history, the prophetic poems of Pushkin and especially Lermontov suggest a state of disengagement, in which empire, like any product of history, is unable to provide a convincing rationale for the sublime, even as it continues to be its abstracted context.

The prophetic poems of Pushkin and Lermontov can thus be read as a lyric individuation of the imperial sublime. In being absorbed into the romantic hero, the sublime was increasingly incapable of finding in history, society, and sometimes even in nature an adequate mirror for the inner workings of the poet's mind. The disjuncture between the subjective and the objective realms would become a source of acute psychological alienation. This change in the romantic poet's self-understanding corresponded to a remarkable shift in the dynamics of the sublime: where once the odic poet had submitted to the sublime only to project its force outward onto an enemy or a disputed territory, the romantic poet-prophet absorbed the violence of the sublime without successfully redirecting it onto an external object. Whether ritually performed or implied through an act of social ostracism, this violence conferred prophetic authority on the poet, without guaranteeing the content of his prophecy an adequate social or ontological space in which to resonate. This, perhaps, is the impasse reached in the last lines of "Prorok," which breaks off before the prophet is able to respond actively to God's exhortation.

The poet-prophet's social isolation, his inability to secure a tangible arena for action, was already an issue for Pushkin and his contemporaries on the eve of the Decembrist uprising. Finding Pushkin all too willing to bask in the aura of exile, Prince Viazemskii, in a letter written in the fall of 1825, cautioned him that "persecution gives sovereign power to the persecuted only where public opinion is split in two. In Russia orthodoxy alone reigns everywhere. Only fame can make you strong in Russia . . . misfortune here cannot buy you even an ounce of strength."[18] The relegation of the poet-prophet to the margins of society would become even more evident in the poetry of Lermontov, written entirely during the repressive reign of Nicholas I, when the educated gentry had been made acutely aware of its own political impotence. Even before 1825, however, an influential lyric rendering of the loss or ebbing away of force was already available to literary consciousness in the form of the elegy.

The Elegiac Sublime

Pushkin's youth coincided with a profound crisis in Russian poetic genres. With the newly ascendant romantic sensibility there came a fundamentally new attitude to genre. In the words of Iurii Lotman, "the value of this or that genre came to be defined by its capacity to express a specific artistic vision and not by its place in an abstract hierarchy. In transposing the norms of one genre onto another Pushkin found an important means for stylistic innovation and dynamism. This is what allowed Pushkin to reject the fundamental division of linguistic resources into the 'high' and the 'low.'"[19] Although Pushkin experimented with most of the existing poetic genres while still a student, the elegy and the friendly epistle were easily his preferred forms. Boris Tomashevskii singled out the elegy as Pushkin's "most productive genre" of the Lycée period, the one in which he "found his own specific language and voice."[20]

The elegy entered modern European poetry as an expression of mourning or lamentation, or as a meditative reflection on the experience of loss. Its dominant mood was one of dejection and melancholy (*unynie*, in Russian), and its themes ranged from the transience of love to the evanescence of life itself. The elegy was first introduced to Russia by Vasilii Trediakovskii, whose "Method" of 1735 defined it as "always teary and mournful" even where it expressed "the exalted [*vazhnoe*] or the amorous."[21] In the eighteenth century the genre was cultivated in Russia only intermittently, most notably by Lomonosov's younger rival, Sumarokov, one of whose elegies explicitly attacked the prevailing dominance of the "inflated, pompous ode."[22] The golden age of the Russian elegy coincided with the beginnings of romanticism. Zhukovskii's 1802 translation of Thomas Gray's "Elegy Written in a Country Churchyard," can be seen as a watershed in this history, after which the elegy was quickly embraced by Konstantin Batiushkov (1787–1855) and the younger poets grouped around Arzamas. The primary models, as always, were French, particularly the tradition of *poésie légère* championed by Évariste de Parny, Charles Millevoye, and André Chenier (the latter rediscovered only in 1819), all of whom exercised a profound influence on Pushkin, whose earliest elegies date back to his years in the Lycée. By the early 1820s the elegy was well into its brief but productive reign as the dominant lyric genre. Küchelbecker's notorious article of 1824 defending the ode against the pervasive fashion of the "gloomy elegy" is an index of how far the pendulum of taste had swung in the opposite direction since Sumarokov's day. As Belinskii would put it, "with [Pushkin's] appearance the elegiac song [*èlegiia-pesnia*] became the exclusive genre of lyric poetry; only old men and the aged were still singing their ceremonial odes."[23] However schematic, Belinskii's observation does convey the generational and generic shift that had occurred in Pushkin's day.

The elegy corroborated an ongoing redefinition within Russian letters of the relationship between public and private life. Even as it evoked an idealized world of shared intimacy and private sentiment, it did so in terms of a codified genre that made profound emotional experience legible to the reading public. It is not by accident, then, notes Monika Greenleaf, "that modern elegiac verse has tended to make its appearance as part of a nation's or city-state's Golden Age, as a correlative of national formation and empire building. Just as the Roman elegiac poets were criticized for trivial, personal pursuits out of keeping with Rome's civic and historical mission, the modern elegy appears to rise on the back of political centralization, either as a product of the civilized leisure and education it enables or as a subversive response to the official discourses of public life."[24]

In Russia, as elsewhere, the private passions dramatized by the elegy by no means served only as a refuge from the political sphere. Rather, the psychological vocabulary developed in the elegy's exploration of passion also provided a newly subjective way of apprehending time and history. The elegy's somewhat narrow emotional range was, in fact, the sentimental correlative to a persistent temporal orientation toward the past. As the romantic aesthetician Aleksandr Galich phrased it in his *Opyt nauki izaishchnogo* (Essay on the science of beauty) (1825), "the elegy, as an anguished or merry song incited by a recollection, is related in its poetry to painful states of the soul that are past or bygone, and which have since cooled to the point that we can already represent them to ourselves in our thoughts without feeling any further agitation."[25] Significantly Galich here sees an awareness of lapsed time rather than a specific emotional state as the elegy's defining trait. If the odic sublime had assumed an incremental vision of history linking past and present, and if the prophetic mode of Decembrism would orient the present to an imminent future, then elegiac time unfolds as an empty present that must be continually filled with the memory of a former plenitude or the anticipation of imminent death. The elegy is *bezvremenna*—not so much timeless as untimely: it dramatizes a fate essentially out of synchrony with the course of events.

The poetry of Konstantin Batiushkov displays the full range of the Russian elegy. Batiushkov's most conventional elegies mourn a transient and debilitating love. Poems such as "Vyzdorovlenie" (Recovery) (1807), "Èlegiia" (Elegy) (1815), or "Moi genii" (My genius) (1815) highlight the close connection between aborted love and poetic inspiration, which together intimate new creative possibilities for the lyric self. The complexities of this fate are fleshed out in the experience of mourning the lost beloved, and the poet's unanswered dialogue with the other is all that remains to prevent the complete erasure of his persona:

Нет, нет! себя не узнаю
Под новым бременем печали!
. . . .

На крае гибели так я зову в спасенье
Тебя, последний сердца друг![26]

No, no! I do not recognize myself
Under the new burden of sorrow!
. . . .
On the brink of ruin I call upon you to save me
You, the last friend of my heart!

Batiushkov's greatest innovation within Russian poetry was to expand the private experience of elegiac mourning into a broader apprehension of history. "In Russian literature," noted Belinskii, "Batiushkov is reputed to have given rise to the specific genre of the *historical* or *epic* elegy. The poet here goes so far as to introduce an event in the form of a recollection suffused with sadness."[27] Batiushkov's poems such as "Vospominanie" (Recollection) (1807–9), "K D[ashko]vu" (To Dashkov) (1813), "Na razvalinakh zamka v Shvetsii" (At the ruins of a castle in Sweden) (1814), "Perekhod cherez Rein" (Crossing the Rhine) (1814), and "Umiraiushchii Tass" (The dying Tasso) (1817) intimate a dramatically new relationship between the lyric subject and the supra-individual forces of history. Significantly the majority of these poems were composed under the immediate impact of contemporary wars against France or Sweden in which Batiushkov took part as a front-line officer. Recalling a battle in Prussia against Napoleon, the poem "Vospominanie" traces the poet's transition from a state of innocent reverie to an apprehension of death as the most disquieting aspect of war:

Да оживлю теперь я в памяти своей
Сию ужасную минуту,
Когда болезнь вкушая люту
И видя сто смертей,
Боялся умереть не в родине моей![28]

May I now revive in my memory
That terrible minute,
When tasting the fierce malady
And seeing a hundred deaths,
I feared to die outside my homeland!

Batiushkov's wartime elegies are among the first poems in the Russian lyric tradition to sketch out an essentially post-odic vision of imperial conflict. Elegiac memory is a psychological category: it historicizes without seeking to objectify. As a consequence, the violence of war is no longer allegorically abstracted, as in the ode, but rawly present as the soldier's fear of death. With this comes a new kind of patriotism, one no longer motivated by the glory accruing to the empire but by a sentimental attachment to hearth and home. "Perekhod cherez Rein," which narrates the poet's experience of the triumphant Russian advance through Germany to Paris, is the most complex of Batiushkov's military elegies. It contains some classically odic topoi such as the "rapture" (*vostorg*) provoked by the "sound of mountain waterfalls" as well as descriptions of the "free, proud, and half-savage" Teutons that read as a striking anticipation of the romantic cult of the Caucasian mountain dwellers. Batiushkov's description of the Russian advance—"from seas covered with ice / from southern streams, from the waves of the Caspian / . . . from the heights of the Caucasus and the Urals," and so on—also corresponds, in part, to a conventional odic topography. Overall, however, Russia's victory over Napoleon is represented in a manner that is no longer odic. Most strikingly the poem is addressed not to the Russian tsar but to the river Rhine: able to recall the struggle of the Germanic tribes against the Roman Empire, the river is evoked as a repository of historical memory that reaches well beyond the chronologies of the French and Russian states. The role of the river as a detached witness to the *longue durée* of history is precisely mirrored in the closing vision of a Russian cavalryman who stands contemplating its flowing waters: separated from his army, "pensive and alone" and "recalling the river of his native parts," the cavalryman can be usefully read as a marker of how differently the elegy and the ode treat the question of poetry and empire.[29]

While the odic poet was subsumed by the victory he celebrated, the elegiac poet survives that victory in order to reconstitute it subjectively in the realm of his private recollections. A patriot but no longer a panegyrist, the elegiac poet affirms his loyalties sentimentally rather than politically. These sentiments, while not openly subversive in the manner of the Decembrists, strike a subtly dissonant note. In the elegy, memory serves to distance the poet from the historical events he depicts, and the deepening of the poet's own subjectivity corresponds to his detachment from the traditional agents of history, such as the Russian state. Patriotic without being jingoistic, Batiushkov's elegies would provide later poets with a means of reconciling national history with an essentially subjective experience of memory and personal fate. Their tone of distanced engagement would find a striking echo in the poetry of Pushkin and Lermontov.

Pushkin's early elegies deal primarily with the travails of the heart. With the experience of passion comes the draining of vital energies, and these poems hover on the tenuous threshold that separates the poet's lost youth from the precocious onset of infirmity:

> You have sped away, days of my joy!
> You have sped away—I weep against my will,
> And wither on the dark morn of my days.
> (1:240)

One of the most complex of Pushkin's early elegies is "Naezdniki" (The horsemen) (1816), in which the elegiac hero is identified in the third person as a "martial poet" who is about to join a partisan raid, probably against Napoleon's army, alongside his comrades in arms. The hero is described as being "gloomy," "pale," and "carried away by a sad thought." When questioned by his friends about his pensiveness before the impending clash, he replies that he has just "foreseen his own desired end" and regrets only that, on hearing of his death, his beloved "will not sigh in secret." Like Batiushkov's poems of the same period, "Naezdniki" reads as an elegiac transformation of the quintessentially odic theme of war. A fearless bard who had once gloried in the poetry of battle suddenly finds himself identifying more deeply with his private pain than with the cause of the nation. Not mourned by his lover, the elegiac poet must mourn himself, and this moment of self-reflexivity acts to detach him from the collective enterprise of war: he sees his impending death reflected not in history but in the nocturnal landscape, whose "deep sleep" mirrors the "long sleep" of the dead (1:205–7).[30]

The elegy most directly related to Pushkin's southern narrative poems is "Pogaslo dnevnoe svetilo" (The diurnal orb has gone out) (1820). Written onboard a ship sailing from Feodosia to Gurzuf on the Crimean Peninsula, this was the first poem of Pushkin's years of southern exile (1820–24) to be published and the first to assimilate vivid elements of the southern landscape into the elegy's generic framework. Its juxtaposition of sentimental crisis and physical geography closely matches an unfinished cycle of elegies by André Chenier entitled "L'orient," whose "defeated" hero, languishing "under the yoke of a cruel woman," flees to the eastern Mediterranean in the hope of finding "dear liberty" on its shores.[31]

Погасло дневное светило;
На море синее вечерний пал туман.
Шуми, шуми, послушное ветрило,
Волнуйся подо мной, угрюмый океан.
Я вижу берег отдаленный,
Земли полуденной волшебные края;
С волненьем и тоской туда стремлюся я,
Воспоминаньем упоенный . . .
И чувствую: в очах родились слезы вновь;
Душа кипит и замирает;
Мечта знакомая вокруг меня летает;
Я вспомнил прежних лет безумную любовь,
И все, чем я страдал, и все, что сердцу мило,
Желаний и надежд томительный обман . . .
Шуми, шуми, послушное ветрило,
Волнуйся подо мной, угрюмый океан.

(2:7)

The diurnal orb has gone out;
The evening mist has descended on the blue sea.
Rattle, rattle, obedient sail,
Keep churning below me, gloomy ocean.
I see a distant shore,
The magical edges of a southern land;
With agitation and anguish I strive to go there,
Enraptured by a recollection . . .
And I feel: in my eyes tears have once more emerged;
My soul seethes and then becomes numb;
A familiar dream flutters around me;
I have remembered the insane love of past years,
And everything that made me suffer, and everything that was dear to my heart,
The oppressive deception of desires and hopes . . .
Be noisy, be noisy, obedient sail,
Keep churning below me, gloomy ocean.

Pushkin's poem establishes a complex dialectic between nature, consciousness, and time that will become the core of what I shall call the elegiac sublime. The piece opens with an evocation of the Black Sea and the Crimean coastline that becomes the poem's refrain, punctuating the text at rhythmic intervals. The gloomy agitation of the sea functions initially as a mirror of the poet's restless state of mind, suggesting a specular relationship between inner and outer worlds. Yet even as the poet finds himself drawn to the "magical lands" of the south, he is assailed by recollections of past loves, the memories of a "lost youth" consumed by passion. Although he exhorts the ship to carry him far away from "the sad shores / Of his foggy homeland," the poet is unable mentally to discard the burden of the past, and the exotic charms of the Crimean landscape quickly yield to an embittered retelling of the betrayals and injuries suffered back home in the name of love and friendship. The text, then, creates a paradoxical time-space that will repeatedly shift the reader's attention away from the poem's ostensible focus: a present figured spatially as landscape is finally overwhelmed by a past that appears as a function of memory. This hypertrophy of memory is typically elegiac and generally functions within the lyric to enrich but also to complicate the terms of the encounter between mind and nature. The role of time in preventing the mirroring of consciousness in nature should not be underestimated, since it is what prevents elegiac landscape from functioning unproblematically as a *paysage d'âme*. Even as it seeks a sympathetic reflection in the outer world, elegiac consciousness always contains excess (a residue of the past or more rarely a premonition of the future) that nature, history, or the beloved cannot adequately reflect, and it is this failure of reciprocity that precipitates the need for mourning. More than just the elegy's theme, mourning is also its temporal condition, preventing the specular reconciliation of subject and object by introducing the phantasm of an unresolved past or an uncertain future.

Although Pushkin continued to write conventionally intimate poems in the elegiac genre, many of the elegies written during the poet's southern exile move manifestly beyond the already standard theme of dejection toward a starker kind of disillusionment.[32] Even as Pushkin's nonelegiac political verse of the early twenties remains enthusiastically engaged in the great issues of the day such as the Greek uprising or the geopolitical legacy of Napoleon,[33] his elegiac verse of the same years betrays a markedly different orientation. In such pieces as "Ia perezhil svoi zhelaniia" (I have outlived my desires) (1821), "Voina" (War) (1821), "V. F. Raevskomu" (To V. F. Raevskii, beginning "Ty prav, moi drug . . .") (1822), "Kto, volny, vas ostanovil . . ." (Who, o waves, halted you . . .) (1823), "Demon" (The demon) (1823), "Svobody seiatel' pustynnyi" (A solitary sower of freedom) (1823), and "K moriu" (To the sea) (1824), the elegiac topos of amorous despair deepens into a broader disenchantment with politics and the world at large.

In the short confessional piece "Ia perezhil svoi zhelaniia," initially conceived as part of a confessional monologue to be uttered by the hero of *Kavkazskii plennik,* the poet declares himself bereft of his former dreams, leaving only "suffering" to fill his "heart's void" (1:282). Central here is the life of the heart, the nuanced cultivation and profligate squandering of feeling. If the eighteenth-century had viewed the passions (*strasti*) as something to be contained through ethical self-mastery, then the romantic poet understood passion as having no limit other than emotional exhaustion or physical death.[34] It is this very discourse of the heart that also serves, in the elegy, to link love and politics. The drama of passion, with its repetitive cycle of hope and despair, desire and its frustration, creates essentially homologous structures by which to live both private and public life. The poem "Voina" is a case in point. Even as it acclaims the cause of Greek independence, the poem is marked by a powerful current of inner torment, restlessness, and self-doubt. Significantly the elegiac poet feels no need to distinguish his act of political solidarity from the expression of a purely personal need for "strong impressions" to fill his inner void:

> Родишься ль ты во мне, слепая славы страсть,
> Ты, жажда гибели, свирепый жар героев?
> Венок ли мне двойной достанется на часть,
> Кончину ль темную судил мне жребий боев?
> И все умрет со мной: надежды юных дней,
> Священный сердца жар, к высокому стремленье,
> Воспоминание и брата и друзей,
> И мыслей творческих напрасное волненье,
> И ты, и ты, любовь! . . . Ужель ни бранный шум,
> Ни ратные труды, ни ропот гордой славы,
> Ничто не заглушит моих привычных дум?
> (2:32–33)

> Will you arise in me, o blind passion for glory,
> You, thirst for death, the fierce ardor of heroes?
> Will it be my destiny to receive a second wreath,
> Has the lot of battle condemned me to an obscure demise?
> And everything will die with me: the hopes of my young days,
> The sacred ardor of the heart, the aspiration toward the sublime,
> The memory of my brother and my friends,
> And the futile agitation of creative thoughts,
> And you, and you, o love! . . . Can it be that neither the noise of battle,
> Nor martial exertions, nor the murmur of proud glory,
> Nothing will deafen my customary thoughts?

War, like all adventures, is an escape. Russia's potential intervention in the Greek uprising against Ottoman rule is here equated with the lyric hero's "blind passion for glory," whose chief virtue lies in its potential to release the poet from the "sublime" but excessively familiar torments of memory, art, and feeling.[35]

Pushkin's political and metaphysical elegies of 1822 and 1823 move beyond the traditionally elegiac topoi of dejection, sloth, and enervation to express a more radical impasse between poetic consciousness and the world at large. This shift has been generally attributed to Pushkin's disappointment at the defeat of national-liberation movements throughout southern Europe at the hands of the Holy Alliance, in which Russia was a leading player.[36] The success of Tsar Alexander's interventionist foreign policy made clear how far the popular masses of Russia and Europe were from adhering to the poet's ideal of liberty. Dismayed at the triumph of reaction, Pushkin began doubting the efficacy of the poet's political mission and calling into question all positive points of reference. Pushkin flirted only in passing with this nihilism, which found its main expression in "Demon." This powerful lyric dramatizes the encounter between the young poet, still agitated by "sublime thoughts, / Liberty, glory and love / And the inspired arts," and a "malicious genius" who casts doubt on the poet's private hopes and public ideals (2:159).

In dallying however briefly with this spirit of radical negation, the Pushkinian elegy engendered a new kind of literary hero, one fated to exceed his elegiac origins and outlive Pushkin's own interest in the romantic paradigm. Restless and mired in the past, the elegiac hero was unable to entertain a sustained rapport with any *external* manifestation of the sublime, be it in nature, art, the beloved, or the realm of imperial history. This failure itself became contemplated as an object of bereavement and was reabsorbed through the act of mourning into the hero's consciousness, where it would engender an alternative sublime of the passions. Whether private or political (and they were often both), the passions generated a specifically elegiac experience of time, rooted in dreams, memories, and impeded desires. In the historical elegies of Batiushkov and Pushkin, elegiac time served to reformulate the relationship of the poet to the myths of nation and empire.

Batiushkov, we remember, wrote as a patriot but not a panegyrist. As an eyewitness to imperial history, Batiushkov depicted the Napoleonic wars as an object of recollection to be sentimentally recoded as a nostalgic love for the fatherland. Pushkin's historical elegies struck a wider range of responses. Knowing full well that the elegy's plaintive tone could also convey abject submission to authority, Pushkin chose consciously not to follow the influential example of Ovid, the exiled poet of

Augustan Rome. In the poem "Iz pis'ma k Gnedichu" (From a letter to Gnedich) (1821) Pushkin distinguishes the "free voice" of his own pipe which "does not sing flattering hymns of gratitude" to Tsar Alexander from Ovid, who "faint-heartedly dedicated his elegiac lyre" to his "deaf idol" Augustus Caesar (2:35). In Pushkin's hands, then, the historical elegy became a vehicle of dissent or disenchantment. Even as it acquired a political charge, the experience of elegiac passion served to internalize the workings of history, assimilating them as part of the restless drama of the self. Both the libertarian politics of revolt and the closely related politics of disengagement thus resonated as subjective projections of the poet's psyche. In Pushkin's great historical elegy, "Andre Shen'e" (André Chenier) (1825), the poet does succeed in transcending his subjective musings, allowing his fate to acquire the genuine pathos of resistance to tyranny. More often, however, darker passions prevailed, precipitating a narcissistic relapse into an alienated self.

Curiously, the elegiac hero and his relationship to imperial history were not definitively fleshed out in the elegy itself. This was the task of another genre, the narrative poem or *poèma,* modeled by Pushkin on Byron's oriental tales, which he later praised for their "fiery depiction of the passions" but also criticized for allowing the author's identification with the main hero to undermine the structure of the work (7:69). The extended narrative possibilities of the romantic *poèma,* as well as its generic hybridity, facilitated a more charged encounter between the narcissistic premise of elegiac time and the vaster chronologies of nation and empire.

Empire, Elegiac Memory, and the Narrative Poem

Vissarion Belinskii long ago recognized the hero of *Kavkazskii plennik* as embodying the "elegiac ideal of a soul disillusioned with life."[37] As Blagoi put it, in the main figure of the prisoner "the 'gloomy' elegiac image acquired those traits of the era's favorite hero which the critics of Pushkin's time dubbed 'Byronic.'"[38] More recently Pushkin's romantic narrative poems have been defined in structural terms as "the transposing of elegiac principles onto an epic genre."[39] How, then, did the psychological premise and the chronotopic patterns of the romantic elegy impinge on the historical theme of *Kavkazskii plennik,* Pushkin's first and most celebrated account of Russia's imperial presence in the south?[40]

Kavkazskii plennik, we recall, recounts the experiences of a young Russian who has fled the stifling constraints of his cultural milieu only to fall captive to a Circassian tribe in the Northern Caucasus. He languishes in chains, observing the landscape and the customs of the local people, before he is befriended and eventually freed by a Circassian maiden, whose love he is unable to return until she, too, in turn rejects his final entreaty to flee with him. The story ends with the girl's apparent suicide and the hero's return to a Cossack encampment. This tragic encounter, in which aborted love also corresponds to the limits of cultural empathy, is in turn framed by a dedication and an epilogue, both of which function to link the main plotline to its two defining contexts: Pushkin's own exploration of the romantic persona and the realm of political history. The structural relationship of the story to its frames is also one of strategic inversion: while the main story presents the Russian as a captive and hence a victim of the mountain dwellers, the dedication and epilogue together essentially reverse this hierarchy, allowing the poet—and with him the Russian army—to establish poetic and then military control over the mountain dwellers' territory.

Pushkin was himself acutely aware of the structural unwieldiness of his poem. In a letter of 1822 he called its main hero "unsuccessful," although he acknowledged the prisoner to be a significant attempt at representing the modern European psyche, "that indifference to life and its pleasures, that premature aging of the soul which have become the distinguishing features of nineteenth-century youth." While he was more content with his descriptions of Circassian customs and mores, he admitted, in a letter of 1822, that they, too, were a "true *hors d'œuvre*" that was "not connected to anything else" (10:49–50). Even for Pushkin himself, it seems, the poem's emphasis on psychology and locale frequently overshadowed the actual storyline.

Significantly these two elements also correspond to the poem's philosophical thesis, which rehearses—but also tests—the Rousseauistic antinomy of civilization and nature. Called an "apostate from worldly society (*sveta*)" and "a friend of nature (*prirody*)," the hero, we learn, has left behind a Russia he equates with a youth of "ruined hopes, joys and desires," the "memory" of which he "has enclosed in his withered heart" (4:109). Having tasted the heady poison of high society, the hero has fled Russia in search of the "merry phantom of freedom," which he identifies with escaping to a "distant land":

> Свобода! он одной тебя
> Еще искал в пустынном мире.
> Страстями чувства истребя,
> Охолодев к мечтам и к лире,

С волненьем песни он внимал,
Одушевленные тобою,
И с верой, пламенной мольбою
Твой гордый идол обнимал.
(4:109–10)

Freedom! You alone
Did he still seek in the desolate world.
Annihilating his feelings with passions,
Becoming coldly indifferent to his dreams and to his lyre,
He heeded with agitation the songs
Animated by you,
And with faith, a flaming prayer
Embraced your proud idol.

The hero's cult of personal freedom is an attempt at resolving the nature/culture dichotomy that governs the poem as a whole: that which culture denies him, he seeks in nature. Yet it turns out that liberty inhabits an entirely different temporal dimension to nature and culture, and cannot successfully interact with the latter elements. If the present is spatialized as the natural landscape and ethnoscape of the Caucasus, then the past is recollected as the Russian high society in which the hero has squandered his youth. Liberty, by contrast, belongs to a chimerical future—defined by wherever the hero is *not* or by the freedom he does *not* currently enjoy. By definition, the elegiac hero cannot integrate these three spatiotemporal dimensions. As a prisoner, the hero becomes a largely passive witness to their manifestation, an unwilling if sporadically engaged spectator to the alpine scenery and the highland way of life, but equally a restless captive to his memories and to his rather inchoate sense of free will:

Воспомнил юноша свой плен,
Как сна ужасного тревоги,
И слышит: загремели вдруг
Его закованные ноги . . .
Все, все сказал ужасный звук;
Затмилась перед ним природа.
Прости, священная свобода!
Он раб.
(4:103)

The youth remembered his captivity,
Like the anxieties of a terrible dream,

And heard: suddenly
His shackled feet began to rattle . . .
The terrible sound told him everything, everything;
Nature became eclipsed before him.
Farewell, sacred freedom!
He was a slave!

The hero's captivity exacerbates his already pronounced capacity for self-absorption, and his surroundings are only visible to the extent that they illuminate his predicament or reflect his mood. The mountains are sometimes described as "splendid paintings" and at other times as "monotonous peaks"; the hero's attention is sometimes described as "fully drawn to the wondrous people" who hold him prisoner, and at other times he is said to watch their "bloody amusements" with "indifference." The hero's fundamentally erratic capacity to engage in his surroundings has seldom been noted by critics, who have often granted the prisoner a heightened sensitivity to nature.

Clearly we are dealing here with a radically different model for representing what the romantics had called locale (*mestnost'*), as remote as can be from the impersonal odic premise of territorial expansion or even the Decembrist premise of radical civic contestation. In his extensive footnotes to *Kavkazskii plennik,* Pushkin pointedly acknowledged Derzhavin's ode to Count Zubov and Zhukovskii's epistle to Voeikov as his predecessors in describing the majestic landscape of the Caucasus. Yet this act of homage also camouflages Pushkin's break with the tradition. For Lomonosov and Küchelbecker, the orient (and increasingly the Caucasus) functioned primarily as a *political* sign: even where personal revolt was conceivable, its significance was immediately elevated through the prophetic mode to the level of the nation. The poems of Derzhavin and Zhukovskii, by contrast, intimated a sublime more oriented toward nature, one that emerged in the dialectic between the traveler's gaze and the magnificence of the alpine scenery: «Там все является очам / Великолепие творенья!» (There the entire grandeur of creation / Appears before the eyes!) (Zhukovskii quoted by Pushkin, 4:133). Pushkin's poem flirts with both the odic and the natural sublimes but finally appears to be seeking a different solution. While it displays many of the motifs of the then evolving prophetic tradition (the "deathly sleep," etc.), the captive's predicament is finally personal, even narcissistic, and does not lend itself immediately to political appropriation. (It is no coincidence that, although Pushkin's poem was initially popular in Decembrist circles, Küchelbecker would eventually dismiss its main character as "weak and undeveloped," and class him alongside Pushkin's elegiac hero as a "whiner.")[41] While the prisoner enjoys fleeting moments of connectedness or reciprocity with his environment—above all during his final encounter with the Circassian girl—his gaze remains unable to experience the prolonged ecstasy needed to sustain the natural sublime. One might thus disagree with Susan Layton, for whom "the prisoner discovers a kinship with the mountains during his captivity" that corresponds to a "romantic equation between the natural sublime and the traveler's intense inner life."[42] Although the poem abounds in sharply observed natural and ethnographic detail of which Pushkin was rightly proud, the true sublimity of the poem surely lies elsewhere.

If the ode was dominated by *rapture,* we might say that *Kavkazskii plennik* is governed primarily by *longing.* A quintessentially elegiac emotion, the hero's longing frustrates all the conciliatory possibilities offered to him by the plot, be it the love of the Circassian maiden or—what amounts to the same thing—the metaphysical resolution of mind and nature. Elegiac longing seeks out an object that is necessarily absent in the present, be it a lost love or a goal yet to be realized. As S. G. Bocharov observes, the hero's "libertarian impulses cannot come into contact or be reconciled with the surrounding freedom of the mountain dwellers. If the latter is their real life, then the former are his ideal aspirations."[43] Since what the hero seeks cannot be found in the present, he can only keep running, although his goal is less a place than a time other than now. The disjuncture between a spatialized present and a recollected past or anticipated future corresponds thematically to the civilizational gap between nature and culture, the Caucasus and Russia: elegiac consciousness cannot close this gap; it can only mourn it.

The dedicatory opening to the poem, which Pushkin addresses to N. N. Raevskii, reformulates the prisoner's elusive goal of liberty, and the temporal structure of elegiac experience itself, as a problem for the poetic enterprise. While identifying himself closely with the fate of the prisoner (both are "victims of slander," mortified by "love's oppressive dream," and "assailed by persecution"), the poet claims to have "fortified his heart with freedom and patience" and boldly presents his poem as an "offering of the free muse." How has the poet achieved what had so eluded the prisoner? What does the poet's freedom consist of? Nothing perhaps, except a capacity to *recollect and record the past:*

Во дни печальные разлуки
Мои задумчивые звуки
Напоминали мне Кавказ,
Где пасмурный Бешту, пустынник величавый,
Аулов и полей властитель пятиглавый,
Был новый для меня Парнас.
Забуду ли его кремнистые вершины,
Гремучие ключи, увядшие равнины,
Пустыни знойные, края, где ты со мной
Делил души младые впечатленья;
. . . .
Ты здесь найдешь *воспоминанья,*
Быть может, милых сердцу дней,
Противуречия страстей,
Мечты знакомые, знакомые страдания
И тайный глас души моей.
(4:105–6; my emphasis)

In the sad days of separation
My pensive sounds
Would *remind* me of the Caucasus,
Where the gloomy Beshtu, majestic hermit,
Five-headed master of auls and fields,
Was for me a new Parnassus.
Will I *forget* its flinty heights,
Its thunderous streams, its withered valleys,
Its sultry deserts, places where you
Shared with me the soul's youthful impressions;
. . . .
You will find here *recollections,*
Of days that were perhaps close to your heart,
The contradictions of passions,
Familiar dreams, familiar sufferings
And the secret voice of my soul.

The poet here invites Raevskii, and with him the reader, to reevaluate elegiac longing, the "contradictions of passions," as a fundamentally valid mode of experience. What the prisoner could contemplate only fleetingly can be experienced retrospectively through the act of poetic recollection. The prisoner's existential predicament is thus viewed by the poet as a positive means of phantasmic appropriation, the very stuff of poetry. As an object of memory rather than of sight, the natural sublimity of the Caucasus is suddenly able to be recuperated, albeit in the evanescent terms of elegiac experience.[44]

In the famous epilogue to *Kavkazskii plennik,* almost as controversial today as it was in 1822, the elegiac recovery of time and place is finally related to—or at least juxtaposed alongside—the historical fact of Russian imperial expansion. The epilogue begins by invoking the elegiac muse, called the "light friend of reverie," as well as the "goddess of songs and story, / filled with recollections" (4:113). Flying to the "confines of Asia" the Muse relives the paradoxical condition of the main hero and of the poem as a whole: in "ripping off (*sryvala*) the wild flowers of the Caucasus" for her wreath, she symbolically reenacts the history of Russian conquest shortly to be celebrated in the epilogue, but in being "captivated" (*ee pleniala*) by the "severe adornments" of the warlike Caucasian tribes, she becomes, like the hero, a "captive" of the Caucasus. From the elegiac mode of longing and recollection, and its narrative embodiment in the hero's captivity, the epilogue abruptly shifts to a confident prediction of Russia's final conquest of the Caucasus:

Богиня песен и рассказа,
Воспоминания полна,
Быть может, повторит она
Преданья грозного Кавказа;
Расскажет повесть дальних стран,
Мстислава древний поединок,
Измены, гибель россиян
На лоне мстительных грузинок;
И воспою тот славный час,
Когда, почуя бой кровавый,
На негодующий Кавказ
Подъялся наш орел двуглавый;
Когда на Тереке седом
Впервые грянул битвы гром
И грохот русских барабанов,
И в сече, с дерзостным челом,
Явился пылкий Цициянов;
Тебя я воспою, герой,
О Котляревский, бич Кавказа!
Куда ни мчался ты грозой—
Твой ход, как черная зараза,
Губил, ничтожил племена.
(4:129–30)

The goddess of songs and story,
Filled with memories,
Perhaps she will repeat
The legends of the menacing Caucasus;

[She] will tell a story of distant countries,
The ancient duel of Mstislav,
The betrayals, the disastrous fate of Russians
On the lap of vengeful Georgian women;
And I will celebrate the glorious hour,
When, sensing a bloody battle,
Our two-headed eagle rose up
Against the indignant Caucasus;
When on the gray Terek
The thunder of battle first roared
And the clamor of Russian drums,
And in the midst of the slaughter, with an audacious brow,
The fiery Tsitsianov appeared;
You I will celebrate, o hero,
O Kotliarevskii, scourge of the Caucasus!
Wherever you race like a storm—
Your passage, like a black plague,
Ruined and destroyed tribes . . .

These extraordinary lines have struck generations of readers as aesthetically aberrant if not ideologically abhorrent. We need only recall Prince Viazemskii's shocked insistence, on reading these lines, that poetry should never stoop to becoming the "ally of butchers," a "celebration of carnage." Strikingly Viazemskii linked his viscerally expressed *political* rejection of Pushkin's apparent embrace of imperialist ideology to his perception of the epilogue's *aesthetic* dissonance: "Such rapture (*vostorg*)," he added, "is a real anachronism."[45] Tomashevskii formulated this "anachronistic rapture" more precisely when he called the epilogue's tone "purely odic," "almost Lomonosovian."[46]

While Viazemskii saw the epilogue as a shameful capitulation to the state's cult of empire, Soviet-era critics were careful to couch their conclusions in more philosophical terms. If *Kavkazskii plennik* is a poetic dramatization of the conflict between European high society and Caucasian "nature," then the epilogue has been seen as presenting an "essential corrective" to the Rousseau-like idealization of primitive society (Tomashevskii),[47] suggesting the "historical necessity" of the triumph of civilization (Blagoi),[48] or even a "harmonious synthesis of naturalness and culture" to be achieved through Russia's military annexation of the Caucasus (Gurevich).[49] For all its sensitivity to the generic hybridity of the poem, Soviet philology ultimately remained imprisoned by the need to legitimate two related narratives of progress: first, the expansion of the Russian state and, second, Pushkin's equally inevitable maturation beyond Byronic romanticism toward a realistic appraisal of human psychology and Russian history. In Zhirmunskii's words, the "objective, supraindividual, state-related historical themes in the epilogue to a lyric-narrative poem that has a novelistic and emotionally coloured plot as well as a private, intimate source of inspiration illustrate best of all which paths Pushkin's art would have to take once it overcame the influence of Byron."[50]

Western scholars have evinced a greater skepticism about the moral and cognitive compass deployed either by Pushkin or his hero in appraising the landscape and people of the Caucasus. Stephanie Sandler has noted suggestively that "the desire to see realism in this quintessentially romantic poem is itself suspect: one of the poem's themes, and hence part of its epistemological attitude, is the consequences of extreme subjectivity." This narcissism is externalized, for Sandler, in gendered terms, as a "will to domination" that resonates both in the epilogue and in the "poem's readiness to use a Circassian woman to liberate a Russian man."[51] Sandler's reading is particularly useful for underlining the masculinist logic that links the homosocial world of the dedication, the Circassian maiden's suicide in the main story, and the imperial violence depicted in the epilogue. One wonders, however, if the prisoner's subjectivity displays nothing more than a "will to domination" that readily complements the imperial project. By contrast, Susan Layton has suggested that, despite its epilogue, *Kavkazskii plennik* seeks rather to deflect attention away from empire toward a "pacific and enriching Russian contact with alpine wilderness. . . . In Pushkin's time . . . romantic poetry's cherished theme of Russian communion with nature averted the eye from military conquest."[52]

I would suggest that, taken as a whole, *Kavkazskii plennik* neither avoids nor simply underwrites the imperial project. Whatever the ideological premise of the epilogue, it is refracted through a complex relationship to the generic forms within and alongside which it functions. Before we examine this correlation of form and content, let us begin by noting the clear evidence confirming Pushkin's support for the Russian conquest of the Caucasus as a bloody but ultimately benign necessity. In a letter of 1820 to his brother, Pushkin wrote:

> The Caucasian region, the torrid boundary of Asia, arouses interest in all respects. Ermolov has filled it with his name and beneficent genius. The savage Circassians have become timorous; their ancient audacity is disappearing. The roads are becoming less dangerous by the hour, and the numerous convoys are becoming superfluous. It is to be hoped that this conquered

> land, which until now has brought no real benefit to Russia, will soon form a bridge between us and the Persians for safe trading, that it will not be an obstacle to us in future wars—and that perhaps we shall carry out Napoleon's chimerical plan of conquering India. (10:17–18)

However deluded in their complacent optimism, these views were commonplaces of the time and would have been willingly echoed by most of Pushkin's contemporaries, both in official circles and in the progressive camp of the Decembrists. The hero's Byronic flight from European civilization, it seems, is not inimical to the civilizing mission of the Russian imperial state: on the contrary, one might argue that the pervasive Russian romantic paradigm of exile (*izgnanie*), whether in Pushkin or Lermontov, functions as a deeply alienated biographical correlative to imperial expansion.

Yet it remains to be seen how—and even whether—Pushkin's imperialist convictions became concretely embodied in literary form. To begin with, it is difficult to view the epilogue as an aesthetically coherent whole. Its presiding muse, in fact, changes generic allegiance several times, beginning in the elegiac vein, then shifting to the mode of epic narrative (in which she "will perhaps repeat the legends [*predan'ia*] of the dreaded Caucasus") and then abruptly giving way again to a first person ("*ia* vospoiu") that seems to reclaim the Lomonosovian tradition of the ceremonial ode. These shifts are numerous and abrupt: the epilogue's triumphant enumeration of Russian military leaders, for example, is suddenly interrupted by several verses to the retired General Kotliarevskii where he is addressed as an elegiac hero who is "weary of the world" and "not gladdened by war," even as the subsequent line—"But lo—the East raises a howl!"—is purely odic (4:130).

The epilogue, then, contaminates two fundamentally distinct forms of poetic—and political—appropriation. Although the historical vision of these lines corresponds to the traditional rhetoric of the odic sublime, it is structurally embedded in an elegiac time-space that is not easily reconciled to imperial ideology. We have already seen that the chronotope of the prisoner's tale consisted of a remembered past and a desired future both of which finally overshadow the present, which is in turn figured spatially as landscape and ethnoscape. The same disjuncture between the past, the future, and the present is reproduced in the epilogue as well. Containing almost no verbs in the present tense, the epilogue is mostly dominated by the imperfective past and the perfective future. Even as it revives the odic theme of empire, the epilogue relegates its actual occurrence to the past and its poetic execution to a strangely receding future: Pushkin does not, for example, say "I celebrate" but "I *will* celebrate" (*ia vospoiu*) the "glorious hour" of Russian conquest. Similarly the closing lines of the poem, in which the mountain dwellers are warned that their defeat at the hands of the Russian forces will one day be related by "the obscure rumors of legend," resound like a chilling but somewhat remote threat. As Susi Frank has noted in a recent and subtle article:

> Like the dedication before them, both parts of the epilogue refer to the Caucasus in the mode of remembrance. On the one hand, the muse's rapture seems to have abated and to belong to the past; on the other hand, the peoples of the Caucasus, depicted here as militantly free, belong to the realm of legend, as do the Tatars with whom they are compared. As a consequence the Caucasus as an exotic orientalist theme appears not only firmly established for Russian literature but also as something the author effectively dismisses. The elegiac mood of the dedication was already the first indication of this. His memory now preserves only "predan'ia," such as the story, just recounted, of the prisoner.[53]

Pushkin never did write an ode or a work in any other genre celebrating Russia's Caucasian adventure. Even his second journey to the Caucasus of 1829, during which he joined a military expedition against Turkey led by General Paskevich, produced only the strangely dispassionate *Journey to Arzrum,* whose preface explicitly forestalls an anticipated attack on Pushkin's failure as an inspired odic or epic chronicler of war: "To *seek inspiration* has always seemed to me to be an amusing and absurd caprice: inspiration cannot be sought out, it must find the poet by itself. For me to go to a war with the intention of celebrating its future exploits would, on the one hand, be too vain, and, on the other hand, too unseemly. I do not get involved in military matters. This is not my affair" (6:640). As in his critique of Küchelbecker, Pushkin here distinguishes inspiration (*vdokhnovenie*) from rapture (*vostorg*): whereas rapture is an index of political commitment, inspiration is a measure of artistic freedom.

Even as they flirt with the odic mode of the sublime, Pushkin's romantic works clearly prefer an elegiac appropriation of history that psychologizes the problem of empire. This dynamic does not deflect history onto nature, as has often been suggested, but rather onto the mental plane of recollection or anticipation. Pushkin's other southern *poèmy* closely mirror the formal orientation I have just outlined. In the closing lines of *Bakhchisaraiskii fontan* (The fountain of Bakhchisarai) (1823) the poet wonders when he "will once more see / the merry shores of the Salgir" and "come upon the slopes of the mountains by the sea, / filled with secret memories" (4:194), while the epilogue to *Tsygany* (The gypsies) (1824), although less strident, still mirrors *Kavkazskii plennik* in the way it raises the theme of imperial conquest only to have it recede into elegiac time:

Волшебной силой песнопенья
В туманной памяти моей
Так оживляются виденья
То светлых, то печальных дней.

В стране, где долго, долго брани
Ужасный гул не умолкал,
Где повелительные грани
Стамбулу русский указал,
Где старый наш орел двуглавый
Еще шумит минувшей славой. . . . .
(4:235)

Through the magic force of song
In my foggy memory
Visions thus revive
Of bright or of sad days.

In a land where for a long, long time
The terrible din of battle did not fall silent,
Where commanding borders
Were shown to Istanbul by the Russian,
Where our old two-headed eagle
Still resounds with its past glory.

Pushkin's romantic *poèmy* were the first investigation of empire in the Russian poetic tradition to break in a significant way with the odic legacy. The powerful elegiac substratum of the narrative poem allowed for the imperial theme to be appraised as a psychological dilemma. Elegiac consciousness did not question the necessity of empire, but nor could it identify completely with its victories: in this lies the essential difference, for our purposes, between the ode and the elegy. In the ode the lyric subject was subsumed by and hence subordinated to the sublime spectacle of history, thus permitting an impersonal identification with empire. In reversing the hierarchy of subject and object, and radically expanding the realm of the former, the elegy effectively abolished the impersonal premise of odic identification, which persisted even in the "prophetic" topos of the Decembrists. In its place the elegy elaborated a new self, restless but enervated, disillusioned but too paralyzed by doubt and self-love to offer a coherent challenge to the present. Yet precisely through its alienated introspection, the elegy was able to intimate a new subjective identity for the Russian poet, one marked by an increasing ambivalence toward the imperial state. The paradoxes of elegiac destiny were vividly outlined by the fate of Pushkin's prisoner. Fleeing the repressive constraints of the metropolis only to find his life journey still determined by the expansionist policies of the state and the native resistance they engendered, the prisoner uncannily anticipated the trajectory of Mikhail Lermontov, the greatest of the Russian romantic poets.

Lermontov and the Politics of Elegiac Identity

Unlike the baldly stated enthusiasms of the ode, the politics of elegiac identity are not always easily read. The generic theme of elegiac mourning could and did occasionally lead to an open denunciation of the existing order. This tendency typified the historical or "civic" elegy, which, during the 1830s, became increasingly informed by elements of satirical invective. More typically, however, the elegy would turn away from the outside world to examine the self for the traces left by the vicissitudes of private emotion and historical change.

The poetry of Mikhail Lermontov (1814–1841) can be read as the most consistently—and complexly—elegiac response to empire ever formulated by a Russian poet. Lermontov wrote at a time when the classical system of genre classification had essentially collapsed. Among his juvenilia we find only two poems that are clearly labeled elegies, both of which are exercises in the "gloomy" tradition of Batiushkov and Zhukovskii.[54] Although no longer explicitly identified as such, an elegiac mood can nonetheless be said to permeate Lermontov's work from an early age, constituting an essential aspect of his lyric self. Lermontov's elegiac sensibility quickly acquired its own defining traits. If the classical Russian elegy had delineated a hero who was private without being unique, Lermontov, by contrast, strove to individuate a consistent and recognizable lyric persona, molded by a specific fate rather than by generic convention. His early poem "Kavkaz" (The Caucasus) (1830) is a case in point:

Хотя я судьбой на заре моих дней,
О южные горы, отторгнут от вас,
Чтоб вечно их помнить, там надо быть раз:
Как сладкую песню отчизны моей,
  Люблю я Кавказ.

В младенческих летах я мать потерял.
Но мнилось, что в розовый вечера час
Та степь повторяла мне памятный глас.
  Люблю я Кавказ.

Я счастлив был с вами, ущелия гор;
Пять лет пронеслось: все тоскую по вас.
Там видел я пару божественных глаз;
И сердце лепечет, воспомня тот взор:
  Люблю я Кавказ! . . . .

(1:75)

Although on the dawn of my days,
O southern hills, I was cut off from you by fate,
In order to remember them eternally, one has to be there once:
Like the sweet song of my fatherland,
  I love the Caucasus.

In my youthful years I lost my mother.
But it seemed that in the rosy hour of evening
That steppe would repeat to me her memorable voice.
  I love the Caucasus.

I was happy to be with you, ravines of the hills;
Five years have passed; I still long for you.
There I saw a pair of divine eyes;
And the heart stammers, recalling that gaze:
  I love the Caucasus!

In these lines elegiac memory delineates the traditional motifs of recollected plenitude and present privation but attributes them to concrete events in the poet's biography, such as the death of his mother and a childhood journey to the Caucasus which is precisely dated as having taken place "five years ago." Although still irrevocable, time can now be quantified, marking the distance between the moment of writing and a feminine Edenic space associated with maternal sustenance and the awkward awakening of adolescent desire.

Nostalgia for a lost homeland, be it the rural idyll of the family estate or an imagined second home situated in the Caucasus, the natural world, childhood, or with God and the angels in heaven, constitutes one aspect of a world that appears radically polarized in the poet's eyes. Lermontov's poetic thinking rests on the irresolvable antinomies of good and evil, earth and sky, happiness and suffering, ephemeral peace and turbulent activity. Yearning for a wholeness denied him by society and unable to secure any harmony within himself, the Lermontovian hero vacillates between a nostalgia for past wholeness and a more active, "demonic" form of resistance to the present, expressed in Byronic terms as an inchoate and ultimately futile revolt against social conventions and the workings of fate. Lermontov's mature elegies, such as "Evreiskaia melodiia" (Hebrew melody) (1836), "Gliazhu na budushchnost' s boiazn'iu" (I look at the future with fear) (1837–38), "Kak chasto, pestroiu tolpoiu okruzhen" (How often, surrounded by a motley crowd) (1840), or "I skushno, i grustno, i nekomu ruku podat'" (I'm both bored and sad, and there's no one to proffer my hand) (1840) move beyond conventional feelings of dejection to reach a starkly pessimistic sense of the poet's place in a world that is revealed to be "an empty and silly joke" (1:468). No longer just an unrequited lover, the poet is an outcast, "a criminal before his execution" (1:435), who responds defiantly to the world's indifference with an "iron verse / drenched in bitterness and malice" (1:467).

The classical "gloomy" elegy clearly could not satisfy the psychological complexity evinced by Lermontov's lyric persona, characterized by a greater capacity for self-analysis, a sharper sense of the social and metaphysical roots of evil, and an acute historical awareness of his generation as the first to have matured in the stagnant aftermath of the Decembrist revolt. From his earliest years, Lermontov also cultivated the historical elegy or *duma,* a genre associated with the Decembrist Ryleev and the tradition of civic poetry.[55] Lermontov's celebrated "Smert' poèta" (Death of a poet) (1837), the poem that brought him instant notoriety, transforms the elegiac task of mourning Pushkin's death into a political denunciation of the fallen poet's assassins. Not unlike "Smert' poèta" in this respect is the poem "Duma" (1838), a tirade whose powerful strain of invective serves effectively to historicize elegiac consciousness. The familiar elegiac traits of inaction, doubt, indifference, the premature loss of vital energy, and the incapacity to feel are all acknowledged by the poet as traits of "our generation," whose ashes will be mocked by posterity "with the severity of a judge and citizen" (1:442–43). This historical contextualization of the elegiac predicament as generational is typical of a deeper shift in Lermontov's poetics. In L. G. Frizman's words: "The elegies Lermontov wrote in the second half of the 1830s contain a new quality, an unprecedented phenomenon that we can call the Lermontovian stage in the history of the Russian elegy: with Lermontov the amorous, political, and philosophical elegies all fuse into one."[56]

Lermontov was to pay a high price for politicizing the elegy: as punishment for circulating his incendiary poem on Pushkin's death, the poet was exiled by Tsar Nicholas to the Caucasus in 1837, where he spent a year. In 1840 another punitive transfer obliged Lermontov to serve in an army regiment stationed in the Caucasus. Compelled to take part in military expeditions against the mountain dwellers, he quickly distinguished himself through his courage in battle but was refused a medal by the tsar. In quantitative terms, the lyric verse directly inspired by Lermontov's sojourns in the Caucasus is dramatically overshadowed by the narrative poems set in the same region, some of which predate even his first exile of 1837.[57] Nevertheless, Lermontov's lyric poetry of the time subtly captures the paradoxes of his own predicament as the agent of a state that regarded him with suspicious disdain.

Lermontov's mature verse on the Caucasus embraces two or three distinct strains. A "folkloric" strain consists of ballads and other lyrics whose chief conceit involves anthropomorphizing elements of the Caucasian landscape. Rivers, cliffs, clouds, and mountains converse freely in these poems, generating dialogues that read as brooding parables on the themes of violent death, erotic longing, and imperial encroachment.[58] A second properly elegiac strain consists of three fine poems written between 1837 and 1841, all of which deal with the poet's fear of dying in battle outside his homeland. The classic elegiac topos of untimely death, already explored in the military context by Batiushkov and Pushkin, here acquires a particular poignancy. In "Spesha na sever izdaleka" (Hastening northward from afar) (1837) the poet addresses Mount Kazbek as he crosses the Caucasus on his way back to Russia:

Но есть еще одно желание!
Боюсь сказать!—душа дрожит!
Что, если я со дня изгнания
Совсем на родине забыт! . . .
. . . .
Или среди могил холодных
Я наступлю на прах родной
Тех добрых, пылких, благородных,
Деливших молодость со мной?
О если так! своей метелью,
Казбек, засыпь меня скорей
И прах бездомный по ущелью
Без сожаления развей.

(1:432–33)

But there is one more desire!
I'm frightened to say it!—My soul trembles!
What if since the day of my exile
I have been forgotten in my homeland! . . .
. . . .
Or will I step among cold graves
Upon the native ashes
Of those fine, ardent, noble ones
Who shared their youth with me?
O, if that is so
Then Kazbek, bury me quickly
With your snowstorm
And scatter without regret
My homeless ashes along the ravine.

These lines convey the poet's fear that the coercive obligations of state service have severed the organic bond that ties him to his native land. To live unremembered is equivalent to dying without the rites of mourning and burial: when the circuit of memory that binds a community is severed, the experience of homecoming itself becomes invalid. In mourning the anticipated failure of the poet's peers to mourn him, "Hastening northward from afar" not only conveys the capacity of empire to destroy a sense of national community but also reads as a metapoetic reflection on the limited efficacy of elegiac bereavement in the face of history.

A thematically related poem of 1839, "Pamiati A. I. O[doevsko]go" (To the memory of A. I. Odoevskii), ponders the "unknown grave" of the Decembrist poet Aleksandr Odoevskii (1802–1839), who had been transferred from Siberian exile to active service in the Caucasus only to perish of malaria during a military expedition on the shores of the Black Sea. Just as Odoevskii's verse would have provided Lermontov with a model of post-Decembrist elegiac despair, so Odoevskii's fate must have also brought home to Lermontov the high cost of using imperial war as a means of repressing domestic dissent.[59] Although Lermontov's elegy successfully buries Odoevskii's heart in the "mute graveyard" of the poet's memory, it is unable to rescue Odoevskii's body, which is once more effectively absorbed into the sublime landscape of the Caucasus (1:461–63). Lermontov's Caucasian verse is permeated by a fear that even a posthumous homecoming may no longer be possible for the poet-soldier. Burial, be it of bodies or of memories, is a symbolic act reconciling the dead and the living and resolving the materiality of death through the promise of transcendence. For Lermontov, it also serves the elusive goal of reconciling the imperial periphery with the motherland. If the rites of mourning and burial are a mark of nostalgia for organic national community, then the abandoned or unburied body suggests the symbolic dislocation of nationhood effected by the imperial state.

The last of Lermontov's Caucasian elegies, and one of his greatest poems, is "Son" (1841), which I have already cited earlier in this chapter as part of the chain of "prophetic" poems that stretches back to Derzhavin's "Na vziatie Izmaila." Here the poet-soldier situates his dying body in a valley of Daghestan. In describing the last moments of the soldier's life—or perhaps the first moments after his death—the poem dramatically straddles a liminal zone where the brute materiality of a wounded body coexists with the still vivid dream-life of a fading consciousness. Lying unburied in a foreign land, the poet-soldier imagines his beloved back home in the Russian heartland, who in turn dreams of him already dead, a "familiar corpse" that lies bleeding in a Daghestani valley:

И снился мне сияющий огнями
Вечерний пир в родимой стороне.
Меж юных жен, увенчанных цветами,
Шел разговор веселый обо мне.

Но в раговор веселый не вступая,
сидела там задумчива одна,
И в грустный сон душа ее младая
Бог знает чем была погружена;

И снилась ей долина Дагестана;
Знакомый труп лежал в долине той;
В его груди дымясь чернела рана,
И кровь лилась хладеющей струей.
(1:530)

And I dreamt of an evening feast gleaming with lights
In my native land.
Young women, their hair wreathed in flowers,
Were talking merrily about me.

But without entering into the merry talk,
One woman sat pensively,
And her young soul was plunged into a sad dream
By God knows what force;

And she dreamt of the valley of Daghestan;
A familiar corpse lay in that valley;
In its heart a wound was turning black,
And blood poured out of it in a cold stream.

The elegiac circuit of recollection that would ideally bind the poet to his loved one serves once more as the tenuous link between nation and empire, the authentic rhythms and human collectivity of rural Russia, on the one hand, and the constraints of the state and military service, on the other. As in the poem to Odoevskii, empire is what impedes the poet's homecoming: killed for and yet abandoned by the imperial cause, the poet's body remains unburied, destined to decompose into the land it fought to occupy.

Although "Son" does not overtly thematize the poet as prophet, it is, in fact, in close dialogue with the prophetic tradition in Russian poetry. We have already noted the vital presence of common motifs and imagery linking all the poems in the tradition: «Как *труп* в пустыне я *лежал*» (Like a corpse I lay in the desert) and «Над ним летает *смертный сон*» (Above him flew a deadly sleep) says Pushkin in "Prorok" and in the opening lines of *Kavkazskii plennik;* «Знакомый *труп лежал* в долине той» (A familar corpse lay in that valley) and «Но спал я *мертвым сном*» (But I slept a deadly sleep) replies Lermontov. "Son" is, in fact, a subtle pastiche, and its unsettling effect on the reader can be partly attributed to the way it combines the first-person perspective of "Prorok" with the third-person narrative that is *Kavkazskii plennik.* Just as the desert landscape of the former and the craggy peaks of the latter are fused in "Son" into a sunburned mountain valley, so the intense solitary "I" of the first lines is inverted into the more distanced vision of the poet who appears in a dream as a "familiar corpse" to his beloved.

In returning explicitly to the oriental landscape of imperial war that was Derzhavin's original point of departure in the Izmail ode, "Son" also serves to *rehistoricize* the figure of the prophet that had become symbolically abstracted in Pushkin's verse: where a seraph had thrust a burning coal into the prophet's breast, we now find a soldier mortally wounded by a bullet. In converting the sublime command of God into an effect of the imperial state, the poem provides further evidence that the prophetic tradition in Russian verse remains consistently, if subtly, within the orbit of the imperial sublime. Indeed, Lermontov's poem might be read as the elegiac end point of the prophetic tradition. As in the past, the fate of the poet-prophet still asks to be read allegorically, as an embodiment of the nation's destiny. Yet where the poet had previously been galvanized by the force of the sublime to become a prophetic vehicle for national renewal, he now simply dies, clinging to the limited solace of mourning and being mourned.

This stark conclusion is even more dramatically confirmed by a handful of late lyric poems by Lermontov that are already post-elegiac and that have been cited by numerous critics as the markings of a new realist or democratic tendency whose development was truncated by the poet's fittingly untimely death at the age of twenty-six.[60] "Valerik" and "Zaveshchanie" (Testament), both written in 1840, are presented by the lyric hero as "artless tales" of the Caucasian war, whose prosaic irony and conversational cadences serve to demystify the heroism of death in battle. Stressing the experiential gap between the lot of the ordinary soldier and the pampered lives of the Russian elite, "Valerik" provides a grimly unadorned account of death and dying in order to strip imperial war of its ideological rationale. Addressing a predictably unfeeling woman from the Petersburg *beau monde,* Lermontov muses:

> . . . И вы едва ли
> Вблизи когда—нибудь видали,
> Как умирают. Дай вам Бог
> И не видать. . . .
>
> (1:504)

> You would have hardly
> Ever seen from close at hand
> How people die. God grant
> You never will. . . .

Remote from the retrospective distortions and biased projections of military strategists and historians, the raw experience of seeing death "close up" impels the poet to pose the scandalous question of why "pitiful man" should fight wars at all when "there is enough space under the heavens for everyone" (1:503–4).[61] Lermontov's use of the phenomenology of dying as a critique of war strikingly anticipates Tolstoi's great epiphanies of death in battle: together they constitute a post-romantic tradition that insisted on the futility of war even as it affirms the simple courage of the Russian soldier.[62]

Tolstoi's "prosaicization" of the sublime falls well beyond the limits of this book. For all his declared hostility toward romanticism, Tolstoi nevertheless shared a crucial premise of the Russian elegiac tradition to which I must now finally turn. In figuring the Russian hero as captive, Pushkin's *Kavkazskii plennik* launched a pervasive myth that would survive intact into the twentieth century.[63] This myth represented Russians as victims rather than aggressors, passive hostages to the violence of the imperial state as well as to the resistance it provoked. In place of the binary opposition of colonizer and colonized, the captive myth aligned the Russian artist initially with "nature" and increasingly with the "people," situating them in implicit opposition to the Russian state no less than to the colonized mountain dwellers. This tripartite opposition was already palpable in the fate of the prisoner, who was compelled to escape *both* the suffocating constraints of Russian society *and* his imprisonment at the hands of the Circassians.

Owing much to the elegiac cult of enfeeblement and loss, the myth of the captive fleshed out one important aspect of what might be called the politics of elegiac identity. Internalizing the violence of imperial conflict without being able to identify unequivocally—"odically"—with the victors, the captive would even begin to see in the defeat of the mountain dwellers an elegiac metaphor for his own political impotence. Lermontov's programmatic lyric "Poèt" (The poet) (1838), written after his first exile to the Caucasus, is the clearest example I know of this tendency:

Отделкой золотой блистает мой кинжал;
  Клинок надежный, без порока;
Булат его хранит таинственный закал—
  Наследье бранного востока.
. . . .
Теперь родных ножон, избитых на войне,
  Лишен героя спутник бедный;
Игрушкой золотой он блещет на стене—
  Увы, бесславный и безвредный!
(1:448–49)

My dagger gleams with a gold finish;
  Its blade is trustworthy and flawless;
Its steel has kept a mysterious temper—
  A legacy of the martial east.
. . . .
But now deprived of its own scabbard worn out in battle,
  Is my hero's poor companion;
It gleams on the wall, like a golden toy—
  Alas, inglorious and harmless!

"Poèt" is essentially an extended simile whose first half involves a tale of transferred ownership: a dagger won by a Cossack in battle from a mountain dweller and then purchased by the poet now hangs, an innocuous trophy, on a wall. The story of the mountain dweller's defeat and the dagger's reduction to decorative impotence is then presented as analogous to the poet's own loss of authority in the modern age:

В наш век изнеженный не так ли ты, поэт,
  Свое утратил назначенье,
На злато променяв ту власть, которой свет
  Внимал в немом благоговенье?
. . . .
Проснешься ли опять, осмеянный пророк?
  Иль никогда на голос мщенья
Из золотых ножон не вырвешь свой клинок,
  Покрытый ржавчиной презренья?
(1:449)

In our pampered age, have you, poet, not similarly
  Lost your mission?
Having exchanged for gold that power which the world
  Heeded in mute veneration?
. . . .
Will you awaken again, mocked prophet?
  Or, responding to the voice of vengeance,
Will you never rip your blade out of its golden scabbard,
  A blade covered with the rust of contempt?

In these lines the conquest of the east becomes a metaphor for the poet-prophet's own political emasculation within Russian society. It is important to note that this alienated identification with the mountain dweller was always partial and never implied an expression of political solidarity on the part of the Russian artist. Even while admiring the mountain dwellers' attachment to freedom, the Russian captive remained an ambivalent symbol of the very state he fled: just as his captivity was a condition of the mountain dwellers' liberty, so his release anticipated the mountain dwellers' subjugation by the Russian state.

This partial "elegiac" identification of the Russian artist with the native mountain dweller found its most detailed and sympathetic elaboration in the myth of the Noble Savage. The native counterpart to the Russian captive, the Noble Savage dominates many of Lermontov's narrative poems.[64] Often a deracinated member of the North Caucasian (Circassian or Daghestani) gentry, the Noble Savage is typically an *abrek*, an outlaw or outcast who roams the ill-defined boundary that separates freedom from utter lawlessness. Inspired by the native custom of vendetta to a personal or political war of revenge, the actions of the savage quickly exceed the logic of either personal grievance or political resistance. Since his struggle is finally against all codified norms, the savage resorts to acts of random violence. A metaphysical affirmation of his freedom, these acts finally alienate him from the constraints of his native culture no less than those of the Russian state. The Noble Savage thus often becomes a political turncoat or at least a cultural hybrid. Lermontov's hero, Izmail-Bei, is a case in point. Having lived among the Russians and been temporarily allied to them, Izmail finds that his partial identification with the enemy only deepens his sense of non-belonging:

«Ты знаешь, верно, что служил
В российском войске Измаил;
Но, образованный, меж нами
Родными бредил он полями,
И всё черкес в нем виден был.
В пирах и битвах отличался
Он перед всеми! Томный взгляд
Восточной негой отзывался:
Для наших женщин был он яд!»
(2:207)

"You probably know that
Izmail served in a Russian regiment;
But [though] educated, among us
He would dream of his native fields,
And the Circassian was always visible in him.
In feasts and battles he stood out
Among everyone! His languid gaze
Was redolent of eastern voluptuousness:
He was poison for our women!"

From this derives the semantic indeterminacy of the Noble Savage: poised on the threshold between Russia and the Caucasus, constraint and freedom, culture and nature, law and crime, his life cannot generate an ideologically coherent message. His revolt is both too personal and too universal; in either case its politics are thereby muted. The literary figure that most eloquently embodied resistance to Russian imperial encroachment thus remains politically ambiguous: tellingly, Izmail Bei—like Tolstoi's Haji Murat after him—perishes at the hands of his own people. Although arguably a victim of empire, the Noble Savage was not primarily a figure of anticolonial protest. He is better read as a native variant of the romantic hero, an allegorical screen on which the Russian gentry writer could project, and deflect, his own political alienation. If the captive embodied the political impotence of the Russian intellectual, then the stubborn but futile libertarianism of the Noble Savage embodied his worthy but misdirected efforts to resist.

Quoting Lermontov's late quasi-elegy "Rodina" (The motherland) (1841), in which the poet declares his indifference to "glory purchased with blood" and a repressive peace "filled with arrogant confidence," Efim Etkind recently concluded that, unlike Pushkin, Lermontov did not write "even one work that celebrated . . . the triumph of imperial might, the grandeur of Peter, the beauty of Petersburg, the victory of the Russian people." Lermontov, he concludes, felt close "not to the state, not to history, but to nature and the natural way of life of the people."[65] Such a conclusion, however, seems too unilateral, and ignores a poem like "Spor" (A quarrel) (1841), in whose account of Russian civilization encroaching on Caucasian nature the critic Pumpianskii heard "an echo of the old ode."[66] Nor does it do justice to the following lines, taken from *Izmail-Bei:*

> Какие степи, горы и моря
> Оружию славян сопротивлялись?
> И где веленью русского царя
> Измена и вражда не покорялись?
> Смирись, черкес! и запад и восток,
> Быть может, скоро твой разделит рок.
> Настанет час—и скажешь сам надменно:
> Пускай я раб, но раб царя вселенной!
> (2:215–16)

> What steppes, mountains and seas
> Have resisted the arms of the Slavs?
> And where have treachery and enmity not been vanquished
> By the command of the Russian tsar?
> Be reconciled, Circassian! Both the west and the east,
> Will perhaps soon share your fate.
> The hour will come—and you yourself will haughtily say:
> I may be a slave, but I am the slave of the king of the universe!

For all their brash jingoism, these lines, written by a still immature poet, can also be read as boldly underlining the dynamic of odic identification. Once conquered, the Circassian is asked to take pride in his subjection, tranfiguring the meaning of his own enslavement by identifying with his master. This, we recall, had also been the essential premise of the eighteenth-century odic poet. It is the abject basis of sublime identification that Lermontov elsewhere turns on its head, "elegiacally" exposing its alienating effects on the ruler as on the ruled. Earlier in the same poem we read:

По берегам темнеют горы;
Их крутизна, их вышина,
Пленяют ум, пугают взоры.
К вершинам их прицеплена,
Нагими, красными корнями,
Кой–где кудрявая сосна
Стоит печальна и одна,
И часто мрачными мечтами
Тревожит сердце: так порой
Властитель, полубог земной,
На пышном троне, окруженный
Льстецов толпою униженной,
Грустит о том, что одному
На свете равных нет ему!
(2:200)

Along the shores the mountains appear darkly;
Their steepness, their height,
Captivate the mind, frighten the gaze.
Chained to their peaks
By bare, red roots
Here and there a curly-headed pine
Stands sad and alone,
And with gloomy dreams often
Troubles the heart: so at times
A ruler, an earthly demigod,
On his sumptuous throne, surrounded
By a humiliated throng of sycophants,
Grieves about the fact that he alone
Has no equal in the world!

Even as it continues to "captivate" and "terrify," the classic landscape of the alpine sublime now elicits melancholia rather than rapture. Compared to the omnipotent despots of the orient, the mountain scenery discovers its own grandeur to be a source of alienation and realizes that the loneliness of despotic power is a direct consequence of the tyrant's humiliation of his subjects. If *Izmail-Bei* still invites the subject to identify with the tsar, then it also suggests that the tsar is no longer able to sustain that identification.

In sum, this chapter has traced the interaction of two lyric genres (and their epic offshoots) as radically divergent means of representing the Russian poet's relationship to empire as well as to his own place within it. In the poetry of Pushkin and Lermontov the odic legacy was only vestigially present and coexisted, often within the same work, with other generic orientations. A quasi-odic topos that flourished in the romantic era was the figure of the prophet. Rhetorically speaking, the prophet's source of inspiration was still the imperial sublime, even when the content of prophecy became increasingly removed from its historical context. By the beginning of the 1820s, the rhetorical trappings of the eighteenth-century sublime had been largely displaced by an aesthetic form closely tied to the elegy. In Pushkin's elegiac or elegiacally inspired "southern" works, a lopsided dialectic is enacted between the Byronic hero and the Caucasian landscape and people. Here the inspirational force of the sublime, formerly attributed to the alpine scenery or to the act of conquest, is largely absorbed into the subjective workings of the mind. The brooding melancholy of the romantic hero is the negative result of this internalization. Unable to identify completely with any external object or historical goal such as empire, the elegist retreats into an alternative world of nostalgic recollection, unrealized hopes, and frustrated desires. In the more historically oriented elegies of Pushkin and Lermontov, the hero's narcissism is revealed to be a kind of psychological compensation for the poet's powerlessness and loss of social agency. The elegy thus intimates a new disillusionment with the powers that be, expressed either as a wistful sense of impotence or as a formless rage. If the ode is the genre of power triumphantly manifested, then the elegy represents power as *absent,* insofar as its vigorous exercise belongs either to the past or to the future or emanates from afar. For the elegist, power exists presently only through the alienating or privative effects it has already realized, and which the poet is no longer able to overcome by identifying with its source. A victim rather than an agent of his own fate, the elegist will internalize the privative aspect of power as his own psychic condition.

Composed at a time when poetic genres were being fused as often as they were dissolved, the romantic poetry of Pushkin and Lermontov was markedly elegiac in tendency but never completely renounced the temptations of odic rapture. This play of genres corresponds to the striking coexistence, in Russian romantic poetry, of imperialist sentiment alongside more dissonant currents of disenchantment, alienation, and even open defiance of the state.

Conclusion

> Pushkin, Tiutchev, Solov'ëv, Blok—this is the most characteristic path that Russian poetic consciousness has taken in the past one hundred years in contemplating the eternal question of Russia and Europe or, more broadly, of East and West.
>
> Ivanov-Razumnik, *Ispytanie v groze i bure*

The Eurasian Sublime: Pushkin, Tiutchev, and Khomiakov

The imperial sublime had a dynamic history that began with the ode and its "lofty style" but which did not end there.[1] It was an evolving tradition, reexamined by each generation, retaining some of its initial features, shedding or transforming others, and adapting to an increasingly diverse literary and political environment. This last chapter, which deals with poems at a considerable remove from the odes of Lomonosov, indicates how far the imperial sublime evolved beyond its earliest ideological commitments, rhetorical choices, and generic orientation. Although the imperial sublime consistently dramatized the interface between poetics and polity, it nevertheless did not amount to a stable ideological position or a fixed poetic form. The elegiac works discussed in this closing chapter are certainly remote from Lomonosov's "high style," yet they do address the imperial theme and exist in a vigorous and at times explicit dialectic with the ode and all it had stood for. I leave it to the reader to decide how well the book has succeeded in articulating the transitions, tensions, and connections between the several historical eras spanned by the imperial sublime, as well as the different political allegiances, poetic preferences, and forms of lyric subjectivity that emerged or prevailed in each period.

Although the previous chapter ended with the death of Lermontov in 1841, it should be said that the imperial sublime had a prolonged afterlife, one that arguably continued well into the twentieth century. In the following pages I trace briefly the evolution of the imperial sublime as a poetics beyond the elegiac sensibility evident in the southern works of Pushkin and Lermontov. In keeping with the summarizing nature of a conclusion, I restrict myself to indicating the defining moments in the Russian poetic sublime after the heyday of romanticism and in the aftermath of Russia's North Caucasian wars.

As early as 1831, another poetic current, post-odic but nonetheless closer in spirit to the ode than to the elegy, became manifest. Responding over the rest of the century to such events as the Polish uprising and the Crimean War, it combined the geopolitical consciousness of the eighteenth-century ode with a new historiosophical sensibility that was richer and subtler, at least in its best moments, than the poetic tradition it superseded. Assuming a geographical perspective significantly broader than the Caucasian theme that had typified the elegiac and Decembrist sublimes, this current envisioned Russia's future in terms that ambitiously straddled both Europe and Asia, even as it realigned Russia against western Europe as the leader of a newly imagined religious, cultural, or ethnic union.

This "geopoetical" shift corresponded in broad terms to the evolution of Russian imperial strategy. The second half of the nineteenth century saw Russia's attention turn from the Caucasus to Turkistan. After the capture of Tashkent by Russian troops in 1865, Central Asia became the arena of what Rudyard Kipling would term the "Great Game." By 1881 Turkmenistan and the strategic emirates to its north had been directly annexed or had fallen under Russian suzerainty, completing Russia's centuries-old southern drive. This final, decisive Central Asian chapter in the history of Russian imperialism, although the object of some journalistic interest, particularly among the Slavophiles, was not destined to figure as powerfully in Russian literature—particularly poetry—as the Caucasian theme had in the works of the romantics. Indeed, it was generally subsumed within the debates that took place under the broader imperial rivalries that spanned the entire Eurasian landmass, linking Russia, Great Britain, Japan, China, and Ottoman Turkey.

To a considerable degree Pushkin's political verse of 1831 set the terms for what were to become the Eurasian and Pan-Slavic tendencies in Russian poetry. "Klevetnikam Rossii" (To the slanderers of Russia) and "Borodinskaia godovshchina" (The anniversary of Borodino) constitute a startling outburst of patriotic sentiment penned in response to the Polish uprising and the sympathy it had elicited in Europe. A passionate defense of Russian state interests, these poems present the conflict between Russians and Poles as a family feud:

> Уже давно между собою
> Враждуют наши племена;
> Не раз клонилась под грозою
> То их, то наша сторона.
> Кто устоит в неравном споре:
> Кичливый лях иль верный росс?
> Славянские ль ручьи сольются в русском море?
> Оно ль иссякнет? вот вопрос.[2]

> For a long time now
> Our tribes have been in conflict;
> Many a time
> Did their side or ours bend under the storm.
> Who will prevail in the unequal argument:
> The haughty Pole or the faithful Russian?
> Will the Slavic streams merge into the Russian sea?
> Will the sea dry out? That is the question.

While rejecting Polish territorial claims and aspirations to autonomy, Pushkin, in fact, excludes the Poles from his "song of grievance," reserving his real ire for western Europe, specifically France.[3] The "orators" of Paris are to blame not only for having forgotten France's own military aggressions under Napoleon but, more fundamentally, for being deaf to the specificities of Slavic history.[4] If the eighteenth-century ceremonial ode celebrated the mere fact of military expansion as a symbol of imperial glory, then, for Pushkin, territorial boundaries and political allegiances were marked by deeper forms of cultural and ethnic solidarity. Despite their differences, Poles and Russians share a common Slavic past that "cannot be judged by European impressions, whatever our way of thinking might be."[5] For all their conventionally odic belligerency, Pushkin's poems of 1831 also signal a new kind of politics, for which the Polish uprising paradoxically became an occasion to proclaim the existence of a common Slavic world and to signal a profound cultural fissure between Russia and western Europe.

Pushkin's poems of 1831 were welcomed by Emperor Nicholas but marked only a momentary rapprochement between poet and tsar. It was the task of Fedor Tiutchev (1803–1873) to elaborate a consistent "ethnocultural" vision of empire during his long career as poet, diplomat, and political thinker. Tiutchev's debt to the eighteenth century was highlighted long ago by Iurii Tynianov, who regarded Tiutchev's poems as a fragmentation and miniaturization of the monumental poetic genres of the previous century.[6] K. Pigarev subsequently nuanced Tynianov's thesis, finding it applicable only to those poems with a didactic "philosophical or socio-political theme," which rhetorically achieve the effects of an ode on a radically reduced scale.[7] Even in this more limited sense, Tiutchev's verse can be seen as a vital sign of the survival—and evolution—of the sublime beyond Pushkin and Lermontov.

An important marker of the "lofty style" in Tiutchev is his repeated insistence on the *prophetic* origins of his metaphysical and political insights. In a poem of 1855, Tiutchev writes:

О вещая душа моя!
О сердце, полное тревоги,
О, как ты бьешься на пороге
Как бы двойного бытия! . . . .

Так, ты жилица двух миров,
Твой день—болезненный и страстный,
Твой сон—*пророчески—неясный,*
Как откровение духов . . .

O, my prescient soul!
O heart full of anxiety,
Oh, how you struggle on the threshold
Of a dual being, as it were! . . .

So, you are an inhabitant of two worlds,
Your day is morbid and passionate,
Your sleep is *prophetically obscure,*
Like the revelation of spirits . . .

In the same year Tiutchev used a nearly identical formula in writing of the consequences he dimly foresaw arising from Russia's catastrophic defeat in the Crimean War:

Стоим мы слепо пред Судьбою.
Не нам сорвать с нее покров . . .
Я не свое тебе открою,
А *бред пророческий духов* . . .

Еще нам далеко до цели,
Гроза ревет, гроза растет,—

И вот в железной колыбели,
В громах, родился Новый Год.[8]

We stand blindly before Fate.
It is not for us to rip off her veil . . .
I will not reveal my own [burden] to you,
But the *prophetic delirium of spirits* . . .

We are still far from the goal,
The storm howls, the storm grows,—
And now in an iron cradle,
In peals of thunder the New Year is born.

Tiutchev's political and philosophical verses derive from a shared prophetic source whose vision involves an impersonal ontological schema that is glimpsed obscurely as if through a veil. In his metaphysical poetry this schema appears static, a perennial confrontation of "two worlds," day and night, the realm of phenomena with their sharply etched but transient contours, on the one hand, and, on the other, an underlying abyss, a boundless infinity with which the threshold consciousness of the poet establishes a fleeting kinship. If the day is "friend to people and gods," then the night "bares the abyss to us / With its terrors and obscurities," a chaos that "terrifies" because it erases "the boundaries between it and us."[9]

In Tiutchev's political verse this ontology acquires the dynamism of a providential plan, whereby the *temporal* dimension of an impending future displaces the terrifying discovery of the abyss that lurks behind the veil of being. The poem "Prorochestvo" (Prophecy) (1850) illustrates this clearly:

Не гул молвы прошел в народе,
Весть родилась не в нашем роде —
То древний глас, то свыше глас:
«Четвертый век уж на исходе, —
Свершится он—и грянет час!»

И своды древние Софии,
В возобновленной Византии,
Вновь осенит Христов алтарь.
Пади пред ним, о царь России, —
И встань как всеславянский царь![10]

It was not the hum of rumor that passed through the nation,
The news did not originate in our race—

> That was an ancient voice, that was a voice from on high:
> "The fourth age is already at its end,—
> It will end—and the hour will strike!"
>
> And the ancient vaults of Hagia Sophia,
> In a renewed Byzantium,
> Will once more be protected by Christ's altar.
> Fall before it, oh tsar of Russia,—
> And rise as tsar of all the Slavs!

These lines revive and modify the perennial Russian dream to liberate Constantinople by adding the unification of the Slavic peoples to the traditional religious imperative of establishing a Christian Empire under Russian leadership. A staunch monarchist throughout his life, Tiutchev viewed Russian autocracy as the providential vehicle of a historical mission that he ascribed to the Russian Empire. We should note straight away how remote Tiutchev's vision was from the politics of "sublime dissent" that, to varying degrees, had typified the prophetic topos from the eighteenth century to the time of the Decembrists. Indeed, Tiutchev's earliest poems express the poet's clear condemnation of the Decembrist cause, and indeed of the political radicalism generally associated with the romantic poet-prophet. "K ode Pushkina na vol'nost'" (On Pushkin's ode to liberty) (1820) thus begins by hailing those who were "born to proclaim sacred truths to hardened tyrants," only to end by urging them to "soften rather than alarm the hearts beneath the brocade of kings."[11]

While many of his later poems on contemporary events bear an embarrassing resemblance to official propaganda, Tiutchev's deepest political convictions, like his metaphysics, always existed at a visionary remove from the real state of Russian affairs. Central to Tiutchev's politics was the question of empire, which Georges Florovsky called "the basic theme and basic category of Tiutchev's historiography."[12] We find his mythology of empire elaborated at some length in his journalistic writings, including the unfinished tract "La Russie et l'Occident" (1848–49): "What then is Russia? What does it represent? Two things: the *Slavic race* [and] the *Orthodox Empire*. . . . There is no political nationhood possible for the Slavs outside Russia. . . . [But] the question of race is only secondary. . . . Russia is orthodox even more than it is Slavic. It is to the extent that it is orthodox that it is the depositary of the Empire. . . . The Empire is one: the Orthodox Church is its soul, the Slavic race its body. If Russia did not result in an Empire, it would come to nothing."[13]

Tiutchev's political vision was messianic rather than simply conservative: his advocacy of empire affirmed the power of Russian autocracy only to the extent that the latter furthered the higher cause of promoting a civilizational and religious unity predestined by fate.[14] A clear case in point is the poem "Kak doch' rodnuiu na zaklan'e" (As [Agamemnon] led his own daughter to her death) (1831), the poet's response to the Polish uprising. Russian blood had been spilled, says Tiutchev, "not for the sake of the Koran of autocracy" but to "maintain the wholeness of the realm" and to "gather kindred generations of Slavs / under the Russian banner." Led to battle by a "higher consciousness," the Russian people had "boldly assumed" the task of "justifying the ways of heaven."[15]

Tiutchev's philosophy of history generated a poetic ideology that was vitally different from the ceremonial or Decembrist ode, even as it displayed some essential continuity. Whether praising or attacking the tsar, the ode had been based on an implicit (ideological or structural) identification between poet and monarch as well as with the monarch's expanding realm. In Tiutchev's case, however, the poet identified with a liminal state of inchoate inspiration that no longer found an immediate analogy in the figure of the tsar. The emperor, where present, was viewed as an agent rather than the protagonist of history and was no longer the poet's constant interlocutor or his structural analogue, while history itself acquired a providential framework that structurally precluded any realization in the present state of affairs. For all its relative conformism, Tiutchev's political verse rarely amounted to a mere celebration of the status quo, or its perpetuation through violence. At least one Soviet-era critic, N. Berkovskii, sought to identify what distinguished Tiutchev from the eighteenth century in terms relevant to our concerns: "[Tiutchev] is related to Derzhavin as a poet of the sublime style. . . . But a characteristic change took place here. The sublime in Derzhavin and his contemporaries is mostly an official sublime, which received its sanction from the church and state." By contrast, suggests Berkovskii, Tiutchev claimed for himself the freedom to decide what, for him, was sublime—"the essential content of life, its general pathos, its main collisions, and not those principles of official faith which inspired the older odic poets."[16]

Berkovskii here intuits a difference that needs to be more carefully delineated. Unrealizable in a given present, the sublime for Tiutchev was to be found in the *boundlessness of space itself*. Figured in his philosophical poems as the "abyss," "chaos," or "oblivion," this spatial infinity did in part recall the endlessly receding horizontal axis of the ceremonial ode. Yet unlike the odic maps of empire, such a space could not be readily charted, since it threatened all boundaries, including those of the poet and the empire. For this reason it could not be mapped, only *prophesied.* In Tiutchev's celebrated poem "Russkaia geografiia" (Russian geography) (1848–49), the tension between metaphysical space and political territory finds its characteristic resolution in a prophetically intuited destiny:

Москва и град Петров, и Константинов град —
Вот царства русского заветные столицы. . . .
Но где предел ему? И где его границы —
На север, на восток, на юг и на закат?
Грядущим временам судьбы их обличат . . .

Семь внутренних морей и семь великих рек . . .
От Нила до Невы, от Эльбы до Китая,
От Волги по Евфрат, от Ганга до Дуная. . . .
Вот царство русское . . . и не прейдет вовек,
Как то провидел Дух и Даниил предрек.[17]

Moscow, Peter's city [Saint Petersburg but possibly also Rome], and the city of Constantine—
These are the cherished capitals of the Russian kingdom . . .
But what are its limits? And where are its boundaries—
To the north, to the east, to the south and where the sun sets?
The fates will reveal them to future times . . .

The seven inner seas and seven great rivers . . .
From the Nile to the Neva, from the Elbe to China,
From the Volga to the Euphrates, from the Ganges to the Danube . . .
That is the Russian kingdom . . . and it will never pass away,
As the Spirit foresaw and Daniel foretold.

The loss of boundaries that tempts and terrifies Tiutchev in his metaphysical poems is here resolved with the anticipated establishment of a Russian Empire whose contours will be discerned in an inevitable but still undetermined future. A vast Eurasian expanse, evoked here in the "from . . . to . . ." formula that Pumpianskii would have described as typically odic, here establishes Russia's potential confines but in a way that makes the territorial entity called Russia indistinguishable from a spiritual utopia. Such a Russia, Tiutchev confidently predicted to Pëtr Chaadaev at the beginning of the Crimean War, would be "associated with so many other elements that would complete and transform her, that her very name will be modified by them. It will not be an empire, it will be a world."[18] At its utopian limit, imperial ambition fades into spiritual universalism, a recurring tendency in Russian poetry and historiosophy inspired by Slavophile ideas.

The theologian Florovsky once complained that "it is difficult to make any connection at all between [Tiutchev's] Orthodox imperialism and the ingenious cosmic intuition that inspired his wonderful lyrics."[19] To this we might reply that Tiutchev's political and metaphysical verses are indeed linked, and in two ways: both claim the authority of prophetic vision, and both exist in an implied dialogue of mutual negation. Whereas the metaphysical poems intuit a chaos underlying the apparent order of things, the political poems affirm, or rather foresee, an ideal civilizational order that is destined to prevail over the chaos of revolution or external aggression.[20] This, broadly speaking, was also the matrix of the French classicist sublime, an experience of *beau désordre* contained within the confines of *bon sens*. Yet just as Lomonosov had pursued lyric disorder beyond the dictates of classicism only to find release in expressing his rapture at the post-Petrine state, so, too, Tiutchev was haunted by an extreme sense of the groundlessness of being whose counterweight was to be a utopian politics of Orthodoxy and empire.

It was the merit of A. S. Khomiakov (1804–1860), a major Slavophile philosopher but a minor poet, to deepen and modify Tiutchev's utopian vision by inserting it into a more authentically lived Christian framework. A poet-prophet in the Küchelbeckerian vein, whose "enraptured voice" aspired to "thunder throughout the universe," Khomiakov wrote an ode in response to the Polish uprising that was not unlike Pushkin's and Tiutchev's related poems in its nuanced defense of Russia's purported goal of a Pan-Slavic empire.[21] Yet in his best political verse Khomiakov went futher than Tiutchev in warning against the two extremes of slavish resignation and excessive pride that threatened the Russian national psyche, the former manifested in the Russian people's perennial submission to tyranny and the latter implicit in the widespread assumption of Russia being a nation anointed by God to fulfill a historic mission:

«Гордись!»—тебе льстецы сказали.—
«Земля с увенчанным челом,
Земля несокрушимой стали,
Полмира взявшая мечом!
Пределов нет твоим владеньям,
И, прихотей твоих раба,
Внимает гордым повеленьям

Тебе покорная судьба.
Красны степей твоих уборы,
И горы в небо уперлись,
И как моря твои озеры . . .»
Не верь, не слушай, не гордись![22]

"Be proud!"—the flatterers told you.—
"O land whose head is crowned,
Land of indestructible steel,
That has conquered half the world by sword!
There are no limits to your dominions,
And, slave to your caprices,
Fate, obedient to you,
Heeds your proud commands.
The adornments of your steppes are beauteous,
And your mountains touch the sky,
And your lakes are like seas . . ."
Don't believe them, don't listen, don't be proud!

The classic topos of imperial boundlessness is here denounced and contrasted to the moral strength of the meek and the godfearing. If, for Tiutchev, Orthodoxy found its primary raison d'être as a unifying ideology and a source of political solidarity, then, for Khomiakov, it also provided the spiritual criteria for a critique of Russia's imperial delusions and national shortcomings.

Panmongolism and the Crisis of Empire

The towering figure of Vladimir Solov'ëv (1853–1900) links the historiosophical poetry of Tiutchev and Khomiakov to the concerns of the Russian Silver Age. A lesser poet than Tiutchev but a far superior metaphysician and philosopher of culture, Solov'ëv deepened Khomiakov's spiritual critique of modern Russia's predicament into a vision that sought to reconcile the world's existing religious and civilizational differences in a universal Christianity, a vision whose evident crisis finally yielded an apocalyptic prediction of the end of history itself.

In the last of his "Tri rechi v pamiat' Dostoevskogo" (Three Dostoevsky memorial lectures) (1881–83), Solov'ëv announced that Russia had been given by "the Christian faith and history" the "great obligation to serve morally both East and West, reconciling them within herself." If in the past "Russia had adequately demonstrated her physical strength to both East and West in her struggle with them,—now she will have to show them her spiritual strength in the [act of] reconciliation." Already hinted at in Tiutchev's more utopian moments, the contrast between *physical* domination through military violence and a *religious* unity attained by "treating one's opponent not humanly but divinely" is made explicit here.[23] Solov'ëv articulated this distinction still more eloquently in his first significant poem on Russia's "Eurasian" dilemma, "Ex oriente lux" (1890). In this poem Solov'ëv retraces the civilizational conflict between east and west from the ancient wars between the Greeks and the Persians right down to his own day. While the "citizens" of the Greek polis, and with them the west, had once triumphed over the "slaves" of Iran, it was finally the east that had given birth to Christ's "spirit of faith and love." History, it seems, is determined not by geography or physical strength alone but also by *ethical* superiority, which is the final arbiter of victory. It was thus Russia's choice to decide "which East" she wished to be—the "Russia of Xerxes or of Christ."[24] Although stylistically the poem reminds us of the prophetic poetry of Küchelbecker and Khomiakov, Solov'ëv goes further here than any of his predecessors in questioning the costs of imperial statehood.

Solov'ëv's universalism, however, had its limits. The philosopher never doubted Christianity's superiority over other faiths, and clung for some time to his dream of a world civilization realized under the auspices of a reunited Church. No less than Christianity's own internal schisms, it was the cultures of the far east that threatened Solov'ëv's early theocratic ideal. "From a Christian point of view," wrote Solov'ëv in "Kitai i Evropa" (China and Europe) (1890), it is not permissible for us to view any people, and hence the Chinese also, as an enemy against whom only weapons must be used. Our antipathy and fears cannot be awakened by the Chinese people itself with its unique character, but only by what separates this people from the remainder of humanity, what makes the basis of its life unique and, in this uniqueness, false."[25] Applying the Hegelian historicist schema that equated the west with historical progress and China with stagnant order and immobility, Solov'ëv nevertheless went beyond Hegel in proposing a synthesis that did not wholly exclude or "sublate" the primary achievements of Chinese culture, its stability and continuity. A "Christian progress that contained within itself the positive principles of order" was thus desirable.[26] By themselves, east and west remain one-sided and incomplete: only a civilization that embodies the "full truth" of Christianity could reconcile both polarities and attain true universality.

The problem here—which was of course not Solov'ëv's alone—lay in extricating the *metaphysical* category of universality from the *political* coercion that allowed it to prevail as a historical force. With the crisis of Solov'ëv's ecumenical dream of reconciling Orthodoxy with Catholicism, the philosopher seems to have turned with greater hope to the Russian imperial state as the vehicle of an east/west synthesis. "A broad all-reconciling policy—imperial and Christian—is the only national policy" possible for Russia, one that is "open to all and excludes none," wrote Solov'ëv in 1896.[27] Empire, then, need not be chauvinistic or sectarian: rather, it must tolerate those differences that it is able to contain within itself. The success of imperial policy, Solov'ëv observed two years later, thus depended equally on internal reform. The catastrophe of the Crimean War was inevitable given the injustice of serfdom and the lawlessness then prevalent in Russia, while the success of reforms promulgated by Alexander II guaranteed the "subjugation of the Caucasus, Central Asia, and the liberation of Bulgaria," which were to be considered as "cultural victories as much as military ones."[28]

Whether projected onto Russia or onto the wider realm of a unified Christendom, Solov'ëv's humanistic and universalizing vision of empire was nevertheless haunted by grave doubts and forebodings. In two poems and a prose text that were destined to exercise an immense influence on the poets of the Silver Age, Solov'ëv elevated his deep fear of a resurgent China into an apocalyptic vision of the end of history itself. The crudest if not the earliest of these texts was "Drakon" (Dragon) (written in 1900 and published posthumously the same year). In this poem Solov'ëv hails the German emperor for sending his troops to quell the Boxer Rebellion in China, an event that assumed a huge importance for Solov'ëv in the final months of his life:

> Полно любовью Божье лоно,
> Оно зовет нас всех равно . . .
> Но перед пастию дракона
> Ты понял: крест и меч—одно.[29]

> The lap of God is full of love,
> It calls to all of us equally . . .
> But faced with the jaws of the dragon
> You understood: the cross and the sword are one and the same.

Solov'ëv here baldly urges a holy war against the Chinese even as he reaffirms his commitment to universal love as a Christian principle.

Six years earlier Solov'ëv had written the still more famous lyric

"Panmongolizm" (Panmongolism) (published partly in 1900 and fully only in 1905). In this poem, perhaps the most disturbing in Solov'ëv's entire work, the "yellow children" of the east are shown gathering for a final war against Christian Europe:

От вод малайских до Алтая
Вожди с Восточных островов
У стен поникшего Китая
Собрали тьмы своих полков.
. . . .
О Русь! забудь былую славу:
Орел двуглавый сокрушен,
И желтым детям на забаву
Даны клочки твоих знамен.[30]

From the waters of Malaysia to Altai
Leaders from the Eastern islands
At the walls of flagging China
Have massed their vast troops.
. . . .
O Russia! Forget your former glory:
The two-headed eagle is smashed,
And to yellow children for their amusement
The shreds of your banners have been given.

Rechristened "panmongolism," the Yellow Peril became, for Solov'ëv, the constitutive element of a historical myth that interpreted the geopolitical tensions of the turn of the century in terms of a historical continuity that linked the remote past (the Mongol invasions of the thirteenth century) to an impending future (the apocalypse). It transformed the dense particularities of Central Asia, Ottoman Turkey, and the far east into a loosely defined Eurasian continent that could be imagined as a traumatic geography, within which ancient historical resentments, fears of racial miscegenation, and millenarian expectations of imminent revolution fueled an anxious exploration of Russia's own role in a new era that was understood to be history's last.

Significantly "Drakon" and "Panmongolizm" diverge noticeably in terms of the historical lesson they actually derive from the threat China posed. Whereas "Drakon" views the resurgence of China as a danger to Christendom that needs to be checked, "Panmongolizm" looks back to Khomiakov's critique of Russia's aspirations to being the "Third Rome" and extends that critique still further. Just as Byzantium's spiritual corruption justified the fall of Constantinople into Turkish hands, so the Yellow Peril is seen in "Panmongolizm" as a "tool of divine punishment," a consequence of Russia's own arrogance in assuming the mantle of Christendom while forgetting Christ's essential message of love. These shifts suggest that Solov'ëv was himself unsure precisely how to situate the orient, as well as the xenophobic sentiments China provoked in him, within the historiosophical scheme he was elaborating.

Solov'ëv's longest account of the "panmongolian" threat is found in "Kratkaia povest' ob Antikhriste" (A short story about the Antichrist), published in 1900 as part of a complex, polyphonic prose work entitled *Tri razgovora* (Three conversations). This story relates the future events of the impending twentieth century, beginning with the unification of east Asia under the leadership of Japan and the subjugation of Russia and Europe by the combined forces of the east. Although Europe finally overthrows its Asiatic rulers, it subsequently falls prey to the Antichrist, a seductive figure who seeks to realize Solov'ëv's once cherished goal of unifying Christendom. The Antichrist temporarily usurps the universal mission Solov'ëv had formerly accorded Russia, while panmongolism belongs to a preliminary period, imminent but not final, that prepares his coming. In both the prosaic and poetic elaborations of his panmongolian myth, Solov'ëv attributed a catalyzing role to a rearmed Asia in preparing the way for a final closure to history. Yet both texts also denounced the spiritual risks and delusions of grandeur implicit in Solov'ëv's own dream of a universal Christian Empire. Solov'ëv's eschatology was thus strikingly double-edged, a critique whose anxious vision of the future spared neither east nor west—nor indeed Solov'ëv himself.[31]

Solov'ëv bequeathed to more than one generation of Russian modernist writers the conviction that *all* art (and not merely the psalm or spiritual ode) possessed prophetic insight insofar as it was able to represent things "from the perspective of their final condition or in the light of the future world."[32] Solov'ëv's "panmongolian" vision specifically provided the symbolists with a prophetic chronotope whose traits were distinct but, at least in one respect, essentially ambiguous. Temporally it anticipated the apocalyptic closure of history such that all contemporary events had to be seen in the light of what they foreshadowed; spatially it configured a vast Eurasian continent sundered into two competing sides, east and west. What remained undecided was Russia's own geographical and cultural orientation in this struggle, its precise role as an empire in the ending of history.

The Sublime and the Symbol: Modernism and Apocalypse

Many of the Russian symbolists were to view the revolution of 1905, alongside the disastrous outcome of the Russo-Japanese war, as a confirmation of Solov'ëv's prophecy, which they updated into their own individual variants of the panmongolian myth. Andrei Belyi's characteristically ambitious article "Apokalipsis v russkoi poèzii" (The apocalypse in Russian poetry) (1905) sought to reinterpret both the politics of the present and the history of Russian poetry through the combined prism of Solov'ëv's eschatology and the epistemological premises of symbolism as a newly ascendant poetics. The technology of modern warfare, said Belyi quoting an eyewitness to the Russo-Japanese conflict, had rendered all things "mysterious, scattered, distant, invisible, abstract." The dematerialization of the phenomenal world under the impact of new military technology corresponded to the epistemology of the poetic symbol, whose role it was to point beyond itself to the existence of another world:

> The immoral application of science is creating the horrors of the contemporary war with Japan—a war in which we see the symbol that has appeared to us of a rising chaos. . . . Japan is a mask behind which there lie invisible things. The question of our victory over the enemy is closely tied to a transition in consciousness directed toward the resolution of profound mystical problems for European humanity. . . . It is necessary to understand that the red dragon hurtling to us from the East is illusory: these are misty clouds and not reality; there is really no war at all: it is a product of our morbid imagination, an external symbol in the struggle of the universal soul with the universal horror, the symbol of the struggle of our souls with the chimeras and hydras of chaos.[33]

For Belyi, imperial war was an illusion or, rather, an epiphenomenon concealing vaster spiritual forces. Being merely one of the many "masks thrown onto reality behind which the Invisible Woman lies hidden," Japan could not be defeated by arms alone, since, like a "hydra," it would sprout as many heads as were severed, combining forces with the "red rooster that has spread its wings over the ancient estates deep in the heart of Russia." The joint forces of Asiatic aggression and social revolution could be countered only by "ripping the mask off the face of the Invisible Woman who is creeping toward us wearing many guises." According to a symbolism inherited from Solov'ëv and closely related to Blok's poetic vision, the feminine allowed for the historical incarnation of a transcendent unity binding heaven and earth. Intuiting this unity was the act of the poet; his aesthetic vision corresponded to a cognitive dissolution of the world of multiplicity and could hasten the advent of a new cosmic order.

It is not possible here to explore the elaboration of these extraordinary ideas in all Belyi's poetry and literary prose. Suffice it to say that Belyi's work as a whole represents, among other things, the most systematic application of symbolist poetics to what we might call the "Eurasian" (as opposed to the Caucasian) sublime as it had evolved from Pushkin and Tiutchev up to and including Solov'ëv. Regarding the political conflicts of his time as manifestations of a "collision between two opposed principles," the "universal struggle of Woman and Beast," Belyi responded by radicalizing the epistemological claims of poetry as prophecy. The tension at the heart of Tiutchev's sublime, between spatial infinity and political territory, was now relocated *within* the poetic symbol itself. *The sublime was thereby interiorized as an act of symbolic cognition,* which discovered within itself the capacity to hasten the end of universal history by discerning a greater reality behind appearances: "The life that surrounds us is a pale reflection of the struggle of human life-forces with fate. Symbolism deepens either the gloom or the light: it transforms possibilities into authentic realities [*podlinnosti*]: it infuses them with being."[34]

How much did the advent of the symbol transform the older tradition of the sublime? Like the sublime, symbolic cognition was the domain of the poet-seer, although now far removed from its odic or psalmic origins. No longer defined by genre, the sublime, as symbol, became a universal attribute of art as prophetic cognition and theurgic creation. It is for this reason, as I have already suggested in the introduction, that the sublime is to be found everywhere and nowhere in Russian symbolist writing. For Belyi, moreover, empire ceased to be a rationalizing historical category, a function it had still served for Tiutchev and Solov'ëv. This had largely to do with Belyi's radical redefinition of history itself: all temporal and spatial phenomena, including empire, were finally mere emanations of vaster spiritual realities. Yet this did not mean that empire ceased to be a concern. Indeed, Belyi's greatest masterpiece, *Peterburg* (Petersburg) (1916) might be read as applying the poetics of the symbol to an exploration of Russia's imminent imperial collapse. A novel that systematically puts into dialogue—and makes ironic—many of Belyi's own cherished epistemological and aesthetic premises, *Peterburg* nonetheless merits our attention as a work that brings together and explodes the organizing spatial tropes of the Russian literary tradition.

A central figure in *Peterburg* is Senator Apollon Apollonovich, patriarch and aging tsarist functionary, scion of a Turkic noble clan that had converted to Christianity and begun to serve the Russian tsars in the eighteenth century. Apollon Apollonovich is described as "being afraid of space": "he had climbed each rung of his career while keeping in view that very same improbable expanse from where the icy hand beckoned, the vastness flew: the Russian Empire."[35] Apollon Apollonovich's life recapitulates the history of his family in its journey from the imperial hinterland to the capital Saint Petersburg, and his psyche will become the battleground on which his repressed oriental origins will lay siege to the modernizing logic of Russian autocracy. It is thus significant that Saint Petersburg represents not only the concentrated power of the state but also the rational organization of space: "Regularity and symmetry calmed the nerves of the senator. . . . Most of all he loved the rectilinear avenue: this avenue reminded him of the flow of time between two points in life" (32). Apollon Apollonovich seeks to hold the messy vastness of empire in check by subordinating it to an abstract grid of lines and squares: "he wanted his carriage to fly forward, the avenues to fly toward him,—avenue after avenue, so that the entire spherical surface of the planet would be caught in snaking rings by the blackish-gray cubes of houses, so that the entire earth, hemmed in by avenues, in its linear cosmic movement would intersect the vast expanse according to the rectilinear law" (33).

In Apollon Apollonovich, as in Saint Petersburg itself, the rationalizing power of European thought collides with inchoate cosmic forces: "There is an infinity of speeding avenues with an infinity of speeding intersecting phantoms. All of Petersburg is the infinity of an avenue raised to the nth power. Beyond Petersburg there is nothing" (34). We have returned here to Tiutchev's binary universe, divided between the phenomenal world and an underlying void or abyss, but now denied the utopian resolution provided by Tiutchev's providential vision. In keeping with Solov'ëv's panmongolian myth, the binary opposition of chaos and order is established according to an east/west axis: Petersburg, and the world of western reason it represents, confronts an orient that has no stable civilizational contours or geographical fixity but possesses the purely negative cosmic power to destroy the world and end history as we know it. Apollon Apollonovich's son, Nikolai, thus at one point fantasizes that he is "an old Turanian—he has become embodied in the flesh and blood of the ancient Russian gentry in order to fulfill a cherished goal: to shatter all foundations; the Ancient Dragon would feed off his bad blood and devour all things with its flame: the ancient east would hail bombs on our time; and Nikolai Apollonovich was an old Turanian bomb: now, as his homeland came into view, he was beginning to explode; and on his face a Mongol expression appeared" (196–97).

In the hybrid genealogy of the Russian gentry the civilizations of east and west become inextricably intertwined. The worlds of order and chaos, still separate for Solov'ëv, collide and interpenetrate. This process is made manifest both in the landscape of the city and in the consciousness and bodies of the novel's protagonists: just as Petersburg can no longer hold at bay the restive populace and boundless expanse of the imperial periphery, so, too, the cognitive operations of the reasoning mind and the genetic inheritance of the body cannot prevent the irruption of "cerebral play," the psychic mechanism by which the individual is traversed and manipulated by superhuman forces.

This contamination of order and chaos is abstractly imaged as a kind of zero point in time and space that Belyi repeatedly calls the *tochka* (point or full stop). The "point" is perhaps the most subtly pervasive motif in Belyi's *Peterburg,* a symbol that links the political conflict of center and periphery to an epistemological inquiry into the nature of space, time, and consciousness. We read in the book's preface that "Petersburg not only seems but turns out to be on maps; in the form of two little concentric circles with a black *point* in the center; and from this *point,* which has no dimension, it energetically proclaims the fact that it—exists, from there, from this very *point,* the swarm of the printed book streams out, from this invisible *point* the circular comes hurtling forth" (24; my emphasis). Located nowhere and without tangible dimension, the "point" is nevertheless the beginning, the end, and the meeting place of all the semiotic systems operating within the novel: the modes of spatialization (imperial cartography, town planning, the domestic interior), temporalization (the linear succession of clock time, the narrative modalities of plot), language (the bureaucratic discourse of the state as well as the creative medium of art), and transcendence (in Belyi's words, "the point is the place where the plane of being touches the spherical surface of the huge astral cosmos" [239]).

As the book's organizing symbol, the "point," or *tochka,* can thus be fruitfully compared and contrasted to the operations of the sublime as they were described in the preceding chapters. Both the sublime and the "point" are abstracting operations that reorganize space as well as the human subject's relation to it. Yet if the sublime permits the ecstatic survey of an expanding infinity, the "point" shrinks that infinity to its moment of origin; the sublime extends vertically and horizontally, whereas the symbol contracts and miniaturizes space into a kind of compressed potency, where it becomes equivalent to an instant in time. The time-space of the "point" acquires its final ironic embodiment in the time bomb that is meant to assassinate Apollon Apollonovich, a bomb that will explode at the book's end but kill nobody and resolve nothing: "the monstrous thing dragged on, for twenty four hours, or—eighty thousand seconds, points [*tochek*] in time: each instant would come . . . : the instant, spreading rather swiftly in circles, was slowly transforming into a swelling ball; this ball would burst open, and the heel would slide into emptinesses: a wanderer might thus slip on time and fall, where one couldn't say, and so on until . . . the new moment" (250). The bomb might be read as Belyi's playful rendering of Solov'ëv's apocalypse, a reduction of the Yellow Peril to an abortive act of terrorism that constitutes the book's tragicomic ending. The closure of history that the bomb fails to accomplish is finally effected on the level of writing by Belyi's central symbol, the "point." Just before the epilogue and a short account of the aftermath of the bomb, the author writes: "And—we shall place here a full stop [*I—stavim zeds' tochku*]" (323). However whimsical, this statement suggests the extent to which, for Belyi, the artistic symbol could transform history into an experience of consciousness and a fact of writing.

Few Russian poets went as far as Belyi in subordinating history to the epistemological ambitions of the symbolist movement: most were content to intuit or hail the future, not to internalize and transform it. In his lyric, "Griadushchie gunny" (The imminent Huns) (1904–5), Valerii Briusov hears the "cast-iron gallop" of the "drunken hordes" from "Pamirs as yet undiscovered" ready to "renew the enfeebled bodies" of the cultured world with a "wave of gleaming blood." While identifying himself with the accumulated spiritual wealth of civilization, Briusov chooses not to condemn the barbarians: "But you who will destroy me / I meet with a hymn of greeting."[36] Briusov's poem is curiously imprecise about the provenance of these barbarians; but, situated as it is within a collection saturated with impressions of the 1905 revolution, the poem can be read as a commentary on the perceived rift *within* Russia itself between the educated bourgeoisie and the populace at large.

Aleksandr Blok's astonishing poem, "Skify" (The Scythians) (1918), renders explicit the shift already hinted at by Briusov and Belyi. Opening with an epigraph that cites the first two verses of Solov'ëv's "Panmongolizm," the poem in fact fundamentally transforms the geographical basis of Solov'ëvian eschatology. Blok recapitulates Pushkin's famous rebuttal to Chaadaev, that Russia had saved Christian Europe by "absorbing the Mongol conquest":

> Мы, как послушные холопы,
> Держали щит меж двух враждебных рас
> Монголов и Европы![37]
>
> We, like obedient lackeys,
> Held the shield between two hostile races
> The Mongols and Europe!

Yet, in absorbing the shock of the Mongol invasion, Blok finds Russia itself to have been fatally orientalized, and thus addresses the west on Russia's behalf as its semi-Asiatic interlocutor: "Yes, we are Scythians! Yes we are Asians, / With slanted and avaricious eyes!" What, for Solov'ëv, had been an *external* Asiatic threat to Christian Russia is viewed by Blok as a territorial and racial mission that Russia has *itself* inherited from the remote past and now reinterpreted as the utopian promise of social revolution. Blok's "Skify" thus completes the identification of the barbarian without (Asia) with the barbarian within (the insurgent Russian people) that had been increasingly evident in the panmongolian myth since the events of 1905.[38] East and west, which Solov'ëv had tended to see as racial or civilizational absolutes, had now collapsed inward: they were no longer dichotomies but perspectival thresholds through which Russia could contemplate the crisis of her imperial destiny.

Overall, what I have tentatively called the "Eurasian sublime" as it evolved from Pushkin and Tiutchev through Belyi and Blok emerges as relatively distinct from the models examined earlier in the book. Most striking is the weakening of the vertical axis of inspiration, whether in the form of the mountainous sublime of the Caucasus or the more abstract experience of odic transport. In its place we find the epistemologically ambitious trope of the symbol, as well as a hypertrophied sense of the horizontal axis, the infinitely receding expanse of Russia's steppes. Horizontality lacks the grandeur of height and the authoritative vision that height affords; it awakens instead a fear of boundlessness or, at the very least, the duller anxiety of monotony. In the most extreme case of Belyi's symbolist novel, *Peterburg*, the horizontal axis contracts to a "point" where center and periphery collide and intermingle. As distances shrink, boundaries also appear increasingly porous: the great texts of Russian modernism reveal a deep vulnerability to the other, a foreignness that can no longer be circumscribed or held at arm's length. In the approach to 1917, this foreignness became identified with the hordes of Asia or with the revolutionary masses themselves, centrifugal forces that would violently end the Petersburg period of Russian history.

Given the essentially statist premise of the Bolshevik Revolution, it should come as no surprise that the imperial sublime revived considerably in Russian poetry in the aftermath of 1917. In addressing the new revolutionary state, Russia's poets were to resuscitate the most archaic elements of the sublime tradition, many of which had been eroded or had fallen into disuse during the declining years of the tsarist regime. These elements entered a diverse literary context of competing post-symbolist currents, creating a striking amalgam of the old and the new. A few examples must suffice here. In Vladimir Maiakovskii's "'Oda revoliutsii" (Ode to the revolution) (1918), as in much of his postrevolutionary production, we find a striking recuperation of the ode, with its civic pathos and celebration of the transformative function of the state:

«Тебе,
освистанная,
осмеянная батареями,
тебе,
изъязвленная злословием штыков,
восторженно возношу
над руганью реемой
оды торжественное
'О'!»[39]

"To you,
heckled,
derided by batteries of guns,
to you,
wounded all over by the spite of bayonets,
I ecstatically raise
over the soaring abuse
the ode's solemn
'O!'"

For the futurist Maiakovskii, the odic theme of praise was always polemical and could thus coexist, linguistically and ideologically, with its opposite: hence the perpetual juxtaposition, in Maiakovskii, of the lofty and the low, and the resulting liberation of the sublime from the constraints of the "high style."[40] Osip Mandel'shtam's volume, *Tristia* (1921), might equally be read as a compendium of the different sublimes that had prevailed in Russian poetic history: the odic or classicist, the Decembrist and the elegiac. This generic and stylistic heterogeneity corresponded directly to the ideological ambiguity at the heart of Mandel'shtam's acceptance of the new Soviet state. His celebrated poem "Sumerki svobody" (The twilight of freedom) (1918) vacillates powerfully between the odic theme of praising the new and the elegiac need for mourning the past:

> Прославим роковое бремя,
> которое в слезах народный вождь берет.
> Прославим власти сумрачное бремя,
> Ее невыносимый гнет.
> В ком сердце есть, тот должен слышать, время,
> Как твой корабль ко дну идет.[41]

> Let us praise the fateful burden,
> Which the people's leader carries in tears.
> Let us praise the crepuscular burden of power,
> Its unbearable weight.
> He who has a heart must hear, o time,
> Your ship sinking to the bottom.

We might finally mention one of the founding figures of the Russian avant-garde, Velimir Khlebnikov, whose influence extended beyond poetry to the plastic arts and the Eurasianist school of thought that flourished in the Russian emigration.[42] Combining experimental poetry with the metalanguages of linguistics and mathematics, Khlebnikov's work can be read as the most ambitious attempt at resuscitating the imperial sublime since the impasse of elegiac romanticism and in the wake of the Eurasian theme so prevalent among the Russian symbolists. In Khlebnikov's culminating work, *Zangezi* (1922), we discover the poet-prophet Zangezi bestriding the summit of a newly constructed vertical axis, propagating his universal alphabet of space and his laws of time. Zangezi's declaration that

> *Эр, Ка, Эль* и *Гэ*—
> Воины азбуки—

Были действующими лицами этих лет,
Богатырями дней[43]

R, K, L and G—
Alphabet war makers—
They were the actors in the drama of those years,
Warrior-heros of those days

is a telling example of Khlebnikov's marriage of linguistic experimentation and historical speculation, the creation of a new "sublime style" whose revelatory power could free Eurasia and the world from the perennial conflict between east and west. But these postrevolutionary developments are best left to future exploration.

Notes

Bibliography

Index

Notes

Introduction

1. Quoted by Derzhavina et al., Introduction, 29–30. Russia's earlier victory against Sweden at Poltava in 1709 was the watershed that prompted Peter to begin seeking the status of emperor; see Vilinbakhov, "Otrazhenie idei absoliutizma v simvolike petrovskikh znamen," 21.

2. Belinskii, "Sochineniia Aleksandra Pushkina. Stat'ia pervaia. Obozrenie russkoi literatury ot Derzhavina do Pushkina," *Polnoe sobranie sochinenii*, 107. The entire quote is even more telling: "Russian literature is not a native plant, but a transplant. . . . Its entire history . . . consists of a constant aspiration to free itself of the results of an artificial transplantation, and find roots in a new soil. . . . The idea of poetry was something sent by mail to Russia from Europe and appeared here like a foreign innovation. . . . It was understood as the art of writing verse for various ceremonial occasions. . . . Lomonosov, the *first* Russian poet, also understood poetry as the 'celebration' of ceremonial occasions, and his first ode (which was at the same time the first Russian poem written in a correct measure) was a song devoted to the capture of Khotin by Russian forces."

3. In her book, *Vasilii Trediakovsky: The Fool of the "New" Russian Literature*, Irina Reyfman has insisted on questioning the later mythologization of Lomonosov as the founding father of Russian letters and the concomitant "demotion" of his contemporary Trediakovskii; on the reception of the Khotin ode see, in particular, 97–98. My point is not to reinforce the Lomonosov myth but to delineate the contemporaneous birth of poetry and empire as a fact greater than any individual author, but to which Lomonosov made the most significant contribution.

4. Belinskii, "Obshchee znachenie slova literatura" (1842), in *Polnoe sobranie sochinenii*, 5:653.

5. Longinus, *On The Sublime*, 1.3. See also Olson's useful summary and discussion, "The Art of Longinus' *On the Sublime*," 232–59.

6. These enunciative shifts have been highlighted by Guerlac, "Longinus and the Subject of the Sublime," 275–89, esp. 275.

7. Monk, *The Sublime*, 233–36.

8. Burke, *A Philosophical Enquiry*, pt. 2, sec. 5.
9. Kant, *Critique of Judgment*, §23 (98), §25 (106).
10. Ibid., §28 (106).
11. Hegel, *Aesthetics*, 1:365, 371, 372, 376.
12. Schwab, *The Oriental Renaissance.*
13. Kant, *Critique of Judgment*, §29 (135). An interesting chapter between Kant and Hegel is Schiller's "On the Sublime" ("Über das Erhabene," *Schillers Sämtliche Werke*, 5:354–70), which opens up the sublime's moral imperative (which Schiller, like Kant, derives from the Old Testament) to the experience of history, thus preparing the way for Hegel.
14. For the notion of oriental despotism as the secular political equivalent of the religious sublime, the relevant pages of the *Aesthetics* must be read alongside Hegel's discussion of the orient in his *Philosophy of History*, 116–222. See also Szondi, "Hegels Lehre von der Dichtung."
15. On the foreignness of the sublime, see Chard, "Rising and Sinking on the Alps and Mount Etna: The Topography of the Sublime in Eighteenth-Century England."
16. See Lyotard, "Le sublime et l'avant-garde," and Marc Richir, *Du sublime en politique.*
17. Twentieth-century Anglo-American critics of the sublime include Monk, *The Sublime;* Abrams, *The Mirror and the Lamp*, 72–78; Weiskel, *The Romantic Sublime;* Bloom, *Poetry and Repression;* Fry, *The Reach of Criticism*, 47–86; Hertz, "A Reading of Longinus," 1–21; Guerlac, "Longinus and the Subject of the Sublime," 275–89; Price: "The Sublime Poem," 31–47; de Bolla, *Discourse of the Sublime;* Ferguson, *Solitude and the Sublime;* Fry, *A Defense of Poetry*, 133–56; and Schönle, "Of Sublimity, Shrinkage, and Selfhood," 467–82.
18. Weiskel, *The Romantic Sublime*, 26–27.
19. Ibid., 29.
20. Guerlac, *The Impersonal Sublime*, 1–3.
21. Wang, *The Sublime Figure of History*, 8, 11–12.
22. Fry, *The Reach of Criticism*, 64–65.
23. We might thus question Hayden White, who, in "The Politics of Historical Interpretation: Discipline and De-Sublimation," 113–37, equates the "aesthetics of the beautiful" with political conservatism of the Right or the Left, insofar as it defuses the utopian vision of history that only the "historical sublime" can provide. The Russian sublime, however, was generally in the service of a hegemonic and essentially repressive historical consciousness. See also Pease, "Sublime Politics," 259–99, esp. 275: "Despite all the revolutionary rhetoric invested in the term, the sublime has, in what we could call the politics of historical formation, always served conservative purposes"; and Shapiro, "From the Sublime to the Political," 213–35.
24. On the introduction of the word *sublime* into English as the modern equivalent of the Greek *hypsos*, see Monk, *The Sublime*, 18–21.
25. Longinus, *O vysokom ili velichestvennom*, iii–iv.
26. These terminological differences are discussed at length in chapters 1 and 2.

27. Pushkin, "Vozrazhenie na stat'i Kiukhel'bekera v 'Mnemozine' " (1949), in *Polnoe sobranie sochinenii,* 7:41–42.

28. Chernyshevskii, *Èsteticheskie otnosheniia iskusstva k deistvitel'nosti,* in *Polnoe sobranie sochinenii,* 2:18–21. See also Chernyshevskii's unpublished article "Vozvyshennoe i komicheskoe" of the same period, which elaborates the same argument at greater length (*Polnoe sobranie sochinenii,* 2:159–95). Discussion of the place of the sublime in Russian literature, whether in Russia or in the west, patchy at best, has picked up considerably in very recent years. David M. Bethea, in *Realizing Metaphors: Alexander Pushkin and the Life of the Poet,* has recently identified the term *vostorg* as "something very close to the Russian sublime" (151): this, effectively, is the topic of my book. Outside the generic confines of the ode, there have been some suggestive articles on the place of the sublime in Russian symbolism: for references see note 33, below. A brilliant discussion of the Russian sublime has also emerged in recent debates on Gogol: see Kotzinger (Frank), "Vozvyshennoe u Gogolia," 3–24; Spieker, "Esthesis and Anesthesia," 161–70; and the major work by Frank, *Der Diskurs des Erhabenen bei Gogol' und die Longinsche Tradition.* Frank's book contains the most elaborate juxtaposition of the western and Russian variants of the sublime existing in any language.

29. See Longinus, *O vysokom, tvorenie Dionisia Longina,* and *O vozvyshennom.*

30. Solov'ëv, "Obshchii smysl iskusstva" (1889), in *Sobranie sochinenii,* 6:84.

31. Solov'ëv, "Krasota v prirode" (1889), in *Sobranie sochinenii,* 6:48–49 n. 3.

32. Ibid., "Poèziia F. I. Tiutcheva" (1895), in *Sobranie sochinenii,* 7:127.

33. Cf. Fieguth, "K voprosu o kategorii 'vozvyshennogo' u Viacheslava Ivanova," 155–70, who suggests that Ivanov "grants the sublime as a 'religious phenomenon' a place outside aesthetics understood as the study of beauty" (162). Both Ivanov and Solov'ëv thus shared a belief in the religious rather than narrowly aesthetic nature of the sublime. The most ambitious and suggestive article on the sublime in Russian modernism is Hansen-Löve's "Zur Typologie des Erhabenen in der russischen Moderne," 166–216.

34. Monk, *The Sublime,* 12.

35. Frank, *Der Diskurs des Erhabenen bei Gogol' und die Longinsche Tradition,* 149.

36. Longinus, *O vysokom ili velichestvennom,* 6–7, 10.

37. Eagleton, *The Ideology of the Aesthetic,* 54.

38. Bloom, *Poetry and Repression,* 23, 254–55.

39. Said, "Orientalism Reconsidered," 1:14, my emphasis; see also Said, *Orientalism,* the book that initiated the debate.

40. See Bassin, "Russia between Europe and Asia," 1–17.

41. Dostoevskii, "Geok-Tepe. Chto takoe dlia nas Aziia?" 27:36–37.

42. Layton, *Russian Literature and Empire.* See also Layton, "The Creation of an Imaginative Caucasian Geography," 470–85; Layton, "Primitive Despot and Noble Savage," 31–45; Scotto, "Prisoners of the Caucasus," 107/2; Greenleaf, *Pushkin and Romantic Fashion;* Barrett, "The Remaking of the Lion of Dagestan," 360; a collection of three articles appearing in *The Russian Review* (July 1994) 53/3, with an opening statement by Alfred J. Rieber, "Russian Imperialism: Popular, Emblematic, Ambiguous," 331–35, in particular Katya Hokanson, "Literary

Imperialism, *Narodnost'* and Pushkin's Invention of the Caucasus," 336–52; Layton, "A Russian Reverie," 6–9; Ram, "Russian Poetry and the Imperial Sublime," 21–49; and Barrett, "Southern Living (in Captivity)," 75–93. To this list we must add two recent books on the subject of Russian literature and empire—Sahni, *Crucifying the Orient;* and Thomson, *Imperial Knowledge:* both books have the considerable merit of going beyond the spatial and temporal framework of Layton's book, addressing Russian representations of Central Asia and reaching well into the twentieth century. What they gain in breadth, however, they lose in attentiveness to literary specificity.

43. Layton, *Russian Literature and Empire,* 8–9.

44. Russian philology and historiography has extensively discussed literary representations of the Caucasus and the Russian "south." Among the major interventions, see Zhirmunskii, *Bairon i Pushkin;* Tomashevskii, *Pushkin. Kniga pervaia;* Gukovskii, *Pushkin i russkie romantiki;* Lotman, "Problema vostoka i zapada v tvorchestve pozdnego Lermontova," 5–22; Eidel'man, *Byt' mozhet za khrebtom Kavkaza;* Gordin, *Kavkaz;* and Zorin, *Kormia dvuglavogo orla . . . literatura i gosudarstvennaia ideologiia.* Zorin's book addresses the role of Russian literature in creating or corroborating the symbolic models that underlay state ideology or policy: its historical scholarship is fascinating, and its methodological choices distinguish it sharply from the dominant Russian critical tradition. Although my book addresses a closely related problem and a similar historical period, I am less interested than Zorin in the actual vicissitudes of state policy and its institutional relationship to literature. If, for Zorin, literature appears as "one of the possible spheres for the production of ideological metaphors" (28), then my view of literature is far less instrumental. If Zorin's goal is to "trace the historically concrete dynamic by which basic ideologemes are elaborated, take form and then displace each other" (29), then mine is to examine poetry and poetics as a textual realm in which the aesthetic and the political are mutually implicated.

More extensive references to Russian scholarship can be found in the notes to subsequent chapters and in the bibliography.

45. Layton, *Russian Literature and Empire,* 34, 38.

46. Ibid., 52–53.

47. Ibid., 39. Frank, "Gefangenen in der russischen Kultur," 61–84, has recently made some interesting observations on the Caucasus as a Russian transposition of the European topos of the Alps (62, 68). For other ways of approaching the sublime as an aesthetics of empire, see Mitter, *Much Maligned Monsters,* 120–40; Suleri, *The Rhetoric of English India,* esp. 65–66; and Schama, *Landscape and Memory,* esp. the chapter "Vertical Empires, Cerebral Chasms" (447–478), which posits a link between eighteenth-century accounts of Alpine crossing and "the fate of the British Atlantic Empire" (461).

48. Tolstoi's "revolt against romanticism" has been extensively discussed by Layton in *Russian Literature and Empire,* 233–51, 263–87.

49. For a discussion of Baratynskii's *Èda* in relation to Pushkin's "southern" poems, see Gasparov, *Poèticheskii iazyk Pushkina,* 291–96; for a stimulating recent discussion of Gogol's *Arabeski,* see Frazier, *Frames of the Imagination;* for a now classic if controversial account of the relationship between the revolutionary

avant-garde and what I would venture to call the "Soviet sublime," see Groys, *The Total Art of Stalinism.*

Chapter 1. Sublime Beginnings

1. Voltaire, *Russia under Peter the Great*, 61; published originally between 1760 and 1763 as *Histoire de l'Empire de Russie sous Pierre-le-Grand.* On Voltaire's book and its reception, see Shmurlo, *Petr velikii v otsenke sovremennikov i potomstva*, 49–60. In fact *tsar* derives from the Greek *kaisar* and referred originally to the Byzantine emperor, although it was also used during the period of Mongol domination to refer to the Tatar khans (who were never called "shahs"). Although some historians, such as Isabel de Madariaga in "Autocracy and Sovereignty," claim that the title of tsar was based on Muscovite "possession of the khanates of Siberia, Astrakhan' and Kazan'" (371), it is worth remembering that Ivan the Terrible officially assumed the title of tsar in 1547, before his conquest of Kazan in 1552, and that the term was also used by earlier monarchs such as Ivan III. In any event, it is clear that the term *tsar* was used to describe Muscovy as well as "Eastern potentates" (371). See also Cherniavsky, "Khan or Basileus," 65–79; Szeftel, "La monarchie absolue dans l'État moscovite et l'Empire russe," 729, and "The Title of the Muscovite Monarch," 59–81.

2. Wortman, *Scenarios of Power*, 1:43. Wortman defines the Muscovite understanding of empire as "first, . . . supreme power unencumbered by other authority," "second, . . . imperial expansion, extensive conquests, encompassing non-Russian lands," and "third, the Christian Empire," the defense of Orthodoxy (1:6). Peter retained the first two definitions, which were also Voltaire's, while weakening the third. For a comparison of Muscovite and Petrine notions of monarchy, see also Rowland, "Did Muscovite Literary Ideology Place Limits on the Power of the Tsar (1540s–1660s)?" 125–55.

3. Klyuchevsky, *Peter the Great*, '76; Klyuchevsky's thesis is confirmed most recently by Anisimov, *Vremia petrovskikh reform*, 122, who emphasizes the "industrial boom" accompanying the militarization of Russian society after 1700, and by Lindsey Hughes in her recent monograph, *Russia in the Age of Peter the Great:* "It is hard to refute the argument that it was foreign policy, rather than domestic needs, which shaped the course of Peter's reign" (63). Miliukov, in *Gosudarstvennoe khoziaistvo Rossii*, also concurs that "the organization of the state [by Peter] was a secondary phenomenon, . . . not a goal in itself but only a means" (545–46).

4. Wortman, *Scenarios of Power*, 1:41; see also Whittaker, "The Reforming Tsar," 77–98, and "The Idea of Autocracy," 32–59.

5. Cherniavksy, *Tsar and People*, 82, 99. Like Cherniavsky, Alain Besançon, in *Le Tsarévitch immolé*, stresses the incomplete and contradictory nature of this transition: "The paradox of the secular state is that it cannot function unless the two figures of the doubled sovereign remain equally alive" (136).

6. Lotman, "Ocherki po istorii russkoi kul'tury," 4:39; see also Zhivov, "Gosudarstvennyi mif," 664, and Lotman and Uspenskii, "Echoes," 53–64.

7. Zhivov and Uspenskii, "Tsar' i Bog," 47–153, esp. 55, 62, 93. See also Baehr, *The Paradise Myth*, 14–40.

8. Raeff, *The Well-Ordered Police State,* 181–250. See also Wortman, *The Development of a Russian Legal Consciousness,* 16–18.

9. *Zhurnal Petra velikogo,* part 1, 25–26; quoted by Serman, "Literaturno-èsteticheskie interesy," 42.

10. Shafirov's *Rassuzhdenie,* 1, ii.

11. "Torzhestvennaia vrata vvodiashchaia v khram Bezsmertnye slavy, perobedimomu imeni . . ." (1703), and "Preslavnoe torzhestvo svoboditelia Livonii" (1704), in Derzhavin et al., *Panegiricheskaia literatura petrovskogo vremeni,* 141–42, 166–67; see also Baklanova, "Otrazhenie idei"; Morozov, "Lomonosov i Barokko," 70–96; Serman, "Literaturno-èsteticheskie interesy," 27–31; Alekseeva, "Zhanr konkliuzii," 7–29; Wortman, *Scenarios of Power,* 1:42–51; and Vilinbakhov, "Osnovanie Peterburga," 46–55. On the importance of Roman antiquity in eighteenth-century Russia, see Kahn, "Readings of Imperial Rome," 745–68.

12. The spectacle is described by Grebeniuk, "Publichnye zrelishcha petrovskogo vremeni," 133–45.

13. The description is Cracraft's in his *Church Reform of Peter the Great,* 26–27. Feofan's main treatise is *Pravda voli monarshei* (1722); see Lentin, *Peter the Great.*

14. Prokopovich, "Panegirikos ili Slovo pokhval'noe o preslavnoi nad voiskami sveiskimi pobede . . ." (1709), in Derzhavina et al., *Panegiricheskaia literatura petrovskogo vremeni,* 184.

15. Prokopovich, "Slovo o Bogodarovannom mire" (1722), in Derzhavina et al., *Panegiricheskaia literatura petrovskogo vremeni,* 268, 271.

16. Prokopovich, *De Arte Rhetorica Libri X Kijoviae 1706,* Book 1, Ch. 8, 53–55. According to Prokopovich's taxonomy, the achievements of empire necessitated a "medium style" whereas national calamities, such as the death of Peter, might call for a "sublime" response. This corresponds in part to his practice, if one were to compare his funeral oration for Peter with many of his earlier speeches. Nonetheless, Prokopovich also permitted the mixing of all three styles in the same oration if the material necessitated it (55). For a sense of Prokopovich's contribution to eighteenth-century poetics, see Kochetkova, "Oratorskaia proza Feofana Prokopovicha," 50–80; for an analysis of his language, see Kutina, "Feofan Prokopovich," 5–51.

17. Simeon Polotskii, "Stisi kraesoglasnii . . ." (1660), in *Izbrannye sochineniia,* 97–98, 100. These lines were declaimed at court during Polotskii's first visit to Moscow in 1660.

18. Polotskii, *Orel rossiiskii,* 14. There is no complete edition of the *Rifmologion;* the 1915 edition of the section entitled "Orel rossiiskii" is, in this sense, an exception. A small part of "Orel rossiiskii" has also been published in Berkov, *Virshi,* 99–100. On "Orel rossiiskii," see also Hippisley, *The Poetic Style of Simeon Polotsky,* 45–48.

19. It has long been known that there is a kinship between the panegyric poets of the seventeenth century and the courtly ode launched by Trediakovskii and Lomonosov in the 1730s; see Sobolevskii, "Kogda nachalsia u nas lozhnoklassitsizm?" 1–6; Pokotilova, "Predshestvenniki Lomonosova v russkoi poèzii," 66–92; Sipovskii, *Russkaia lirika,* 1–11; Gukovskii, *Russkaia poèziia XVIII veka,* 11; Serman, "Lomonosovs Oden," 129–41; Uspenskii and Zhivov, "Zur Spezifik des

Barock in Rußland," 25–56; Sazonova, "Ot russkogo panegirika," 103–26; and Zhivov, *Iazyk i kul'tura,* 245. The categorical statement that "the origins of odic poetics are thus to be sought in the Baroque literature of Southwest Russia" (Uspenskii and Zhivov, "Zur Spezifik des Barock in Rußland," 47), however, risks obscuring the real differences between the older panegyric style and what I will call the "imperial sublime."

20. Polotskii, "Privetsvo 2," from the cycle "Gusl'dobroglasnaia," in *Izbrannye sochineniia,* 127; see also Eremin's afterword to this edition of *Izbrannye sochineniia,* "Simeon Polotskii—poèt i dramaturg," 247–48.

21. Polotskii, *Orel rossiiskii,* 49.

22. In Panchenko, "Istoriia i vechnost'," 187–99. Panchenko sees Polotskii as already representing a new philosophy of history, for which "history is not an ideal, but an illustration" (195), as against the eschatological beliefs of Muscovite traditionalists. This, however, is less applicable to Polotskii's panegyric poetry than to his other collection, *Vertograd mnogotsvetnyi.* In another article, "Dva ètapa russkogo barokko," 100–106, Panchenko clarifies his understanding of the Baroque sense of history. As Panchenko puts it, the Baroque envisions a world "full of movement, but subject to a singular 'civilizational' time" (102), in which biblical and pagan antiquity coexist alongside present-day Russia. This anticipates the taste for historical allegory in the odic poets but not their sense of history, which derives—at least in Lomonosov's case—from a secular, purposeful, and diachronic sense of time. The Baroque sense of the "transience of being" is, however, very palpable in Derzhavin.

23. On Baroque notions of the linguistic sign and their conflict with Russian tradition, see Uspenskii and Zhivov, "Zur Spezifik des Barock in Rußland."

24. Polotskii, "Zhelanie tvortsa," in *Izbrannye sochineniia,* 159. Marcus Levitt has informed me that this poem was not included in the copy of the book presented to the tsar, suggesting that the poem indeed struck a somewhat dissonant note. On Polotskii's self-understanding as a writer, see Panchenko, *Russkaia stikhotvornaia kul'tura,* 177; and on the importance of verbal creation in Polotskii's worldview, see his "Slovo i Znanie," 232–41. Two surveys of the changing status of the writer, from Polotskii up to the Petrine period, are Panchenko, "O smene pisatel'skogo tipa v petrovskuiu èpokhu," 112–28; and Jones, "The Image of the Eighteenth-Century Russian Author," 57–74.

25. Feofan Prokopovich, "Èpinikion siest' pesn' pobednaia o toeizhde preslavnoi pobede," in *Sochineniia,* 209.

26. Prokopovich, "De arte poetica," in *Sochineniia,* 275–76.

27. Prokopovich, "Èpinikion," 212.

28. Polotskii, "Raznstvie," in *Izbrannye sochineniia,* 16.

29. Serman, *Russkii klassitsizm,* 42.

30. Kutik, *The Ode and the Odic,* 2. Although I would hope that my privileging of the ode in this book is justified, a full account of the imperial sublime would also need to examine epic accounts of empire such as Kheraskov's *Rossiiada* (1779).

31. See Maddison, *Apollo and the Nine;* and Jump, *The Ode.*

32. See Gasparov, "Poèziia Pindara," 361–93; Pindar, *The Odes of Pindar.*

33. Pumpianskii, "Ocherki po literature," 115.

34. See Boileau-Despréaux, "Discours sur l'ode" (1693), in *Oeuvres complètes de Boileau,* 3:14; and *L'Art poétique,* Canto I, in *Oeuvres complètes de Boileau,* 2:85, verses 131–34. This opinion was echoed by Trediakovskii, in his "Epistola ot Rossiiskoi poèzii k Apollinu," in *Izbrannye proizvedeniia,* 391.

35. The analogy between Pindar and the Psalms was made by Boileau, "Discours sur l'ode" (1693), 12.

36. See Pumpianskii, "Trediakovskii i nemetskaia shkola razuma," 157–86, and his related article "Lomonosov i nemetskaia shkola razuma," 3–44. On the poetic culture of this period, also see Berkov, *Lomonosov i literaturnaia polemika ego vremeni;* Silbajoris, introduction to *Russian Versification,* 1–35; and Morozov, "Sud'by russkogo klassitsizma," 3–27; on the relationship of the German poets Junker and Stehlin to the Academy of Sciences during the 1730s and beyond, see Pekarskii, *Istoriia Imperatorskoi Akademii nauk v Peterburge,* 1:479–93, 538–67. Smoliarova provides a sophisticated if brief account of the history of the European and Russian ode and its relationship to performance in her *Parizh 1928: Oda vozvrashchaetsia v teatr,* 7–13.

37. Quoted by Berkov, *Lomonosov i literaturnaia polemika ego vremeni,* 25. On Trediakovkii's literary reputation, see Reyfman, *Vasilii Trediakovsky.*

38. Trediakovskii, "Rassuzhdenie o ode voobshche," Appendix 5 to his *Vasilij Kirillovic Trediakovskij Psalter 1753,* 536. It is worth noting that the later—and better known—1752 redaction of the article, "Rassuzhdenie ob ode voobshche," in *Sochineniia Tred'iakovskogo,* 1:278–81, which differs considerably from the first, speaks of the ode treating "noble and solemn matters, seldom tender or pleasant ones, in highly poetic and grandiose speeches" (278). The greater elasticity accorded to the ode here is probably a polemic with Lomonosov.

39. Trediakovskii, "Rassuzhdenie o ode voobshche," in *Vasilii Kirillovic Trediakovskij Psalter 1753,* 537–39. The mention of Horace as Pindar's equivalent in Latin is absent in Boileau and seems inappropriate. Most of the statements quoted above are, in fact, citations translated from the Boileau article "Discours sur l'ode."

40. Cf. Polotskii, "Stisi kraesoglasnii . . ." (1660), in *Izbrannye sochineniia,* 97: "My heart filled with joy, / when you had occasion to appear, / O God-given Orthodox tsar. . . ."

41. Cf. Achinger, *Der französische Anteil an der russischen Literaturkritik,* 27–29; Zhivov, *Iazyk i kul'tura v Rossii XVIII veka,* 249–64; and Alekseeva, "'Rassuzhdenie o ode voobshche' V. K. Trediakovskogo," 13–22.

42. Trediakovskii, "Oda torzhestvennaia o sdache goroda Gdanska," in *Izbrannye proizvedeniia,* 129. The oxymoronic phrase "trezvoe pianstvo" (sober intoxication) does not correspond directly to Boileau's "sainte et docte ivresse" (holy and learned intoxication), and probably refers to Longinus's idea that "even in Bacchic transport sobriety is required."

43. Trediakovskii, *Izbrannye proizvedeniia,* 133.

44. Boileau, "Ode sur la prise de Namur," in *Oeuvres complètes de Boileau,* 3:15. Boileau's second stanza, which does not mention the king at all, reaffirms the self-sustaining sweetness, and power, of poetry, while Trediakovskii's equivalent stanza immediately compares his lyric talent to his loyalty to the empress.

On the relationship of Trediakovskii's poem to its prototype, see Grishakova, "Trediakovskii i traditsiia russkoi ody," in his *M. V. Lomonosov i russkaia kul'tura,* 31–35.

45. Trediakovskii, *Izbrannye proizvedeniia,* 130–32.

46. Ibid., 365–420.

47. Trediakovskii, "O drevnem, srednem i novom stikhotvorenii rossiiskom" (1755), in *Izbrannye proizvedeniia,* 442. The question was first raised during a poetic competition that took place in 1744 between Trediakovskii, Lomonosov, and Sumarokov to translate Psalm 143. In the introduction to the published version of these translations, Trediakovskii (although not explicitly identified) clearly expresses his belief that meter and subject matter are unrelated. See Trediakovskii, "Dlia izvestiia," in *Izbrannye proizvedeniia,* 421–24.

48. Trediakovskii, "Sposob k slozheniiu rossiiskikh stikhov, protiv vydannogo v 1735 gode ispravlennyi i dopolnennyi" (1752), in *Sochineniia Tred'iakovskogo,* 1:167.

49. Cf. Pumpianskii, "Trediakovskii i nemetskaia shkola razuma," 185, who, however, makes no connection between Trediakovskii's commitment to formal variety and court ideology.

50. See Pekarskii, *Istoriia Imperatorskoi Akademii Nauk v Peterburge,* 2:259–892.

51. Belinskii, "Sochineniia Aleksandra Pushkina," in *Èstetika i literaturnaia kritika v dvukh tomakh,* 2:138. Such definitions are, of course, somewhat arbitrary: Lomonosov had already translated one ode by Fénélon in trochaic tetrameter by this time, and Trediakovskii had already written an ode to Baron von Korff in tonic verse in 1734, followed by the numerous examples provided in his Method of 1735. Whatever the case, it is worth noting that most of the early experiments in syllabo-tonic verse (not counting Lomonosov's juvenilia) were primarily odes.

52. The 1752 edition of "Sposob k slozheniiu rossiiskikh stikhov, protiv vydannogo v 1735 gode ispravlennyi i dopolnennyi," in *Sochineniia Tred'iakovskogo,* 1:167–78, accepts Lomonosov's reforms in most of its ramifications. The same edition also provides a new rendering of the ode on Gdansk in trochaic tetrameters, 271–77. On the impact of Lomonosov and Trediakovskii's response, see "Ob otnosheniiakh Lomonosova k Trediakovskomu po povodu Ody na vziiatiia Khotina. (Vmesto Vvedeniia)," in Kunik, *Sbornik materialov,* viii–lvi; and Berkov, *Lomonosov i literaturnaia polemika ego vremeni,* 25.

53. Lomonosov, "Pis'mo o pravilakh rossiiskogo stikhotvorstva," in *Polnoe sobranie sochinenii,* 7:15; my emphasis.

54. Lomonosov, "Razgovor s Anakreonom," in *Polnoe sobranie sochinenii,* 8:762.

55. Lomonosov, "Pis'mo o pravilakh rossiiskogo stikhotvorstva," in *Polnoe sobranie sochinenii,* 7:9–10, 12.

56. Boileau, *L'Art poétique,* Canto I, in *Oeuvres complètes de Boileau,* 2:82, verses 27–34.

57. For an account of the *honnête homme* as a French cultural model, see the *Dictionnaire des lettres françaises,* 501–3.

58. Boileau, "Discours sur l'ode," in *Oeuvres complètes de Boileau,* 3:12.

59. Boileau, *L'Art poétique*, Canto II, 58–64, 71–72.

60. See Brody, *Boileau and Longinus;* and Marin, "1674: On the Sublime, Infinity, Je ne sais quoi," 340–45.

61. Boileau, preface to *Oeuvres complètes de Boileau*, 4:45.

62. Lomonosov's notes are preserved in TsGADA (Moscow), F.17, ed. khr. 9, l.2–7; see also the notes to his *Polnoe sobranie sochinenii*, 8:871, and Dan'ko, "Iz neizdannykh materialov o Lomonosove," 248–75, for the history of the manuscript and its context. These notes suggest a reader for whom the sublime is first and foremost a form of stylistics: Longinus is a rhetorician who can choose and appraise select pieces of verse or prose for their merit and whose conclusions are always grounded in ready citations. Lomonosov quotes Longinus's own act of quoting: if his notes seem indecisive on the level of content—"La sublimité vient ou de la grandeur de l'âme ou de l'imagination, ou de l'imitation"—his pattern of attention to the original text bespeaks a constant attempt to verify judgment through citation, as if to guarantee the adequacy of literature to its critical model. Yet this search for stylistic norms also bespeaks a relation between Longinus and Lomonosov that is itself sublime: each citation allows Lomonosov a fictive identification with the source of utterance as a norm-giving authority. As Suzanne Guerlac observes, in "Longinus and the Subject of the Sublime": "the structure of citation appears embedded in the very operation of sublimity" (275–76).

63. It is worth noting that in his "Discours sur l'ode" Boileau insists far less on simplicity, speaking even of a "magnificence des mots," Lomonosov's formula precisely. On the reception of Boileau in Russia, see Achinger, *Der französische Anteil an der russischen Literaturkritik*, and Klein, "Sumarokov und Boileau," 254–304.

64. Gottsched, *Versuch einer Critischen Dichtkunst*, 371–72.

65. Lomonosov, "Kratkoe rukovodstvo k krasnorechiu," in *Polnoe sobranie sochinenii*, §239, 7:284–85.

66. Lomonosov, "Predislovie o pol'ze knig tserkovnykh v rossiiskom iazyke," in *Polnoe sobranie sochinenii*, 7:589. On the history of the "three styles" in Russia, see Vomperskii, *Stilisticheskoe uchenie M. V. Lomonosova;* more generally, see Vinogradov, *The History of the Russian Literary Language*.

67. Lomonosov, "Predislovie o pol'ze knig tserkovnykh v rossiiskom iazyke," in *Polnoe sobranie sochinenii*, 7:590.

68. On this question, see Zhivov, *Iazyk i kul'tura v Rossii XVIII veka*, 243–64, 334–36.

69. Lotman, "Ocherki po istorii russkoi kul'tury," 4:93.

70. The quote is from Pushkin's poem "Poètu" (To the poet) (1830).

71. Lotman, "Ocherki po istorii russkoi kul'tury," 89.

72. Trediakovkii, "Rassuzhdenie ob ode voobshche," in *Sochineniia Tred'iakovskogo*, 1:280–81.

73. Geldern, "The Ode as a Performative Genre," 934.

74. Trediakovskii, "Preduvedomlenie," *Psaltir' ili knigi Psalmov Blazhennogo Proroka i Tsaria Davida*, republished as *Vasilii Kirillovic Trediakovskij Psalter 1753*, 5.

75. See Trediakovskii's "Dlia izvestiia," 422, 423–24. Interestingly the title reserves the term *psalm* only for the Church Slavic text; the poetic reworkings are termed *odes*. On the poetics of the Psalms, see Alter, *The Literary Guide to the Bible*, 244–62.

76. Trediakovskii, "Oda vtoraia iambicheskaia," in Kunik, *Sbornik materialov*, 429.

77. Lomonosov, "Oda tretia khoreicheskaia," in Kunik, *Sbornik materialov*, 432.

78. See Levitsky, "Russian Sacred Verse," 572; see also Dorovatovskaia, "O zaimstvovaniiakh Lomonosova iz Biblii," in Sipovskii, *1711–1911 M. V. Lomonosov, Sbornik statei*, 3–65; Motol'skaia, *Istoriia russkoi literatury v desiati tomakh*, 3:338–48; Serman, *Poèticheskii stil' Lomonosova*, 39–45, 170.

79. Lomonosov, "Prelozhenie psalma 34," in *Polnoe sobranie sochinenii*, 8:377.

80. See Dorovatovskaia, "O zaimstvovaniiakh Lomonosova iz Biblii," in Sipovskii, *1711–1911 M. V. Lomonosov, Sbornik statei*, 40; Levitsky, "Russian Sacred Verse," 572; Pekarskii, *Istoriia Imperatorskoi Akademii Nauk v Peterburge*, 2:338–45; Serman, *Mikhail Lomonosov*, 30–31.

81. Lomonosov, "Prelozhenie psalma 145," in *Polnoe sobranie sochinenii*, 8:185. In this poem Lomonosov warns us not to "place forever one's hopes on the vain power of earthly princes."

82. Zhivov, "Koshchunstvennaia poèziia," 4:727. See also Lomonosov, *Kratkoe rukovodstvo k krasnorechiu* (§109), in *Polnoe sobranie sochinenii*, 7:178, in which Lomonosov quotes Cicero's definition of poetry: "Other sciences consist of rules and doctrine, but poets . . . are inspired by some divine spirit." The topos of poet-prophet, in fact, did appear at least once before the period—and the genre—in question: Feofan Prokopovich's short poem, "K sochiniteliu satir" (1730), written in response to Kantemir's first satire, hails the latter as "proroche rogatyi" (horned prophet). Although the formal context of Feofan's poem is pre-odic and still syllabic, its ideological premise is radically secular and Petrine. The image of the poet here is transitional: he occupies a more exalted status than that claimed by the earlier Baroque poets, but he is praised for his virtue, his learning, and his commitment to eradicating ignorance rather than for his poetic merit. The notion of divine transport is nominally present but does not really define any tangible aesthetic experience. On the meaning of the phrase "proroche rogatyi," see Alekseev, "'Proroche rogatyi' Feofana Prokopovicha," 17–43.

83. Cf. Pumpianskii, "K istorii russkogo klassitsizma": "The language of the Psalms gave birth in Russian poetic language to a new poetics, clearly distinguishable from the poetics of literature in general, but just as clearly distinguishable from the language of the church" (322).

84. Serman, *Poèticheskii stil' Lomonosova*, 133; Gukovskii, *Russkaia poèziia XVIII veka*, 17–18.

85. Pogosian, *Vostorg russkoi ody*, 101.

86. Pumpianskii, "K istorii russkogo klassitsizma," 310.

87. Ibid.

88. Klein, "Reforma stikha Trediakovskogo," 21.

Chapter 2. The Ode and the Empress

1. Geldern, in "The Ode as a Performative Genre," 927, argues that the ode was read aloud, but most scholars, including Panov and Ranchin, in "Torzhestvennaia oda i pokhval'noe slovo Lomonosova," 176–77, have found no evidence that Lomonosov's odes were declaimed as a part of court ceremony.

2. Lomonosov, "Oda na vziatie Khotina," in *Polnoe sobranie sochinenii,* 8:17. All future citations of Lomonosov's poetry are taken from this edition, with references provided in parentheses in the main body of the chapter. The original 1739 version of the ode has not been found; nonetheless, the 1751 redaction of the poem was widely understood then and subsequently as the "beginning" of modern Russian poetry.

3. See Boileau, "Ode sur prise de Namur," in *Oeuvres complètes,* 3:15; Günther, "Auf den zwischen Ihrer Romisch Kayserlichen Majestät," 339; and Kirchner, "Lomonosov und Johann Christian Günther," 483–97.

4. Lomonosov, "Slovo pokhval'noe . . . Imperatritse Elisavete Petrovne" (1749), in *Polnoe sobranie sochinenii,* 8:252.

5. The term *poddanstva znak* [sign of subjection] appears in other poems by Lomonosov, for example, Ode 21 (1741), 36. In all cases the poems make an analogy between poetic homage and imperial conquest.

6. Pumpianskii, "Lomonosov i nemetskaia shkola razuma," 44. Cf. Makogonenko, "Puti razvitiia russkoi poèzii": "Lomonosov's 'rapture' is 'Russia's metamorphosis' as it is experienced internally by the poet's personality" (32).

7. Solov'ev, *Istoriia Rossii,* book 5, 22:556–58. On the utopian, paradisial, and cosmogonic elements in eighteenth-century imperial mythology, see also Baehr, *The Paradise Myth,* and the recent article by Bukharkin, "Topos 'tishiny' v odicheskoi poèzii M. V. Lomonosova," 3–12.

8. Pumpianskii, "Ocherki po literature," 129. See also Berkov, who argues, in *Lomonosov i literaturnaia polemika ego vremeni,* that the conflict between the middle gentry and the elite is the basis of the dispute between Lomonosov and his literary opponents (100–102).

9. Cf. Pumpianskii, "Lomonosov i nemetskaia shkola razuma," 28.

10. Gleason, "The Two Faces of the Monarch," 403.

11. Lomonosov, "Kratkoe rukovodstvo k krasnorechiiu," in *Polnoe sobranie sochinenii,* §158, 7:228–29.

12. Bassin, "Asia," 69.

13. See the notes to the poem in Lomonosov, *Polnoe sobranie sochinenii,* 8:1170–75; and Chernov, "M. V. Lomonosov v odakh 1762 g.," 1331–80.

14. Sumarokov, "Iz traktata Longinova," 219–24.

15. See Sumarokov, *Izbrannye proizvedeniia,* 287–92. On the circumstances surrounding the poems and their censoring, see Pekarskii, *Istoriia Imperatorskoi Akademii Nauk v Peterburge,* 2:653–55.

16. Concerning Lomonosov, Sumarokov, and the minor odic poets, see Grechishcheva, "Khvalebnaia oda," 93–149; Zapadov, *Poèty XVIII veka;* and Klein and Zhivov, "Zur Problematik und Spezifik," 234–88.

17. The most vivid account of Derzhavin's life is Khodasevich's *Derzhavin;* for Derzhavin's views on state service and the writer's profession, see Wortman, in-

troduction to "Gavrila Romanovich Derzhavin and his *Zapiski*," 1–8; and Fomenko, "Avtobiograficheskaia proza G. R. Derzhavina," 143–64.

18. On the constitutive gap between state ideals and state practice under Catherine, see Lotman and Uspenskii, "K semioticheskoi tipologii russkoi kul'tury XVIII veka," 4:434; on Catherinian enlightenment as a "mythological attribute" of the Russian state, see Zhivov, "Gosudarstvennyi mif," 4:666–79.

19. Billington, *The Icon and the Axe*, 233.

20. Derzhavin, "Prilozhenie k ode 'Na vziatie Varshavy.' Iz pis'ma k Merzliakovu ot 26 avgusta 1815g. iz Zvanki," in *Sochineniia Derzhavina*, 1:455. The nineteenth-century Grot edition remains the most exhaustive and is the source of all future Derzhavin quotations in this book, with references henceforth provided within parentheses in the text.

21. Belinskii believed that Derzhavin had reconciled Kantemir's satire and Lomonosov's ode; Gukovskii suggested that Derzhavin had replaced genre and concept with the human persona; Tynianov spoke of Derzhavin's "destruction of the ode as a closed, canonical genre."

See Belinskii, "Vzgliad na russkuiu literaturu 1847 g. (stat'ia 1-aia)," in *Èstetika i literaturnaia kritika v dvukh tomakh*, 2:652; Gukovskii, "O russkom klassitsizme," 24; and Tynianov, "Oda kak oratorskii zhanr," in *Arkhaisty i novatory*, 75. Cf. also Hart, "Continuity and Change in the Russian Ode," 45–62; and Stepniak, "Lomonosov i Derzhavin," 235–67. See also Mayer's doctoral dissertation, "Models for Creativity and the Image of the Author in the Poetry of G. R. Derzhavin," for a useful summary of the critical debates.

22. Pushkin, in a letter to A. A. Del'vig, June 1825, polemically dismisses Derzhavin for his defiance of grammar and euphony (*Perepiska A. S. Pushkina v dvukh tomakh*, 1:381).

23. In *Sochineniia Derzhavina* cf. "Na priobretenie Kryma" (On acquiring the Crimea) (1784), *Sochineniia*, 1:126–28; "Na vziatie Izmaila" (On the taking of Izmail) (1790), 1:237–47; "Na vziatie Varshavy" (On the Taking of Warsaw) (1794), 1:443–49; "Na pokorenie Derbenta" (On the subjugation of Derbent) (1796), 1:507–8; "Na perekhod Al'piiskikh gor" (On crossing the Alps) (1799), 2:173–82. Other odes of empire, such as "Osen' vo vremia osady Ochakova" (Autumn during the seige of Ochakova) (1788), 1:156–59, involve transformations of the older imperial theme that I will treat shortly.

24. Wortman, *Scenarios of Power*, 1:122–23, 138–39.

25. Reddaway, Letter XV (29 May / 9 June 1767), in *Documents of Catherine the Great*, 17–18; see also Madariaga, *Russia in the Age of Catherine the Great*, 150; and Alexander, *Catherine the Great*, 107–12.

26. Quoted in Alexander, *Catherine the Great*, 109.

27. On the Chitalagai odes, see Hart, *G. R. Derzhavin*, 19–27; Etkind, "Rozhdenie 'krupnogo sloga,'" 163–84; and Vroon, "'Chitalagaiskie ody,'" 185–201.

28. Vroon, "'Chitalagaiskie ody,'" 195.

29. Gukovskii, *Russkaia literatura XVIII veka*, 416–17; Blagoi, "Gavrila Romanovich Derzhavin," 29; Serman, *Derzhavin*, 108–9.

30. Serman, "Derzhavin v novom veke," 27:56.

31. Longinus, *O vysokom ili velichestvennom*, 46–47.

32. Crone, "Doing Justice to Potemkin," 393–418.

33. Cf. Serman, *Derzhavin*, 67–68; Zapadov, *Gavrila Romanovich Derzhavin*, 97–104; and Kondrashov, "'Plan obshirnyi ob"emletsia smelost'iu zamysla,'" 31–42. See also Khodasevich, *Derzhavin*, 138–39.

34. See Zorin, "Krym v istorii russkogo samosoznaniia," 124. See also Zorin, "Russkaia oda kontsa," 5–29; and Schönle, "Garden of the Empire," 1–23.

35. Trediakovskii, "Rassuzhdenie o ode voobshche," in *Vasilii Kirillovic Trediakovskij Psalter 1753*, 539.

36. From a poem written to mark Elizabeth's birthday, written in 1741 (Lomonosov, *Polnoe sobranie sochinenii*, 7:55).

37. Serman, in "Poèziia Lomonosova v 1740-e gody," 3–69, argues that some delineation of Elizabeth's real features can be noted in certain of Lomonosov's poems.

38. Marin, *Portrait of the King*, 89; see also Marin, *Cross-Readings*, 137–56.

39. Montesquieu, *De l'Esprit des lois*, book 5, chap. 14. Other references, mostly negative, to Russia in Montesquieu's work are 5:14, 6:16, 11:2, 14:2, 15:6, 17:3, and 19:14. On Montesquieu, see Althusser, *Montesquieu*, 83, 91–92: "Despotism is indeed a political *idea* . . . the idea of the very limits of the political as such. . . . It is very clear that Montesquieu had wished to represent in this figure of despotism something entirely different from the state formations found in the orient: *the abdication from the political itself* . . . despotism is a geographical illusion only to the extent that it is a historical allusion." Althusser's essay contains precious insights on the time and space of despotism—"a space without place, a time without duration" (87)—and on the constitutive gap between ruler and ruled: "The paradox of despotism is that it is unleashed so powerfully on the great and powerful that the people appear to be spared." For a genealogy of the term *despotism* from Greek antiquity to the Enlightenment, see Koebner's "Despot and Despotism," while Franco Venturi's "Despotismo orientale" is useful in showing how Montesquieu's ideas were contested by the early oriental philologists such as Anquetil-Duperron. A more recent Marxist summary of this earlier debate is Turner's "Orientalism and the Problem of Civil Society in Islam." The debate has been revived in our time by Wittfogel's *Oriental Despotism*, a book deeply traumatized by a Stalinism for which it seeks to provide an Asiatic ancestry and morphology. In the case of both Montesquieu and Wittfogel, "historical allusion" is decisive, threatening to empty the term *despotism* of any referential status with respect to the east. Perry Anderson seeks to rebut Wittfogel in *Lineages of the Absolutist State*, 463.

40. Montesquieu, *De l'Esprit des lois*, 8:17, 19.

41. Ibid., 18:6.

42. Ekaterina II, "Iz 'Nakaza,'" 23. The texts by Catherine and Montesquieu correspond right down to grammatical structure and lexical choice; these and other correspondences have also been noted by W. F. Reddaway, editor of the English version *Documents of Catherine the Great*, 322ff. Where Montesquieu has "autorité despotique" (despotic authority), Catherine has "samoderzhavnuiu vlast" (autocratic power) in Russian and "autorité souveraine" (sovereign authority) in her French version. Other discussions of the textual and ideological import of the "Nakaz" are Chechulin, "Ob istochnikakh 'Nakaza'"; Taranovskii, "Politicheskaia doktrina v Nakaze Imperatritsy Ekateriny II"; Miliukov, *Ocherki*

po istorii russkoi kul'tury, vol. 3; Druzhinin, "Prosveshchennyi absoliutizm v Rossii," 428–59; Rasmussen, *Catherine II and Peter I,* chap. 3; Madariaga, "Catherine the Great," 289–311.

43. The passage is copied almost verbatim from Montesquieu, *De l'Esprit des lois,*14:14 (see also 17:3), but Montesquieu's version also condemns as "tyrannical" the means Peter employed to modernize Russia.

44. Ekaterina II, *Antidote,* 7:82.

45. Ekaterina II, *Sochineniia,* 485. Catherine's espousal of enlightened absolutism remained a point of controversy in her dialogue with the French Lumières. In Leonard Krieger's *Essay on the Theory of Enlightened Despotism,* we read a letter Diderot wrote to Catherine in 1774 arguing that "two or three consecutive reigns of a just and enlightened despotism" would be "one of the great misfortunes that could occur in any free nation," since any despot, "be he the best of men, . . . is a good shepherd who reduces his subjects to the level of animals" (20). See also Whittaker, "The Idea of Autocracy," 32–59, who points to historians of the period who sought to defend Russian autocracy against the charge of despotism (42–46).

46. Kubacheva, "'Vostochnaia povest', 305.

47. For both stories, see Ekaterina II, *Sochineniia,* 118–36.

48. In "Tale of the Crown Prince Fevei," where the role of the Turkic nomads is more negative, the prince's response is one of benign superiority: the people of the Golden Horde are meant to "learn a more amicable way of treating people and other virtues" from the Prince's example (*Sochineniia,* 136).

49. Serman, *Russkii klassitsizm,* 82.

50. Lotman, "Ocherki po istorii russkoi kul'tury," 105–6.

51. Billington, *The Icon and the Axe,* 233.

52. My argument here has benefited from Judith Butler's *The Psychic Life of Power.*

53. Hart, *G. R. Derzhavin,* 57. Much has been made of the prose and the poetic variants of "The Murza's Vision," the former far bolder than the latter: see Makogonenko, *Ot Fonvizina do Pushkina,* 376–431. The gap between the two suggests the limits of the ceremonial ode in realizing an autonomous literary or political vision.

54. Hart, *G. R. Derzhavin,* 58.

55. Most critics either defend Derzhavin's didacticism as proof of his independence, for example, Zapadov, *Masterstvo Derzhavina,* or Makogonenko, *Ot Fonvizina do Pushkina,* 367–431, or (less frequently) condemn his panegyrics as proof of his political venality: yet surely neither extreme is really true.

56. The most sophisticated analysis of the ambiguities of Derzhavin's "self" is I. Z. Serman's, in *Russkii klassitsizm* (80–96), and *Derzhavin* (108–9), but even Serman does not go beyond a model based on a "complex system of relations between the "I, the ode's narrator, and a concrete embodiment of the odic ideal—Felitsa" (89).

57. Zhivov, "Gosudarstvennyi mif," 4:672–73. E. Ia Dan'ko, in "Izobrazitel'noe iskusstvo v poèzii Derzhavina," 243–44, has suggested that Derzhavin's pictorial representations of ethnicity derive from a porcelain dinner set commissioned between 1780 and 1790 for the Russian court.

58. Cf. Blagoi, *Istoriia russkoi literatury XVIII veka,* 293, who describes the Murza as an "artificial 'Tatar' disguise." Richard Wortman also discusses another journey of 1787 which took Catherine as far as the recently conquered territories on the Black Sea and whose objective was to present a "spectacular confirmation of the motifs of conquest and transformation" (*Scenarios of Power,* 1:141); for another perspective on this journey, see Panchenko, "'Potemkinskie derevni' kak kul'turnyi mif," 93–104. This journey might have provided an additional historical precedent for aspects of "Izobrazhenie Felitsy."

59. On the details of Catherine's policy toward the Tatar Muslims, and the role of the Legislative Commission in the evolution of her ideas, see Fisher, "Enlightened Despotism," 4:552–53; Kappeler, *Russlands erste Nationalitäten,* esp. 298–307, 370–77; and Barthold, *La Découverte de l'Asie,* 249–50.

60. It has long been suggested that Derzhavin's choice of the Murza as a lyric persona has a biographical basis (see Grot's notes in Derzhavin, 1:91, 94), but the broader historical significance of the lyric persona has been neglected.

61. In Horace's original poems (*Odes,* III:30 and II:20) references to empire serve only to corroborate the breadth of the poet's fame; in Derzhavin, empire is the poet's inhabited space and an integral part of his literary mission.

62. Derzhavin's posthumously published poem, "Lirik" (dated approximately between 1801–1816), bridges the gap between the eighteenth-century perception of King David's "psalmic odes" and the Decembrist notion of the poet-prophet: "Did not a pastor, through his rapture, / Become king, establishing commerce with God himself?" (3:411).

63. Lotman, "Ocherki po istorii russkoi kul'tury," 4:95.

Chapter 3. Sublime Dissent

1. Exemplary manifestos of "Karamzinism" are Karamzin, "Otchego v Rossii malo avtorskikh talantov?" (1802), in *Izbrannye stat'i i pis'ma,* 101–4 ; and Batiushkov, "Rech' o vliianii legkoi poèzii na iazyk" (1816), in *Opyty v stikhakh i proze,* 8–19.

2. See Todd, *Fiction and Society in the Age of Pushkin,* 10–44, esp. 25.

3. Ibid., 26.

4. Tynianov, "Arkhaisty i Pushkin," 23–121.

5. Radishchev, *Puteshestvie iz Peterburga v Moskvu,* 1:388–89. On Radishchev, see McConnell, *A Russian philosophe.*

6. Radishchev, "Vol'nost'," in *Polnoe sobranie sochinenii,* 1:15–17, verses 48–54. Radishchev reaffirms his spatial theory of empire in the gloss to the poem that he supplies in *Puteshestvie iz Peterburga v Moskvu:* "The following eight stanzas contain predictions on the future lot of the fatherland, which will separate into parts, all the more quickly the more spatially extended it is" (1:361). This idea is oddly contradicted by a brief note on Montesquieu and Rousseau written in roughly the same period, in which the equation of territorial size with coercion is questioned (*Polnoe sobranie sochinenii,* 3:47, fragment VII). On Radishchev's ode, "Liberty," and his views on Lomonosov, see Gukovskii, "Vokrug Radishcheva," 141–43, 174–75; on Radishchev's influence on the Decembrists, see

Kochetkova, "Oratorskaia proza dekabristov," 100–120; and Lotman, "Otrazhenie etiki i taktiki revoliutsionnoi bor'by," 2:134–58.

7. Radishchev, *Journey from Petersburg to Moscow,* in *Polnoe sobranie sochinenii,* 1:354.

8. See Shishkov, "Rassuzhdenie o starom i novom sloge rossiiskogo iazyka" (1803), in *Sobranie sochinenii,* 2:1–352. For discussion of the Colloquy of Lovers of the Russian Word, see Altshuller, *Predtechi slavianofil'stva v russkoi literature;* and Liamina, "Arkhaisty i nenovatory," 27:67–81.

9. Shishkov, "Rech' pri otkrytii Besedy liubitelei ruskago [*sic*] slova," *Sobranie sochinenii,* 4:140–41, 136.

10. Serman, "Derzhavin v novom veke," 63. The nature and extent of Derzhavin's involvement in the Colloquy remains a topic of controversy.

11. Tynianov, "Arkhaisty i Pushkin," 26, 35.

12. Cf. Sobolev, "Teoriia iziashchnogo—teoriia deistviia (o svoeobrazii èstetiki dekabristov)," 107–42; Pul'khritudova, "Literaturnaia teoriia dekabristskogo romantizma," 232–92; and Frizman, "Literaturnaia kritika dekabristov," 5–24.

13. Gukovskii, *Pushkin i russkie romantiki,* 180. The term *revolutionary romanticism* was applied earlier to the Decembrists by Presniakov, "Motivy real'noi politiki v dvizhenii dekabristov," 33. See also Pul'khritudova, "Romanticheskoe i prosvetitel'skoe," 39–72. Another critic to concur with Gukovskii in differentiating the eighteenth century from the Decembrists, albeit for different reasons, is Gofman, "Ryleev-poèt," 1–73. Gofman argues that a "functional shift" occurred in the import of civic verse, such that the pragmatic need to promote real change, clearly present in the Decembrist tradition, was absent in the ode: "The 'civic' nature of the classical tradition manifested itself above all as a semantic characteristic which motivated a semantic 'thunder' within the verse itself" (35). One might agree that the ode never really constituted an active intervention in political life, but this does not make the ceremonial ode any less political.

14. Gukovskii, *Pushkin i russkie romantiki,* 180.

15. Ginzburg, "O probleme narodnosti i lichnosti v poèzii dekabristov," 66. Here Ginzburg seems to contradict a statement made in her earlier book, *Tvorcheskii put' Lermontova,* that "the romantic demand for grandeur is not, of course, to be equated with the classicist notion of the sublime (*vysokogo*)" (6).

16. Zholkovsky, "The Obverse of Stalinism," 67 (my emphasis).

17. Freidin, "By the Walls of Church and State," 156.

18. Ibid., 156–57.

19. Zhivov, "Gosudarstvennyi mif," 4:678. Zhivov is not speaking specifically of the Decembrists but of a broader cultural tendency that began with Derzhavin.

20. Ryleev, "Grazhdanskoe muzhestvo," in *Dekabristy,* 24–25. The poem was not published in Ryleev's lifetime but would have circulated widely in manuscript form.

21. On revolutionary neoclassicism, its French roots, and its Russian adaptations, see Gasparov, *Poèticheskii iazyk Pushkina,* 24–52.

22. Ryleev, "Na smert' Beirona," in *Dekabristy,* 25–26.

23. I am summarizing the debate between Gukovskii, *Pushkin i russkie romantiki,* 180ff., and Ginzburg, "O probleme narodnosti i lichnosti v poèzii dekabristov," 65ff.

24. Other instances of the same topos of animating or personifying specific mountains are Zhukovskii's "K Voeikovu poslanie (otryvok)" (An epistle to Voeikov [a fragment]) (1814), Pushkin's "Otvet F. T." (An answer to F. T.) (1826) and "Monastyr' na Kazbeke" (The monastery on Kazbek) (1829), S. D. Nechaev's "Vospominaniia" (Recollections) (1825), V. N. Grigor'ev's "Beshtau" (Beshtu) (1826), and V. G. Tepliakov's "Kavkaz" (The Caucasus) (1828); numerous instances from Lermontov's long poems could also be provided.

25. Cf. Ryleev's poem "A. P. Ermolovu," (1821), in *Dekabristy,* 4. On Ermolov's role in the Decembrist political project, see Shaduri, *Drug Pushkina A. A. Shishkov i ego roman o Gruzii,* 69ff.; Nechkina, *Griboedov i dekrabristy,* 220–58; Shostakovich, *Diplomaticheskaia deiatel'nost' A. S. Griboedova,* 28–33.

26. Tomashevskii, *Pushkin. Kniga pervaia,* 407.

27. Pestel', *Russkaia pravda,* 107–9. For a comprehensive account of Decembrist views on the "southern question," see Syroechkovskii, "Balkanskaia problema," 216–303.

For a suggestive commentary on Pestel' and other ideologians of the Caucasian conquest, see Gordin, *Kavkaz,* 6–10 ; see also Lotman, *Aleksandr Sergeevich Pushkin,* 79–83.

28. Pestel', *Russkaia Pravda,* 167.

29. Ibid., 167–69.

30. Gukovskii, *Pushkin i russkie romantiki,* 258–59.

31. Belinskii, "Stikhotvoreniia M. Lermontova," *Polnoe sobranie sochinenii,* 4:544.

32. Lazarev, "'Da, aziaty my . . .' (Vmesto Predisloviia)," 14. There is a sizable secondary literature on Griboedov and the orient: see Enikolopov's several monographs *A. S. Griboedov v Gruzii i Persii, Griboedov v Gruzii,* and *Griboedov i vostok;* Shostakovich, *Diplomaticheskaia deiatel'nost' A. S. Griboedova;* the documentary collections Popova, *A. S. Griboedov v Persii,* Shaduri and Buachidze, *Tam, gde v'etsia Alazan',* and.Harden, *The Murder of Griboedov.* Shorter articles on Griboedov's orientalism include Krasnov, "Putevye pis'ma Griboedova," 206–11; Arinshtein, "Persidskie pis'ma po povodu gibeli Griboedova," 108–32; Iakubova, "A. S. Griboedov," 265–70; and Murav'eva, "Zamysel A. S. Griboedova," 271–78.

33. These definitions correspond somewhat to Edward Said's in "Orientalism Reconsidered," 1:14 (my emphasis); cf. also Said, *Orientalism,* the book that initiated the debate.

34. Griboedov, "O razbore vol'nogo perevoda Biurgerovoi ballady 'Lenory,'" in *Sochineniia,* 391.

35. Griboedov, "Pis'mo k izdateliu ('Syna otechestva') iz Tiflisa ot 21 ianvaria 1819g.," in *Sochineniia,* 400. The Lomonosov quote (analyzed in chapter 2) is from his "Oda na den' vosshestviia na prestol Elisavety Petrovny 1748 goda."

36. Griboedov, *Sochineniia,* 401, 403.

37. Ibid., 404.

38. Griboedov, Letter to S. I. Mazarovich, 12 October 1818, in *Sochineniia,* 533.

39. Griboedov, Letter to S. N. Begichev, 29 January 1819, in *Sochineniia*, 420.

40. Griboedov, "Proèkt uchrezhdeniia Rossiiskoi Zakavkazskoi kompanii," in *Sochineniia*, 497–520.

41. Tynianov, "Siuzhet 'Goria ot uma,'" 359; on rumor as a motif linking Griboedov's politics and literature, see also 355–58.

42. Griboedov, "Otryvki iz pervoi redaktsii 'Gore ot uma,'" in *Sochineniia*, 141.

43. It is not until we reach Tolstoi's Caucasian works of the 1850s, such as "Rubka lesa" (Felling the forest) (1853–55), that we shall see a more systematic dismantling of the vertical "poetic" axis in favor of a more pragmatic "horizontal" understanding of the administrative and military underpinnings of imperial power. These developments, which take place primarily in prose genres, are outside the scope of this book.

44. Griboedov, Letter to S. N. Begichev, 29 January 1819, in *Sochineniia*, 420.

45. Griboedov, Letter to S. N. Begichev, 10–13 February 1819, in *Sochineniia*, 436.

46. Griboedov, "Putevye zapiski. VII. Krym," 30 June 1825, in *Sochineniia*, 459.

47. Griboedov, "Proèkt uchrezhdeniia Rossiiskoi Zakavkazskoi kompanii," in *Sochinenia*, 515, 520. The project was composed jointly with P. D. Zavileiskii, but most scholars attribute the text and its ideas primarily to Griboedov; cf. Enikolopov, *Griboedov v Gruzii*, 57ff. Enikolopov quotes General Paskevich's statement that Georgia should remain a source of raw materials for Russian manufacturing rather than become an industrial center in its own right (*Griboedov v Gruzzii*, 79): Paskevich's views were essentially contrary to Griboedov's.

48. See Levchenko, "Griboedov i russkaia ballada," 265–70; cf. also Orlov, "Khudozhestvennaia problematika Griboedova," 60–62.

49. Griboedov, Letter to S. N. Begichev, 7 December 1825, in *Sochineniia*, 596. The letter was written shortly after the poem was composed. Cf. also Enikolopov, *Griboedov i vostok*, 54–55.

50. Griboedov, "Khishchniki na Chegeme," in *Sochineniia*, 366.

51. Griboedov, "Rodamist i Zenobiia," in *Sochineniia*, 337.

52. Griboedov, Letter to S. N. Begichev, 10–13 February 1819, in *Sochineniia*, 436.

53. For a general survey of Decembrist poetry, see Frizman, *Poèziia dekabristov*, 3–64.

54. This point has been made earlier, e.g., Koroleva, "V. K. Kiukhel'beker," 1:31. What has yet to be analyzed is the relationship of nation and empire in the individuation of the lyric voice and in the articulation of the civic or political dimension of Decembrist poetry.

55. Tynianov, "Pushkin i Kiukhel'beker," 240; cf. also Tynianov, "Arkhaisty i Pushkin," 90–94. In the poet's juvenilia (1814–21), still marked by what Küchelbecker would later criticize as a "banal descriptive-elegiac" tone, the sublime is intermittently, if increasingly, present, often registering the irruption of the historical present and its concerns into the poem's descriptive logic. Cf. Küchelbecker's comments concerning his own poem "Massiliia" (1821) in his prison diaries, 4 December 1833, *Puteshestvie, dnevnik, stat'i*, 287–88.

56. Küchelbecker, "[Lektsiia Kiukhel'bekera o russkoi literature i russkom iazyke, prochitannaia v Parizhe v iiune 1821 g.]," 366.

57. Küchelbecker, "Dnevnik," 3 January 1832, *Puteshestvie, dnevnik, stat'i,* 77. Cf. also Tynianov, "Arkhaisty i Pushkin," 90. The scattered comments on Griboedov in Küchelbecker's diary have been collected in *A. S. Griboedov. V vospominaniiakh sovremennikov,* 257–63. In fact, Küchelbecker appears to have already met Griboedov earlier, in the summer of 1817: see Pul'khritudova, "Kiukhel'beker," 3:253–58. See also Maz'ia, "A. S.Griboedov v stikhakh i dnevnike B. K. Kiukhel'bekera," 174–84.

58. Gukovskii writes that with Glinka "the oriental style in its biblical recension definitively matured as a Decembrist style" (*Pushkin i russkie romantiki,* 268).

59. Griboedov, "David," in *Sochineniia,* 358. Glinka translated the same Psalm, calling it "Pobeda," *Opyty sviashchennoi poèzii* (1826).

60. Küchelbecker, "Griboedovu" (1821), *Izbrannye proizvedeniia,* 1:151.

61. Küchelbecker, "A. S. Griboedovu pri peresylke k nemu v Tiflis moikh Argivian" (1823), *Izbrannye proizvedeniia,* 1:170–71.

62. Küchelbecker, "Nachalo poèmy o Griboedove" (1822–23), *Izbrannye proizvedeniia,* 1:347–49. It has been suggested that the narrator is the Azerbaijani historian and poet Abbas Kuli-Agha Bakikhanli, who served over several decades as a cultural mediator between the Russian imperial administration and the Transcaucasian Muslim community. While Bakhikanli knew Küchelbecker and Griboedov, he would have been very young in the early twenties, whereas the narrator is described as an old man. Perhaps a composite figure is involved here. Cf. E. M. Akhmedov, "Vydaiushchiisia azerbaidzhanskii myslitel'," especially 17–24.

63. Küchelbecker, "O napravlenii nashei poèzii, osobenno liricheskoi, v poslednee desiatiletie," in *Puteshestvie dnevnik stat'i,* 454.

64. Ibid., 458.

65. Ibid., 456.

66. Ibid., 457–58.

67. Küchelbecker, "Minuvshego 1824 goda voennye, uchenye, i politicheskie dostoprimechatel'nye sobytiia v oblasti rossiiskoi slovesnosti," in *Puteshestvie, dnevnik, stat'i,* 500.

68. Gukovskii, *Pushkin i russkie romantiki,* 238. Cf. also Gukovskii, "Stil' grazhdanskogo romantizma 1800-kh–1810-kh godov i tvorchestva molodogo Pushkina," in Blagoi and Kirpotin, *Pushkin—rodonachal'nik novoi russkoi literatury,* 167–91; and Gusev, "Vklad dekabristov v otechestvennuiu ètnografiiu," 80–104.

69. Ginzburg, "O probleme narodnosti i lichnosti v poèzii dekabristov," 55, 80. See also Gukovskii, *Pushkin i russkie romantiki,* 291ff., and also G. P. Makogonenko, "O romanticheskom geroe dekabristskoi poèzii," 6–24.

70. Küchelbecker, "O napravlenii nashei poèzii, osobenno liricheskoi, v poslednee desiatiletie," in *Puteshestvie dnevnik stat'i,* 458.

71. Küchelbecker, *Evropeiskie pis'ma,* 2:162–63. I would like to acknowledge Chris Caes's help in developing this argument.

72. Ibid., 2:153. The inertia of the Soviet tradition is so great that E. M. Pul'khritudova, in "Literaturnaia teoriia dekabristskogo romantizma," 237, in-

terprets the *European Letters* as embodying the view that the main force of history is national liberation.

73. Küchelbecker, *Evropeiskie pis'ma*, 2:167.

74. Küchelbecker, "Russkii Dekameron,"in *Puteshestvie dnevnik stat'i*, 510.

75. Ibid., 516; my emphasis.

76. Küchelbecker, *Zorovavel'*, 1:475. In content and form, *Zerubbabel* closely resembles Küchelbecker's earlier unfinished poem, "Nachalo poèmy o Griboedove," mentioned above.

77. Küchelbecker, *Zorovavel'*, 1:501.

78. Ibid., 1:502.

79. Küchelbecker, "Prorochestvo," in *Izbrannye proizvedeniia*, 1:158. In his diary Küchelbecker recalls writing this poem in Georgia after his encounter with Griboedov, in the wake of a Greek victory against the Ottomans (25 May 1845, *Puteshestvie Dnevnik Stat'i*, 428).

80. Küchelbecker, "Prorochestvo," in *Izbrannye proizvedeniia*, 159.

81. Küchelbecker, "Prokliatie," in *Izbrannye proizvedeniia*, 161.

82. Küchelbecker, "Ermolovu" and "Uchast' poètov," in *Izbrannye proizvedeniia*, 150, 185.

83. Küchelbecker, "Smert' Bairona," in *Izbrannye proizvedeniia*, 201–2.

84. Ryleev, "Na smert' Beirona" (1824), in *Dekabristy*, 26.

85. Küchelbecker, "Smert' Bairona," in *Izbrannye proizvedeniia*, 202.

86. Cf. Pushkin's "Pogaslo dnevnoe svetilo" (The diurnal orb has gone out) (1820), "Kto, volny, vas ostanovil" (Who halted you, o waves) (1823), and "K moriu" (To the sea) (1824), in *Polnoe sobranie sochinenii*, 2:7–8, 151, 198–200, respectively. The latter was also published in Odoevskii and Küchelbecker's *Mnemozina*.

87. Küchelbecker, "Smert' Bairona," in *Izbrannye proizvedeniia*, 203.

88. Ibid., 206.

89. Küchelbecker, "Zhrebii poèta," in *Izbrannye proizvedeniia*, 190.

Chapter 4. Pushkin, Lermontov, and the Elegiac Sublime

1. Ginzburg, *Tvorcheskii put' Lermontova*, 9.

2. Pushkin, "Vospominaniia v Tsarskom Sele" and "Vol'nost'," in *Polnoe sobranie sochinenii v desiati tomakh*, 1:83–88, 1:321–24. All future citations from Pushkin are to*Polnoe sobranie sochinenii v desiati tomakh*, with references provided in the main body of the text. Other relevant political poems by the young Pushkin are "K Litsiniiu" (To Licinius) (1815), "Napoleon na El'be" (Napoleon on the Elbe) (1815), "K Chaadaevu" (To Chaadaev) (1818), and "Derevnia" (The countryside) (1819). On Pushkin's early political verse and its relationship to "civic romanticism," see Gukovskii, "Stil' grazhdanskogo romantizma 1800-kh - 1810-kh godov i tvorchestvo molodogo Pushkina," in Blagoi and Kirpotin, *Pushkin rodonachal'nik novoi russkoi literatury*, 167–91.

3. Tomashevskii argues, in *Pushkin, kniga pervaia*, 56–63, that the poem owes less to Derzhavin than to Batiushkov and that its strophic pattern is taken from Batiushkov's historical elegy "On the Ruins of a Castle in Sweden" (1814). At the

same time Tomashevskii points out that Pushkin called the poem "lyrical," which was "almost equivalent to the word 'ode.'" Although "Pushkin did not write ceremonial odes in the proper sense of the word," in poems such as "Memories in Tsarskoe Selo" Pushkin "[came] closest to approaching an odic sensibility" (61). Lotman, in "Pushkin. Ocherk tvorchestva," 190, has called the poem a synthesis of Batiushkov's historical elegy and Derzhavin's ode. For a still more formally oriented reading, see Vickery, "Vospominaniia v Tsarskom sele" (1814) i "Pamiatnik": k voprosu o strofike," 485–97. A recent and suggestive reading of the same poem can be found in Bethea, *Realizing Metaphors*, 154–72. Bethea's book is perhaps the primary work to have recently taken up the question of a Russian sublime in the context of a dialogue between Pushkin and the odic tradition. On Pushkin and Derzhavin, see also Tatishcheva, "Pushkin i Derzhavin," 106–16; and Makogonenko, "Pushkin i Derzhavin," 113–26.

4. On Pushkin and Küchelbecker, see Tynianov, "Pushkin i Kiukhel'beker," 233–94.

5. In his article "Arkhaisty i Pushkin," Tynianov was the first to identify this poem as a critique of the young archaist revival of the odic sublime and not just an attack on the ceremonial ode in general.

6. Lidiia Ginzburg has discussed this problem in the context of the disintegration of the genre system in Russian poetry: see her "O probleme narodnosti i lichnosti," 90–91.

7. V. E. Vatsuro, "Prorok," in *Zapiski kommentatora*, 16.

8. Cf. Lerner, "Vosstan', vosstan', prorok Rossii . . .," 18–29; and idem, *Rasskazy o Pushkine*, 94–107; Fridman, "Obraz poeta-proroka v lirike Pushkina," 88–98; Tsiavlovskaia, Commentary, 2:689–90; Blagoi, *Tvorcheskii put' Pushkina*, 268ff., 533–42; B. S. Meilakh, "Pushkin i dekabristy," 2:201; and Gorodetskii, *Lirika Pushkina*, 106–8. A more factual account is Tsiavlovskaia, "Otkliki na sud'by dekabristov v tvorchestve Pushkina," 195–218.

9. Gasparov, *Poèticheskii iazyk Pushkina*, 229; cf. 348 n. 10. Other critics, who have minimized the political or didactic significance of the poem, include Bondi, *O Pushkine*, 145–52; Nepomniashchii, "Prorok," 132–52; and Stennik, *Pushkin i russkaia literatura XVIII veka*, 184.

10. Stepanov, *Lirika Pushkina*, 348, 353.

11. Bethea, *Realizing Metaphors*, 186–87.

12. See Cherniaev, *"Prorok" Pushkina*, 1–75; Koplan, "K stikhotvoreniiu 'Prorok,'" 327–28; Kashtaleva, "'Podrazhaniia Koranu'"; Fridman, "Obraz poeta-proroka," 88–98; Tomashevskii, *Pushkin, kniga vtoraia*, 18–45; Ivanov, "Temy i stili vostoka v poèzii zapada," 431–38; and Stennik, *Pushkin i russkaia literatura XVIII veka*, 184–90. On the "Imitations of the Koran," see also Vickery, "Towards an Interpretation of Pushkin's 'Podrazhaniia Koranu,'" 61–74, and Fomichev, "'Podrazhaniia Koranu,'" 22–45. A general discussion of Pushkin's relationship to linguistic archaism can be found in Vinogradov, *Iazyk Pushkina*, 111–94. On orientalism in Pushkin or as a tendency of Russian romantic poetry, see Lobikova, *Pushkin i vostok;* Kaganovich, *Russkii romantizm i vostok;* and idem, "Nekotorye osobennosti russkoi oriental'noi poèzii," 5–35.

13. Derzhavin, "Na vziatie Izmaila," in *Sochineniia*, 1:241–42.

14. Küchelbecker, "Prorochestvo," in *Izbrannye prozvedeniia*, 1:158. Küchel-

becker wrote the poem before April or May 1822, the time of his departure from Georgia, and hence before reading Pushkin's *Prisoner of the Caucasus,* which he did not receive before the end of the same year (see Tynianov, "Pushkin i Küchelbecker," in *Pushkin i ego sovremenniki,* 260–61). We can, however, speak of a reverse influence: "Prophecy" has been widely cited as an intertext for Pushkin's "The Prophet"; see Meilakh, *Pushkin i russkii romantizm,* 181 n. 1.; and Stepanov, *Lirika Pushkina,* 349–50. Although never published in Küchelbecker's lifetime, the poem was definitely known to Pushkin by September 1822 (see Pushkin's letter to his brother, 4 September 1822, *Polnoe sobranie sochinenii,* 10:43–44).

15. Lermontov, *Sobranie sochinenii v chetyrekh tomakh,* 1:530.

16. Stennik, *Pushkin i russkaia literatura XVIII veka,* 163–92, has traced the prophetic topos back to the tradition of the psalmic or religious odes.

17. Yet another relevant poem is Pushkin's "Istanbul Is Now Praised by the Giaours" (1830), a poem in which the vertical axis of Islamic piety, linking God, the Prophet Muhammad, and the community of believers is juxtaposed alongside a bloody episode of oriental despotism, the repression of the janissary rebellion of 1826 by the Ottoman sultan Mahmud II. Some critics have read the poem as an allegory of the Decembrist revolt: see Fridman, "Obraz poeta-proroka v lirike Pushkina," 102.

18. Viazemskii, letters of 28 August and 6 September 1825, in Pushkin, *Perepiska A. S. Pushkina v dvukh tomakh,* 223.

19. Lotman, "Pushkin. Ocherk tvorchestva," 188–89.

20. Tomashevksii, "Poèticheskoe nsaledie Pushkina (Lirika i poèmy)," in *Pushkin, kniga vtoraia,* 361.

21. Trediakovskii, "Novyi i kratkii sposob k slozheniiu rossiiskikh stikhov," in *Izbrannye proizvedeniia,* 395. On the Russian elegy, cf. Gukovskii, "Elegiia v XVIII veke," 48–102; Frizman, *Zhizn' liricheskogo zhanra,* "Èvoliutsiia russkoi romanticheskoi èlegii," 73–106, and "Dva veka russkoi èlegii," 5–48; Senderovich, *Aleteiia,* 109–59; and Greenleaf, *Pushkin and Romantic Fashion,* 89. On the elegy outside Russia, cf. Potts, *The Elegiac Mode;* Kirchmeir, *Romantische Lyrik and Neoklassizistische Elegie;* Sacks, *The English Elegy;* and Vatsuro, "Frantsuzskaia èlegiia kontsa XVIII veka," 8–48.

22. Sumarokov, "Stradai, priskorbnyi dukh! Terzaisia, grud' moia" (1768), in *Izbrannye proizvedeniia,* 160.

23. Belinskii, "Razdelenie poèzii na rody i vidy," in *Polnoe sobranie sochinenii,* 5:52. Pushkin would himself acknowledge the clash between the ode and the elegy as a central issue of the time in *Eugene Onegin,* chap. 4, stanzas 32–33. The same transition also occurred in France, only earlier: cf. Kirchmeir, *Romantische Lyrik and Neoklassizistische Elegie,* 119, who notes the "flowering of the elegy toward the end of the eighteenth century" and the "displacement of the lofty ode by the elegy as the dominant new lyric genre of romanticism." Tomashevskii, in *Pushkin, kniga pervaia,* 530, and *Pushkin. Kniga vtoraia,* 376–77, suggests that Küchelbecker's critique signaled but did not cause the elegy's rapid decline in Russia after 1825. Yet if these were the last years of the elegy proper, then a generally elegiac tone can be said to permeate much of Lermontov's lyric verse, which generally defies narrow generic definition (see below).

24. Greenleaf, *Pushkin and Romantic Fashion,* 89.

25. Galich, *Opyt nauki izaishchnogo*, 262.

26. Batiushkov, *Polnoe sobranie stikhotvorenii*, 198–99.

27. Belinskii, "Razdelenie poèzii na rody i vidy," in *Polnoe sobranie sochinenii*, 5:50.

28. Batiushkov, "Vospominanie," in *Polnoe sobranie stikhotvorenii*, 93.

29. Batiushkov, "Perekhod cherez Rein," in *Polnoe sobranie stikhotvorenii*, 212.

30. The poem was first published posthumously in 1841. It nonetheless falls readily into the prophetic genealogy we have just constructed and is likely to have been an intertext for Lermontov's poem "The Dream": cf., in particular, the lines just quoted, which echo the "sleep" motif that is an intrinsic part of the tradition: "glubokii *son* v *doline* brannoi" (deep sleep in the valley of battle) and "Skazhite: milaia slezoiu / Vash usladit li dolgoi *son*?" (Tell me: will your beloved / Sweeten your long sleep with a tear?) (my emphasis). Cf. also Tomashevskii's interesting analysis of the poem in "Poèticheskoe nasledie Pushkina," *Pushkin, kniga vtoraia*, 357.

31. Pushkin discovered Chenier at precisely this time. See Chenier, "L'Orient," part 3 of "Voyage en Italie, projet de voyage en orient," in *Oeuvres complètes d' André Chenier*, 3:28–29. In 1829 Pushkin made a very free translation of this precise poem: see *Frantsuzskaia èlegiia XVIII-XIX vekov v perevodakh poètov pushkinskoi pory*, 219–21; cf. also Tomashevskii, "Pushkin—chitatel' frantsuzskikh poètov," 210–28; and idem, *Pushkin. Kniga pervaia*, 388–90.

32. See Medvedeva, "Pushkinskaia èlegiia 1820-x godov i 'Demon'," 6:51–71, esp. 70–71; Blagoi, "Stikhotvoreniia Pushkina," 1:535; and Tomashevskii, *Pushkin. Kniga pervaia*, 530, who notes that although the elegy does not numerically dominate Pushkin's lyric production, it is still "fairly typical" of it.

33. Cf. the following poems by Pushkin of 1821: "The Dagger," "Napoleon," "Faithful woman of Greece, do not weep, he fell a hero," and "To General Pushchin."

34. Passion (*strast'*) should not be confused with feeling (*chuvstvo*): As Gurevich notes in "Ot 'Kavkazskogo plennika' k 'Tsyganam,'" 69: "Passions—the powerful and fiery movements of the soul—are destructive and tragic," whereas feelings are "an expression of a full emotional life."

35. On "war" and the question of passion, see Tomashevskii, *Pushkin. Kniga pervaia*, 532–34.

36. See Tomashevskii, *Pushkin. Kniga pervaia*, 563–66, and *Pushkin. Kniga vtoraia*, 377–78; Blagoi, *Tvorcheskii put' Pushkina*, 279–312; and Lotman, *Aleksandr Sergeevich Pushkin*, 77ff. Vickery provides a useful non-Soviet account of the evolution of Pushkin's politics in "Pushkin: Russia and Europe," 15–38, esp. 22–24.

37. Belinskii, *Polnoe sobranie sochinenii*, 7:372.

38. Blagoi, *Tvorcheskii put' Pushkina*, 259.

39. Lotman, "Pushkin. Ocherk tvorchestva," 193. Cf. also Mann, *Dinamika russkogo romantizma*, 133–34.

40. Of the vast literature on *Kavkazskii plennik* and Pushkin's romantic *poèmy*, see, in particular, Zhirmunskii, *Bairon i Pushkin*; Semenov, *Pushkin na Kavkaze*; Blagoi, *Tvorcheskii put' Pushkina*, chap. 6, 246–70; Sandomirskaia, "'Estestvennyi chelovek' i obshchestvo," 184–90; Gurevich, "Ot 'Kavkazskogo plennika' k

'Tsyganam.'" 63–84; Austin, "The Exotic Prisoner in Russian Romanticism," 217–71; Hokanson, "Literary Romanticism," 336–52; Sandler, *Distant Pleasures*, esp. chap. 4; Greenleaf, *Pushkin and Romantic Fashion;* Layton, *Russian Literature and Empire;* Susi Frank, "Gefangen in der russischen Kultur," 61–84; and my own "Russian Poetry and the Imperial Sublime," 21–49.

41. Küchelbecker, "O napravlenii nashei poèzii," 457. Cf. Ginzburg, *Tvorcheskii put' Lermontova*, 30.

42. Layton, *Russian Literature and Empire*, 42–43.

43. Bocharov, *Poètika Pushkina. Ocherki*, 6.

44. The classic treatment of mourning and memory as a form of desire is by Freud, "Mourning and Melancholia," 14:246ff. The validating of mourning as a form of phantasmic appropriation I owe to Giorgio Agamben, in *Stanze*, pp. 25–26.

45. Prince Viazemskii's negative reaction, never publicly aired, can be found in a letter to Turgenev, dated 27 September 1822, cited in the notes to Viazemskii, *Èstetika i literaturnaia kritika*, 393: "Poetry is not an ally of butchers; . . . the hymns of a poet should never be a celebration of carnage." On Pushkin's epilogue, see Vickery, "Pushkin: Russia and Europe," 21.

46. Tomashevskii, *Pushkin. Kniga pervaia*, 405.

47. Ibid., 409.

48. Blagoi, *Tvorcheskii put' Pushkina*, 271.

49. Gurevich, "Ot 'Kavkazskogo plennika' k 'Tsyganam,'" 70.

50. Zhirmunskii, *Bairon i Pushkin*, 86.

51. Sandler, *Distant Pleasures*, 150, 164. See also Andrew, "'The Caresses of Black-eyed Captive Women,'" 103–23.

52. Layton, *Russian Literature and Empire*, 37, 53.

53. Frank, "Gefangen in der russischen Kultur," 70–71.

54. Lermontov, "O, esli b dni moi tekli . . ." (1829) and "Drobis', drobis', volna nochnaia" (1830), in Lermontov, *Sobranie sochinenii v chetyrekh tomakh*, 1:60, 123. All future references to Lermontov are to this edition and are provided in the main body of the text.

55. See "Napoleon" (1829), "Umiraiushchii gladiator" (1836), "Smert' poèta" (1837), and "Duma" (1838), *Sobranie sochinenii*, 1:45–47, 403–4, 412–14, 442–43.

56. Frizman, "Dva veka russkoi èlegii," 38. Cf. also Eikhenbaum, *Lermontov*, 17–18: "The struggle of the ode and the elegy had to lead to the dissolution of both these genres and produce, on the one hand, Tiutchev's lyric, where the ode was compressed and transformed into a lyric "fragment" even as it retained its oratorical pathos (Tynianov), and, on the other hand, Lermontov's poetry, where the elegy lost its airy classical traits and appeared in the form of a declamatory meditation or 'duma.'"

57. On Lermontov's representation of the Caucasus and the east in general, see Semenov, *Lermontov i fol'klor Kavkaza;* Ginzburg, *Tvorcheskii put' Lermontova*, 120–24; Grossman, "Lermontov i kul'tury vostoka," 43–44:673–744; Andronikov, *Lermontov;* Kholmukhamedova, "Vostok v russkoi poèzii," 57–67; Scotto, "Prisoners of the Caucasus," 246–60; Reid, "Ethnotope in Lermontov's Caucasian Poems," 217–74; and Lotman, "Problema vostoka i zapada," 5–22.

58. For example, "Tri pal'my" (1839), "Dary Tereka" (1839), "Kazach'ia kolybel'naia pesnia" (1840), "Utes" (1841), "Spor" (1841), "Tamara" (1841), in Lermontov, *Sobranie sochinenii,* 1:454–56, 458–60, 470–71, 525, 526–29, 535–36. Of these poems only "Spor" (1841) is an explicit commentary on empire.

59. On Lermontov and Odoevskii, see Korovin, "Lermontov i russkaia lirika ego vremeni," 311–40.

60. See Pumpianskii, "Stikhovaia rech' Lermontova"; Maksimov, *Poèziia Lermontova,* 168–70; and Iusufov, *Dagestan v russkoi literature,* 213–19.

61. For two recent readings of "Valerik," see Briggs, "The Seven Voices of *Valerik,*" 35–63; and Layton, *Russian Literature and Empire,* 222–29.

62. Tolstoi viewed his own Caucasian writings as deromanticizing the legacy of Lermontov and Bestuzhev-Marlinskii, whom he had read in his youth. See Tolstoi, "Zapiska o Kavkaze: Poezdka v Mamakai-iurt," in *Polnoe sobranie sochinenii,* 3:215; Pumpianskii, "Stikhovaia rech' Lermontova," 390, 412–13, 418; and Layton, *Russian Literature and Empire,* 233–51. It is worth noting that the deromanticization of the Caucasian war in Lermontov's late works was anticipated by the poetry of A. I. Polezhaev: see his "Erpeli" (1830) and "Chir-iurt" (1832) in *Stikhotvoreniia i poèmy,* 227–60, 281–309.

63. After Pushkin, the main texts to perpetuate the myth of the captive are Lermontov, *Kavkazskii plennik,* in *Sobranie sochinenii* , 2:17–39; Tolstoi, "Kavkazskii plennik (Byl')," in *Sobranie sochinenii,* 10:225–48; Bitov, *Kavkazskii plennik;* Makanin, "Kavkazskii plennyi," 449–77; and Bodrov's film *Kavkazskii plennik,* released in English as *Prisoner of the Mountains* (1996). To this list one might add Gaidai's film *Kavkazskaia plennitsa, ili novye prikliucheniia Shurika* (1966), a screwball comedy. For a more exhaustive account of the "captive" as a literary topos in Russia, a list of the lesser-known eighteenth- and nineteenth-century texts in this tradition, and some valuable insights into the metaphysics of captivity, see Austin, "The Exotic Prisoner in Russian Romanticism," 217–74. Cf. also my "Kavkazskie plenniki: Kul'turnye mify i medial'nye reprezentatsii v chechenskom konflikte," 78–108; and Susan Layton's suggestive exploration of the same myth with respect to the poet Polezhaev, "Aleksandr Polezhaev and Remembrance of War in the Caucasus," 559–84.

64. The Noble Savage effectively dominates the following texts by Lermontov (all in *Sobranie sochinenii,* vol. 2): *Kally* (1830–31), *Izmail Bei* (1832), *Aul Bastundzhi* (1833–34), *Khadzhi Abrek* (1833), and *Beglets* (late 1830s). The discussion that follows is derived from a reading of these texts. The more spiritually evolved Caucasian protagonists of *Mtsyri* (1839) and *Demon* (1841), also by Lermontov, are closely related. On the figure of the outcast, or *abrek,* see Semenov, *Lermontov i fol'klor Kavkaza,* 30. A useful discussion of the status of the savage in the western tradition can be found in White, *Tropics of Discourse,* 150–96; particularly valuable is White's insistence on the figurative role of the Noble Savage as "an idea to belabor nobility, not to redeem the savage" (190). Cf. also Layton, "Primitive Despot and Noble Savage," 31–45; and idem, "Nineteenth-Century Russian Mythologies of Caucasian Savagery," 80–99.

65. Etkind, "Poèticheskaia lichnost' Lermontova," 17. For Lermontov's poem, see "Rodina," in *Sobranie sochinenii,* 1:509.

66. Pumpianskii, "Stikhovaia rech' Lermontova," 414.

Conclusion

1. The text in the epigraph to this chapter was published as a preface to the publication of Aleksandr Blok's *Skify* and *Dvenadtsat'* whose antecedents it was Ivanov-Razumnik's stated goal to trace.

2. Pushkin, "Klevetnikam Rossii," in *Polnoe sobranie sochinenii v desiati tomakh,* 3:222.

3. Pushkin, "Borodinskaia godovshchina," in *Polnoe sobranie sochinenii,* 3:224–26.

4. Pushkin, "Klevetnikam Rossii," in *Polnoe sobranie sochinenii,* 3:222.

5. Pushkin, letter to P. Viazemskii, 1 June 1831, in *Polnoe sobranie sochinenii,* 10:351.

6. Tynianov, "Vopros o Tiutcheve," 367–85.

7. Pigarev, *Zhizn' i tvorchestvo Tiutcheva,* 272. Other useful interventions on Tiutchev's relationship to the "lofty style" are Pumpianskii, "Poeziia F. I. Tiutcheva," 9–57; and Afanas'eva, "'Odizm' ili 'tragizm'? Razmyshleniia na temu 'Tiutchev i Derzhavin,'" 80–97.

8. Tiutchev, "O veshchaia dusha moia," and "1856," in *Polnoe sobranie stikhotvorenii,* 113–14 (my emphasis).

9. Tiutchev, "Den' i noch'," in *Polnoe sobranie stikhotvorenii,* 76.

10. Tiutchev, "Prorochestvo," in *Polnoe sobranie stikhotvorenii,* 91–92. Cf. Eikhenbaum, "Pis'ma Tiutcheva," 50–61, one of the earliest attempts at relating Tiutchev's ontology of space and time to the question of prophecy.

11. Tiutchev, "K ode Pushkina na vol'nost'," in *Polnoe sobranie stikhotvorenii,* 29–30. Cf. also the famous poem "14 dekabria 1825" (December 14th, 1825) (1826), in *Polnoe sobranie stikhotvorenii,* 37, which ambiguously condemns the Decembrists both for having sought to undermine a social order in which the people still had faith and for having believed that their "meager blood," although "corrupted by Autocracy," was sufficient to heat Russia's "eternal Arctic."

12. Florovsky, "Tiutchev and Vladimir Solov'ev," in *Theology and Literature,* 11:40.

13. Tiutchev, "La Russie et l'Occident," in *Fedor Ivanovich Tiutchev,* 97:215. On Tiutchev's political views, also see, in the same volume, Tvardovskaia, "Tiutchev v obshchestvennoi bor'be poreformennoi Rossii," 132–70, as well as Kozhinov's suggestive but apologetic introduction to the article "La Russie et l'Occident," 183–200. Other useful critical works are Strémoukhoff, *La poésie et l'idéologie de Tiouttchev;* and Conant, *The Political Poetry and Ideology of F. I. Tiutchev.*

14. Cf. Tiutchev, "Russia and Germany" (1844), in *Polnoe sobranie sochinenii F. I. Tiutcheva,* 441, which defends Russia's "extraordinary expansion" as its "apparent conquests" and "violence" were, in fact, the most "organic affair . . . to have ever occurred in history . . . a vast act of restoration." Tiutchev's "Lettre à m. le docteur Gustave Kolb, rédacteur de la 'Gazette Universelle'" (1844), in *Polnoe sobranie sochinenii,* 519–41, expresses similar opinions.

15. Tiutchev, *Polnoe sobranie stikhotvorenii,* 53–54.

16. Berkovskii, "F. I. Tiutchev," 163.

17. Tiutchev, *Polnoe sobranie stikhotvorenii,* 81.

18. Tiutchev, Letter dated 1853, "Pis'ma F. I. Tiutcheva k P. A. Chaadaevu," 415.

19. Florovsky, "The Historical Premonitions of Tiutchev," in *Theology and Literature*, 11:53–54. By this Florovsky is referring to the gap between Tiutchev's ontological vision, which is richly suggestive, and his sense of history, which is, despite appearances, spiritually impoverished; in this Florovsky is right, of course.

20. Cf. Lotman, "Poèticheskii mir Tiutcheva," 108–41: "Formless space . . . is nonbeing. It swallows, floods, and transforms things into nothing. The state is a form of space—in the poem "Russian Geography" it is its political and providential idea, realized in the form of boundaries . . . boundedness/boundlessness are two related edges of the same opposition, within which Tiutchev's poetry of space unfolds" (125, 131).

21. See "Razgovor" and "Oda" (both 1831), in Khomiakov, *Stikhotvoreniia i dramy*, 94, 90.

22. See Khomiakov's "Rossii" (1839), "V al'bom V. V. Ganki" (1847), and "My rod izbrannyi,—govorili" (1851), in *Stikhotvoreniia i dramy*, 110–12, 124–25, and 130–31.

23. Solov'ëv, "Tri rechi v pamiat' Dostoevskogo," in *Sobranie sochinenii Vladimira Sergeevicha Solov'ëva*, 3:215–16. On these questions, see also Serbinenko, *Vladimir Solov'ëv*, esp. 60–62, 104.

24. Solov'ëv, "Ex oriente lux," in *Stikhotvoreniia i shutochnye p'esy*, 80–81.

25. Solov'ëv, "Kitai i Evropa," *Sobranie sochinenii*, 6:97.

26. Ibid., 6:148.

27. Solov'ëv, "Mir vostoka i zapada" (The world of east and west), in *Sobranie sochinenii*, 7:383.

28. Solov'ëv, "Pis'mo o vostochnom voprose" (A letter on the eastern question) (1898), in *Sobranie sochinenii*, 9:170–71.

29. Solov'ëv, "Drakon," in *Stikhotvoreniia i shutochnye p'esy*, 137.

30. Solov'ëv, "Panmongolizm," in *Stikhotvoreniia i shutochnye p'esy*, 104.

31. When the Boxer Rebellion broke out shortly after the publication of *Tri razgovora*, Solov'ëv felt vindicated: "I really did have some foresight or foreboding of these events and of all that they threaten to bring with them in the future. . . . The drama of history has been played out, and only one epilogue remains" ("Po povodu poslednikh sobytii. Pis'mo v redaktsiiu" [On the latest events. A letter to the editor] [1900]), in *Sobranie sochinenii*, 9:223, 226. On Solov'ëv and the Silver Age, see Bethea, *The Shape of Apocalypse in Modern Russian Fiction*, 110–16. Judith Deutsch Kornblatt, in "Solov'ëv on Salvation," 68–87, has made the subtle argument that the "short story about the Antichrist" represents a parody rather than a radical repudiation of Solov'ëv's previous views, but even Kornblatt acknowledges that Solov'ëv had become "disenchanted with the external forms into which he had tried to place his beliefs" (84)—namely, church and empire.

32. Solov'ëv, "Obshchii smysl iskusstva," in *Sobranie sochinenii*, 6:85.

33. Belyi, "Apokalipsis v russkoi poèzii," 409–10. For Belyi's views on Solov'ëv, see also his "Vladimir Solov'ev. Iz vospominanii" (1907), 387–94; and the correspondence between Belyi and Aleksandr Blok, particularly in the year 1911, in Orlov, *Aleksandr Blok–Andrei Belyi Perepiska*, 245–81. See also Leonid An-

dreev's phantasmagoria of the Russo-Japanese War, "Krasnyi smekh. Otryvki iz naidennoi rukopisi" (Red laughter. Fragments of a found manuscript) (1904), 1:475–531, which is closely tied to Belyi's way of relating symbolism and history.

34. Belyi, "Simvolizm," in *Simvolizm kak miroponimanie*, 256. See also Cioran, *Apocalyptic Symbolism*.

35. Belyi, *Peterburg*, 77. All further quotes from this novel are provided in parentheses in the text.

36. Briusov, "Griadushchie gunny" (1904–5), in *Sobranie sochinenii v semi tomakh*, 1:433. The poem originally appeared as part of the collection *Stephanos* (1905).

37. Blok, "Skify," in *Sobranie sochinenii v shesti tomakh*, 3:244. Pushkin's rebuttal is found in his letter to P. Ia. Chaadaev, 19 October 1836, in *Polnoe sobranie sochinenii*, 10:596–98.

38. This identification has an older history in Blok's work, namely, the lyric cycle "Na pole Kulikovom" (On the field of Kulikovo) (1908), in *Sobranie sochinenii*, 3:158–62, which should be read through Blok's article "Narod i intelligentsiia" (The people and the intelligentsia) (1908), in *Sobranie sochinenii*, 5:259–68. In the article the historic Battle of Kulikovo that pitted the Russians against the Mongols is read as an allegory of the conflict between Russian intelligentsia and the people (*narod*). Between 1908 and 1918 Blok achieves a kind of anxious identification with the revolutionary masses whom he had feared earlier, a shift not uncommon among intellectuals of the period.

39. Maiakovskii, "Oda revoliutsii," 1:144.

40. Cf. Tynianov, "Promezhutok," in *Arkhaisty i novatory*, 553.

41. Mandel'shtam, "Sumerki svobody," in *Sobranie sochinenii v trekh tomakh*, 1:72.

42. Eurasianism was an intellectual current launched in the Russian diaspora with the publication, in 1921, of the collection *Iskhod k vostoku* by N. S. Trubetzkoy, P. N. Savitskii, G. V. Florovskii, and P. P. Suvchinskii. A fuller account of the relationship between orientalism and empire in postrevolutionary Russian culture would have to articulate the links between the Scythianism of Blok and Ivanov-Razumnik, the linguistic experimentalism of Khlebnikov, and the philosophy of history promoted by the Eurasianist school; part of this work has been done by Lo Gatto, "*Panmongolismo* di V. Solov'ëv, 296–300; and Nivat, "Du 'panmongolisme' au 'mouvement eurasien,'" 460–78.

43. Khlebnikov, *Zangezi*, in *Tvoreniia*, 479. The English translation is from *Velimir Khlebnikov: The King of Time. Poems, Fictions, Visions of the Future*, trans. Paul Schmidt, ed. Charlotte Douglas (Cambridge, Mass.: Harvard University Press, 1985), 202.

Bibliography

Abrams, M. H. *The Mirror and the Lamp: Romantic Theory and the Critical Tradition.* New York: Oxford University Press, 1953.

Achinger, Gerda. *Der französische Anteil an der russischen Literaturkritik des 18. Jahrhunderts unter besonderer Berücksichtigung der Zeitschriften (1730–1780).* Berlin: Verlag Gehlen, 1970.

Afanas'eva, K. A. "'Odizm' ili 'tragizm'? Razmyshleniia na temu 'Tiutchev i Derzhavin.'" In *Tiutchev segodnia. Materialy IV Tiutchevskikh chtenii,* ed. Evgenii N. Lebedev, 80–97. Moscow: Izdatel'stvo literaturnogo instituta, 1995.

Affergan, Francis. *Exotisme et altérité. Essai sur les fondements d'une critique de l'anthropologie.* Paris: Presses universitaires de France, 1987.

Agamben, Giorgio. *Stanze. La parola e il fantasma nella cultura occidentale.* Turin: Einaudi, 1977.

Akhmedov, E. M. "Vydaiushchiisia azerbaidzhanskii myslitel'." In A.-K. Bakikhanov, *Sochineniia, zapiski, pis'ma,* 6–59. Baku: Elm, 1983.

Al-Azmeh, Aziz. "The Articulation of Orientalism." In *Orientalism, Islam, and Islamists,* ed. Asaf Hussain, Robert Olson, and Jamil Qureishi, 89–124. Brattleboro, Vt.: Amana, 1984.

Alekseev, M. P. "'Proroche rogatyi' Feofana Prokopovicha." In *Iz istorii russkikh literaturnykh otnoshenii XVIII–XX vekov,* 17–43. Moscow: Izdatel'stvo Akademii nauk SSSR, 1959.

Alekseeva, M. A. "Zhanr konkliuzii v russkom iskusstve kontsa XVII–nachala XVIII v." In *Russkoe iskusstvo barokko. Materialy i issledovaniia,* ed. T. V. Alekseeva, 7–29. Moscow: Nauka, 1977.

Alekseeva, N. Iu. "'Rassuzhdenie o ode voobshche' V. K. Trediakovskogo." *XVIII vek. Sbornik* (1996) 20: 13–22.

Alexander, John T. *Catherine the Great: Life and Legend.* New York: Oxford University Press, 1989.

Alter, Robert. *The Literary Guide to the Bible.* Edited by Robert Alter and Frank Kermode. Cambridge, Mass.: Harvard University Press, Belknap Press, 1987.

Althusser, Louis. *Montesquieu. La politique et l'histoire.* Paris: Presses universitaires de France, 1974.

Altshuller, Mark. *Predtechi slavianofil'stva v russkoi literature: obshchestvo "Beseda liubitelei russkogo slova."* Ann Arbor: Ardis, 1984.

Anderson, Perry. *Lineages of the Absolutist State.* 3rd ed. London: New Left Books, 1977.

Andreev, Leonid. "Krasnyi smekh. Otryvki iz naidennoi rukopisi." In *Povesti i rasskazy v dvukh tomakh,* 1:475–531. 2 vols. Moscow: Khudozhestvennaia literatura, 1971.

Andrew, J. "'The Caresses of Black-eyed Captive Women': Narrative, Desire and Gender in Pushkin's *The Prisoner of the Caucasus.*" In *Studies in Poetics: Commemorative Volume for Krystyna Pomorska (1928–1986),* ed. Elena Semeka-Pankratov, 103–23. Columbus, Ohio: Slavica, 1995.

Andronikov, I. *Lermontov. Issledovaniia i nakhodki.* Moscow: Khudozhestvennaia literatura, 1968.

Anisimov, E. V. *Vremia petrovskikh reform.* Leningrad: Lenizdat, 1989.

———. *Gosudarstvennye preobrazovaniia i samoderzhavie Petra Velikogo v pervoi chetverti XVIII veka.* St. Petersburg: Izdatel'stvo "Dmitrii Bulanin," 1997.

Arinshtein, L. M. "Persidskie pis'ma po povodu gibeli Griboedova." In *A. S. Griboedov. Materialy k biografii,* ed. S. A. Fomichev, 108–32. Leningrad: Nauka, 1989.

Austin, Paul M. "The Exotic Prisoner in Russian Romanticism." *Russian Literature* 16–18 (October 1984): 217–74.

Baddeley, John F. *The Russian Conquest of the Caucasus.* New York: Russell and Russell, 1969.

Baehr, Stephen Lessing. "From History to National Myth." *Russian Review* 37, no. 1 (January 1978): 1–14.

———. *The Paradise Myth in Eighteenth-Century Russia: Utopian Patterns in Early Secular Russian Literature and Culture.* Stanford: Stanford University Press, 1991.

Baklanova, A. "Otrazhenie idei absoliutizma v izobrazitel'nom iskusstve pervoi chetverti XVIII v." In *Absoliutizm v Rossii (XVII–XVIII vv.),* 101–58. Moscow: Nauka, 1964.

Barrett, Thomas. "The Remaking of the Lion of Dagestan: Shamil in Captivity." *Russian Review* 53 (July 1994): 357–65.

———. "Southern Living (in Captivity): The Caucasus in Russian Popular Culture." *Journal of Popular Culture* 31, no. 4 (spring 1998): 75–93.

Barthold, V. V. *La Découverte de l'Asie. Histoire de l'orientalisme en Europe et en Russie.* Paris: Payot, 1947.

Bassin, Mark. "Russia between Europe and Asia: The Ideological Construction of Geographical Space." *Slavic Review* 50 (spring 1991): 1–17.

———. "Asia." In *The Cambridge Companion to Modern Russian Culture,* ed. Nicholas Rzhevsky, 57–85. Cambridge: Cambridge University Press, 1998.

Batiushkov, K. N. *Polnoe sobranie stikhotvorenii.* Moscow: Sovetskii pisatel', 1964.

———. *Opyty v stikhakh i proze.* Moscow: Nauka, 1977.

Belinskii, V. G. *Polnoe sobranie sochinenii.* 13 vols. Moscow: Izdatel'stvo Akademii nauk SSSR, 1955.

———. *Èstetika i literaturnaia kritika v dvukh tomakh.* 2 vols. Moscow: GIKhL, 1959.

Belyi, Andrei. "Vladimir Solov'ev. Iz vospominanii." In *Arabeski,* 387–94. Moscow: Musaget, 1911.

———. *Peterburg.* Moscow: Khudozhestvennaia literatura, 1979.
———. *Simvolizm kak miroponimanie.* Moscow: Respublika, 1994.
———. "Apokalipsis v russkoi poèzii." In *Simvolizm kak miroponimanie,* 409–10. Moscow: Respublika, 1994.
Benningsen, Alexandre, and Chantal Lemercier-Quelquejay. *Islam in the Soviet Union.* Translated by Geoffrey E. Wheeler and Hubert Evans. London: Pall Mall, 1967.
Benningsen Broxup, Marie. *The North Caucasian Barrier: The Russian Advance on the Muslim World.* London: Hurst, 1992.
Berkov, P. *Lomonosov i literaturnaia polemika ego vremeni. 1750–1765.* Moscow: Izdatel'stvo Akademii nauk SSSR, 1936.
———, ed. *Virshi. Sillabicheskaia poèziia XVII–XVIII vekov.* Moscow: Sovetskii pisatel', 1935.
Berkovskii, N. Ia. "F. I. Tiutchev." In *O russkoi literature,* 155–199. Leningrad: Khudozhestvennaia literatura, 1985.
Besançon, Alain. *Le Tsarévitch immolé. La symbolique de la loi dans la culture russe.* Paris: Librairie Plon, 1967.
Bethea, David M. *The Shape of Apocalypse in Modern Russian Fiction.* Princeton, N.J.: Princeton University Press, 1989.
———. *Realizing Metaphors: Alexander Pushkin and the Life of the Poet.* Madison: University of Wisconsin Press, 1998.
Bhabha, Homi. "Difference, Discrimination, and the Discourse of Colonialism." In *The Politics of Theory: Essex Sociology of Literature Conference,* ed. Francis Barker et al., 194–211. Colchester: University of Essex Press, 1983.
———. "Interrogating Identity: The Postcolonial Prerogative." In *The Anatomy of Racism,* ed. David Theo Goldberg, 183–209. Minneapolis: University of Minnesota Press, 1990.
———, ed. *Nation and Narration.* London: Routledge, 1990.
Billington, James. *The Icon and the Axe: An Interpretive History of Russian Culture.* New York: Vintage, 1970.
Bitov, Andrei. *Kavkazskii plennik.* In *Imperiia v chetyrekh izmereniiakh.* Vol. 3. Moscow: TKO-AST/Folio, 1996 (written in 1969). Translated into English, by Susan Brownsberger, as *A Captive of the Caucasus: Journeys in Armenia and Georgia.* London: Harvill, 1992.
Blagoi, D. D. *Istoriia russkoi literatury XVIII veka.* Moscow: Izdatel'stvo Narkomprosa RSFSR, 1945.
———. *Tvorcheskii put' Pushkina (1813–1826).* Moscow: Izdatel'stvo Akademii nauk, SSSR, 1950.
———. "Gavrila Romanovich Derzhavin." In *G. R. Derzhavin. Stikhotvoreniia,* 5–30. Leningrad: Sovetskii pisatel', 1957.
———. "Stikhotvoreniia Pushkina." In *A. S. Pushkin. Sobranie sochinenii v desiati tomakh.* Moscow: Gosudarstvennoe izdatel'stvo khudozhestvennoi literatury, 1959.
Blagoi, D. D., and V. Ia. Kirpotin, eds. *Pushkin—rodonachal'nik novoi russkoi literatury.* Moscow: Izdatel'stvo Akademii nauk, 1941.
Blok, Aleksandr. *Sobranie sochinenii v shesti tomakh.* 6 vols. Moscow: Pravda, 1971.

Bloom, Harold. *Poetry and Repression: Revisionism from Blake to Stevens.* New Haven: Yale University Press, 1976.

Bocharov, S. G. *Poètika Pushkina. Ocherki.* Moscow: Nauka, 1974

Boichenko, V. A., ed. *Kavkaz v russkoi poezii.* Rostov-na-Donu: Izdatel'stvo Rostovskogo universiteta, 1986.

Boileau-Despréaux, Nicolas. *Oeuvres complètes de Boileau.* 7 vols. Paris: Société des Belles Lettres, 1934–43.

Bondi, S. *O Pushkine. Stat'i i issledovaniia.* Moscow: Khudozhestvennaia literatura, 1978.

Briggs, A. D. P. "The Seven Voices of *Valerik.*" In *Mikhail Lermontov: Commemorative Essays,* ed. A. D. P. Briggs, 35–63. Birmingham: Birmingham Modern Languages Publications, University of Birmingham, 1992.

Briusov, Valerii. *Sobranie sochinenii v semi tomakh.* 7 vols. Moscow: Khudozhestvennaia literatura, 1973–75.

Brody, Jules. *Boileau and Longinus.* Geneva: Librairie E. Droz, 1958.

Broxup, Marie Benningsen, ed. *The North Caucasian Barrier: The Russian Advance on the Muslim World.* London: Hurst, 1992.

Bukharkin, P. E. "Topos 'tishiny' v odicheskoi poèzii M. V. Lomonosova." *XVIII vek. Sbornik* (1996) 20: 3–12.

Burke, Edmund. *A Philosophical Enquiry into the Origin of Our Ideas of the Sublime and the Beautiful.* Edited by James T. Boulton. London: Routledge and Kegan Paul, 1958.

Butler, Judith. *The Psychic Life of Power: Theories in Subjection.* Stanford: Stanford University Press, 1997.

Butler, William E. Introduction to *Discourse Concerning the Just Causes of the War between Sweden and Russia: 1700–1721.* P. P. Shafirov. New York: Oceana, 1973.

Carter, Paul. *The Road to Botany Bay: An Exploration of Landscape and History.* Chicago: University of Chicago Press, 1987.

Catherine II. *Sochineniia.* Moscow: Sovremennik, 1990.

———. *Sochineniia Imperatritsy Ekateriny II.* 5 vols. Edited by A. N. Pypin. St. Petersburg: Tipografiia Imperatorskoi Akademii nauk, 1901–1907.

Chard, Chloe. "Rising and Sinking on the Alps and Mount Etna: The Topography of the Sublime in Eighteenth-Century England." *Journal of Philosophy and the Visual Arts* 1, no. 1 (1989): 61–69.

Chechulin, N. D. "Ob istochnikakh 'Nakaza.'" *Zhurnal Ministerstva Narodnago Prosveshcheniia* 340 (April 1902).

Chenier, André. *Oeuvres completes d' André Chenier.* Edited by Paul Dimoff. 3 vols. Paris: Librairie Delagrave, 1908–19.

Chereiskii, L. *Pushkin i severnyi Kavkaz.* Stavropol': Stavropol'skoe knizhnoe izdatel'stvo, 1986.

Cherniavksy, Michael. *Tsar and People: Studies in Russian Myths.* New Haven: Yale University Press, 1961.

———. "Khan or Basileus: An Aspect of Russian Mediaeval Political Theory." In *The Structure of Russian History: Interpretive Essays,* ed. Michael Cherniavsky, 65–79. New York: Random House, 1970.

Cherniaev, N. I. *"Prorok" Pushkina v sviazi s ego zhe "Podrazhaniiami Koranu."* Moscow: Tipografiia Iuzhnogo Kraia, 1898.

Chernov, S. N. "M. V. Lomonosov v odakh 1762 g." In *XVIII vek. Sbornik statei i materialov*, ed. A. S. Orlov, 133–80. Moscow: Izdatel'stvo Akademii nauk, 1935.

Chernyi, Karp. *Pushkin i Kavkaz*. Stavropol': Kraiizdat, 1950.

———. *Kavkaz podo mnoiu*. Stavropol': Knizhnoe izdatel'stvo, 1965.

Chernyshevskii, N. G. *Polnoe sobranie sochinenii*. 16 vols. Moscow: Gosudarstvennoe Izdatel'stvo Khudozhestvennoi literatury, 1939–53.

Chichagova, M. N. *Shamil na Kavkaze i v Rossii. Biograficheskii Ocherk*. Petersburg: S. Muller and I. Bogel'man, 1889.

Cioran, Samuel D. *The Apocalyptic Symbolism of Andrej Belyj*. The Hague: Mouton, 1973.

Cohen, Ariel. *Russian Imperialism: Development and Crisis*. London: Praeger, 1996.

Conant, Roger. *The Political Poetry and Ideology of F. I. Tiutchev*. Ann Arbor: Ardis, 1983.

Cracraft, James. *The Church Reform of Peter the Great*. London: Macmillan, 1971.

———. "Empire vs. Nation: Russian Political Theory under Peter I." *Harvard Ukrainian Studies* 10, nos. 3–4 (December 1986): 524–33.

———, ed. *Peter the Great Transforms Russia*. 3rd ed. Lexington, Mass.: Heath, 1991.

Crone, Anna Lisa. "Doing Justice to Potemkin: Paradox, Oxymoron, and Two Voices in Derzhavin's 'Waterfall.'" *Russian History* 21, no. 4 (winter 1994): 393–418.

Daniel, Noman. *Islam and the West: The Making of an Image*. Edinburgh: Edinburgh University Press, 1960.

Dan'ko, E. Ia. "Iz neizdannykh materialov o Lomonosove." *XVIII vek*. 2 (1940): 248–75.

———. "Izobrazitel'noe iskusstvo v poèzii Derzhavina." *XVIII vek*. 2 (1940): 243–44

de Bolla, Peter. *The Discourse of the Sublime: Readings in History, Aesthetics, and the Subject*. Oxford: Basil Blackwell, 1989.

Derzhavin, G. R. *Sochineniia Derzhavina s ob"iasnitel'nymi primechaniiami Ia. Grota*. 7 vols. 2nd ed. St. Petersburg: Tipografiia Akademiia nauk, 1868–78.

Derzhavina, O. A., et al. Introduction to *Panegiricheskaia literatura petrovskogo vremeni*. Moscow: Nauka, 1979.

Dictionnaire des lettres françaises. Le Dix-septième siècle. Paris: Librairie Arthème Fayard, 1954.

Djaït, Hichem. *Europe and Islam*. Translated by Peter Heinegg. Berkeley: University of California Press, 1985.

Dostoevskii, F. M. *Polnoe sobranie sochinenii v tridtsati tomakh*. 30 vols. Leningrad: Nauka, 1972–90.

———. "Geok-Tepe. Chto takoe dlia nas Aziia?" Published as part of the *Dnevnik pisatelia, 1881*. In F. M. Dostoevskii, *Polnoe sobranie sochinenii v tridtsati tomakh*, 27: 32–40. 30 vols. Leningrad: Nauka, 1972–90.

Douglas, Charlotte. "Kindred Spirits." In *Collected Works of Velimir Khlebnikov*, ed. Charlotte Douglas, 7–32. Cambridge: Cambridge University Press, 1987.

Druzhinin, V. M. "Prosveshchennyi absoliutizm v Rossii." In *Absoliutizm v Rossii (XVII–XVIII vv.)*, 428–59. Moscow: Nauka, 1964.

Duganov, R. V. *Velimir Khlebnikov: priroda tvorchestva.* Moscow: Sovetskii pisatel', 1990.

Eagleton, Terry. *The Ideology of the Aesthetic.* Oxford: Basil Blackwell, 1990.

Eidel'man, N. Ia. *Byt' mozhet za khrebtom Kavkaza.* Moscow: Nauka, 1990.

Eikhenbaum, B. M. "Pis'ma Tiutcheva." In *Skvoz' literaturu. Sbornik statei,* 50–61. Leningrad: Voprosy poètiki, 1924.

———. *Lermontov. Opyt istoriko-literaturnoi otsenki.* Munich: Wilhelm Fink Verlag, 1967 [1924].

Enikolopov, I. K. *A. S. Griboedov v Gruzii i Persii: istoriko-biograficheskii ocherk.* Tiflis: Zakkniga, 1929.

———. *Griboedov v Gruzii.* Tbilisi: Zaria Vostoka, 1954.

———. *Griboedov i vostok.* Erevan: Aiastan, 1974.

Etkind, Efim. "Poèticheskaia lichnost' Lermontova ('Dialektika dushi' v lirike)." In *Mikhail Lermontov. Simpozium, posviashchennyi 175-letiiu so dnia rozhdeniia. Norwich Symposia on Russian Literature and Culture.* St. Petersburg: Maxima, 1992.

———. "Rozhdenie 'krupnogo sloga.' Derzhavin i poèziia Fridrikha Vtorogo Prusskogo." In *Symposium Dedicated to Gavriil Derzhavin: Norwich Symposia on Russian Literature and Culture,* 4:163–84. Northfield, Vt.: The Russian School of Norwich University, 1995.

Fabian, Johannes. *Time and the Other: How Anthropology Makes Its Object.* New York: Columbia University Press, 1983.

Fanon, Frantz. *Black Skin, White Masks.* New York: Grove, 1967.

Ferguson, Frances. *Solitude and the Sublime: Romanticism and the Aesthetics of Individuation.* New York: Routledge, 1992.

Fieguth, Rolf. "K voprosu o kategorii 'vozvyshennogo' u Viacheslava Ivanova." *Cahiers du Monde russe* 35, nos. 1–2 (January–June 1994): 155–70.

Fisher, Alan W. "Enlightened Despotism and Islam under Catherine II." *Slavic Review* 27, no. 4 (December 1968): 542–64.

Florovsky, Georges. *Theology and Literature: The Collected Works of Georges Florovsky.* 11 vols. Vol. 11. Vaduz: Büchervertriebsanstalt, 1989.

Fomenko, I. Iu. "Avtobiograficheskaia proza G. R. Derzhavina i problema professionalizatsii russkogo pisatelia." *XVIII vek. Russkaia literatura XVIII–nachala XIX veka v obshchestvenno-kul'turnom kontekste* 14 (1983): 143–64.

Fomichev, S. A."'Podrazhaniia Koranu.' Genezis, arkhitektonika i kompozitsiia tsikla." In *Vremennik pushkinskoi komissii,* 22–45. Leningrad: Nauka, 1978.

———, ed. *A. S. Griboedov. Materialy k biografii.* Leningrad: Nauka, 1989.

Frank, Susi. "Gefangenen in der russischen Kultur. Zur Spezifik der Aneinung des Kaukasus in der russischen Literatur." *Die Welt der Slaven* 43 (1998): 61–84.

———. *Der Diskurs des Erhabenen bei Gogol' und die Longinsche Tradition.* Munich: Wilhelm Fink Verlag, 1999.

Frazier, Melissa. *Frames of the Imagination: Gogol's Arabesques and the Romantic Question of Genre.* New York: Peter Lang, 2000.

Freidin, Gregory. "By the Walls of Church and State: Literature's Authority in Russia's Modern Tradition." *Russian Review* 52 (April 1993): 150–61.

Freud, Sigmund. "Mourning and Melancholia." In *The Standard Edition of the Complete Psychological Works of Freud.* Vol. 14. London: Hogarth, 1963.

Fridman, N. V. "Obraz poeta-proroka v lirike Pushkina." In *Uchenye zapiski MGU. Trudy kafedry russkoi literatury* 118, no. 2 (1947): 88–98.

Frizman, L. G. *Zhizn' liricheskogo zhanra. Russkaia elegiia ot Sumarokova do Nekrasova.* Moscow: Nauka, 1973.

———. "Èvoliutsiia russkoi romanticheskoi èlegii." In *K istorii russkogo romantizma,* 73–106. Moscow: Nauka, 1973.

———. *Poèziia dekabristov.* Seriia literatury. Moscow: Znanie, 1974.

———. "Literaturnaia kritika dekabristov." In *Literaturno-kriticheskie raboty dekabristov,* 5–24. Moscow: Khudozhestvennaia literatura, 1978.

———. "Dva veka russkoi èlegii." In *Russkaia èlegiia XVIII-nachala XX veka,* 5–48. Leningrad: Sovetskii pisatel', 1991.

Fry, Paul. *The Reach of Criticism: Method and Perception in Literary Theory.* New Haven: Yale University Press, 1983.

———. *A Defense of Poetry: Reflections on the Occasion of Writing.* Stanford: Stanford University Press, 1995.

Gadzhiev, A. Dzh. *Kavkaz v russkoi literature pervoi poloviny XIX veka.* Baku: Iazychy, 1982.

Gadzhiev, V. G., and A. M. Pikman. *Velikie russkie revoliutsionnye demokraty o bor'be gortsev Dagestana i Chechni.* Makhachkala: Tipografiia Dagestanskogo filiala AN SSSR, 1972.

Galich, A. *Opyt nauki iziashchnogo.* In *Russkie èsteticheskie traktaty pervoi treti XIX veka,* 205–75. Moscow: Iskusstvo, 1974 [1825].

Gasché, Rodolphe. "Hegel's Orient or the End of Romanticism." In *History and Mimesis. Occasional Papers III by Members of the Program in Literature and Philosophy, Spring 1983,* ed. Irving Massey and Sung-Won Lee. New York: State University of New York at Buffalo, 1983.

Gasparov, B. M. *Poèticheskii iazyk Pushkina kak fakt istorii russkogo literaturnogo iazyka. Wiener Slawistischer Almanach.* Vienna: Gesellschaft zur Förderung slawistischer Studien, 1992.

Gasparov, M. L. "Poèziia Pindara." In *Pindar. Vakhilid. Ody. Fragmenty,* 361–93. Moscow: Nauka, 1980.

Geldern, James von. "The Ode as a Performative Genre." *Slavic Review* 4 (winter 1991): 927–39.

Ginzburg, Lidiia. *Tvorcheskii put' Lermontova.* Leningrad: Khudozhestvennaia literatura, 1940.

———. "O probleme narodnosti i lichnosti v poezii dekabristov." In *O russkom realizme XIX veka i voprosakh narodnosti literatury. Sbornik statei,* 100–51. Moscow: Gosudarstvennoe izdatel'stvo khudozhestvennoi literatury, 1960.

Gleason, Walter. "The Two Faces of the Monarch: Legal and Mythical Fictions in Lomonosov's Ruler Imagery." *Canadian-American Slavic Studies* 16, nos. 3–4 (fall 1982): 388–409.

Gofman, V. "Ryleev-poèt." In *Russkaia poèziia XIX veka,* 28–61. Leningrad: Academia, 1929.

Gordin, Ia. "Chto uvleklo Rossiiu na Kavkaz?" *Zvezda* 10 (1997): 94–111.

———. *Kavkaz: zemlia i krov'. Rossiia v kavkazskoi voine XIX veka.* St. Petersburg: Zhurnal "Zvezda," 2000.

Gorodetskii, B. P. *Lirika Pushkina.* Leningrad: Prosveshchenie, 1970.

Gottsched, Johann Christian. *Versuch einer Critischen Dichtkunst.* Leipzig: Verlag Beinhard Christoph Breitkopf, 1751 [1733].

Grebeniuk, V. P. "Publichnye zrelishcha petrovskogo vremeni i ikh sviaz' s teatrom." In *Novye cherty v russkoi literature i iskusstve XVII–nachalo XVIII v.*, 133–45. Moscow: Nauka, 1976.

Grechishcheva, E. "Khvalebnaia oda v russkoi literature XVIII v." In *M. V. Lomonosov. Sbornik statei,* ed. V. V. Sipovskii, 93–149. St. Petersburg: Ia. Basmakov, 1911.

Greenleaf, Monika. *Pushkin and Romantic Fashion: Fragment, Elegy, Orient, Irony.* Stanford: Stanford University Press, 1994.

Griboedov, A. S. *Sochineniia.* Edited by V. Orlov. Moscow: Gosudarstvennoe izdatel'stvo khudozhestvennoi literatury, 1956.

———. *A. S. Griboedov v vospominaniiakh sovremennikov.* Moscow: Khudozhestvennaia literatura, 1980.

Grishakova, M. F. "Trediakovskii i traditsiia russkoi ody." In *M. V. Lomonosov i russkaia kul'tura. Tezisy dokladov konferentsii, posviashchennoi 275-letiiu so dnia rozhdeniia M. V. Lomonosova (28–29 noiabria 1986 g.),* 31–35. Tartu: Tipografiia TGU, 1986.

Grosrichard, Alain. *Structure du serail. La fiction du despotisme asiatique dans l'Occident classique.* Paris: Seuil, 1979.

Grossman, L. "Lermontov i kul'tury vostoka." *Literaturnoe nasledstvo.* Moscow: Akademiia, 1941.

Groys, Boris. *The Total Art of Stalinism: Avant-garde, Aesthetic Dictatorship, and Beyond.* Translated by Charles Rougle. Princeton, N.J.: Princeton University Press, 1992.

Guenther, Johannes von. *Ein Leben im Ostwind. Zwischen Petersburg und München.* Munich: Biederstein Verlag, 1969.

Guerlac, Suzanne. "Longinus and the Subject of the Sublime." *New Literary History* 16, no. 2 (1985): 275–89.

———. *The Impersonal Sublime. Hugo, Baudelaire, Lautréamont.* Stanford: Stanford University Press, 1990.

Gukovskii, G. A. *Russkaia poèziia XVIII veka.* Leningrad: Academia, 1927.

———. "O russkom klassitsizme." In *Poètika. Vremennik otdela slovesnykh iskusstv gosudarstvennogo instituta istorii iskusstv. Vypusk V,* 21–65. Leningrad: Academia, 1929.

———. "Vokrug Radishcheva." In *Ocherki russkoi literatury XVIII veka.* Leningrad: Goslitizdat, 1938.

———. *Russkaia literatura XVIII veka.* Moscow: Uchpedgiz, 1939.

———. *Pushkin i russkie romantiki.* Moscow: Khudozhestvennaia literatura, 1965.

Gukovskii, G. A., and V. A. Desnitskii, eds. *Literatura XVIII veka.* Vols. 1–2 of *Istoriia russkei literatury.* Moscow: Izdatel'stvo Akademii nauk SSSR, 1941.

———. *Istoriia russkoi literatury.* 10 vols. Moscow: Izdatel'stvo Akademii nauk SSSR, 1941–54.

Günther, Johann Christian. "Auf den zwischen Ihrer Romisch Kayserlichen Majestät und der Pforte geschlossenen Frieden." In *Werke,* ed. Reiner Bolhoff, 339. Frankfurt: Deutscher Klassiker Verlag, 1998.

Gurevich, A. "Ot 'Kavkazskogo plennika' k 'Tsyganam.'" In *V mire Pushkina. Sbornik statei,* ed. S. Mashinskii, 63–84. Moscow: Sovetskii pisatel', 1974.

Gusev, V. E. "Vklad dekabristov v otechestvennuiu ètnografiiu." In *Dekabristy i russkaia kul'tura,* ed. B. S. Meilakh, 80–104. Leningrad: Nauka, 1975.

Hansen-Löve, Aage A. "Zur Typologie des Erhabenen in der russischen Moderne." *Poetica. Zeitschrift für Sprach- und Literaturwissenschaft* 23, nos. 1–2 (1991): 166–216.

Harden, Evelyn J. *The Murder of Griboedov: New Materials.* Birmingham: Slavonic Materials No. 6. Department of Russian Language and Literature, University of Birmingham, 1979.

Hart, Pierre R. "Continuity and Change in the Russian Ode." In *Russian Literature in the Age of Catherine the Great: A Collection of Essays,* ed. A. G. Cross, 45–62. Oxford: Willem A. Meeuws, 1976.

———. *G. R. Derzhavin: A Poet's Progress.* Columbus, Ohio: Slavica, 1978.

Hauner, Milan. *What Is Asia to Us? Russia's Asian Hinterland Yesterday and Today.* Boston: Unwin Hyman, 1990.

Hegel, H. *The Philosophy of History.* Translated by J. Sibree. New York: Dover, 1956.

———. *Aesthetics: Lectures on Fine Art.* Translated by T. M. Knox. Oxford: Clarendon, 1975.

Hertz, Neil. "A Reading of Longinus." In *The End of the Line: Essays on Psychoanalysis and the Sublime,* 1–21. New York: Columbia University Press, 1985.

Hippisley, Anthony. *The Poetic Style of Simeon Polotsky.* Birmingham: Birmingham Slavonic Studies, 1985.

Hokanson, K. "Literary Imperialism, Narodnost' and Pushkin's Invention of the Caucasus." *Russian Review* 53, no. 3 (July 1994): 336–52.

Hughes, Lindsey. *Russia in the Age of Peter the Great.* New Haven: Yale University Press, 1998.

Iakubova, M. A. "A. S. Griboedov v derevoliutsionnoi raznoiazychnoi pechati Azerbaidzhana." In *A. S. Griboedov. Materialy k biografii,* ed. S. A. Fomichev, 265–70. Leningrad: Nauka, 1989.

Iusufov, R. F. *Russkii romantizm nachala XIX veka i natsional'nye kul'tury.* Moscow: Nauka, 1970.

———. *Dagestan v russkoi literature kontsa XVIII i pervoi poloviny XIX v.* Moscow: Nauka, 1964.

Ivanov, Viacheslav Vs. "Temy i stili vostoka v poèzii zapada." In *Vostochnye motivy. Stikhotvoreniia i poèmy,* 431–38. Moscow: Nauka, 1985.

Ivanov-Razumnik. *Ispytanie v groze i bure.* Berlin: Skify, 1920.

Jakobson, Roman. *Noveishaia russkaia poèziia.* Prague: Politika, 1921.

———. *Language in Literature.* Cambridge, Mass.: Harvard University Press, Belknap Press, 1987.

Jakobson, Roman, C. H. van Schooneveld, and Dean S. Worth, eds. *Slavic Poetics: Essays in Honor of Kiril Taranovsky.* The Hague: Mouton, 1973.

Janowitz, Anne F. *England's Ruins: Poetic Purpose and the National Landscape.* Cambridge, Mass.: Blackwell, 1990.

Jones, Gareth. "The Image of the Eighteenth-Century Russian Author." In *Russia in the Age of the Enlightenment: Essays for Isabel de Madariaga,* ed. Roger Bartlett and Janet Hartley, 57–74. New York: St. Martin's, 1990.

Jump, John D. *The Ode.* London: Methuen, 1974.

Kaganovich, S. L. *Russkii romantizm i vostok.* Tashkent: Izdatel'stvo "FAN" Uzbekskoi SSR, 1988.

———. "Nekotorye osobennosti russkoi oriental'noi poèzii pervoi treti XIX v. (formirovanie stilevoi traditsii)." In *Russkaia literatura i vostok (osobennosti khudozhestvennoi orientalistiki XIX–XX vv.),* 5–35. Tashkent: Izdatel'stvo "FAN" Uzbekskoi SSR, 1988.

Kahn, Andrew. "Readings of Imperial Rome from Lomonosov to Pushkin." *Slavic Review* 52, no. 4 (winter 1993): 745–68.

Kant, Immanuel. *Critique of Judgment.* Translated by Werner S. Pluhar. Indianapolis: Hackett, 1987.

Kappeler, Andreas. *Russlands erste Nationalitäten. Das Zarenreich und die Völker der Mittleren Volga vom 16. bis 19. Jahrhundert.* Cologne: Böhlau Verlag, 1982.

Karamzin, N. *Izbrannye stat'i i pis'ma.* Moscow: Sovremennik, 1982.

Karimov, È. A., ed. *Russkaia literatura i vostok (Osobennosti khudozhestvennoi orientalistiki XIX–XX vv).* Tashkent: Izdatel'stvo "FAN" Uzbekskoi SSR, 1988.

Kashtaleva, K. S. "'Podrazhaniia Koranu' Pushkina i ikh pervoistochnik." *Zapiski Kollegii vostokovedov* 5 (1930): 101–13.

Khlebnikov, Velimir. *Tvoreniia.* Edited by V. P. Grigor'ev and A. E. Parnis. Moscow: Sovetskii pisatel', 1986.

———. *Velimir Khlebnikov. The King of Time. Poems, Fictions, Visions of the Future.* Edited by Charlotte Douglas, translated by Paul Schmidt. Cambridge, Mass.: Harvard University Press, 1985.

Khodasevich, V. *Derzhavin.* Moscow: Kniga, 1988 [1931].

Kholmukhamedova, N. N. "Vostok v russkoi poèzii 30-x godov XIX veka. (V. K. Kiukhel'beker i M. Iu. Lermontov)." *Seriia literatury i iazyka* (1985): 57–67.

Khomiakov, A. S. *Stikhotvoreniia i dramy.* Leningrad: Sovetskii pisatel', 1969.

Kirchmeir, Karl-Wilhelm. *Romantische Lyrik and Neoklassizistische Elegie. Studien zur Theorie der Lyrik in Frankreich im 18. Jahrhundert und in der Romantik.* Munich: Wilhelm Fink Verlag, 1976

Kirchner, P. "Lomonosov und Johann Christian Günther." *Zeitschrift für Slawistik* 6, no. 4 (1961): 483–97.

Klein, Joachim. "Sumarokov und Boileau. Die Epistel 'Über die Verskunst' in ihrem Verhältnis zur 'Art poétique': Kontextwechsel als Kategorie der vergleichenden Literaturwissenschaft." *Zeitschrift für Slavische Philologie* 50, no. 1 (1990): 254–304.

———. "Reforma stikha Trediakovskogo v kul'turno-istoricheskom kontekste." *XVIII vek. Sbornik* 19 (1995): 21.

Klein, Joachim, and Viktor Zhivov. "Zur Problematik und Spezifik des russischen Klassizismus: Die Oden des Vasilij Majkov." *Zeitschrift für Slavische Philologie* 48, no. 2 (1989): 234–88.

Klyuchevsky, Vasili. *Peter the Great.* Translated by Liliana Archibald. New York: Macmillan, St. Martin's, 1969.

Kochetkova, N. D. "Oratorskaia proza Feofana Prokopovicha i puti formirovaniia literatury klassitsizma." *XVIII vek. Sbornik* 9 (1974): 50–80.

———. "Oratorskaia proza dekabristov i traditsii russkoi literatury XVIII veka (A. N. Radishchev)." In *Literaturnoe nasledie dekabristov,* 100–120. Leningrad: Nauka, 1975.

Koebner, R. "Despot and Despotism: Vicissitudes of a Political Term." *Journal of the Warburg and Courtauld Institutes* 14 (1951): 38–57.

Kondrashov, S. N. "'Plan obshirnyi ob"emletsia smelost'iu zamysla.' (Nekotorye sotsial'no-èticheskie motivy stikhotvoreniia G. R. Derzhavina 'Vodopad')." In *Zhanrovoe svoeobrazie russkoi poèzii i dramaturgii,* 31–42. Kuibyshev: Kuibyshevskii gosudarstvennyi pedagogicheskii institut, 1981.

Koplan, B. I. "K stikhotvoreniiu 'Prorok.'" In *Pushkinskii sbornik pamiati prof. S. A. Vengerova. Pushkinist,* 4:327–28. Moscow: n.p., 1922.

Kornblatt, Judith Deutsch. "Solov'ëv on Salvation: The Story of the 'Short story of the Antichrist.'" In *Russian Religious Thought,* ed. Judith Deutsch Kornblatt and Richard F. Gustafson, 68–87. Madison: University of Wisconsin Press, 1996.

Koroleva, N. V. "V. K. Kiukhel'beker." In V. K. Küchelbecker, *Izbrannye proizvedeniia v dvukh tomakh,* 1:31. Moscow: Sovetskii pisatel', 1967.

Korovin, V. "Lermontov i russkaia lirika ego vremeni." In *Tvorchestvo M. Iu. Lermontova,* 311–40. Moscow: Nauka, 1964.

Kotzinger (Frank), Susi. "Vozvyshennoe u Gogolia: Vlast' ritoriki i vozvyshennoe iskusstvo." In *Traditsii i novatorstvo v russkoi klassicheskoi literature (. . . Gogol' . . . Dostoevskii . . .), Mezhvuzovskii sbornik nauchnykh trudov,* ed. L. G. Savel'eva, 3–24. St. Petersburg: Obrazovanie, 1992.

Krasnov, P. S. "Putevye pis'ma Griboedova (ot Tiflisa do Tegerana)." In *A. S. Griboedov. Tvorchestvo, Biografiia, Traditsii,* 206–11. Leningrad: Nauka, 1977.

Krasnov, S. A., ed. *Griboedov: zhizn' i tvorchestvo.* Moscow: Russkaia kniga, 1994.

Krieger, Leonard. *An Essay on the Theory of Enlightened Despotism.* Chicago: University of Chicago Press, 1975.

Kubacheva, V. N. "'Vostochnaia povest' v russkoi literature XVIII–nachala XIX veka." *XVIII vek. Sbornik* 5 (1962): 295–316.

Küchelbecker, V. K. "[Lektsiia Kiukhel'bekera o russkoi literature i russkom iazyke, prochitannaia v Parizhe v iiune 1821g]." In *Literaturnoe Nasledstvo. Dekabristy-Literatory* 1, 59: 360–67. Moscow: Izdatel'stvo Akademii nauk SSSR, 1954.

———. *Izbrannye prozvedeniia v dvukh tomakh.* 2 vols. Moscow: Sovetskii pisatel', 1967.

———. *Evropeiskie pis'ma.* In *Dekabristy. Antologiia v dvukh tomakh,* ed. Vl. Orlov, 2:151–70. Leningrad: Khudozhestvennaia literatura, 1975.

———. *Puteshestvie, dnevnik, stat'i.* Leningrad: Nauka, 1979.

Kunik, A., ed. *Sbornik materialov dlia istorii Imperatorskoi Akademii nauk v XVIII veke.* St. Petersburg: Tipografiia Imperatorskoi Akademii nauk, 1865.

Kutik, I. *The Ode and the Odic. Essays on Mandelstam, Pasternak, Tsvetaeva and Mayakovsky.* Stockholm: Almqvist and Wiskell International, 1994.

Kutina, L. I. "Feofan Prokopovich, slova i rechi. Leksiko-stilisticheskaia kharakteristika." In *Literarturnyi iazyk XVIII veka. Problemy stilistiki*, 5–51. Leningrad: Nauka, 1982.

Kuzmin, Mikhail. *Izbrannye proizvedeniia*. Leningrad: Khudozhestvennaia literatura, 1990.

Lachmann, Renata. *Demontazh krasnorechiia. Ritoricheskaia traditsiia i poniatie poèticheskogo*. St. Petersburg: Akademicheskii proekt, 2001.

Layton, Susan. "The Creation of an Imaginative Caucasian Geography." *Slavic Review* 45 (fall 1986): 470–85.

———. "Primitive Despot and Noble Savage: The Two Faces of Shamil in Russian Literature." *Central Asian Survey* 10, no. 4 (1991): 31–45.

———. *Russian Literature and Empire: Conquest of the Caucasus from Pushkin to Tolstoi*. Cambridge: Cambridge University Press, 1994.

———. "A Russian Reverie: Chechnya's Literary Legacy." *History Today* 47 (February 1997): 5–20.

———. "Nineteenth-Century Russian Mythologies of Caucasian Savagery." In *Russia's Orient: Imperial Borderlands and Peoples, 1700–1917*, ed. Daniel Brower and Edward J. Lazzerini, 80–99. Bloomington: Indiana University Press, 1997.

———. "Aleksandr Polezhaev and Remembrance of War in the Caucasus: Constructions of the Soldier as Victim." *Slavic Review* (fall 1999): 559–84.

Lazarev, M. S. "'Da, aziaty my . . .' (Vmesto Predisloviia)." In N. Ia. Eidel'man, *Byt' mozhet za khrebtom Kavkaza*, 3–18. Moscow: Nauka, 1990.

Le Donne, John P. *Absolutism and Ruling Class*. New York: Oxford University Press, 1991.

Lefebvre, Henri. *La production de l'espace*. 2nd ed. Paris: Editions Anthropos, 1980.

Lentin, A., ed. and trans. *Peter the Great: His Law on the Imperial Succession in Russia 1722. The Official Commentary*. Oxford: Headstart History, 1996.

Lermontov, M. Iu. *Sobranie sochinenii v chetyrekh tomakh*. 4 vols. Moscow: Izdatel'stvo A.N.S.S.R., 1958–62.

Lerner, N. O. "Vosstan', vosstan', prorok Rossii . . ." In *Pushkin i ego sovremenniki*, 18–29. St. Petersburg: n.p., 1910.

———. *Rasskazy o Pushkine*. Leningrad:Priboi, 1925.

Levchenko, O. A. "Griboedov i russkaia ballada 1820-kh gg. ('Gore ot uma' i 'Khishchniki na Chegeme'). In *A. S. Griboedov. Materialy k biografii. Sbornik nauchnykh trudov*, ed. S. A. Fomichev. Leningrad: Nauka, 1989.

Levitsky, Alexander. "Russian Sacred Verse from Simeon of Polotsk to Derzhavin." In *Vasilii Kirillovic Trediakovskij Psalter 1753*, 541–664. Paderborn: Ferdinand Schöningh, 1989.

Liamina, E. Ia. "Arkhaisty i nenovatory." *Novoe literaturnoe obozrenie* 27 (1997): 67–81.

Lobikova, N. M. *Pushkin i vostok: Ocherki*. Moscow: Nauka, 1974.

Lo Gatto, Ettore. "*Panmongolismo* di V.Solov'ëv, *I venienti Unni* di V.Briusov e *Gli Sciti* di A.Blok." In *For Roman Jakobson*, 296–300. The Hague: Mouton, 1956.

Lomonosov, M. V. *Polnoe sobranie sochinenii*. 11 vols. Moscow: Izdatel'stvo Akademii nauk, 1950–83.

Longinus. "Iz traktata Longinova, o vazhnosti slova s perevoda Boalova." *Trudoliubivaia pchela* 4 (1759) 219–24.

———. *O vysokom ili velichestvennom. Tvoreniia Dionisa Longina.* Translated by I. I. Martynov. St. Petersburg: n.p., 1803.

———. *O vysokom, tvorenie Dionisia Longina. Perevod I. Martynova s grecheskogo iazyka, s primechaniiami perevodchika.* Translated by I. I. Martynov. St. Petersburg: n.p., 1826.

———. *O vozvyshennom.* Translated by by N. A. Chistiakova. Moscow: Nauka, 1966.

———. *On the Sublime.* Translated by James A. Arieti and John M. Crossett. New York: Edwin Mellen, 1985.

Lotman, Iu. M. *Aleksandr Sergeevich Pushkin. Biografiia pisatelia.* Leningrad: Prosveshchenie, 1983.

———. "Problema vostoka i zapada v tvorchestve pozdnego Lermontova." In *Lermontovskii sbornik,* 5–22. Leningrad: Nauka, 1985.

———. "Poèticheskii mir Tiutcheva." In *Tiutchevskii sbornik. Stat'i o zhizni i tvorchestve Fedora Ivanovicha Tiutcheva,* 108–41. Tallinn: Eesti raamat, 1990.

———."Otrazhenie ètiki i taktiki revoliutsionnoi bor'by v russkoi literature kontsa XIX veka." In *Izbrannye stat'i,* 2:134–58. Tallinn: Aleksandra, 1992.

———. "Pushkin. Ocherk tvorchestva." In *Pushkin,* 175–90. St. Petersburg: Iskusstvo-SPB, 1995.

———. "Ocherki po istorii russkoi kul'tury XVIII–nachala XIX veka." In *Iz istorii russkoi kul'tury (XVIII–nachalo XIX veka),* 4:13–337. Moscow: Shkola "Iazyki russkoi kul'tury," 1996.

Lotman, Iu. M., and B. A. Uspenskii. "K semioticheskoi tipologii russkoi kul'tury XVIII veka." In *Iz istorii russkoi kul'tury (XVIII–nachalo XIX veka),* 4:425–49. Moscow: Shkola "Iazyki russkoi kul'tury," 1996.

———. "Echoes of the Notion 'Moscow as the Third Rome' in Peter the Great's Ideology." In *The Semiotics of Russian Culture,* ed. Ann Shukman, 53–64. Ann Arbor: Michigan Slavic Contributions, 1984.

Lyotard, Jean-Francois. "Le sublime et l'avant-garde." *L'inhumain. Causeries sur le temps.* Paris: Editions Galilée, 1988.

Madariaga, Isabel de. *Russia in the Age of Catherine the Great.* New Haven: Yale University Press, 1981.

———. "Autocracy and Sovereignty." *Canadian-American Slavic Studies* 16, nos. 3–4 (fall–winter 1982): 369–88.

———. "Catherine the Great." *Enlightened Absolutism: Reform and Reformers in Later Eighteenth-Century Europe.* Ann Arbor: University of Michigan Press, 1990.

Maddison, Carol. *Apollo and the Nine: A History of the Ode.* Baltimore, Md.: Johns Hopkins University Press, 1960.

Maiakovskii, Vladimir. "Oda revoliutsii." In *Sochineniia v trekh tomakh.* 3 vols. Moscow: Khudozhestvennaia literatura, 1978.

Makanin, V. S. "Kavkazskii plennyi." In *Kavkazskii plennyi,* 449–77. Moscow: Panorama, 1997.

Makogonenko, G. P. *Ot Fonvizina do Pushkina. Iz istorii russkogo realizma.* Moscow: Khudozhestvennaia literatura, 1969.

———. "Pushkin i Derzhavin." In *XVIII vek. Sbornik 8. Derzhavin i Karamzin v literaturnom dvizhenii XVIII–nachala XIX veka,* 113–26. Leningrad: Nauka, 1969.

———. "Puti razvitiia russkoi poèzii XVIII veka." In *Poèty XVIII veka,* 5–72. Leningrad: Sovetskii pisatel', 1972.

———. "O romanticheskom geroe dekabristskoi poèzii." In *Literaturnoe nasledie dekabristov,* ed. V. G. Bazanov and V. E. Vatsuro, 6–24. Leningrad: Nauka, 1975.

Maksimov, D. E. *Poèziia Lermontova.* Moscow: Nauka, 1964.

Malherbe. *Oeuvres poetiques.* Paris: Garnier Frères, 1874.

Mandel'shtam, Osip. *Sobranie sochinenii v trekh tomakh.* 3 vols. Edited by G. P. Struve and B. A. Filippov. Washington: Inter-Language Literary Associates, 1967–81.

Mann, Iu. *Dinamika russkogo romantizma.* Moscow: Aspekt, 1995.

Manuilov, V. A., et al., eds. *Lermontovskaia èntsiklopediia.* Moscow: Sovetskaia èntsiklopediia, 1981.

Marin, Louis. *Portrait of the King.* Translated by Martha M. Houle. Minneapolis: University of Minnesota Press, 1988.

———. "On the Sublime, Infinity, Je ne sais quoi." In *A New History of French Literature,* ed. Denis Hollier, 340–45. Cambridge, Mass.: Harvard University Press, 1989.

———. *Cross-Readings.* Translated by Jane Marie Todd. Atlantic Highlands, N.J.: Humanities, 1992.

Markov, Vladimir. *Svoboda v poèzii. Stat'i. Esse. Raznoe.* St. Petersburg: Izdatel'stvo Chernysheva, 1994.

Mayer, Alis Gayle. "Models for Creativity and the Image of the Author in the Poetry of G. R. Derzhavin." Ph.D. dissertation, Brown University, 1997.

Maz'ia, M. P. "A. S. Griboedov v stikhakh i dnevnike V. K. Kiukhel'bekera." In *A. S. Griboedov. Materialy k biografii,* 174–84. Leningrad: Nauka, 1989.

McConnell, Allen. *A Russian Philosophe: Alexander Radishchev, 1749–1802.* The Hague: Martinus Nijhoff, 1964.

Medvedeva, I. "Pushkinskaia èlegiia 1820-x godov i 'Demon.'" *Vremennik pushkinskoi komissii* 6 (1941): 51–71.

Meilakh, B. *Pushkin i russkii romantizm.* Moscow: Izdatel'stvo Akademii nauk SSSR, 1937.

———. "Pushkin i dekabristy v period posle porazheniia vosstaniia 1825 g." *Pushkin. Issledovaniia i materialy* 2 (1958): 201.

Miliukov, Pavel. *Gosudarstvennoe khoziaistvo Rossii v pervoi chetverti XVIII stoletiia i reformy Petra.* 2nd ed. St. Petersburg: Tipografiia M. M. Stasiulevicha, 1905.

———. *Ocherki po istorii russkoi kul'tury.* 3 vols. Moscow, 1930.

Mitter, Partha. *Much Maligned Monsters: A History of European Reactions to Indian Art.* 2nd ed. Chicago: University of Chicago Press, 1992.

Monk, Samuel H. *The Sublime: A Study of Critical Theories in 18th-Century England.* Ann Arbor: University of Michigan Press, 1960.

Montesquieu. *De l'Esprit des lois.* Paris: Garnier Frères, [1748].

Morozov, A. "Lomonosov i Barokko." *Russkaia literatura* 2 (1965): 70–96.

———. "Sud'by russkogo klassitsizma." *Russkaia literatura* 1 (1974): 3–27.

Moskvich, Grigorii. *Putevoditel' po Kavkazu.* 15th ed. Odessa: I. Kopel'man, 1910.

Murav'eva, O. S. "Zamysel tragediia A. S. Griboedova 'Gruzinskaia noch.'" In *A. S. Griboedov. Materialy k biografii,* ed. S. A. Fomichev, 271–78. Leningrad: Nauka, 1989.

Nechkina, M. *Griboedov i dekabristy.* Moscow: Khudozhestvennaia literatura, 1977.

Nepomniashchii, V. "Prorok. Khudozhestvennyi mir Pushkina i ego sovremennost'." *Novyi mir* (January 1987): 132–52.

Nivat, Georges. "Du 'panmongolisme' au 'mouvement eurasien.' Histoire d'un thème littéraire." *Cahiers du monde russe et soviétique* 3 (1966): 47–62.

Olson, Elder. "The Art of Longinus' *On the Sublime.*" In *Critics and Criticism, Ancient and Modern,* 232–59. Chicago: University of Chicago Press, 1961.

Orlov, V. "Khudozhestvennaia problematika Griboedova." *Literaturnoe Nasledstvo* 47/48 (1946): 60–85.

———, ed. *Aleksandr Blok–Andrei Belyi Perepiska.* Munich: Wilhelm Fink Verlag, 1969 [1940].

Ovsiannikov, M.-F., ed. *Russkie èsteticheskie traktaty pervoi treti XIX veka.* Moscow: Iskusstvo, 1974.

Panchenko, A. M. "Slovo i Znanie v èstetike Simeona Polotskogo (na materiale 'Vertograda mnogotsvetnogo')." In *Trudy otdela drevnerusskoi literatury. XXV. Pamiatniki russkoi literatury X–XVII vv.,* 232–41. Moscow: Nauka, 1970.

———. *Russkaia stikhotvornaia kul'tura XVII veka.* Leningrad: Nauka, 1973.

———. "O smene pisatel'skogo tipa v petrovskuiu èpokhu." *XVIII vek. Sbornik* 9 (1974): 112–28.

———. "Dva ètapa russkogo barokko." In *Tekstologiia i poètika russkoi literatury XI–XVIII vekov,* 100–106. Leningrad: Nauka, 1977.

———. "Istoriia i vechnost' v sisteme kul'turnykh tsennostei russkogo barokko." In *Kulikovskaia bitva i pod"em natsional'nogo samosoznaniia,* 187–99. Leningrad: Nauka, 1979.

———. "'Potemkinskie derevni' kak kul'turnyi mif." *XVIII vek. Sbornik 14. Russkaia literatura XVIII–nachala XIX veka v obshchestvenno-kul'turnom kontekste* (1983): 93–104.

Panov, S. I., and A. M. Ranchin. "Torzhestvennaia oda i pokhval'noe slovo Lomonosova: obshchee i osobennoe v poètike." In *Lomonosov i russkaia literatura,* 175–89. Leningrad: Nauka, 1972.

Parry, Benita. "Problems in Current Theories of Colonial Discourse." *Oxford Literary Review* 9, nos. 1–2 (1987).

Pease, Donald E. "Sublime Politics." *Boundary* 2 12, no. 3 (spring 1984); 13, no. 1 (fall 1984): 259–99.

Pekarskii, Petr. *Istoriia Imperatorskoi Akademii nauk v Peterburge.* 2 vols. St. Petersburg: Tipografiia Imperatorskoi Akademii nauk, 1873.

Pestel', Pavel. *Russkaia pravda.* Moscow: Progress-Akademiia, 1993.

Pierre R. *G. R. Derzhavin: A Poet's Progress.* Columbus, Ohio: Slavica, 1978.

Pigarev, K. *Zhizn' i tvorchestvo Tiutcheva.* Moscow: Izdatel'stvo Akademii nauk SSSR, 1962.

Pindar. *The Odes of Pindar.* Translated by Richard Lattimore. Chicago: University of Chicago Press, 1971.

Pogosian, Elena. *Vostorg russkoi ody i reshenie temy poèta v russkom panegirike 1730–1762 gg.* Tartu: Tartu Ulikooli Kirjastus, 1997.

Pokotilova, M. "Predshestvenniki Lomonosova v russkoi poèzii XVII-go i nachala XVIII-go stoletii." In *1711–1911 M. V. Lomonosov, Sbornik statei*, ed. V. V. Sipovskii, 66–92. St. Petersburg: Trud, 1911.

Polezhaev, A. I. *Stikhotvoreniia i poèmy.* Edited by V. V. Baranov. Leningrad: Sovetskii pisatel', 1957.

Polotskii, Simeon. *Orel rossiiskii.* Edited by N. A. Smirnov. St. Petersburg: Tipografiia M. A. Aleksandrova, 1915.

———. *Izbrannye sochineniia.* Edited by I. P. Eremin. Moscow: Izdatel'stvo Akademii nauk, 1953.

Popova, O. I. *A. S. Griboedov v Persii: 1818–1923 gg.: po novym dokumentam.* Moscow: Kooperativnoe izdatel'stvo "Zhizn' i Znanie," 1929.

Portal, R. "Les Bachkirs et le gouvernement russe au XVIII siècle." *Revue des etudes slaves* (1946): 113–35.

Potts, Abbie Findlay. *The Elegiac Mode: Poetic Form in Wordsworth and Other Elegists.* Ithaca, N.Y.: Cornell University Press, 1967.

Pratt, Mary Louise. *Imperial Eyes: Travel Writing and Transculturation.* London: Routledge, 1992.

Presniakov. "Motivy real'noi politiki v dvizhenii dekabristov." In *Bunt dekabristov.* Leningrad: Byloe, 1926.

Price, Martin. "The Sublime Poem: Pictures and Powers." In *Poets of Sensibility and the Sublime*, ed. Harold Bloom, 31–47. New York: Chelsea House, 1986.

Prokopovich, Feofan. *Sochineniia.* Moscow: Izdatel'stvo Akademii nauk SSSR, 1961.

———. *De Arte Rhetorica Libri X Kijoviae 1706.* Edited by Renate Lachmann. Cologne: Böhlau Verlag, 1982.

Pul'khritudova, E. M. "Literaturnaia teoriia dekabristskogo romantizma v 30-e gody XIX veka." In *Problemy romantizma*, ed. U. R. Fokht, 232–92. Moscow: Iskusstvo, 1967.

———. "Romanticheskoe i prosvetitel'skoe v dekabristskoi literature 20-x godov XIX veka." In *K istorii russkogo romantizma*, 39–72. Moscow: Nauka, 1973.

———. "Kiukhel'beker." In *Russkie pisateli, 1800–1917. Biografiecheskii slovar'*, 3:253–58. Moscow: Bol'shaia rossiiskaia èntsiklopediia, 1994.

Pumpianskii, L. V. "Poeziia F. I. Tiutcheva." *Uraniia. Tiutchevskii al'manakh.* Leningrad: Priboi, 1928.

———. "Trediakovskii i nemetskaia shkola razuma." In *Zapadnyi sbornik*, 157–86. Moscow: Izdatel'stvo akademii nauk SSSR, 1937.

———. "Stikhovaia rech' Lermontova." *Literaturnoe nasledstvo* 43–44 (1941): 389–424.

———. "Lomonosov i nemetskaia shkola razuma." *XVIII vek. Sbornik 4* (1983): 3–44.

———. "K istorii russkogo klassitsizma (poètika Lomonosova)." In *Kontekst. 1982 Literaturno-teoreticheskie issledovaniia*, 303–34. Moscow: Nauka, 1983.

Pushkin, A. S. *Polnoe sobranie sochinenii.* 17 vols. Leningrad: Izdatel'stvo Akademii nauk SSSR, 1937–59.

———. *Polnoe sobranie sochinenii v desiati tomakh.* 10 vols. Moscow: Izdatel'stvo Akademii nauk SSSR, 1962–66.

———. *Perepiska A. S. Pushkina v dvukh tomakh.* 2 vols. Moscow: Khudozhestvennaia literatura, 1982.

———. *Polnoe sobranie sochinenii.* 19 vols. Moscow: Voskresenie, 1994–97.

Radishchev, A. *Polnoe sobranie sochinenii.* 3 vols. Moscow/Leningrad: Izdatel'stvo Akademii nauk, 1938–52.

Raeff, Marc. "Patterns of Russian Imperial Policy towards the Nationalities." In *Soviet Nationalities Problems,* ed. E. Allworth, 134–82. New York: Columbia University Press, 1971.

———. *The Well-Ordered Police State: Social and Institutional Change through Law in the Germanies and Russia (1600–1800).* New Haven: Yale University Press, 1983.

———, ed. *Peter the Great Changes Russia.* 2nd ed. Lexington, Mass.: Heath, 1972.

Ram, Harsha. "Russian Poetry and the Imperial Sublime." In *Russian Subjects: Empire, Nation, and the Culture of the Golden Age,* ed. Monika Greenleaf and Stephen Moeller Sally, 21–49. Evanston, Ill.: Northwestern University Press, 1998.

———. "Kavkazskie plenniki: Kul'turnye mify i medial'nye reprezentatsii v chechenskom konflikte." *Novoe literaturnoe obozrenie* 34, no. 6 (1998): 78–108.

Rasmussen, Karen Malvey. *Catherine II and Peter I: The Idea of a Just Monarch. The Evolution of an Attitude in Catherinian Russia.* Ph.D. dissertation, University of California at Berkeley, 1973.

Reddaway, W. F., ed. *Documents of Catherine the Great.* Cambridge: Cambridge University Press, 1931.

Reid, Robert. "Ethnotope in Lermontov's Caucasian Poems." *Russian Literature* 31 (May 1992): 555–73.

Reyfman, Irina. *Vasilii Trediakovsky: The Fool of the "New" Russian Literature.* Stanford: Stanford University Press, 1990.

Riasanovsky, Nicholas. *The Image of Peter the Great in Russian History and Thought.* New York: Oxford University Press, 1985.

Richir, Marc. *Du sublime en politique.* Paris: Éditions Payot, 1991.

Rieber, Alfred J. "Russian Imperialism: Popular, Emblematic, Ambiguous." *Russian Review* 53, no. 3 (July 1994): 331–45.

Robbins, Bruce, et al. "Edward Said's *Culture and Imperialism.* A Symposium." *Social Text* (fall 1994): 103–29.

Rodinson, Maxine. "The Western Image and Western Studies of Islam." In *The Legacy of Islam,* ed. C. E. Bosworth and Joseph Schacht, 334–87. Oxford: Clarendon, 1974.

Rowland, Daniel. "Did Muscovite Literary Ideology Place Limits on the Power of the Tsar (1540s–1660s)?" *Russian Review* 49 (1990): 125–55.

Ryleev, Kondratii. *Dekabristy. Poèziia, dramaturgiia, proza, publitsistika, literaturnaia kritika.* Edited by Vl. Orlov. Moscow: Gosudarstvennoe izdatel'stvo khudozhestvennoi literatury, 1951.

Rywkin, Michael, ed. *Russian Colonial Expansion to 1917.* London: Mansell, 1988.

Sahni, Kalpana. *Crucifying the Orient: Russian Orientalism and the Colonization of Caucasus and Central Asia.* Oslo: White Orchid, 1997.

Said, Edward W. *Orientalism*. New York: Vintage, 1978.

———. "Orientalism Reconsidered." In *Europe and Its Others: Proceedings of the Essex Conference on the Sociology of Literature, July 1984*, 14–27. Colchester: University of Essex, 1985.

———. *Culture and Imperialism*. New York: Vintage, 1994.

Sacks, Peter M. *The English Elegy: Studies in the Genre from Spenser to Yeats*. Baltimore, Md.: Johns Hopkins University Press, 1985.

Samorodova, O. "Poèt na Kavkaze." *Zvezda* 6 (1972): 186–93.

Sandler, Stephanie. *Distant Pleasures: Alexander Pushkin and the Writing of Exile*. Stanford: Stanford University Press, 1989.

Sandomirskaia, V. "'Estestvennyi chelovek' i obshchestvo. 'Kavkazskii plennik' v tvorchestve poèta." *Zvezda* 6 (1969): 184–90.

Sarkisyanz, Emanuel. "Russian Imperialism Reconsidered." In *Russian Imperialism from Ivan the Great to the Revolution*, ed. Taras Hunczak, 45–81. New Brunswick, N.J.: Rutgers University Press, 1974.

Sazonova, L. I. "Ot russkogo panegirika XVII v. k ode M. V. Lomonosova." In *Lomonosov i russkaia literatura*, 103–126. Moscow: Nauka, 1987.

Schama, Simon. *Landscape and Memory*. New York: Vintage, 1996.

Schiller, F. *Schillers Sämtliche Werke*. Leipzig: Insel, 1924.

Schönle, Andreas. "Of Sublimity, Shrinkage, and Selfhood in the Works of Bruno Schulz." *SEEJ* 42, no. 3 (1998): 467–82.

———. "Garden of the Empire: Catherine's Appropriation of the Crimea." *Slavic Review* 60, no. 1 (spring 2001): 1–23.

Schwab, Raymond. *The Oriental Renaissance: Europe's Rediscovery of India and the East, 1680–1880*. Translated by Gene Patterson Black and Victor Reinking. New York: Columbia University Press, 1984.

Scotto, Peter. "Prisoners of the Caucasus: Ideologies of Imperialism in Lermontov's 'Bela.'" *PMLA* 107, no. 2 (March 1992): 246–60.

Semenov, L. P. *Pushkin na Kavkaze*. Piatigorsk: Severo-Kavkazskoe kraevoe gosudarstvennoe izdatel'stvo, 1937.

———. *Lermontov i fol'klor Kavkaza*. Piatigorsk: Ordzhonikidzevskoe kraevoe izdatel'stvo, 1941.

Senderovich, S. "Aleteiia. Èlegiia Pushkina "Vospominanie" i problemy ego poètiki." Vienna: *Wiener Slawistischer Almanach*, 1982.

Serbinenko, V. V. *Vladimir Solov'ëv: zapad, vostok i Rossiia*. Moscow: Nauka, 1994.

Serman, I. Z. "Poèziia Lomonosova v 1740-e gody." *XVIII vek. Sbornik* 5 (1962): 3–69.

———. *Poèticheskii stil' Lomonosova*. Moscow: Nauka, 1966.

———. *Derzhavin*. Leningrad: Prosveshchenie, 1967.

———. *Russkii klassitsizm. Poèziia, drama, satira*. Leningrad: Nauka, 1973.

———. "Literaturno-èsteticheskie interesy i literaturnaia politika Petra I." In *Russkoe isskusstvo barokko. Materialy I issledovaniia*, ed. T. V. Alexeeva, 27–31. Moscow: Nauka, 1977.

———. "Lomonosovs Oden und die Poetik des Schuldramas." In *Slavische Barockliteratur II. Gedenkschrift für Dmitrij Tschizewskij (1894–1977)*, 129–43. Munich: Wilhelm Fink Verlag, 1983.

———. *Mikhail Lomonosov: Life and Poetry*. Jerusalem: Lexicon, 1988.

———. "Derzhavin v novom veke." *Novoe literaturnoe obozrenie* 27 (1997): 54–67.
Shaduri, Vano. *Pervyi russkii roman o Kavkaze.* Tbilisi: Zaria Vostoka, 1947.
———. *Drug Pushkina A. A. Shishkov i ego roman o Gruzii.* Tbilisi: Zaria vostoka, 1951.
———. *Dekabristskaia literatura i gruzinskaia obshchestvennost'.* Tbilisi: Zaria Vostoka, 1958.
Shaduri, Vano, and T. Buachidze, eds. *Tam, gde v'etsia Alazan: 180 let so dnia rozhdeniia A. S. Griboedova.* Tbilisi: Merani, 1977.
Shafirov, P. P. *Rassuzhdenie, kakie zakonnye prichiny ego tsarskoe velichestvo Petr I k nachatiiu voiny protiv korolia Karola XII shvedskogo v 1700 godu imel.* St. Petersburg: n.p., 1717. Reissued in a facsimile edition in Russian with an English translation as *Discourse Concerning the Just Causes of the War between Sweden and Russia: 1700–1721.* Introduction by William E. Butler. Dobbs Ferry, N.Y.: Oceana, 1973.
Shapiro, Gary. "From the Sublime to the Political: Some Historical Notes." *New Literary History* 16, no. 2 (1985): 213–35.
Shishkov, A. S. *Sobranie sochinenii i perevodov Admirala Shishkova.* 16 vols. St. Petersburg: Tipografiia Imperatorskoi Rossiiskoi Akademii, 1818–34.
Shostakovich, S. V. *Diplomaticheskaia deiatel'nost' A. S. Griboedova.* Moscow: Izdatel'stvo sotsial'no-èkonomicheskoi literatury, 1960.
Shmurlo, E. *Petr velikii v otsenke sovremennikov i potomstva.* St. Petersburg: Senatskaia tipografiia, 1912.
Silbajoris, Rimvydas. *Russian Versification: The Theories of Trediakovskij, Lomonosov, and Kantemir.* New York: Columbia University Press, 1968.
Sipovskii, V. V. *Russkaia lirika. Vypusk 1. XVIII vek.* Petrograd: Ia. Basmakov, 1914.
———, ed. *1711–1911 M. V. Lomonosov, Sbornik statei.* St. Petersburg: Trud, 1911.
Smoliarova, T. I. *Parizh 1928: Oda vozvrashchaetsia v teatr.* Moscow: Rossiiskii gosudarstvennyi gumanitarnyi teatr, 1999.
Sobolev, P. V. "Teoriia iziashchnogo—teoriia deistviia (o svoeobrazii èstetiki dekabristov)." In *Dekabristy i russkaia kul'tura,* ed. B. S. Meilakh, 107–42. Leningrad: Nauka, 1975.
Sobolevskii, A. I. "Kogda nachalsia u nas lozhnoklassitsizm?" *Bibliograf* 1 (1890): 38–47.
Solov'ev, S. M. *Istoriia Rossii s drevneishikh vremen.* 10 vols. St. Petersburg: Obshchestvennaia pol'za, 1894.
Solov'ëv, Vladimir. *Sobranie sochinenii Vladimira Sergeevicha Solov'ëva.* 10 vols. St. Petersburg: Prosveshchenie, 1911–14.
———. *Stikhotvoreniia i shutochnye p'esy.* Leningrad: Sovetskii pisatel', 1974.
Spieker, Sven. "Esthesis and Anesthesia: The Sublime in *Arabesques.*" In *Gogol: Exploring Absence. Negativity in 19th-Century Russian Literature,* ed. Sven Spieker. Bloomington, Ind.: Slavica, 1999.
Stepanov, N. *Lirika Pushkina. Ocherki i ètiudy.* Moscow: Sovetskii pisatel', 1959.
Stennik, Iu. V. "Lomonosov i Derzhavin." In *Lomonosov i russkaia literatura,* 235–67. Moscow: Nauka, 1987.
———. *Pushkin i russkaia literatura XVIII veka.* St. Petersburg: Nauka, 1995.
Strémoukhoff, D. *La poésie et l'idéologie de Tiouttchev.* Paris: Les Belles Lettres, 1937.

Suleri, Sara. *The Rhetoric of English India.* Chicago: University of Chicago Press, 1992.

Sumarokov, A. P. *Izbrannye proizvedeniia.* Leningrad: Sovetskii pisatel', 1957.

Sumner, Benedict Humphrey. *Peter the Great and the Ottoman Empire.* Oxford: Backwell, 1949.

Syroechkovskii, B. E. "Balkanskaia problema v politicheskikh planakh dekabristov." In *Iz istorii dvizheniia dekabristov,* 216–303. Moscow: Izdatel'stvo moskovksogo universiteta, 1969.

Szeftel, Marc. "La monarchie absolue dans l'État moscovite et l'Empire russe (fin XVe siècle–1905)." In *Russian Institutions and Culture up to Peter the Great,* 201–34. London: Variorum Reprints, 1975.

———. "The Title of the Muscovite Monarch." *Canadian-American Slavic Studies* 13, nos. 1–2 (spring–summer 1979): 59–81.

Szondi, Peter. "Hegels Lehre von der Dichtung." *Poetik und Geschichtsphilosophie.* Frankfurt: Suhrkamp, 1974.

Tamakhin, V. M., ed. *Russkaia literatura i Kavkaz.* Stavropol': Stavropol'skii gosudorstvennyi pedagogicheskii institut, 1974.

Taranovskii, F. V. "Politicheskaia doktrina v Nakaze Imperatritsy Ekateriny II." In *Sbornik statei po istorii prava posviashchennyi M. F. Vladimirskomu-Budanovu,* ed. M. N. Iasninskii, 18–41. Kiev: n.p., 1904.

Tatishcheva, G. S. "Pushkin i Derzhavin." *Vestnik Leningradskogo universiteta. Seriia istorii, iazyka i literatury* 14 (1965): 106–16.

Thomson, Ewa M. *Imperial Knowledge: Russian Literature and Colonialism.* Westport, Conn.: Greenwood, 2000.

Tiutchev, F. I. "Pis'ma F. I. Tiutcheva k P. A. Chaadaevu." *Russkii arkhiv* 3, no. 11 (1900): 415.

———. *Polnoe sobranie sochinenii F. I. Tiutcheva.* Edited by P. V. Bykov. 6th ed. St. Petersburg: Tovarishchestvo A. F. Marksa, 1912.

———. *Polnoe sobranie stikhotvorenii.* Leningrad: Sovetskii pisatel', 1939.

———. *Fedor Ivanovich Tiutchev. Kniga pervaia. Literaturnoe nasledstvo.* Vol. 97. Moscow: Nauka, 1988.

Todd, William Mills. *Fiction and Society in the Age of Pushkin. Ideology, Institutions, and Narrative.* Cambridge, Mass.: Harvard University Press, 1986.

Tolstoi, L. N. *Polnoe sobranie sochinenii.* 90 vols. Moscow: Gosudarstvennoe izdatel'stvo khudozhestvennoi literatury, 1928–58.

———. *Sobranie sochinenii.* 20 vols. Moscow: Gosudarstvennoe izdatel'stvo khudozhestvennoi literatury, 1960–65.

Tomashevskii, Boris. "Pushkin—chitatel' frantsuzskikh poètov." In *Pushkinskii sbornik pamiati professora Semena Afanas'evicha Vengerova. Pushkinist. IV,* 210–28. Moscow: Gosudarstvennoe izdatel'stvo, 1923.

———. *Pushkin. Kniga pervaia (1813–1824).* Moscow: Izdatel'stvo Akademii nauk SSSR, 1956.

———. *Pushkin, kniga vtoraia. Materialy k monografii (1824–37).* Moscow: Izdatel'stvo Akademii nauk SSSR, 1961.

Trediakovskii, Vasilii. *Sochineniia Tred'iakovskogo.* 3 vols. Edited by Aleksandr Smirdin. St. Petersburg: Tipografiia Voenno-Uchebnykh Zavedenii, 1849.

———. "Dlia izvestiia." Introduction to *Tri ody parafrasticheskie Psalma 143, sochi-*

nennye chrez trekh stikhotvortsev, iz kotorykh kazhdoi odnu slozhil osoblivo (1754). Republished in *Sbornik materialov dlia istorii Imperatorskoi Akademii nauk v XVIII veke*, ed. A. Kunik. St. Petersburg: Tipografiia Imperatorskoi Akademii nauk, 1865.

———. *Izbrannye proizvedeniia*. Moscow: Sovetskii pisatel', 1963.

———. "Preduvedomlenie," in *Psaltir' ili knigi Psalmov Blazhennogo Proroka i Tsaria Davida*. Republished as *Vasilii Kirillovic Trediakovskij Psalter 1753*. Edited by Alexander Levitsky. Paderborn: Ferdinand Schöningh, 1989.

———. *Vasilij Kirillovic Trediakovskij Psalter 1753*. Edited by Alexander Levitsky. Paderborn: Ferdinand Schöningh, 1989.

Trubetzkoy, N. S., et al. *Iskhod k vostoku: Predchuvstviia I svershenia. Utverzhdeniia evraziitsev*. Sophia: Balkan, 1921.

Tsiavlovskaia, T. G. Commentary. In *A. S. Pushkin, Sobranie sochinenii v desiati tomakh*, 2:689–90. Moscow: Gosudarstvennoe izdatel'stvo khudozhestvennoi literatury, 1959.

———. "Otkliki na sud'by dekabristov v tvorchestve Pushkina." In *Literturnoe nasledie dekabristov*, 195–218. Leningrad: Akademkniga, 1965.

Turner, Bryan. *Marx and the End of Orientalism*. London: Allen and Unwin, 1978.

———. "Orientalism and the Problem of Civil Society in Islam." In *Orientalism, Islam, and Islamists*, ed. Asaf Hussain, Robert Olson, and Jamil Qureishi, 23–42. Brattleboro, Vt.: Amana, 1984.

Tynianov, Iurii. "Oda kak oratorskii zhanr." In *Arkhaisty i novatory*, 48–56. Munich: Wilhelm Fink Verlag, 1967 [1929].

———. "Vopros o Tiutcheve." In *Arkhaisty i novatory*, 367–385. Munich: Wilhelm Fink Verlag, 1967 [1929].

———. "Arkhaisty i Pushkin." In *Pushkin i ego sovremenniki*, 105–15. Moscow: Nauka, 1969.

———. "Pushkin i Kiukhel'beker." In *Pushkin i ego sovremenniki*, 233–94. Moscow: Nauka, 1969.

———. "Siuzhet 'Goria ot uma.'" In *Pushkin i ego sovremenniki*, 347–79. Moscow: Nauka, 1969.

Uspenskii, B. A., and Viktor M. Zhivov. "Zur Spezifik des Barock in Rußland." *Forum Slavicum* 54 (1983): 25–57.

Vatsuro, V. E. "Frantsuzskaia èlegiia kontsa XVIII veka–pervoi chetverti XIX veka." In *Frantsuzskaia èlegiia XVIII–XIX vekov v perevodakh poètov pushkinskoi pory*, 8–48. Moscow: Raduga, 1989.

———. *Zapiski kommentatora*. St. Petersburg, Akademicheskii proèkt, 1994.

Venturi, Franco. "Despotismo orientale." *Rivista storica italiana* 72 (1960): 117–26.

Viazemskii, P. A. *Èstetika i literaturnaia kritika*. Moscow: Iskusstvo, 1984.

Vickery, Walter N. "Pushkin: Russia and Europe." *Review of National Literatures* 3, no. 1 (spring 1972): 15–38.

———. "'Vospominaniia v Tsarskom sele'" (1814) i 'Pamiatnik': k voprosu o strofike." In *Slavic Poetics: Essays in Honor of Kiril Taranovsky*, ed. Roman Jakobson, C. H. van Schooneveld, and Dean S. Worth, 485–97. The Hague: Mouton, 1973.

———. "Towards an Interpretation of Pushkin's 'Podrazhaniia Koranu.'" *Canadian-American Slavic Studies* 11, no. 1 (spring 1977): 61–74.

Vilinbakhov, G. V. "Otrazhenie idei absoliutizma v simvolike petrovskikh znamen." In *Kul'tura i iskusstvo Rossii XVIII veka. Novye materialy i issledovania. Sbornik statei*, 7–26. Leningrad: Iskusstvo, 1981.

———. "Osnovanie Peterburga i imperskaia èmblematika." *Semiotika goroda i gorodskoi kul'tury: Peterburg. Trudy po znakovym sistemam* 18 (1984): 46–55.

Vinogradov, B. S. *Kavkaz v russkoi literature 30-kh godov XIX veka (Ocherki).* Groznyi: Checheno-Ingushskoe knizhnoe izdatel'stvo, 1966.

Vinogradov, V. V. *Iazyk Pushkina. Pushkin i istoriia russkogo literaturnogo iazyka.* Moscow: Academia, 1935.

———. *The History of the Russian Literary Language from the Seventh Century to the Nineteenth.* Madison: University of Wisconsin Press, 1969.

Viswanathan, Gauri. *Masks of Conquest: Literary Study and British Rule in India.* New York: Columbia University Press, 1989.

Voller, Jack G. *The Supernatural Sublime: The Metaphysics of Terror in Anglo-American Romanticism.* Urbana: Northern Illinois University Press, 1994.

Voltaire. *Russia under Peter the Great.* Translated by M. F. O. Jenkins. London: Associated University Press, 1983.

Vomperskii, V. P. *Stilisticheskoe uchenie M. V. Lomonosova i teoriia trekh stilei.* Moscow: Izdatel'stvo Moskovskogo universiteta, 1970.

Vroon, Ronald. "'Chitalagaiskie ody.' (K istorii liricheskogo tsikla v russkoi literature XVIII veka)." *A Symposium Dedicated to Gavriil Derzhavin: Norwich Symposia on Russian Literature and Culture*, 185–201. Northfield, Vt.: Russian School of Norwich University, 1995.

Wang, Ban. *The Sublime Figure of History: Aesthetics and Politics in Twentieth-Century China.* Stanford: Stanford University Press, 1997.

Weiskel, Thomas. *The Romantic Sublime: Studies in the Structure and Psychology of Transcendence.* Baltimore, Md.: Johns Hopkins University Press, 1976.

White, Hayden. *Tropics of Discourse: Essays in Cultural Criticism.* Baltimore, Md.: Johns Hopkins University Press, 1978.

———. "The Politics of Historical Interpretation: Discipline and De-Sublimation." *Critical Inquiry* 9, no. 1 (December 1982): 113–37.

Whittaker, Cynthia. "The Reforming Tsar: The Redefinition of Autocratic Duty in Eighteenth-Century Russia." *Slavic Review* 51, no. 1 (spring 1992): 77–98.

———. "The Idea of Autocracy among Eighteenth-Century Russian Historians." In *Imperial Russia: New Histories for the Empire*, ed. Jane Burbank and David I. Ransel, 32–59. Bloomington: Indiana University Press, 1998.

Wittfogel, Karl A. *Oriental Despotism: A Comparative Study in Total Power.* New Haven: Yale University Press, 1957.

Wortman, Richard. Introduction to "Gavrila Romanovich Derzhavin and his *Zapiski*." In *Zapiski Derzhavina*, 32–59. Cambridge: Oriental Research Partners, 1973.

———. *The Development of a Russian Legal Consciousness.* Chicago: University of Chicago Press, 1976.

———. *Scenarios of Power: From Peter the Great to the Death of Nicholas I.* Vol. 1. Princeton, N.J.: Princeton University Press, 1995.

Zapadov, A. V. *Masterstvo Derzhavina.* Moscow: Sovetskii pisatel', 1958.

———. *Gavrila Romanovich Derzhavin. Biografiia.* Moscow: Prosveshchenie, 1965.

———. *Poèty XVIII veka.* Moscow: Izdatel'stvo Moskovskogo universiteta, 1984.

Zhirmunskii, V. M. *Bairon i Pushkin. Iz istorii romanticheskoi poèmy.* Leningrad: Nauka, 1978 [1924].

Zhivov, V. M. "Gosudarstvennyi mif v èpokhu prosveshcheniia i ego razrushenie v Rossii kontsa XVIII veka. In *Iz istorii russkoi kul'tury,* 4:657–85. Moscow: Shkola, 1996.

———. "Koshchunstvennaia poèziia v sisteme russkoi kul'tury kontsa XVIII–nachala XIX veka." In *Iz istorii russkoi kul'tury (XVIII–Nachalo XIX veka),* 4:701–55. Moscow: Shkola, 1996.

———. *Iazyk i kul'tura v Rossii XVIII veka.* Moscow: Shkola, 1996.

Zhivov, V. M., and B. A. Uspenskii. "Tsar' i Bog. Semioticheskie aspekty sakralizatsii monarkha v Rossii." In *Iazyki kul'tury i problemy perevodimosti,* ed. B. A. Uspenskii, 47–154. Moscow: Nauka, 1987.

Zholkovsky, Alexander. "The Obverse of Stalinism: Akhmatova's Self-Serving Charisma of Selflessness." In *Self and Story in Russian History,* ed. Laura Engelstein and Stephanie Sandler, 46–68. Ithaca, N.Y.: Cornell University Press, 2000.

Zhurnal Petra Velikogo. St. Petersburg: n.p., 1770.

Zorin, Andrei. "Russkaia oda kontsa 1760-kh–nachala 1770-kh godov, Vol'ter i 'grecheskii proèkt' Ekateriny II." *Novoe literaturnoe obozrenie* 24 (1997): 5–29.

———. "Krym v istorii russkogo samosoznaniia." *Novoe literaturnoe obozrenie* 31 (1998): 123–44.

———. *Kormia dvuglavogo orla . . . literatura i gosudarstvennaia ideologiia v Rossii v poslednei treti XVIII–pervoi treti XIX veka.* Moscow: Novoe literaturnoe obozrenie, 2001.

Index